Cap Anson

Also by David L. Fleitz
and from McFarland

*Ghosts in the Gallery at Cooperstown:
Sixteen Little-Known Members
of the Hall of Fame* (2004)

*Louis Sockalexis:
The First Cleveland Indian* (2002)

*Shoeless: The Life and Times
of Joe Jackson* (2001)

Cap Anson
The Grand Old Man of Baseball

DAVID L. FLEITZ

McFarland & Company, Inc., Publishers
Jefferson, North Carolina, and London

LIBRARY OF CONGRESS CATALOGUING-IN-PUBLICATION DATA

Fleitz, David L., 1955–
    Cap Anson : the grand old man of baseball / David L. Fleitz.
    p.   cm.
    Includes bibliographical references and index.

    ISBN 0-7864-2238-6 (softcover : 50# alkaline paper) ∞

    1. Anson, Adrian C. (Adrian Constantine), 1852–1922. 2. Baseball player-managers—United States—Biography. I. Title.
GV865.A64F54   2005
796.357'092—dc22
[B]   2005018506

British Library cataloguing data are available

©2005 David L. Fleitz. All rights reserved

No part of this book may be reproduced or transmitted in any form or by any means, electronic or mechanical, including photocopying or recording, or by any information storage and retrieval system, without permission in writing from the publisher.

Cover images: (foreground) Cap Anson in his Chicago uniform (National Baseball Hall of Fame Library, Cooperstown, New York); (background) Anson in 1887 (author's collection)

Manufactured in the United States of America

McFarland & Company, Inc., Publishers
  Box 611, Jefferson, North Carolina 28640
  www.mcfarlandpub.com

Acknowledgments

I would like to thank a few people without whom this book would not have been possible.

The online archives of the University of Notre Dame proved helpful, and David F. McCartney, Denise Anderson, and the archivists at the University of Iowa were generous with their assistance. So were Ralph Christian of the Iowa Historical Society and Carole Winkleblack of the Marshalltown (Iowa) Public Library.

Bill Burdick and the staff at the photographic department of the National Baseball Library in Cooperstown, New York, offered helpful assistance in rounding up photographs for this book, as did Mark Rucker of Transcendental Graphics. The Eugene C. Murdock collection of baseball books and materials at the Cleveland Public Library was invaluable, and Eric Enders of Triple E Productions provided valuable research information. The SABR (Society for American Baseball Research) Lending Library, my source for microfilmed copies of *The Sporting News* and *Sporting Life*, was a great help, and the ProQuest online newspaper archive, offered by SABR to its members, opens up new horizons in baseball research. This book would have taken much longer to write without it.

I would also like to thank my wife Deborah for her editing skills and moral support.

Acknowledgment

Contents

Acknowledgments v
Introduction 1

1. Beginnings 3
2. From Marshalltown to Rockford 16
3. The Philadelphia Athletics 29
4. Across the Ocean 41
5. William Hulbert and the White Stockings 53
6. Manager in Training 68
7. Captain of the Chicagos 81
8. Champions of the National League 94
9. Controversy 107
10. Back on Top 120
11. King of Kickers 133
12. A New Beginning 145
13. Second Place 158
14. Around the World 172
15. The Brotherhood War 188
16. A Disputed Pennant Race 203
17. The Grand Old Man 214
18. Anson and His Colts 225

19. Cap Anson on Broadway	239
20. The Final Season	252
21. An Unemployed Manager	265
22. Baseball, Business, and Politics	278
23. "The Best I Can"	292
24. Epilogue	306
Appendix A: Cap Anson's First Professional Baseball Contract	313
Appendix B: Cap Anson's Statistical Record	315
Appendix C: Cap Anson's Statistical Record (Projected to 162–Game Seasons)	317
Chapter Notes	319
Bibliography	329
Index	333

Introduction

I enjoy reading baseball biographies.

I like all kinds of historical works, but I have been a baseball fan since I was a child, and have always been interested in the life stories of baseball personages.

The first baseball biography I ever read was *The Babe Ruth Story*, which was dictated by Ruth to sportswriter Bob Considine in 1948, mere months before Ruth died. Many more books on Ruth have appeared since then, and the total number of Babe Ruth biographies is probably over 100 by now. I also read Ty Cobb's book *My Life in Baseball: The True Record*, along with several other works on Cobb by Charles Alexander and others. The lives of later ballplayers, including Ted Williams, Mickey Mantle, Henry Aaron, and many more, have been detailed in literally hundreds of books.

However, there is one long-ago player who seems to have escaped public recognition entirely. Adrian Constantine (Cap) Anson was, without a doubt, baseball's first superstar, the outstanding performer of the first three decades of major league baseball. He was the first player to make 3,000 hits, and posted a batting average of .300 or better in 24 of his record 27 seasons. He won four batting championships, led the National League eight times in runs batted in, and was the most dangerous hitter of his era. Anson was the man who set all the career batting records (for hits, runs scored, games played, times at bat, doubles, and runs batted in) that Cobb, Ruth, and others now hold. He was almost unanimously recognized as the greatest first baseman in the game's history until the 1930s, when Lou Gehrig of the New York Yankees surpassed him in the esteem of the nation's sportswriters.

Anson spent 22 seasons with the Chicago White Stockings, the National League team now known as the Cubs. For 19 of those 22 years, he served as manager of the ballclub, leading it to five pennants and four second-place finishes between 1879 and 1897. He won more games and more league championships than any other manager of the 19th century, and defined the role for all who followed. Anson was baseball's greatest player and its most successful manager, simultaneously. If San Francisco Giants star Barry Bonds, baseball's outstanding hitter of the present day, had also managed the Giants to five pennants, he would be as dominant a force in the game as was Cap Anson more than 100 years ago.

More importantly, Anson played a major role in establishing major league baseball as a permanent part of the American scene. He came of age when professional baseball was in its infancy, struggling for survival against such potentially fatal threats as gambling, player dishonesty, fan violence, and financial pressures. Cap Anson was baseball's biggest star, and his popularity drew legions of fans to the sport and helped to make a mere bat-and-ball game into the national pastime of a growing nation.

Cap Anson's life encompassed many interesting events. He took to the stage and headlined a Broadway play, one which was written to take advantage of his fame. He was present at the first public performance of "Casey at the Bat," the most famous piece of baseball literature ever produced. He participated in baseball's first tour of England in 1874, and 14 years later helped organize a round-the-world excursion that introduced the sport to Australia, Egypt, Europe, and other far-flung outposts. He was elected to political office after his baseball career ended, and spent his later years touring the vaudeville circuit. Anson also, regrettably, vehemently opposed the presence of African-Americans in baseball, and played a major role in the segregation of the game during the 1880s.

Surprisingly, only one biography of Cap Anson has ever been published, and that was produced by Anson himself in 1900. Titled *A Ball Player's Career*, it was the first baseball autobiography. More than 100 years have passed since anyone else has attempted to create a full-length work on the life of baseball's first great player. I believe that Cap Anson's interesting and eventful life deserves a new biographical treatment, and this book is the result.

David L. Fleitz
June 2005

CHAPTER 1

Beginnings

> *Looking back over my youthful experiences I marvel that I have ever lived to relate them, and that I did not receive at least a hundred thrashings for every one that was given me. I know now that I fully deserved all that I received, and more, too.*
> — Adrian C. Anson, 1900[1]

Adrian (Cap) Anson, the hard-hitting first baseman and pennant-winning manager of the Chicago baseball team now known as the Cubs, is the most famous person ever born in Marshalltown, Iowa. He was the son of the founder of the town, and lived there for the first 18 years of his life before he set out to find success as a professional athlete, a journey that took him to Chicago and, eventually, to the Baseball Hall of Fame in Cooperstown, New York.

Cap Anson is nearly forgotten today, but his plaque at the Baseball Hall of Fame states, with admirable simplicity, that he was the "greatest hitter and greatest National League player-manager of [the] 19th century." He was the first major league player to amass 3,000 base hits and the first to win four batting championships. Anson batted .300 or better in all but two of his major league campaigns, and upon his retirement in 1897, he held the all-time records for games played, times at bat, hits, runs scored, doubles, and runs batted in. He also served as manager of the Chicago ballclub, winning five pennants and finishing in the top half of the league in 15 of his 19 seasons. Baseball truly became the national pastime during the last three decades of the 19th century, and Cap Anson of Marshalltown was the game's first and biggest star. As such, he was one of the most well-known and widely admired men in the United States.

Marshalltown today is a city of about 26,000 inhabitants, and a local map of the city reveals such landmarks as Anson Street, Anson Creek, Anson Elementary School, and Anson Middle School. However, these were not named for the town's most prominent athlete. They were intended to honor the baseball player's father, Henry, founder of the city and an interesting character in his own right. The story of Cap Anson begins in Marshalltown, and the story of Marshalltown starts with Henry Anson.

The Anson family was a fixture in Dutchess County, New York, for several generations. They descended from one John Austin, an immigrant from England who founded the village of Stamford, Connecticut, in 1657. Since the family claimed a famous British naval hero, Lord Anson, as an ancestor, Henry Anson's great-grandfather Silas Austin Junior changed his last name to Anson sometime during the late 1700s. Warren Anson, Henry's father, was a cooper by trade who began the westward movement of the Anson family. After marrying, he established a home in Canandaigua, New York, near Rochester, about 200 miles west of Dutchess County.

Henry Anson, founder of Marshalltown, Iowa. (Transcendental Graphics)

Henry Anson was born in Canandaigua in April 1826, at a time when settlement in his home state was virtually complete and the more adventurous souls looked to the west for open spaces and new challenges. The Ansons relocated to Erie County, Ohio, when Henry was seven years old, and they took up residence near the present-day town of Castalia in Margaretta Township. New towns and villages were springing up all over northern Ohio at the time, but statehood had been achieved more than 30 years before, and the Ansons arrived too late to take part in the first wave of pioneers. Warren Anson moved the family around for a few years afterward, always edging westward, looking for the next opportunity. Henry

1. Beginnings

and his family spent some time in the southern Michigan counties of St. Joseph, Hillsdale, and Cass, near towns named Sturgis and Constantine and Adrian, and most likely passed through other Michigan settlements as well.

People called Henry Anson "the redheaded Yankee" from an early age. An athletic young man, he was a crack shot with a rifle and an enthusiastic billiards player. However, he never allowed play to interfere with work. Henry was determined to become successful, and his father had taught him to strive toward new goals. Henry Anson was never afraid of hard work, and viewed the frontier of the rapidly expanding nation as an avenue to help make his mark on the world.

The Ansons passed through in the town of Marshall, Michigan, during the 1840s, and it was there that Henry decided on his course in life. Marshall was the Calhoun County seat, located near the center of the lower peninsula of Michigan, which had achieved statehood only a few years before. The Michigan legislature had not yet determined the location of the permanent state capital, and Marshall was one of several towns competing for the honor. In 1839, the town fathers set aside a parcel of land for the future home of state government, and two years later, when a Marshall resident became the governor of Michigan, it appeared that Marshall had the inside track. It did not come to fruition, because in 1847 the legislature moved the capital to Lansing, where it resides today. Henry Anson gained a firsthand look at the triumphs and disappointments of Marshall, Michigan, and he was determined to start his own town and build it into prominence.

Henry was a man in a hurry. In 1846, at age 19, he returned to Erie County, Ohio, and married the 17-year-old Jeanette Rice. She was the daughter of a prominent family of the area, one with its own share of ambitious would-be pioneers, and Henry grew close to Jeanette's older brother Wells, a businessman. Wells Rice shared Henry's passion in creating a town, but Ohio and Michigan were well settled by 1846, so the two men set their sights on the new states emerging in the west.

The Ansons were still living in Ohio when their first son, Sturgis Ransome Anson, was born in 1850.[2] Soon afterward, Henry moved his family west to Bureau, Illinois. Their new home was only temporary, as Henry was already focused on the new state of Iowa, which joined the Union in the same year that Henry and Jeannette were married. In the spring of 1851 Henry left Jeanette and Sturgis in Illinois while he traveled alone, on horseback, to Iowa to find a suitable site for a settlement. He concentrated his search on the central part of the state, for he was already formulating big plans. He envisioned his new town as not only a county seat, like Marshall,

Michigan, but also as the eventual capital of Iowa. Henry Anson was determined to succeed where the boosters of Marshall had failed.

The spring of 1851 was one of the rainiest in the history of the state, and the bad weather caused serious flooding, making Henry's task more difficult. Roads and riverbanks were nearly impassable, but the determined pioneer forged ahead until he found his ideal place in the newly organized Marshall County. His journey brought him to a valley along the Iowa River, where he met a chief of the friendly Pottawattamie Indians. The chief, who had adopted the name Johnny Green, advised Anson not to stay in the valley, but to continue north and settle in an expanse of fertile prairie with gently rolling hills in the valley between Linn Creek and the Iowa River. "Build your homes between the river and the creek," said the chief, "because a tornado will never touch down between them."[3]

Henry chose an elevated area in which to stake his claim, and as a local historical atlas published in 1875 put it, he "was so pleased with the natural beauty of the spot that ... he caught his hat from his head, and throwing it high in the air, exclaimed, 'I've found the prettiest place in Iowa, and here I'll live and lay my bones.'" Perhaps he did not say those words exactly, but Henry was convinced that this land was his ticket to success. "It seemed to be the one particular spot where nature had lavished its richest gift," recalled Anson years later, and he immediately laid out the future Main Street and built a cabin on the property.[4] He called the town Marshall, not only for the name of the county but also for his former Michigan home, and then rushed to the land office in Dubuque to register his claim.

The only barrier to Henry's plan was that a settler named Ralls owned a 300-acre spread adjoining Anson's claim south of the river. Anson, wanting no competition, returned to Illinois to fetch his wife and son, and also talked Wells Rice into giving the Ralls family $400 to move its homestead several miles to the east. Henry, Jeanette, and their son, along with Wells Rice and other members of the Rice and Anson families, boarded a covered wagon and made the trek to Iowa in late 1851. On April 17, 1852, in the settlement that Henry Anson founded and in the log cabin he built, the first white child was born in Marshall County, Iowa. The baby boy was named Adrian Constantine Anson.

While Jeanette busied herself with her young sons, Henry strived to build Marshall, Iowa, into prominence. He had the site surveyed, and when the plat was recorded on August 15, 1853, the town of Marshall was ready for settlement. Wells Rice, one of the most prominent businessmen in the new town, opened the first general store on West Main Street, and in 1854 he became the town's first postmaster. A few years later, Jeanette's father built the Anson Hotel at the corner of Main and Center streets. The town grew so quickly that lumber for building became scarce, so in 1854 Henry Anson imported a steam-powered sawmill from Ohio and put it into operation. Within two years a flourmill and a foundry opened for business in the little settlement.

Henry was exactly the kind of man that a growing town needed to succeed. Ambitious, plainspoken, and honest to a fault, Anson commanded respect and admiration for his business acumen and civic endeavors. He worked tirelessly, and used his forceful personality to persuade others to work alongside him through good times and bad. A fire in the spring of 1856 destroyed the sawmill and interrupted the growth of Marshall, but Henry refused to be discouraged, and the fire proved no more than a temporary setback. Marshall continued to thrive, and by 1860 it was home to nearly 1,000 residents, thanks largely to the efforts of Henry Anson.

Henry was Marshall's most enthusiastic builder and booster, and he tackled every task that was necessary for the town's success. There was no dentist in Marshall in its first few years of existence, so Henry extracted teeth with a pair of bullet molds. He began his own surveying business and served as the local land agent for many years. Whenever land was needed to attract businesses or build schools, Henry could be counted on to make it available. He was the main property owner in town, and donated land for schools, parks, and the courthouse. He was Marshall's first justice of the peace and its first county supervisor, and he maintained friendly relations with Johnny Green and the Pottawattamie Indians.

As the biggest landowner in Marshall, Henry cleverly used his holdings to increase the town's population. He made a standing offer of a free lot to any man who wanted to make his home in Marshall, and the proposition attracted hundreds of eager settlers, adding scores of names to Marshall's voting rolls. The resulting surge in population increased Marshall's influence in the affairs of Marshall County, as Henry had anticipated. By 1856, the patriarch believed that his new town was ready to take the next step toward prominence. In that year, Henry Anson began a campaign to designate Marshall the county seat.

The founder of Marshall had a fight on his hands. In the same year that Henry arrived in Iowa, the Marshall County commissioners chose an undeveloped spot a few miles from Marshall, named it Marietta, and laid out a new town, intending to make it the county seat. Marshall grew much faster than Marietta, and Anson began campaigning for the seat of government to move to Marshall. He sparked a bitter feud between the two towns, but the redheaded Yankee never shied from a fight. A countywide vote in 1856 left the county seat in Marietta, but the undeterred Henry convinced his fellow townsmen to continue the battle. They built a courthouse in Marshall in 1857, on land that was donated by Henry Anson, and soon afterwards a delegation of Marshall men raided the courthouse in Marietta and made off with the county files and documents. It was a drastic move, but it succeeded, and in 1859 the Iowa Supreme Court declared Marshall the permanent seat of Marshall County.

As Marshall grew, Anson and his fellow town fathers discovered another village in Iowa that bore the same name, so in 1863 they adopted the name Marshalltown, by which the place is known to this day. Henry regretted that the protracted battle with Marietta kept Marshall out of the running to become the state capital, which was awarded to Des Moines in 1857. "If the same effort in time and money had been spent during the seven-year war over the county seat," wrote Henry many years later, "Marshalltown would today be the capital of Iowa."[5] The town boosters were disappointed, but the arrival of the Iowa and Nebraska Railroad in 1863 gave the new town another jolt of prosperity. In 1869 the transcontinental railroad, which passed through Marshalltown, was completed, and Henry Anson's settlement became a stopping point for businessmen and others traveling from one coast to the other.

Henry had achieved his dream of building his own prosperous town, and today Marshalltown pays homage to its founder with a street, a creek, and two schools named for him. Henry Anson found success on the plains of Iowa, but he experienced his share of tragedy as well. Melville Anson, the third son of the family, lived for only a few years, and in December 1859 Jeanette took ill and died suddenly. She left Henry to raise his remaining children, Sturgis and Adrian, by himself. Sturgis was a good student, a well-mannered boy and a hard worker like his father. Adrian, however, was much more of an individual, and Henry would have his hands full in raising this headstrong second son.

Adrian Constantine Anson, named after two towns in southern Michigan that his father had admired, lost his mother when he was seven years old. "I remember her now as a large, fine-looking woman," said Adrian many years later, "who weighed something over two hundred pounds, and she stood about five feet ten and a half inches in height. This is about all the recollection that I have of her."[6] After her death, the Anson household was an all-male affair, and, as Adrian later put it, "my father and I were more like a couple of chums at school together than like father and son." Henry Anson busied himself with the affairs of the growing town, traveling often to Chicago or the state capital at Des Moines, and often left Sturgis and Adrian in the care of relatives for weeks at a time. Adrian found many opportunities for creative mischief making during his father's frequent absences.

Teasing the local Indians was one of the favorite pastimes among the boys of Marshalltown. The Sioux were still active in Iowa when Marshalltown was settled, and carried out a massacre of settlers near Spirit Lake as late as 1857 before the United States Army quelled their uprising. Fortunately, the only Indians near Marshalltown were the peaceful Pottawattamie, whose teepees dotted the landscape outside of town during Adrian Anson's childhood. The Indians respected the honest and forthright Henry Anson, but Adrian and the other boys of the settlement enjoyed tormenting them at every opportunity. Henry had relied on the advice of the Pottawattamie chief, Johnny Green, in selecting a location for the town, but Adrian later described the chief dismissively as being "as fond of fire-water as any of them." It appears that Adrian developed many of his attitudes toward minorities during his childhood through his contacts with the Indians.

Adrian inherited his father's reddish-blond hair and his enthusiasm for sports, and received his height from his mother. He was a tall, strongly built boy, with a ruddy complexion that grew red easily when embarrassed or angry. His skin was so pink and his hair so light that many people assumed that he possessed Scandinavian ancestry. In adulthood, people dubbed him "Swede" for that reason, though Adrian always corrected them, for he was proud of his English forebears. With his strapping build, Adrian seemed like a boy who should have been able to put in countless hours of physical labor like his hard-working father. Instead, Adrian reveled in play. "I was possessed of an instinctive dislike both to study and to work, and I shirked them at every opportunity,"[7] as he later explained. Adrian was, in his own words, a "natural-born kicker," always ready to argue his way out of work, much to Henry Anson's exasperation. "I was as averse to work as I was to study," related Adrian, "and I had a way of avoiding it at times that was peculiarly my own."[8]

Henry and the town fathers had built a schoolhouse for the new settlement, but Adrian was not interested in obtaining an education. He resented being cooped up in a classroom while fun activities awaited him outside, and he played hooky at every opportunity. Henry punished Adrian often for skipping school, but Adrian had also inherited Henry's stubbornness, and the young man continued to shirk his chores, both at home and at school.

"Sport of any kind," said Adrian, "and particularly sport of an outdoor variety, had for me more attractions than the best book ever published."[9] The boys of Marshalltown played a game that they called "soak ball," a precursor to baseball in which a fielder retired a baserunner by throwing the ball at him. They fished and swam in the Linn River and hunted for birds and game in the woods outside of town. Adrian also became an expert at billiards after his father installed a primitive game table in the Anson Hotel, and Adrian spent hours practicing with a cue stick until he could beat anyone for miles around. To Adrian, playing billiards and bat-and-ball games were much more appealing than sitting in a classroom or doing the chores.

Henry tried to instill in Adrian a sense of responsibility. On one occasion, before the elder Anson left on a trip to Chicago, he promised he would give the boy his prized silver pocket watch if Adrian would cut and stack a large pile of wood before his return. Adrian coveted the watch, but he was less interested in performing the work necessary to earn it, so he rounded up a group of his friends from the neighborhood and set them to work on the woodpile. After the task was completed, Adrian paid them for their efforts with cakes and cookies from the larder of the Anson Hotel. Henry was impressed when he returned to Marshalltown and saw the neatly stacked supply of firewood, and only later did he realize that his son had subcontracted the job to his friends and paid them for their labors with Henry's own food.

During another of Henry's business trips, Adrian traded one of the elder Anson's prized guns for a hunting dog, a Llewellyn setter. This brought Henry's temper to full boil, but his anger was somewhat mollified when the dog proved its worth on a subsequent hunting trip. Shortly thereafter, a neighbor accidentally killed the dog, and a judge awarded Henry $200 for his loss, a far greater sum than the gun was worth. Though this incident turned out to Henry's advantage, it demonstrated that Adrian was increasingly resistant to his father's example and advice. Adrian admired his father, and all his life he referred to Henry as the "old gentleman," a term of great respect, but the young man still found trouble at every turn.

Henry grew frustrated with his willful second son. When Adrian was 14 years old, the elder Anson decided to send both of his sons to a school with a reputation for strict discipline. Though the Ansons were not Roman Catholic, Henry enrolled them at the all-male College of Notre Dame in South Bend, Indiana, in the fall of 1866. As Adrian later put it, Notre Dame "was selected as being the proper place for 'breaking me into harness,' provided that the said 'breaking in' performance could be successfully accomplished anywhere."[10]

Notre Dame, in the years immediately following the Civil War, was an institution with about 500 students. It accepted those as young as 14, and admitted almost anyone able to pay the $245 annual tuition. Since

Adrian was much too young to begin college studies, he entered a two-year preparatory program similar to a present-day high school course of instruction. This program provided instruction in Latin grammar, primary Greek, reading, arithmetic, geography, and history. The college also offered business courses, and it is probable that Henry Anson intended for both of his sons to concentrate on that course of study.

From all available evidence, it appears that Adrian behaved himself at Notre Dame, and in later life he looked back fondly on the two years that he spent in South Bend. Still, he was more interested in baseball, football, and skating than in his studies. Baseball had been introduced on campus in 1865 by some of the seniors, and the sport became so popular that the students assembled their own teams and played each day from the end of classes till sundown. One of the main teams on campus was called the Juanitas, and both Adrian and Sturgis were welcomed into the Juanita lineup when they arrived in South Bend. Adrian Anson excelled at the second base position, but Sturgis became the star of the team. He played center field and owned the strongest throwing arm in the student body, and the two Anson boys turned the Juanitas into the powerhouse of the campus.

Adrian enjoyed "fancy skating" in the wintertime, and boasted of his prowess on the ice many years later in his autobiography. Notre Dame provided Adrian with an outlet for his athletic skills, though the scholarly atmosphere of the campus made little impression upon the teenager. "If I acquired any honors in the way of scholarships in the brief time I was there," said Adrian, "I have never heard of them."[11] Notre Dame helped Adrian to become a fine athlete, like his older brother and father, and athletics, especially the rapidly growing sport of baseball, became his primary focus when he returned to Marshalltown in the summers.

Baseball fever swept the Midwest shortly after the Civil War, and Marshalltown was only one of the many small towns in Iowa that surrendered to the mania for the sport. Communities of all sizes assembled teams that battled their nearby rivals, and baseball soon became an important facet of civic pride for small towns with ambitions of growth. Marshalltown was no different, and in the summer of 1866 Henry Anson and the town fathers created their own community baseball team. The patriarch of Marshalltown was already 40 years old, but the "old gentleman" was still one of the best athletes in town, and starred for the team at bat and in center field.

Sturgis Anson played first or third base, while the 14-year-old Adrian was relegated to the second team due to his youth. This status did not sit well with Adrian, and baseball gave the boy a sense of direction and purpose that he had sorely lacked. Adrian envied his father and older brother, and resolved to earn a place in the Marshalltown starting lineup. For the first time in his life, he found a goal for which he was willing to work, and to put in long hours if necessary. "I was practicing early and late," recalled Adrian years later, "and if I had any great ambition it was to play in the first nine, and with this end in view I neglected even my meals in order that I might become worthy of the honor."[12]

Adrian batted and threw from the right side, and during his teenage years he developed the batting style that he used, with little change, for his entire career. He did not straddle the plate, as most batters do today; instead, he faced the pitcher with feet nearly together, almost perpendicular to a line from the plate to the mound. He held his hands below his waist during the pitcher's windup, and as the ball approached the plate, Anson lifted the bat, brought his left foot around and stepped into the pitch, swinging his bat through the ball with his powerful shoulders and arms. His strength enabled him to swing his thick-handled bats, which were made of dense hickory wood and were longer and heavier than any used in the major leagues today. His level swing produced bullet-like line drives that were difficult for infielders to handle, especially in the earliest days of the sport when no one, not even the catchers, wore gloves on the field. Adrian practiced, by himself or with others, at every opportunity, and would not be satisfied until he gained a position beside his father and brother on the Marshalltown club.

Adrian possessed two other attributes that served him well on the baseball field. He owned a large, booming voice and an argumentative nature. In the early days of baseball, a player rarely argued with an umpire, but Adrian was so competitive that he put up a fuss whenever he found his team on the receiving end of a poor decision. *The Sporting News* once related a story about Adrian, told by a General Sanford, one of Marshalltown's leading citizens:

> [Anson] was a kicker, even in his tender years. I remember one afternoon that he was playing ball when his father was umpiring the game. Adrian was captain of his team and kicked vigorously from start to finish.
> "Look here," said Cap to the old gentleman finally when the latter had rendered a decision, "that won't do. That man wasn't out."
> "Yes, he was," said Anson senior.
> "No sir, he was not," retorted the younger limb.
> "Don't you tell me I lie, sir," said the old gentleman.
> "Well, don't you lie so like h__l then," muttered young Anson, at the same time dodging the butt of his father's cane.[13]

The Marshalltown baseball team, circa 1868. Adrian Anson is on the far right. (Transcendental Graphics)

While Adrian impatiently bided his time with the second-stringers, Henry Anson's ballclub quickly became one of the leading aggregations in the state of Iowa. With Henry and Sturgis in the lineup and Adrian cheering from the bench, they won a state tournament at Waterloo in the summer of 1867. In a later competition at Belle Plaine, the other teams refused to play Anson's men unless some accommodation was made for the prowess of the Marshalltown nine. Henry agreed to give the opponents six outs in an inning instead of the usual three, but Marshalltown still managed to win the tournament.

Baseball provided Adrian and his father a common interest, as Henry shared his son's enthusiasm for the sport. After a long day's work, Henry returned to the Anson house, where he and Adrian ate their dinner as quickly as possible and then headed for the local baseball field to practice until nightfall. Sturgis came later; he liked baseball too, but he ate in a more leisurely fashion before joining the others for practice. Adrian's hard work eventually paid off. In late 1867 or early 1868, Henry gave his younger son a spot on the first team, declaring that although Adrian was "only a kid," he played as well as anyone in town.

In the summer of 1868, a team called the Crescents from the state capital in Des Moines challenged Marshalltown for the state title. It was an exciting game, with Henry and Sturgis scoring three times each and Adrian scoring twice, and the teams battled to an 18–18 tie after seven innings. Marshalltown scored three times in the eighth, but the Crescents scored three runs of their own in the ninth to send the game into extra innings, which were rarely seen in those days. Neither side scored in the tenth, but the Crescents won the game with two runs in the eleventh and returned to Des Moines with the championship banner. This defeat inflamed Adrian's competitive passion, and the 16-year-old set out to assemble a team to win the pennant back. Des Moines accepted the challenge, and with Adrian at second base, Henry at third, and Sturgis in center field, Marshalltown defeated the Crescents and brought the prized championship banner back to Marshalltown.

As the reputation of Marshalltown's baseball team grew, the formerly unreliable Adrian invested all his energy in the sport. One day the teenager surveyed the public square in the center of the town, land that had been donated by his father, and decided that it would hold a baseball diamond very nicely but for the trees on the property. Adrian procured an ax and went to work. "When it came to weeding a garden or hoeing a field of corn, I was not to be relied upon," said Adrian, "but at laying out a ball field I was a whole team."[14] He took great pride in the field he created, because he had finally found, in baseball, an outlet for his strength and enthusiasm.

Henry Anson believed in the value of an education, and he did not want to send his sons out into the world without one more attempt at formal schooling. In the fall of 1869, Henry sent both Sturgis and Adrian to the new state college at Iowa City, the present University of Iowa, about 50 miles from Marshalltown. The brothers enrolled in the Introductory program, which until then had been called the Preparatory course. This program taught high-school level material to its students as a means of preparing them for real college work.

Adrian was now 17 years old, with two years of preparatory studies at Notre Dame under his belt, but he failed the state college entrance examination. He passed the test on his second attempt, and he and Sturgis began their education in Iowa City. However, Adrian was no more of a scholar in Iowa City than he had been at Marshalltown and South Bend. "I was as wild as a mustang and as tough as a pine knot," recalled Adrian, "and the scrapes that I got into were too numerous to mention."[15] Adrian learned very little at the state college, spending only one year there before returning to Marshalltown, where he immersed himself once again in baseball.

His future was still undecided, and Adrian did not yet know what he wanted to do with his life. Professional baseball had barely made its appearance on the American scene; though a few teams paid their players for their efforts, it was still an amateur sport in the late 1860s. Baseball was a pastime, not a career choice, and although Adrian Anson worked diligently to improve his skill at the sport, it remained to be seen how, or if, his efforts would translate into success in the adult world.

CHAPTER 2

From Marshalltown to Rockford

> *I first saw Anson playing on the old Lake Front Grounds in Chicago [in 1871] ... I shall never forget the wonderful work he did then. He stood over six feet in height, was straight and slender as an arrow, could run with the fleetness of a deer, and could hit the ball harder than any man I had ever seen.*
> — Alfred H. Spink, founder of *The Sporting News*, 1910[1]

Adrian Anson's big break came in the summer of 1870 when the Forest City team of Rockford, Illinois, arrived in Marshalltown to play the Iowa state champions. Rockford, a small city of 11,000 people about 100 miles west of Chicago, boasted one of the leading ballclubs in the Midwestern states. A coterie of Rockford businessmen had organized the team five years earlier as a way to publicize the merits of the town, and they managed to sign and develop several players who went on to star in professional ball. Rockford's biggest win came in August 1867 when they defeated the powerful Washington Nationals, 29–23, in a tournament in Chicago, mere days after the Nationals had bombed a strong Chicago club, the Excelsiors, by a 49–4 score. It was the only loss suffered by the Nationals on their western trip, and the people of Rockford celebrated for a week after their team's stunning victory.[2] The Rockford nine further distinguished itself during the summer of 1870 when they defeated the Cincinnati Red Stockings, undefeated national champions of 1869, by a 12–5 score.

Rockford's greatest star was only 20 years old in 1870, but had already established himself as the finest pitcher in the Midwest. Albert Goodwill Spalding, a tall, thin righthander from Byron, Illinois, pitched the Forest

2. From Marshalltown to Rockford 17

Citys to 45 wins in 58 games from 1867 to 1870, and in one trip through the eastern states, Spalding and the Rockford squad won 13 games, lost only three, and tied one against the nation's strongest teams. Spalding threw straight underhand, as required by the rules of the time, and combined a good fastball with an excellent change of pace and a measure of craftiness on the mound. Rockford boasted several other fine players, but Al Spalding was the star of the team and the primary reason for the success of the Forest City ballclub.

Tiny Marshalltown had never encountered a team like the Forest Citys or a pitcher like Al Spalding, but the local fans dutifully placed their faith in Henry Anson's ballclub and came out to cheer their team. The crowd was swelled by the presence of "sportsmen" from Rockford and Chicago who followed the Forest Citys and wagered with the locals on the number of runs scored and the margin of Rockford's impending victory.

Adrian played second base for Marshalltown, with Henry in center field and Sturgis at third, and the Marshalltown nine gave the Rockfords a tough battle. As expected, the Forest Citys defeated the locals, but the final score of 18–3 surprised all observers. Rockford was used to walloping its opponents by 30 to 50 runs or more, and the Forest City backers lost most of their wagers that day. The Rockford men quickly arranged to play Marshalltown again the next day to give the sportsmen a chance to win some of their money back.

On the following afternoon, the Rockford nine gave the Marshalltown team a lesson in the tricks of the game. Anson's team supplied the baseball for the first contest, but the Rockford club offered to provide the ball for the second game. In the early 1870s, good-fielding teams liked to play with the "Ryan Dead Ball," which was recognized as official by most sporting organizations, but good-hitting aggregations preferred much livelier baseballs with more rubber at the core. Henry Anson insisted ever after that the Forest Citys stitched a Ryan Dead Ball cover onto a much livelier "Bounding Rock" baseball and used it in the second game of the series. When the Marshalltown fielders took their positions in the second game, they saw line drives whizzing past them for the first few innings until they adjusted.

The second game ended in a 35–5 Rockford win, but the 18-year-old Adrian Anson, "a big, rawboned, loose jointed fellow" as Spalding later described him, impressed the Forest Citys with his hard hitting and enthusiastic play. Adrian spent the entire game shouting encouragement to his teammates, dashing around the infield making plays, and sprinting madly around the bases. He was the best player on the field for Marshalltown, and the Rockford club directors made a mental note of the strong-armed teenager. As Spalding stated many years later, "We found that the main strength of the Marshalltown team was the Anson family ... they put up a rattling game, especially the two sons, and they were the hardest fighters I ever saw in my life."[3]

Henry Anson impressed Spalding for a different reason. The umpire was a Rockford man who was not inclined to call balls against Al Spalding, and Spalding pitched outside the strike zone all day in an effort to get his opponents to swing at bad pitches. Henry Anson patiently waited Spalding out, and the Rockford hurler changed his tactics and threw inside to drive the "old gentleman" away from the plate. Henry stood his ground, and Spalding hit Henry with a pitch early in the second game. On Henry's next trip to the plate Spalding struck him again, and the red-headed Yankee stormed to the mound, demanding to know if Spalding had thrown at him intentionally. The young pitcher quickly made his apologies to the fuming town patriarch. "He scared me," remarked Spalding many years later, "so that I kept the ball away from the plate after that for fear of reaching him again."

After this series, Adrian was more convinced than ever that he could play baseball on the highest level. There was money to be made playing the game, as he discovered one day when a team from Clinton, Iowa, offered Adrian $50 to play for them against their rivals from Des Moines. Fifty dollars, at that time, was "more money than I had ever had at any one time in my life," as Adrian described it years later, and so he agreed to disguise himself and travel to the state capital for the game. Adrian was already well known in Iowa baseball circles, so he dyed his hair and stained his skin before he went to the Marshalltown train station on game day to catch the express for Des Moines.

Unfortunately for Adrian, Henry heard of his son's promised windfall, and the "old gentleman" met Adrian at the station and asked him what on earth he thought he was doing. "When he got there," recalled Adrian, "he gave me a lecture, told me that such a proceeding on my part was not honest and would ruin my reputation. In fact, he made me thoroughly ashamed of myself."[4] Adrian learned a valuable lesson about honesty, one that he remembered for the rest of his life. He also spent the next several days washing the dye out of his hair and off of his skin. Adrian mourned the loss of $50, but he would soon find a way to earn money at the sport he loved without resorting to deception or disguise.

By the fall of 1870, Henry Anson had resigned himself to the fact that the lure of baseball was too strong for his son to resist. With professionalism slowly taking its place in the sport, many of the nation's most prominent teams declared themselves as all-professional nines. One of those teams was the famous Chicago White Stockings, who claimed the unofficial national championship in 1870 and chose to assemble an all-paid team of players for the 1871 campaign. Henry, at Adrian's urging, wrote a letter to Chicago manager Jimmy Wood, requesting a tryout for the 18-year-old Adrian. Wood turned the Ansons down, explaining that the Chicago ballclub was only interested in hiring experienced players.

Adrian was disappointed with Wood's reply, but it did not take long for him to find a place in professional ball. Not long after it departed Marshalltown, the Rockford club decided to join the professional ranks for its 1871 campaign. The Forest Citys had "spread the fame of Rockford far and wide" and the club members agreed "that it would be to our pecuniary advantage to put our hands deep down in our pockets ... to maintain a first class club."[5] However, they would have to compete in the future without the services of Al Spalding. The 20-year-old pitcher had signed with the new Boston Red Stockings, a ballclub that was managed by Harry Wright and included four other members of the undefeated 1869 Cincinnati national champions. The Rockford club was further crippled when two other stars, second baseman Ross Barnes and outfielder Fred Cone, departed for Boston with Spalding.

Rockford needed players to fill its roster, and the team directors remembered the feisty team from Marshalltown and the redheaded Anson men. They had already signed two Marshalltown players, shortstop Sam (Pony) Sager and outfielder Pete Hoskins, both of whom played for the Forest Citys during the last few weeks of the 1870 season. Hoskins did not remain with the team for 1871, but Sager did, and the Rockford directors decided to raid Marshalltown for more talent. They mailed contract offers to Adrian Anson, the best player on the team, and to Sturgis and Henry Anson as well.

Henry may have been flattered by the Rockford offer, but he was 44 years old and had no intention of abandoning his business concerns in Marshalltown to play ball for pay. Besides, Henry had remarried, taking the sister of one of his business associates as his second wife in 1869. Sturgis was not interested in professional ball either; he was a fine player, but he had injured his arm at Notre Dame and no longer threw with the strength that he once possessed. Adrian, in contrast, viewed the contract as a golden opportunity. Henry might have preferred to send his sons back to school at Iowa City in the fall of 1870, but college life held no appeal for Adrian. He wanted to play ball, and though Henry and Sturgis declined the Rockford offer, Henry permitted Adrian to accept it.[6]

Adrian and shortstop Sam Sager, who was five years older than Adrian, spent the winter months practicing in Henry Anson's barn. In March of

1871 Adrian boarded a train for Rockford and the start of his career in professional baseball. He was 18 years old and had never seen a city bigger than Des Moines.

Baseball in the early 1870s, as historian Bill James has pointed out, more closely resembled fast-pitch softball of the present day than the modern game of baseball. The pitcher stood in a box, not on a mound, and he delivered the ball while standing between two iron plates set at a distance of 45 feet and 51 feet from home plate. He was required to deliver the ball underhanded, with his arm perpendicular to the ground; though umpires allowed some latitude for wrist-snaps and the like, the pitcher could not release the ball above his waist for any reason. In 1872 the pitching rules were relaxed, and although the ball was still released below the waist, the hurler was allowed to bend his elbow or wrist, or throw with a more sidearm delivery. This brought the curveball into the game and radically changed the balance of power between the hitters and the pitchers.

Few batters walked, because it took nine balls, not four, for the batter to be awarded first base. Actually, each third pitch outside the strike zone was a "called ball," and it took three called balls—nine bad pitches in total—for the umpire to give the batter his base. Some umpires allowed the pitchers leeway in the number of called balls, and sometimes a batter would let as many as 13 bad pitches go by before taking first base on a walk. There were also few strikeouts, partially because an underhand pitch was easier for a batter to hit, but also because a batter was expected to make a reasonable effort to hit the ball. Foul balls were not regarded as strikes, and would not be until the 1880s, but a foul ball caught on the first bound was an out. The batter was allowed to call for a high or low pitch, above or below the belt. Adrian Anson always requested high pitches, which allowed him to use his considerable upper body strength to best advantage.[7]

Perhaps the most remarkable feature of baseball in the early 1870s lay in the fact that no fielders, not even the catchers, wore gloves, and catchers did not wear masks until the middle of the decade. Because all defensive players were barehanded, sharp line drives, not long fly balls, were the order of the day. The fences were so far away that few men could hit a ball over them, and home runs were such a rarity that even a strongman like Adrian Anson failed to hit one during his first five years of professional play. Anson's forte was the "line hit," what we now call the line drive, and his bullet-like hits were almost impossible for an infielder to stop without endangering life and limb.

Prior to 1871, the most powerful teams in the country, amateur and professional, arranged their own matches and played each other on an irregular basis. In some seasons, the national champion was obvious to all, as in 1869 when the Cincinnati Red Stockings won all their games and defeated all of the nation's best teams. In other years, several teams lay claim to the championship, with a resultant controversy similar to that which surrounds college football today. The 1870 season ended without a universally recognized titlist. One claimant was the Atlantic club of Brooklyn, which defeated the defending champs from Cincinnati in June of that year, but the Chicago White Stockings and New York Mutuals compiled better records and flew their own self-awarded championship flags. Many baseball enthusiasts longed for a way to identify a champion in a more organized fashion.

In the spring of 1871, the leading teams in the nation met at a tavern in New York and created the first all-professional baseball circuit, the National Association of Professional Base Ball Players. It was more of a loose confederation of teams than an actual league, and any professional or semiprofessional team could join the Association by posting a ten-dollar fee. The new circuit attracted the strongest teams in the country, such as the Athletics of Philadelphia, the Mutuals of New York, and the Chicago White Stockings, and the league promised to award a banner, called a "whip-pennant," to the first-place team at the end of the season. Each team would play a series of five games against each other team, and the club which won the most series—not necessarily the most games—would win the whip-pennant.

The Rockford Forest City nine had held its own against the nation's best, so the Rockford backers enthusiastically paid the entry fee and entered their club onto the National Association roster. Within months the lineup for the 1871 season was set, with clubs representing six large cities (Philadelphia, New York, Washington, Boston, Cleveland, and Chicago) and three smaller ones (Rockford, Fort Wayne, Indiana, and Troy, New York). The Cincinnati Red Stockings, champions of 1869, had disbanded, but several of their star players and manager Harry Wright moved to Boston and created a new team, also called the Red Stockings. Wright signed the former Rockford star Al Spalding as Boston's pitcher, and the Red Stockings appeared to be the class of the new association. It remained to be seen how the small-town clubs from Fort Wayne, Troy, and Rockford would fare against their big-city rivals.

Historians have described the Rockford ballpark as the poorest in major league history, and though no photographs of the place survive, we know that it was far inferior to a Little League field of the present day. It was called Fairgrounds Park, and was built on the grounds of the Agricultural Society, where Winnebago County's annual fair was once held. There must not have been much open space on the Society property, because so

OSBORN

RYAN

ADDY

HAM

SAGER

FISHER

BIRD

MACK

ANSON

FOREST CITYS 1871
HASTINGS 1871

many trees surrounded the field that it was nearly impossible for the players to chase foul balls. The fielders also had to beware of an open drainage ditch at the edge of the outfield.

A Rockford resident named John Clifford gave a description of the field to a local newspaper in 1939. "The games were played on the fair grounds and a poorer field, to my mind, has never been known," recalled Clifford. "The catcher was hemmed in by trees with the exception of a space about 30 by 50 feet. An umpire could not see a foul unless it hit back of the plate or a few feet on either side of the base lines. Between the plate and second base, the terrain was fairly level, but approaching third base, there was a noticeable rise, and from third to the plate there was a depression and the base runner had to dig in for life."[8] The bleachers, made of planking from a torn-down bridge, seated between 300 and 500 people.

Adrian Anson arrived in Rockford in March of 1871 and reported to Fairgrounds Park for practice. The weather was cold, and Adrian shivered as he stood in to hit against Rockford's new pitcher, William (Cherokee) Fisher, a fast underhand thrower. Anson had batted successfully against Al Spalding, the greatest pitcher in the Midwest, but Fisher threw faster than anyone Adrian had ever seen. Adrian swatted a few liners to the outfield and was assured by the club president, a Rockford businessman named Hiram Waldo, that he was "all right." If he could hit Cherokee Fisher's pitching, he could stand in against any professional pitcher in the nation.

On March 31, Adrian signed his official contract for the 1871 season. In it, the directors of the Rockford ballclub attested that Adrian had "represented ... that he is a first class base ball player and possessed of the skill, and physically competent to play said game as a member of a first class club." In return, Adrian agreed to "abstain from the use of alcoholic Liquors," to "abstain from profane language," and to practice at least two and a half hours per day. The contract, which covered the six-month period from April 15 to October 15, 1871, called for the directors to pay Adrian the sum of $66.66 on the first day of each month, beginning in June and ending in November. Adrian was also required to pay for his own uniform, a white outfit with a white cap, green stockings, and "Rockford" stitched in green letters across the chest.

Spring practice began in early March, but the teenaged ballplayer would not receive any salary until June 1, though Adrian did not complain. "It was a fairly good salary for a ball player," remarked Anson years later,

Opposite: The 1871 Rockford Forest Citys, who finished in last place in the National Association. (Transcendental Graphics)

"and especially one who was only eighteen years old and a green country lad at that."⁹

The Rockford field manager and catcher, Winfield Scott Hastings, had not yet arrived in town. He had played for the Forest Citys in 1870 and then spent the spring months in New Orleans, where he joined an independent club. Hastings played his last game down South in mid–April and returned to Rockford in early May. In his absence, the Forest City team practiced and prepared for their first National Association contest, a home game against the Cleveland club on May 6. Adrian Anson, who turned 19 in April of 1871, was the youngest man on the team, but his confidence grew with each day of practice at the Agricultural Society grounds.

Adrian gained a cluster of nicknames in Rockford. Some newspapers dubbed him the "Marshalltown Infant," due to his youth, while Hiram Waldo called the young man "Addie," but his teammates labeled him "Hoss" or "Old Hoss" because of his size. Adrian was six feet and two inches tall and already weighed nearly 200 well-muscled pounds. He was the biggest and strongest man on the team by a wide margin, and he was probably the biggest man on the field in every game he played that season. Strong, durable, and fearless, he played third base without a glove and stopped punishing line drives with his chest. In those days, many players excelled in "fair-foul" hitting, because a ball that struck in fair territory and rolled foul was still considered to be a fair ball. The first and third basemen of the early 1870s played in front of the bag for this reason, and it took a courageous soul to play third base well.

Adrian received an unwelcome surprise when he appeared at the park for his first major league game on May 6, 1871. Scott Hastings arrived at the game late, so Adrian, who said later that he "looked forward to this game with fear and misgivings," was ordered to go behind the bat and catch the deliveries of Cherokee Fisher. Catchers were more prone to injury than any other player on the field, since they wore no masks or gloves then, but Anson caught the entire game, and only three of Fisher's pitches managed to elude him for passed balls. Anson batted sixth in the lineup and managed one hit, a double, in four trips to the plate, and although the Rockford club lost the game to Cleveland by a 12–4 score, Adrian was pleased with his performance. He caught only a few more times in the 1871 season, much to his relief, as Hastings resumed his position and Anson returned to third base.

There was no formal schedule of games in professional baseball's first season. Each club was expected to arrange its own series of contests with its competitors, and before long it became apparent that Rockford was at a disadvantage in this regard. Rockford was the westernmost city in the league, and the teams in New York and Boston were not anxious to travel all the way to western Illinois for a match, not when they could play lucrative exhibitions in the eastern states. The Rockford club was obliged to spend most of its time on the road, and the club played only seven home games that counted in the official league standings that year.

The Forest Citys defeated the Olympics of Washington, 15 to 12, in Rockford on May 17, then headed east. They lost 15–6 at Chicago on May 22, although Adrian Anson whacked three hits and impressed the sportswriter from the *Chicago Tribune*. "The new [Forest City] nine seems to be fortunate in the possession of an excellent third baseman," said the *Tribune* on May 23, "one who will make Pinkham [the Chicago third sacker] look to his laurels before the season is through." The Rockford nine then traveled to Fort Wayne and beat the Kekionogas of that city by a 17–13 count in ten innings.

However, Scott Hastings' sojourn in New Orleans came back to haunt the Rockford club. The National Association had passed a rule barring any player from joining a club until three months had elapsed since his last professional engagement. Hastings played his last game in New Orleans on April 16, and the other clubs protested that he was not eligible to play for Rockford until July 16. Hastings played while Rockford appealed, and in early June the Forest Citys traveled to Philadelphia and defeated the league leading Athletic nine by scores of 11 to 10 and 10 to 7. Unfortunately, Rockford lost its appeal in the Hastings controversy, and the league declared all Rockford wins before July 16 as forfeited. This ruling put the Forest Citys at the bottom of the standings, where they remained all season long.

The Rockford ballclub also ran into scheduling problems in the eastern states. They tried to arrange playing dates with the New York Mutuals and the Brooklyn Eckfords, but those two clubs demanded a much larger cut of the gate than the Rockford club was willing to surrender. Eastern clubs drove hard bargains with the teams from smaller cities, but the Rockford directors would not knuckle under, and Rockford declined to play the Mutuals and Eckfords on their eastern trip in May. Rockford managed to work out an agreement with the Mutuals for two games in early June, both of which they lost.

The National Association learned an important lesson in 1871. Teams from Rockford, Troy, and Fort Wayne could not compete on an equal basis with the richer teams of the eastern states, and they did not draw enough attendance at their home games to enable visiting teams to meet their expenses. All three teams struggled, and in late August the Kekionogas of Fort Wayne withdrew from the league. Rockford competed well against non-league competition — they bombed a team from Hamilton, Ontario, by a 50–6 score in July—but they stayed on the bottom of the National Association standings, thanks to the Hastings ruling. Cherokee Fisher was a good pitcher, but the Forest Citys missed Al Spalding, whose Boston nine defeated them in May by a 25–11 score. On July 10, Spalding and the Bostons bested Rockford again by a 21–12 count.

Each National Association team was required to play five games against each of their fellow league members, but the teams also faced each other in games that did not count in the standings. Club directors might arrange a four-game series in which only one or two games were designated as "championship contests," so Rockford played more games than the total of 25 that shows in the Association standings for 1871. One such non-championship tilt, held in Rockford on July 5, found the Forest Citys trailing the Chicago White Stockings by a 12–8 score after five innings. Rockford scored 14 runs in the sixth to pull out a 29–14 victory in a game that the *Chicago Tribune* called "the worst [that] the Whites have ever played in the field." Anson managed only one hit, but a home run by Bob Addy and a bevy of fielding miscues by the White Stockings gave Rockford the win. "The details are unworthy of notation," stated the *Tribune*. "The only word to express the play is damnable."[10]

On the Fourth of July, the White Stockings defeated Rockford at Chicago by a 17–13 score despite three hits by Rockford's rookie third baseman. Anson had begun to be noticed by the newspapers, especially in Chicago, where the *Tribune* praised him as a "sturdy stripling." By midseason, manager Hastings moved his young star to the second spot in the batting order, and Anson's hitting improved as he grew accustomed to major league pitching. He probably had not yet seen a pitcher throw a curveball, since the pitch did not appear in the Association until 1872, but Adrian was quick enough to hit the best fastballs from the hardest throwers in the circuit.

Adrian Anson, a teenager from a small town on the Western frontier, had his horizons broadened considerably in 1871. The Rockford club journeyed by train to New York, Boston, and other large cities in the United States and Canada, and Adrian, in his words, "learned more regarding the country I lived in and its wonderful resources than I could have learned in going to school for half a lifetime." The Rockford players traveled in sleeping cars on overnight trips, two to a berth, but "we did not look upon this as an especial hardship," said Anson, "as would the players of these latter days, many of whom are inclined to grumble because they cannot have the use of a private stateroom on their travels."[11]

The Rockford club, thanks to the Hastings ruling, remained winless until the end of July. They were well out of the pennant race by then, but finally won an official game on July 31 against the New York Mutuals by a score of 18 to 5. Three days later Cherokee Fisher "Chicagoed" the Kekionogas in Fort Wayne; a shutout was called a "Chicago" game then, and the Forest Citys beat Fort Wayne 4–0 for one of only four shutouts completed all season in the National Association. In August Rockford finally gained momentum, winning at Chicago and again at Cleveland to complete a four-game winning streak. They then went to Canada for five exhibition games, all of which they won by lopsided scores, then traveled to Brooklyn on September 1 and overwhelmed the Atlantics in a non-league game by a score of 39 to 5. They followed that win with a 14–9 victory over the Brooklyn Eckfords on September 2, though that game also did not count in the standings. If Rockford had hit its stride a few months earlier, and if the Hastings controversy had not caused the team to forfeit several of its wins, the Forest Citys might have finished near the top of the Association.

The Rockfords were scheduled to continue their season at Chicago in early October, but the Forest Citys and the White Stockings never got the chance to meet. On October 9, 1871, the Rockford players, approaching Chicago by train, saw a thick layer of smoke that hung over the entire city. The Great Chicago Fire had begun the night before and raged for more than two days, destroying most of the city, along with the White Stockings' ballpark and equipment. Adrian and his teammates returned to Rockford, where they finished the season with two contests against the Troy Haymakers, and in mid–October the city's first and only season of major league baseball came to an end. With an official won-lost record of 4–21, the Forest Citys became professional baseball's first last-place team.

The disappointing performance of the Rockford squad exacerbated the financial pressure on the club, and the directors realized that they could not afford to keep their star players. Adrian Anson was one of the brightest young players in the Association, and although he enjoyed playing in Rockford, he had already attracted the notice of the richer eastern teams. He impressed the league-leading Philadelphia Athletics when Rockford played there in early June, and after the game, a Philadelphia team official spoke with the teenager about playing for the Athletic club in 1872. In July, the directors made Adrian a firm offer at a salary of $1,250, more than three times the pay the young man received from Rockford.

Adrian preferred to stay in Rockford, and in September he approached team president Hiram Waldo and offered to remain with the Forest Citys for a salary of $100 a month. However, Waldo counseled Adrian to take the Philadelphia offer, since he was not certain that Rockford could afford to field a team in the Association in 1872. Waldo's advice was sound, because the team proved a failure at the gate and, despite their good play in August and September, on the field as well. The club won only eight games of the 25 they played that counted in the standings, and four of those wins were forfeited because of the Hastings controversy. Rockford's official 4–21 record brought up the rear of the Association, and the Forest City club did not return to the circuit in 1872.

Despite the team's troubles, "Hoss" Anson performed well at bat and in the field. He led the team in batting with a .325 mark, though the average was then expressed as "average first base hits" with a figure of 1.64. Anson also led the league in doubles with 11 in the 25 official league games. The versatile teenager played every position except pitcher and shortstop, and he was the only Rockford player to bat above the .300 mark.

Because of the confusion caused by the Rockford forfeits and the failure of the Fort Wayne Kekionogas to finish their season, the National Association called a meeting in November 1871 to decide which team would receive the championship whip-pennant. Two of the forfeited Rockford wins were awarded to the Philadelphia Athletics, and those two additions to the Philadelphia win column allowed the Athletics to nose out Boston for the title. The city of Philadelphia celebrated its victory, and the chance to play for the championship team of the Association appealed to Adrian Anson as much as the tripling of his salary. The Athletics, for their part, looked forward to adding Rockford's only .300 hitter to their already powerful lineup.

Adrian decided to accept the Philadelphia offer. He did not consult his father about the matter — indeed, he had not returned to Marshalltown since he left the previous March — and in the latter months of 1871 he moved to Philadelphia, joined a gymnasium, and began working out to prepare for the 1872 campaign. Adrian had made a success of himself in professional baseball, and was making his own decisions now. He would not see Marshalltown again for nearly five years.

CHAPTER 3

The Philadelphia Athletics

> *Philadelphia is a good city to live in, at least I found it so, and had I had my own way I presume that I should still be a resident of the city that William Penn founded instead of a citizen of Chicago....*
> — Adrian Anson, 1900[1]

The Philadelphia Athletics were one of the most well-known and successful teams in the nation. The leading sports organization in the city, the Athletic Club of Philadelphia, founded the team as a cricket club in 1859 before its focus switched to the fast-growing baseball arena. During the Civil War, the Athletic nine became a force in the amateur baseball world. In 1866 they lost only two games all season and claimed a share of the unofficial national championship. On October 1, 1866, more than 30,000 people showed up to see the Athletics play the Atlantics of Brooklyn in the first game of a series to decide the national title, but the crowd swarmed onto the field, forcing the postponement of the match. In a rain-shortened two-inning game a few weeks later, the Athletics defeated the Brooklyn club by a 31–12 score, but a dispute over the division of gate receipts kept the rest of the series from being completed.

That same year, the Athletics secretly began paying three of their star players $20 per week, and within a few years the Athletic ballclub was, overtly or otherwise, professional in every sense. The Athletics also compiled the best record in the country in 1868, with 47 wins and only three losses, a year before the all-professional Cincinnati Red Stockings completed their unprecedented undefeated season. Late in 1868 the editor of the *New York Clipper* awarded a gold medal to the best hitter in the nation at each position, and five of the nine medal winners were members of the Philadelphia Athletics.

Adrian Anson joined a ballclub that retained the remnants of the powerful Civil War–era champions. The field captain, what we would today call a manager, was pitcher Dick McBride, who joined the Athletic team as a cricket player in 1860 and won the *Clipper* gold medal as the nation's best hitting pitcher seven years later. McBride was a righthander who threw straight underhand with speed, though he had not mastered the curveball delivery that slowly took its place in the game in the early 1870s. Two other gold medallists, infielders West Fisler and Al Reach, also remained from the championship contenders of the previous decade, and they spearheaded the team that won the first National Association "whip-pennant" in 1871.

Though the Athletics won the inaugural National Association championship, the team directors moved to revamp the roster for the 1872 campaign. Some of the Athletic players were aging, while others departed the Quaker City to sign with rival ballclubs; in all, the Athletics changed personnel at six of the nine positions on the field for the new season. McBride installed Adrian Anson at third base, moved incumbent third baseman Levi Meyerle to right field, sent veterans Al Reach (who was also a club director) and John (Count) Sensenderfer to the bench, and juggled the remainder of the infield and outfield. The 1872 edition of the Athletics bore only a slight resemblance to the 1871 championship team.

Despite — or perhaps as a result of — its success, the Athletic ballclub was the least popular outfit in the Association. In those days, the home and visiting clubs were required to jointly choose an acceptable umpire to work the game, and the Athletics were famous for their endless squabbles with visiting ballclubs. They seemed to prefer umpires who could be intimidated into calling close plays in their favor, and they were probably the first club to gain an advantage through their bullying tactics. The sporting press labeled the Athletics as the "champion kickers" of the league, and Anson, who learned how to argue with the umpires on the sandlots of Marshalltown, promised to fit right in with his new teammates.

Anson joined his new team in March, and after a few weeks of practice the Athletics played their first exhibition game against a "picked nine" of local players in Gloucester, New Jersey, on April 3. Several Athletic players were absent, including manager and pitcher Dick McBride, and the team had to recruit two locals to fill in. Nonetheless, the Athletics defeated their opponents by a 19–5 score in a game that featured the "terrific hitting" of Anson, according to the *New York Clipper*. Anson impressed his new teammates with two hits and four runs scored in his first appearance with his new team. The powerfully built young man cut an imposing figure in his white Athletic uniform, with blue stockings, white cap, blue ascot, and the word "Athletic" spelled out in blue letters across his chest.

Adrian found the home park of the Athletics to be a vast improvement over the hilly Rockford baseball field. The Jefferson Street Grounds, located at 23rd and Jefferson streets, was Philadelphia's first enclosed ballfield, seating about 2,000 people. The center field fence stood more than 500 feet away from home plate, and management often handled overflow crowds by making standing room available behind ropes in the outfield. The Athletic club management kept the field well groomed, and boasted to out-of-towners that it was as level as a billiards table. Though scant information survives about the ballpark, which was used by several different teams until 1890, the Jefferson Street Grounds certainly qualified as one of the Association's two or three best facilities.

The Athletics believed in hitting and plenty of it. They were the hardest-hitting team in the Association, having led the circuit with an average of more than 13 runs scored per game in 1871, and preferred to use a lively baseball and not the Ryan dead ball favored by the better-fielding teams. The home team supplied the baseballs in the earliest years of the sport, and the choice of balls was limited only by the National Association rules, which stated that a ball must weigh between 5 and 5.25 ounces and measure between 9 and 9.25 inches in circumference. The core of a ball was made of rubber (the present cork-centered ball was not introduced until 1910 or so) and the density of rubber inside a baseball determined its liveliness. The Athletics always used the liveliest balls that they could buy, a policy that resulted in many high-scoring slugfests at the Jefferson Street Grounds. "In some of the games we played that season," remarked Anson, "the fielders had a merry time of it and found at least plenty of exercise in chasing the ball."[2]

The Athletics were not known for their fielding prowess, but their heavy batting, coupled with their skill at intimidating the umpires (especially at home), made them the team to beat as the 1872 campaign began. In the first game of the season, played at the Jefferson Street Grounds on May 1, the Athletics took advantage of the lively ball and windy weather to pound the Baltimore club 34–19 with 33 hits, six of them by third baseman Adrian Anson.[3] The Athletics beat Troy into submission by a 25–5 score on May 13, and defeated Cleveland 31–7 eight days later as Anson drilled five hits and scored five runs. His batting average rose to nearly .500 early in the season, and the "Marshalltown Infant," or "Baby" Anson, immediately became a fan favorite. Though he remained in the seventh spot in the lineup for most of the campaign, Anson quickly became the most dangerous hitter in the Athletic lineup.

One of the biggest controversies of 1872 occurred during the early weeks of the season. The Athletics faced the Baltimore Canaries (so called because of their bright yellow stockings) on the road on May 20, and after seven innings the score was tied at 4. Baltimore took the lead with three runs in the top of the eighth, but the Athletics rallied, putting Adrian Anson on second and Mike McGeary on first with Denny Mack at bat. Anson attempted to steal third base on a 2–2 count (it took three called balls for a walk under the rules of the time) and the catcher threw Anson out just as the umpire called "ball three." Manager McBride immediately appealed, and after a period of intense discussion Anson was allowed to take third, with McGeary moving to second and Mack to first.

The Athletics won this argument, but the umpire's next decision caused a much bigger fracas. While McBride made his case to the umpire, McGeary wandered off of second base. The umpire had not called time, so Baltimore's Lip Pike got the ball and tagged McGeary out. The umpire let this play stand, but McBride ordered McGeary to remain on second base. Neither the manager nor the umpire would budge, and McBride took his team off the field in protest. Baltimore pitcher Bobby Mathews, at the umpire's direction, then threw several pitches to the plate, with no batter present, and when McBride failed to send a batter to the plate the umpire declared the game forfeited to the Canaries.

Protested games and umpire disputes were then handled by a Judiciary Committee, but three of the five members of the panel were Philadelphians, and the committee later ruled that the game was a tie and ordered it replayed. This decision rewarded the Athletics for their "kicking" and incensed many of the other teams in the league. "The first effect of the disgraceful row," said the *Brooklyn Eagle*, "was a loss of prestige by the Athletic club, and a general desire — outside of Philadelphia — to see them defeated in every game they played."[4]

The two teams played three more games at Baltimore that season, with a large police presence at each contest, and no more incidents occurred despite what the *Eagle* called a "general ill-feeling" that permeated the crowd. However, the Philadelphia fans pelted the Baltimore players with stones in a game at the Jefferson Street grounds in June, and the *Eagle* harshly criticized the crowd for its "insulting language" and objectionable behavior. "The Athletic management had better put a stop to this style of thing," stated the *Eagle*. "If this is what the professional championship is going to bring about, the sooner the people stop patronizing the game the better."[5]

The Athletics also enjoyed a lively rivalry with the New York Mutuals, who played at the Union Grounds in Brooklyn. The Athletics won their first six decisions of the season (not including the disputed game in Baltimore) before the Mutuals defeated them in Brooklyn, 3–2, on June 1 behind curveball specialist Candy Cummings, despite the 100 to 40 odds laid on the Athletics before game time. Philadelphia returned the favor at the Jefferson Street Grounds seven days later with a 19–0 victory, but on July 13 Cummings and the Mutuals "Chicagoed" the Athletics by an 8–0 score in front of a crowd of 6,000 people. Cummings allowed only five hits and fooled the free-swinging Athletics with his tricky curve ball. Pool betting and other forms of baseball gambling flourished in New York, and the Mutual fans who took their team at 162 to 100 odds that day were big winners.

Though the Athletics still held second place with a 14–4 record, the 8–0 defeat was the first shutout ever pitched against them, and the Philadelphia papers sharply criticized the ballclub. "This is the worst defeat the Athletics have ever had," complained the Philadelphia City Item, and also labeled the shutout loss "a disgrace to Philadelphia."[6] The Quaker City papers took baseball very seriously, reacting and overreacting to every twist and turn in the fortunes of the ballclub, and newspaper criticism became a fact of life for Adrian Anson and the rest of the his teammates.

Baseball gambling was another accepted practice in Philadelphia. Gambling had accompanied sporting events and competitions of all kinds throughout human history, but with the post–Civil War boom in baseball's popularity came a renewed interest in wagering on the game. In the 1860s and early 1870s bookmakers set their own odds and brokered individual bets, a practice that led to countless disagreements. Pool-selling, introduced in 1871, streamlined the betting process and made wagering easier and more widespread than before. In 1872, *The New York Times* lamented, "Base ball, so far as it can claim to be a typical American institution at all, is simply a contrivance for gambling that most honest men would cheerfully see suppressed."[7] National Association executives publicly bemoaned the influence of gambling on the sport, but the weakly organized circuit was unable to curb what Henry Chadwick called "the gambling evil" that threatened the integrity of the game.

Players as well as fans were caught up in the betting atmosphere. Tim Murnane, who played with Anson on the Athletics and later became a renowned sportswriter for the *Boston Globe*, recalled in 1900 that "just outside the grounds was a club-house where pools were sold before the games, and it was no uncommon thing to see players in uniform putting down a few bets before they started for the ball field." The Athletics had allowed pool-sellers on the grounds in previous seasons, but banished them by 1872; however, the team could not control betting outside of the ballpark, and gamblers made up a sizable percentage of the attendance at the Jefferson Street Grounds. Betting on one's team was not considered unusual at the time, and some Philadelphia ballplayers attempted to augment their salaries with well-placed wagers. So far as anyone knows, Anson limited his betting to the billiards table, but many other players wagered both for and against their own teams in the early 1870s.

With the increase in betting activity came the inevitable upsurge in fan misbehavior, since many, if not most, of the attendees at the ballpark on any given day were financially interested in the outcome of the contest. In mid-season 1872, the Philadelphia papers criticized the Athletics management for tolerating wagering and failing to control the fans. "There is a bad influence within the Athletic Club," complained the *Philadelphia City Item*. "It is the influence of meanness, or vulgarity, and it ought to be corrected. What is the reason we so seldom see ladies at the matches? In the old days the seats were all occupied by bright, pure, good women!

"Come, Directors! Let there be reform! Throw out the betting men, the rummies, and the beats! Restore the old club to its former honorable standing!"[8]

The National Association began the 1872 campaign with 12 teams, but several of those had no realistic expectation of challenging for the whip-pennant. The league welcomed any ballclub willing to post the ten-dollar entry fee, and several "co-op" teams entered the field that year. Co-op teams, usually from smaller towns, paid their players from available gate receipts, not on a salary basis, and they existed only because their proximity to bigger cities allowed them to schedule matches against nines that were passing through. The league accepted a club from Middletown, Connecticut, which dropped out of the circuit after only 24 games, and five other teams failed to complete the 1872 season. In late July the Association decreed that its remaining teams play a series of nine games, not five, against each other to decide the championship.

The defending champion Athletics disappointed their fans when they fell behind the Boston Red Stockings in the pennant chase, but the fans found much to admire in their new third baseman. Though Adrian Anson made 57 errors in only 46 games that year for a fielding percentage of .738, such an error total was in no way unusual for the era, and his fielding was considered adequate, if not extraordinary. Anson represented a significant upgrade at the third base position from Levi Meyerle, who posted an incredible .492 batting average in 1871 but was probably the worst fielding third sacker in the Association. Meyerle was prone to committing errors in bunches, especially when booed by the Philadelphia crowds, and his .654 fielding percentage forced his move to right field for the 1872 campaign.

Anson made his greatest contribution to the Athletics with his bat. He belted National Association pitching for a .415 average, finishing third in the league in batting, and his on-base percentage of .455 led the league. The 20-year-old hitting sensation did his best to keep the Athletics within striking distance of the streaking Boston Red Stockings, who won more than 80 percent of their games and held the league lead from May forward.

In early September, the Athletics traveled to Boston for a series, needing to win to remain in the pennant chase. The *Philadelphia Mercury* declared that the team was "confident of winning in Boston, as they could easily defeat the [Red Stockings] five times out of six."[9] However, the Boston club preferred to play with the Ryan dead ball to negate the heavy hitting of the Athletics, and they defeated the Athletics 16–4 on September 5. Adrian Anson belted five hits off Boston pitcher Al Spalding, but only Dick McBride managed more than one among the other Athletics, and after the game McBride decided to move Anson to the third spot in the batting order. He remained there for the rest of the season, but the move came too late as the Bostons ran away with the pennant. A 10–3 loss to Candy Cummings and the Mutuals on September 17 finally quashed the Athletic pennant hopes for 1872.

Anson was involved in a strange play on September 14, when the Athletics led Boston 4–1 going into the seventh inning at the Jefferson Street grounds. Anson and Al Reach opened the inning with singles, and Fergy Malone followed with a pop-up to Boston shortstop George Wright. Wright surprised the Athletics when he caught the ball in his hat, and when Anson and Reach froze on the bases, Wright touched third and threw to second to complete what he claimed was a double play. Wright knew that a player cannot legally catch a ball in his hat, so he insisted that the ball was still in play and that Anson and Reach were forced out at third and second respectively.

The Philadelphia players and fans let out a collective howl at this unusual interpretation of the rules, and the incident led to a long and angry argument. Finally, the umpire decided to allow Malone to bat again and sent the runners back to their bases. It wasn't the correct decision, but it mollified the unruly crowd and allowed the game to continue. The Athletics won the contest by a score of 6 to 4, and after the season was over the rules committee specifically outlawed the practice of catching the ball in a fielder's hat.[10]

The last glimmer of hope for the Athletics faded on September 25 in Philadelphia. On that day, the New York Mutuals sent curveball specialist Candy Cummings, the nemesis of the Athletics, to the mound, and the Mutuals built a 14–5 lead that they carried into the ninth inning. In the bottom of the ninth, the Mutual defense fell apart, as both Ned Cuthbert and Adrian Anson reached base on errors. Two more errors, a walk, and a bases-clearing triple by West Fisler sparked an eight-run rally, and the score stood at 14–13 when Anson came to bat for the second time in the inning with two out and a man on first. Anson walloped a long foul ball that New York's John McMullen caught on the first bounce, an out by the rules of the time, and the Mutuals escaped with a 14–13 victory.

The Athletics split their eight games with Boston evenly, winning four games in Philadelphia and dropping four in Boston, but the Red Stockings lost only four other games all year and ran away with the 1872 pennant. The race was so one-sided that the fans around the nation lost interest. Subsequently, the teams from Boston, Philadelphia, and New York staged a "Grand Tournament" in October to rekindle fan support. The three teams played for $1,800 in prize money, but this concept failed to excite the fans, and the Athletics and Red Stockings split the prize at the end of the tourney.

The only highlight of the tournament came on October 15 at the Union Grounds in Brooklyn, where six players, including Adrian Anson, participated in a throwing contest. Anson, hurling from center field to home plate, managed a heave of 330 feet, but Brooklyn's John Hatfield broke his own four-year-old record with a throw that measured 400 feet and seven and a half inches on the fly.

The season of 1872 was a difficult one for all the teams in the Association. The Philadelphia Athletics were one of the few ballclubs that made money that year, though they earned only $8.39 on gross receipts of $26,047.23. The pennant-winning Boston Red Stockings finished more than $5,000 in the hole and, reportedly, sent their players home for the winter without their final paychecks. Despite the gloomy financial outlook, four new teams entered the Association for the 1873 campaign. These included a second team in Baltimore called the Marylands, a new team in Washington called the Blue Legs, and the 1872 New Jersey state champions, the Elizabeth Resolutes, who believed they could compete on the higher level.

The other new team was formed in Philadelphia and provided competition for the established Athletic nine. This new club was called the White Stockings, though most newspapers simply called them the Philadelphias to avoid confusion with the more famous team from Chicago. The Philadelphias, who shared the Jefferson Street Grounds with the Athletics, struck a blow against their cross-town rivals when they induced five Athletic players (Meyerle, Cuthbert, Mack, Malone, and Treacy) to jump to the new team. Adrian Anson remained loyal to the Athletics, but the raid left the established ballclub with major holes to fill. The Athletic ballclub needed to replace its catcher, its first baseman, and its entire outfield.

3. THE PHILADELPHIA ATHLETICS

The Athletics and the Philadelphias play at the Jefferson Street Grounds on April 21, 1873. The Philadelphias won the game by a score of 11 to 3. (Author's collection)

McBride and the Athletic directors moved quickly to strengthen their club. Catcher John Clapp and outfielder Tim Murnane came from the disbanded Middletown nine, while Adrian's old Rockford teammate, Cherokee Fisher, joined the club from Baltimore as a right fielder and substitute pitcher for McBride, who had thrown all of the Athletics' innings in 1872. Ezra Sutton, one of the best third basemen in the Association, arrived from the defunct Cleveland team and took over the hot corner from Adrian, who moved to first base. Anson had played only one game at first during his first two professional seasons, but his sure hands and size made him the obvious candidate to replace Denny Mack at that position.

The presence of the Philadelphias provided the Athletics with another heated rivalry. The teams met for the first time on April 21 at the Jefferson Street Grounds, and the Philadelphias came away with an easy 11–3 win before a crowd of 6,000. On May 14, Adrian Anson belted four of the nine Athletic hits, but the Philadelphias won the game in 13 innings by a score of 5–4. This was the longest contest ever played in the professional ranks up to that time, and *The New York Times* called it "the finest game of base ball that ever took place in Philadelphia."[11]

The Athletics then won their next nine games, with a 22–3 walloping of the New York Mutuals bringing them to within three games of the league lead, but three more losses to the Philadelphias dropped them back to the middle of the pack. Though the Athletics defeated the defending champions from Boston in the early part of the campaign, they lost all of their first six matches with the new Philadelphia ballclub.

On July 21, the Athletics and Baltimore met in an exciting 13-inning game in which Anson played a key role. Baltimore scored four runs in the first inning, but the Athletics scored three times in the fourth, and Anson singled to start another three-run rally in the fifth that gave the Athletics a 6–4 lead. In the ninth, with the Athletics leading by one, Anson singled again but was forced out by Fisler as the Baltimores escaped the inning without allowing a run. Baltimore tied the game in the bottom of the ninth, but the Athletics scored three more times in the tenth, two of the runs being driven home by a sharp single by Anson.

Baltimore knotted the game once more in the bottom of the tenth, and in the thirteenth inning, Anson singled for the third time in the game. He surprised the Baltimores by attempting to steal second, but Baltimore catcher Cal McVey threw Anson out, ending the rally. In the bottom of the inning, Baltimore's Everett Mills singled, went to third on a throwing error by Anson, and scored the winning run on a single by John Radcliffe.

This game highlighted Anson's strengths and weaknesses as a ballplayer. Never more than an adequate fielder, he was a sure-handed first baseman, but his range was merely average, and he possessed a strong throwing arm that was not consistently accurate. He had played third base exclusively in 1872, but in 1873 McBride moved Anson all over the field, with 36 games at first base, 11 at third, and three each at catcher, second base, and the outfield. He was a versatile, if not outstanding, defensive player.

Once again, his real value on the field lay in his batting. He batted .398 in 1873, second in the Association to Boston's Ross Barnes, and the 22-year-old Anson was already the chief run producer for the Athletic ballclub. In August of that year, the Athletic board of directors signed Anson to a contract for the 1874 season, a move that kept the young star from considering offers from the cross-town Philadelphias and other rival nines. The papers reported that his $1,200 salary was one of the highest on the team, topped only by pitcher and manager Dick McBride and equaled by two other veterans, Ezra Sutton and West Fisler.

The Athletics took a three-week vacation in late July and early August, a practice that was also followed by other ballclubs during the hottest part of the summer. They trounced the Washington Blue Legs by a 14–0 score in their first game back, but seven losses in an eight-game stretch knocked the Athletics out of the pennant chase. The Philadelphias entered September with a comfortable lead over the Boston Red Stockings, but the new ballclub withered under the pressure and slowly relinquished their lead. The Red Stockings had managed to schedule some of its weaker opponents in the season's final month, and six consecutive wins against Washington moved Harry Wright's ballclub back into the race. On September 29, the Athletics finally defeated the Philadelphias for the first time in the 1873 season and crippled their rivals' hopes for the whip-pennant. Boston went on a late-season tear, with 24 wins in 26 decisions, to overtake the Philadelphias and win the flag for the second year in a row.

Anson as a member of the Philadelphia Athletics. This picture appeared in *Harper's* magazine on July 25, 1874. (Author's collection)

By the end of the 1873 season, Adrian Anson, the recognized "heavy hitter" of the Athletic lineup, was one of the most popular athletes in Philadelphia. He had come a long way from the pioneer settlement of Marshalltown, Iowa, and reveled in the money and fame he received from his exploits on the ball field. He had reached his full adult height of six feet and two inches, but, as Anson later admitted, he still had some growing up to do. "I was just at that age," Anson once recalled, "when, in my estimation, I knew a heap more than did the old man, and that idea had not been entirely knocked out of my head when I arrived in Philadelphia." The young ballplayer had "a constitution that a young bull might envy," but, as Adrian admitted, "good advice was, to a greater or less extent, thrown away upon me."[12]

Adrian was strong enough to play ball during the day and party well into the night, and he became a regular customer of the bars and pool halls in the nightlife districts of Philadelphia. His many hours of practice on the pool table in the Anson Hotel paid off handsomely, for he was an excellent billiards player, probably the best in the baseball world. He won a lot of money challenging players from the Athletics and other ballclubs, and in February of 1875 he won a three-ball match for $100 a side against James Lantz, one of the leading professional billiards players in the city. There were plenty of worshipful female fans at the Philadelphia ballpark, but Adrian paid little attention to them, preferring to concentrate on his baseball career and his extracurricular billiard activities.

His attitude changed when he met a young woman at a ball during the 1872 season. Virginia Fiegal was the daughter of John Fiegal, a bar and restaurant owner who ran an establishment in Philadelphia's 10th ward, not far from the Jefferson Street grounds. The brunette and brown-eyed Virginia was seven years younger than Adrian, and was only 13 years old when she made the acquaintance of the 20-year-old ballplayer. Virginia immediately captivated Adrian, despite their difference in ages, and he began calling on the Fiegals regularly. "I also began to hunt up excuses of various kinds for visiting the house ... and some of these were of the flimsiest character," admitted Adrian years later.[13]

Another ballplayer, catcher Charlie (Pop) Snyder, also pursued Virginia, and Adrian became annoyed on those occasions when he arrived at the Fiegal house and found Snyder already there. After a while Adrian ordered Snyder out of the picture, for he had already decided that Virginia was the girl he wanted to marry. He would have to wait a few years, due to Virginia's youth, but Adrian was willing to do so. He would establish himself in his baseball career and then, with his future secured, he would ask John Fiegal for Virginia's hand in marriage.

CHAPTER 4

Across the Ocean

> Anson is the heavy weight of the Athletic nine, and plays on the bases as well as at right field. He is the least active fielder of the nine, but excels in heavy batting. He is quite a fine billiard player, and can make a good score in either the French or the American game, as can half of the entire party for that matter, any style of ball-playing coming handy to them.
> — Henry Chadwick, 1874[1]

During the early 1870s, the rules of baseball changed every year as the leaders of the National Association continued to tinker with the game and the manner in which it was played. One innovation was the introduction in 1874 of the first batter's box. Previously, a batter was required to stand at the plate with one foot on a line drawn across the center of the home plate area. If a batter struck a pitch without having a foot on the line, the umpire disallowed the resulting blow and called the batter back to the plate. The batter's box measured six feet by three feet in 1874, and was increased to its present size of six-by-four in 1886.

Another suggestion, which did not take hold, was Henry Chadwick's proposal that baseball become a 10-man game of 10 innings in length. On November 6, 1873, the Athletics and the Philadelphias played such a contest as a benefit for injured player Ned Cuthbert. Each team employed a five-man infield with three basemen and two shortstops as the Athletics won the game by a score of 14 to 10. Chadwick's brainchild drew a great deal of negative reaction, and baseball has remained a 9-man, 9-inning game ever since.

As baseball's popularity increased in the United States and Canada, the game's promoters investigated the feasibility of exporting the national game to Europe and the rest of the world. Boston Red Stockings manager

Harry Wright, who was born in England, had long harbored a desire to bring the sport of baseball to his native land, and his dream became a reality in 1874. In January of that year, Wright sent his star pitcher, Al Spalding, to England to make arrangements for two National Association clubs, the Red Stockings and the Athletics, to introduce baseball to the British. Spalding managed to secure the cooperation of England's foremost cricket institution, the famed Marylebone Cricket Club of London, and scheduled a series of baseball and cricket matches to be played in London and other cities in late July and early August. Both the Red Stockings and the Athletics had taken mid-season vacations during the previous few seasons; in 1874, they would use those weeks to give their British hosts a look at America's national pastime.

While Spalding and Wright planned the trip to England, the lineup of teams in the National Association changed once again. The Elizabeth Resolutes and the Washington Blue Legs dropped out, and the Chicago White Stockings rejoined the National Association after the two-year hiatus imposed by the Great Fire. The Hartford Dark Blues also joined, giving the circuit eight teams and raising hopes that the Association would, for the first time, complete a season without losing any teams along the way.

Anson in 1874. (National Baseball Hall of Fame Library, Cooperstown, New York)

The leader of the new Chicago ballclub was William Hulbert, a hard-driving coal merchant and member of the Chicago Board of Trade who had been a club official of the previous team administration. Hulbert was a competitive sort who viewed the revival of the White Stockings as a powerful metaphor for the renaissance of the city of Chicago, still struggling to rebuild after the disastrous fire. The impatient Hulbert had no interest in building his team gradually; instead, he declared his intention to challenge Boston for the whip-pennant immediately. Hulbert, with solid financial backing from a group of Chicago businessmen and community leaders, induced six members of the Philadelphias to leave their home city and join the revitalized White Stockings. Four of the new Chicago players were the same men who jumped from the Athletics to the Philadelphias one year before, and Hulbert's coup decimated the Philadelphias, who began calling themselves the Pearls in 1874 due to their off-white uniform stockings. Hulbert's new ballclub, according to the papers, carried the highest payroll in the Association, and many observers counted the White Stockings as Boston's main rival for the 1874 pennant.

As for the Philadelphia Athletics, the club directors had protected their roster by signing Adrian Anson and other key players to contracts before the previous season had ended. The Pearls were now suffering as the Athletics had suffered the year before, and the Athletics defeated the Pearls in their first meeting of the season on April 23 by a score of 10 to 6. The Pearls had won eight of nine contests against the Athletics in 1873, but Hulbert's raid on the Pearls enabled the Athletics to regain the top position in Philadelphia baseball. Early June found the Pearls floundering in the middle of the standings, while Anson and the Athletics held second place behind the defending champions from Boston.

Anson continued to bounce from one position to another as needed for the Athletics, appearing in 24 games at first base, 20 at third, eight in the outfield, and three more at catcher during the 1874 campaign. "I was looked upon as a sort of general-utility man, who could play in one position about as well as in another," remarked Anson in his autobiography. Anson would have preferred to remain in one position on the field, because, as he once stated, "The jack-of-all-trades is the master of none."[2] He was not a bad fielder, and although not a master at any position, he was adequate at almost any spot on the diamond. His versatility, if not his fielding brilliance, kept his powerful bat in the lineup and afforded manager McBride some flexibility in dealing with injuries and slumps.

The talk of the baseball world in 1874, however, was the upcoming excursion to England by the Red Stockings and the Athletics. On July 15, in their last game before the start of the voyage to Europe, the Athletics defeated the Red Stockings at Boston by a score of 6–4. The following afternoon, 18 ballplayers from the first-place Boston club and the second-place Athletics, accompanied by writers, team executives, and boosters of the two ballclubs, boarded the steamship *Ohio* for an 11-day voyage to the British Isles. In all, nearly 200 American baseball enthusiasts traveled to England to introduce the national game to the British.

Adrian Anson had never made a sea voyage before. He was amazed by the vastness of the ocean; with nothing but water as far as the eye could see, Anson remarked, "I wished that I might be able to devise some plan for bottling it up and sending it out West to [Henry] to be used for irrigating purposes." Though seasickness afflicted many of the traveling party, Anson found the trip an enjoyable one. The players distracted themselves with cards, shuffleboard, and other games, and the amusements on board, in Anson's words, "helped us to forget that the old gentleman with the scythe and hourglass was still busily engaged in making his daily rounds."[3] On July 27, the *Ohio* dropped anchor at Liverpool, and Anson saw, for the first time, the land of his forebears.

Spalding had scheduled 14 baseball games and seven cricket matches in several British cities. He added a trip to Dublin, capital of Ireland, to the itinerary at the suggestion of Harry Wright. "We must take Dublin in," said Wright in a letter to Athletic team president James Ferguson, "for with all our Mc's and O'R's [among the players], a game there would surely prove attractive and pay handsomely."[4] The tight schedule left little time for sightseeing, particularly early in the trip. The first game was to be played only three days after the ship docked, and Spalding wanted to give his players time to get their bearings on land after 11 days at sea. The teams practiced for two days at Liverpool, where the British press remarked favorably on the visitors' appearance. "A smarter collection of athletes or a finer-looking body of men it would be impossible to find," stated one paper, "all of them being lithe, active, and wonderfully agile in the field."[5]

The first baseball game of the tour was played on July 30 at Liverpool, where the Athletics defeated the Bostons by a 14–11 score in ten innings. Boston evened the series with a 23–18 win the following day. The travelers then proceeded to Manchester, with the Athletics winning a 13–12 decision, and then to London, the most important city on the tour.

Upon his arrival in London, Spalding discovered to his horror that his hosts displayed little interest in seeing their guests play baseball. Londoners were more excited about the cricket matches than Spalding had promised; in Spalding's words, "We found the British public thoroughly advised of the forthcoming cricket matches, and only slightly informed about the exhibition ball games."[6] Spalding had scheduled a match against the Marylebone club, the strongest cricket team in England, almost as an afterthought, but he now realized that the match might turn into an embarrassing fiasco due to the Americans' inexperience at the British national game. Only three of the Americans (McBride and the Wright brothers) were experienced cricket players, and few of the remaining Red Stockings and Athletics had ever played the game. Many of the Americans had never seen a cricket match in their lives, so Harry Wright gave his teammates a crash course in the unfamiliar English game.

In cricket, there are two batters, called strikers, each of whom stands in front of a wooden wicket. The bowler (or pitcher) throws the ball on one bounce to one of the waiting strikers. If the ball gets past the striker and knocks over the wicket, the striker is "put out," but if the striker hits the ball, he and his fellow striker score by running between the two wickets. A striker may also be put out if he hits a ball that is caught by one of the fielders, or if the ball is returned to one of the two wicket keepers (or catchers) before the striker has returned to it. A team bats until all hands have been put out, and then the other team bats until all of its members have been put out. Cricket is a much slower game than baseball, because every man bats once in each inning, and a striker may score an unlimited number of runs before the other team manages to put him out. For this reason, a championship cricket match may last for several days.

Harry Wright had been a professional cricket player before entering baseball, and he strove to acquaint Anson and the other Americans with the nuances of the English game. Wright stressed the importance of scientific play, or "good form," which demanded that the striker defend his wicket by fouling off, or blocking, balls that head straight for it. English players believed that their main purpose lay in defending the wicket, with run scoring as their secondary objective; therefore, they swung only at off-target pitches, those that were thrown "off the wicket." A baseball player, following the same logic, would swing only at pitches thrown outside the strike zone and purposely foul off those thrown over the plate.

Spalding, with his gift for analysis, realized that the inexperienced Americans could never match the English at scientific play. He reasoned that his men would score more runs if they swung hard at the good pitches, not the bad ones, especially since the English cricket paddle was a wide, flat piece of wood and not a long, thin one like a baseball bat. "With the great board paddle now in my hands," said Spalding, "it just seemed impossible to miss." Wright objected, dismissing Spalding's proposed style of play as "wild slugging" and "bad form," but Spalding did not want to be embarrassed with a lopsided loss, and was determined to play cricket his own way.

The two sides agreed to play a one-inning match, in which each player would come to the bat once, and the British hosts graciously allowed the Americans to play all 18 of their men instead of the customary 11 or 12. Monday, August 3, was a bank holiday in England, and more than 5,000 curious people descended on the Marylebone cricket grounds to see the American athletes. The fans were probably more interested in how the Americans would fare at cricket against the strongest team in the nation, but they also came to see the first baseball game ever held in England between professional teams.

The cricket match commenced promptly at noon, and though the Americans managed to cover almost the entire field with defenders, the first six English strikers put up 45 runs in the first inning against bowlers Harry Wright and Dick McBride. At four o'clock, the umpire halted the cricket match and turned the field over to the baseball teams. The Red Stockings defeated the Athletics by a score of 24 to 7 in a game that lasted about two hours, and then, with darkness approaching, the two teams retired to dinner, agreeing to complete the cricket match the following day.

When the match resumed, the English side completed its inning with a total of 105 runs and took the field as the Americans came to bat. The two most experienced cricket players, Harry Wright and Dick McBride, were the first pair of strikers for the American side. Playing in strictly good form, Wright managed to tally only one run, while McBride was put out after five runs. With Wright and McBride retired, Al Spalding and Adrian Anson advanced to the wickets.

The English bowler decided to pitch first to Spalding, who was more convinced than ever that "good form" was a worthless concept as far as the Americans were concerned. Spalding swung from the heels at the first pitch and walloped it completely off the grounds for four runs. He blasted the next two pitches off the lot as well, to the amusement of the Americans and the astonishment of the Englishmen. Spalding then made several more safe hits, with he and Anson dashing madly between the wickets, and put up 23 runs before the bowler managed to put him out. The English were impressed with the American pitcher; as one newspaper put it, "If Mr. Spalding would deign to put a polish on his style, and study the art of defence as well as that of hitting, he might at once take rank with some of our foremost English professionals."[7]

Anson tried to imitate Spalding, but was retired after tallying only two runs. However, Spalding's display of power instilled confidence in his teammates, and the other Americans decided to follow his lead. George Wright, who combined good form with slugging, tallied 12 runs, while Cal McVey and Andrew Leonard reached double figures by ignoring form and walloping every ball that they could reach. By the end of the inning, the Americans had scored 107 runs and defeated the English at their own game.

The visitors played six more cricket matches during the tour and won all of them, mostly by lopsided scores. Adrian Anson finished in eighth place among the Americans in run scoring with 48 tallies, though in one match in Dublin, he surpassed Spalding's performance with 27 tallies in a single inning. In the baseball games, Anson led all of the visitors with a .437 average as the Red Stockings won eight of the 14 contests.

The crowds were sparse after the London match, partly due to inclement weather, but also due to the massive disinterest in baseball among the English people. The British were amazed at the fielding and throwing ability of the Americans, though they dismissed baseball as being too similar to the bat-and-ball games that English children play before graduating to cricket. "The game of base-ball which during the last ten years has grown so rapidly in favour on the other side of the Atlantic," stated the *London Graphic,* "that it is now regarded by our American cousins as their national pastime, appears to an English spectator very much like the simple game of rounders with which he was familiar in his youth."[8] Spalding and Wright had hoped to see baseball gain a foothold in England, but, as a London newspaper observed, "Cricket ... is more than a game, it is an institution, and baseball will never supersede or do the slightest injury to our own natural sport in any way."[9]

Pitcher and manager Dick McBride in 1874. (Author's collection)

Anson thoroughly enjoyed himself in England. On one occasion, he and teammate Tim Murnane were strolling in Hyde Park when they were stopped by an army officer, who asked if such a fine physical specimen as Anson would consider joining the British military. Anson informed the officer that he was an American, but, as Murnane later put it, "It was no wonder that John Bull saw in the young American a boy who might do some clean fighting as a soldier in the ranks." Anson was "six feet tall in his stockings and weighing 190 pounds, while as straight as an arrow,"[10] recalled Murnane, and although all the Americans impressed their hosts as fine athletes, the powerfully-built Anson stood out among them.

The most important result of the trip for Anson, in retrospect, was the opportunity to develop a friendship with Al Spalding. The star Boston pitcher was, like Anson, a product of the Midwest, and although he was less than two years older than Anson, Spalding had already begun to display his acumen as a businessman. The 23-year-old Spalding had successfully planned and executed the overseas excursion, a venture that excited the imaginations of baseball fans and boosters across America, and Anson could not help but be impressed. Al Spalding, like Henry Anson, was a builder and organizer *par excellence*, and Spalding provided Adrian Anson with his second great role model and mentor.

The venture was a money-loser — Anson complained that the "Argonauts of Base-Ball" had "brought back but little of the golden fleece" — but he fully agreed with Spalding's opinions regarding the sport of cricket and its relation to America's national game:

> Cricket is a gentle pastime [wrote Spalding in 1911]. Base ball is war! Cricket is an athletic sociable, played and applauded in a conventional, decorous, and English manner. Base ball is an athletic turmoil, played and applauded in an unconventional, enthusiastic, and American manner.
>
> Base ball, I repeat, is war! And the playing of the game is a battle in which every contestant is a commanding general, who, having a field of occupation, must defend it; who, having gained an advantage, must hold it by the employment of every faculty of his brain and body, by every resource of his mind and muscle.[11]

Spalding recognized that baseball had come a long way from the amateur "game of gentlemen." Baseball was now a profession, not a mere pastime, and winning was the sole objective of the ballplayer's efforts. Spalding was already known for "crowding the umpire," though his manager Harry Wright still believed in the gentlemanly style of play that was fast disappearing from the professional scene. Anson, an accomplished "kicker" himself, saw in Spalding a man who possessed a competitive drive to match his own. It seemed only natural that these two men, so similar in age and background, would find reasons to admire each other.

The *Ohio* returned to America on September 10 after another 11-day voyage, and three days later Spalding and the Red Stockings defeated the Athletics in Philadelphia by a score of 5 to 4. Boston picked up where it left off, posting a 22–10 record in September and October and sweeping to its third consecutive pennant, while the Athletics slumped to a 10–12 mark and finished third behind Boston and the resurgent New York Mutuals. The Athletics, at least, regained the top spot in Philadelphia, as the Pearls ended the season in fourth place with the new Chicago White Stockings a disappointing fifth.

Anson's batting average dropped to .336 in 1874, though he posted the second-best mark on the Athletics. He was not regressing, as his average was still the eighth-best in the Association. Averages dropped all over the circuit in 1874, a phenomenon that Anson, in his autobiography, credited to a general improvement in fielding skill among players in the professional ranks. The advent of professional ball, in Anson's view, caused the general level of playing skill to increase each year as players applied themselves to their new jobs. Some games still featured many errors, as on April 25, 1874, when the Athletics and the Pearls combined for 44 errors on a cold and windy day in Philadelphia, but such contests became less common by the mid–1870s. The total number of runs scored per game in the Association dropped from 23 in 1871 to less than 14 in 1874, a phenomenon that can be at least partially explained by better fielding.

The introduction of the curve ball was undoubtedly another crucial factor in the offensive decline. In 1872 Candy Cummings of the New York Mutuals was the only pitcher who threw the curve regularly, but by 1874 Tommy Bond and Bobby Mathews, among others, had added the pitch to their arsenals. The curveball was changing the game, and Adrian Anson and the rest of the free-swinging Athletics, who had been stymied many times in the previous few seasons by Cummings and his curve, would have to learn how to hit the tricky delivery as it gained in popularity among pitchers in the National Association.

While the Athletics prepared to battle the Boston Red Stockings for the 1875 pennant, Chicago team president William Hulbert grew disillusioned with the National Association. The new White Stockings proved an embarrassment to Hulbert with their poor performance in 1874, especially during a month-long eastern trip in June. On the 15th, Philadelphia's Candy Cummings struck out a record six White Stockings in succession, a feat that made national headlines in an era of few strikeouts. Three days later, the Chicago ballclub traveled to Brooklyn and lost to the New York Mutuals by a score of 38 to 1. The White Stockings made only two hits and committed 36 errors in what was certainly one of the most poorly played professional games in baseball history. A 29–6 loss to Al Spalding at Boston on the 29th proved only a bit less shameful to an ambitious, competitive man like Hulbert. The White Stockings were not meeting Hulbert's expectations, given that the new Chicago ballclub carried the highest payroll in the Association, higher even than the salary list of the perennial champions from Boston.

Hulbert fortified the team with a few new players for 1875, including Anson's old Rockford manager Scott Hastings, but the White Stockings fell another notch in the standings to sixth place, finishing seven games under the .500 mark. In July of 1875, the Chicago club suffered another humiliation when rookie pitcher Joe Borden of the Pearls shut them out without a hit. Borden's performance made the White Stockings the victims of the first no-hitter in baseball history, in either the professional or the high amateur ranks.

Hulbert was disgusted, not only with his team's play, but also with the weakness of the National Association. "Hippodroming," the fixing of games at the behest of gamblers, was a growing concern in the baseball world, but the Association appeared powerless to engage firm action to stop the problem. Several players were suspected of selling out games to gambling interests, but when the Philadelphia Pearls suspended John Radcliffe for dishonesty late in 1874, a new Philadelphia club, the Centennials, began play in 1875 with Radcliffe on its roster. Hulbert suspected men on his own team of throwing games, especially star pitcher George Zettelein and outfielder Fred Treacy, both of whom were suspended and released for suspicious play in August of 1874. Without league backing, Hulbert was powerless to combat the growing problem, and his frustration with the Association built throughout the 1875 season.

The final straw for Hulbert concerned a controversy surrounding his star shortstop, Davy Force. In mid–1874, the shortstop reached an agreement with Hulbert to return to Chicago in 1875, but because the Association did not allow players to sign contracts until season's end, the Association ruled the agreement invalid. In November 1874 Force signed again with Chicago, but a short time later, changed his mind and signed a second contract with the Philadelphia Athletics. The matter went to the Association board, which awarded Force to the White Stockings for 1875, but a few weeks later C. H. Sperling, the president of the Athletics, gained a seat on the board and re-opened the Force case. The new Association board reversed the previous decision and awarded Force to the Athletics, a move that left Hulbert fuming.

The Force case was merely the latest in a string of battles between Hulbert and the two Philadelphia ballclubs, the Athletics and the Pearls. The Philadelphians resented the White Stockings for using their city as prime recruiting ground, especially in 1874 when the Pearls lost six of their stars to the Chicago club. Hulbert, in turn, hated the Athletics for their rowdy fans, their indifference to pool selling, and their blatant use of bullying tactics against the umpires at the Jefferson Street Grounds. In Adrian Anson's four years with the Athletics, the team posted a won-lost record of 91–25 at home but finished one game under the break-even point on the road at 53–54, a statistic which seems to support the notion that the Athletics held an unfair home field advantage. "I don't think we can win from Philadelphia," wrote Hulbert angrily to a friend in 1875.

Hulbert figured that if the eastern teams could raid the White Stockings of its star players, two could play at that game. Al Spalding summarized

Hulbert's frame of mind many years later when he wrote, "It was borne to [Hulbert] one day that the reason why Chicago, whose phenomenal achievements on other lines were attracting the wonder of all the world, could make no better showing on the diamond was because the East was in league against her; that certain Base Ball magnates in the Atlantic States were in control of the game; were manipulating things to the detriment of Chicago and all Western cities; that if the Chicago Club signed an exceptionally strong player he was sure to be stolen from her; that contracts had no force, because the fellows down East would and did offer players increased salaries and date new contracts back to suit their own ends."[12]

By the start of the 1875 season, William Hulbert was convinced that the National Association had outlived its usefulness and was dying under the weight of its many long-term problems. Though he stated in a letter to a St. Louis club official that he wanted to "give the governing and playing rules [of the Association] a thorough overhauling — they sadly need it,"[13] he had something much more radical in mind. He began laying plans to create his own organization, a new circuit with stable membership, businesslike management, and the total elimination of gambling and pool-selling from the baseball scene. Adrian Anson did not yet know it, but William Hulbert prepared to launch what the *New York Clipper* would call "a startling *coup d'état*" in the baseball world, and Anson himself would play a central role in the uprising.

While the National Association battled its many problems, Adrian Anson reached a turning point in his personal life during the 1875 season. He, like most of his teammates, was a fun-loving and hard-drinking fellow who spent most of his evenings frequenting the pool halls and taverns near the Jefferson Street Grounds. "I was as full of unbroken spirits as is an unbroken thoroughbred colt," said Anson many years later, "and as impatient of restraint." He drank, made wagers at billiards (which he usually won), played pranks on his teammates, and took boxing lessons from a local prizefighter named Billy McLean. Before long, Anson became quite proficient at "the noble art of self-defense," at least in his own estimation, and "when the beer was in and the wit was out," Adrian thought he could, as he put it, "lick a whole army of wildcats."[14]

His short-lived interest in boxing prompted a change in his life. Anson and some of his teammates were drinking in a local tavern one evening when a loud discussion of the local boxing scene led to a confrontation between the inebriated ballplayer and a local policeman. Anson, who fancied himself an expert in the pugilistic arts, decided to test his boxing skills against the policeman, so he belted the cop and started a brawl. Unfortunately for the young ballplayer, several other officers came to their colleague's rescue and subdued the young ballplayer with their clubs. The disturbance ended with Anson being led in handcuffs to the police station. Fortunately for Adrian, the president of the Athletics at the time was a police commissioner, and a sympathetic judge turned him loose the next morning.

Anson and his friends then repaired to another bar, where "I started in to celebrate a victory that was, after all, a good deal more like a defeat." In his intoxicated state, Anson, much to his embarrassment, happened to run into the young woman that he had recently been dating. He was, no doubt, as surprised to see Virginia Fiegal walking down the street that day as she was mortified to see her steady beau in his unsteady state. Since her father was a bar owner, she had seen her share of drunken men, and did not want to marry one. Virginia delivered this sharply worded opinion to her suitor, and then stalked off.

Adrian's dream of a life with Virginia Fiegal was threatened when she spotted him stumbling down the street that morning in 1875. This humiliation marked a turning point for Adrian Anson. It "ended the wild oats business for me," as he stated many years later, and from that day forward Anson rarely drank, and never to intoxication. He stopped going to bars, though he still enjoyed beating his teammates at billiards, and concentrated his energies on playing baseball and pursuing Virginia Fiegal. By the middle of the 1875 season, the 23-year-old Adrian and the 16-year-old Virginia were dating each other exclusively and planning a future together.

CHAPTER 5

William Hulbert and the White Stockings

> *[Anson] seemed enormous at the plate.... His legs were solid and seemed especially so in his tight knee pants. His body was straighter than a tree, and his stance erect. He held his bludgeon of a bat easily in large supple hands. His clear, expressionless eyes never seemed to leave the pitcher, and his swing was almost effortless, as if the big bat he wielded were a small stick of no account.*
> — Robert Smith, 1947[1]

The 1875 season found the National Association still struggling with the same problems that had plagued it since its beginning four years before. Though the Association scored a coup by expanding to the baseball-mad city of St. Louis for the first time, the circuit allowed itself to be hobbled once again by admitting teams with no realistic chance of competing successfully. Washington, a city that had seen two previous teams fail, entered the Association once again in 1875, while the league also admitted the Iowa state champions from Keokuk to full membership. Rockford's ballclub had failed in 1871 mostly because it was too far west, but Keokuk was a smaller city located even farther afield. The Keokuk team disbanded after only 13 games, and several other new clubs failed to finish the season. "Unless the present Professional Association leadership adopts rules to limit the number of teams allowed to participate in the Championship season," said the *Chicago Tribune*, "all clubs will go broke."[2]

The Association also, for reasons that remain unclear, decided to allow a third team to play in Philadelphia in direct competition with the established Athletics and Pearls. The new team was dubbed the Centennials and shared the Jefferson Street Grounds with the other two ballclubs. Predictably, three teams in one city proved to be at least one too many, and none of the Philadelphia clubs drew enough fan support to turn a profit. In late May the Centennials collapsed after losing 12 of its 14 games. They then had the distinction of being the first professional team to sell a player when they arranged for the transfer of two of their stars, Bill Craver and George Bechtel, to the Athletics for a small sum of money, reportedly $1,500. Some observers believed that the Athletics simply bought out the money-losing Centennials, inducing them to drop out of the league in exchange for the cash payment and receiving the services of the two players as a bonus.

The dominance of the Boston Red Stockings posed another dilemma for the National Association. The Athletics started the season well, but Boston zoomed out of the gate and built a formidable lead in the pennant chase once again. At the same time, the teams at the bottom of the league lost games with stunning frequency. The New Haven nine lost its first eight games, while the Washington club dropped its first 11 in a row and the Brooklyn Atlantics, a powerhouse in the days of amateur ball, won only two of the 44 games they played before the team disbanded. Boston triumphed in nearly 90 percent of its games and the Athletics in more than 70 percent, but five other clubs could not even manage to win one of every five contests. The gulf between the best and worst teams widened with each passing year, and fan interest dwindled as Boston ran away with its fourth consecutive pennant.

Gamblers also grew bolder in 1875, and Adrian Anson received a first-hand glimpse of the influence of gambling on the sport. On June 28, the Boston club played the Athletics at Philadelphia, and the score was tied 10–10 after nine innings when rain halted the contest. The two teams resumed play after the skies cleared, with the Bostons taking the lead with two runs in the top of the tenth. The gamblers in the crowd did not want to chance losing their wagers with a Boston victory, so the crowd swarmed the field and refused to leave. The umpire declared the game a tie, and Boston manager Harry Wright was so incensed that he informed the papers that he would never again bring his team to Philadelphia.

Though manager Dick McBride kept the Athletics in second place, he came under a barrage of criticism both from the local newspapers and his own bosses. Attendance was down at the Jefferson Street Grounds, partly due to fan rowdiness as well as low morale, as the Athletics had lost all hope of catching the streaking Red Stockings by mid-season. The Athletics were losing money, and the team board of directors split into two warring factions, those that supported McBride and those who opposed him. One director in the latter group, Al Reach, was still an active player, making him both the superior and the subordinate of McBride. This awkward situation contributed to the club's failure to thrive, and by the end of the 1875 season the Athletic ballclub found itself more than $5,000 in debt, teetering on the edge of collapse.

On the field, McBride once again kept Anson bouncing from one position to another. The "Marshalltown Infant" displayed his versatility with 32 games at first base, five at third, 25 in the outfield, and 13 more behind the plate. He led the team in batting average with a .325 mark and in runs scored with 84 in only 59 games. He was one of the most feared hitters in the game at the age of 24, with a career batting average of .360, and his heavy hitting attracted the notice of William Hulbert of the Chicago White Stockings.

Hulbert's zeal to build a winning team that could wrest the pennant away from the Association's Eastern power base burned brighter than ever, and in June of 1875 Hulbert made his move. Though the rules of the National Association clearly outlawed contract negotiations during the season with players belonging to other teams, Hulbert ignored the rule, as had many other owners before him, and resolved to bring the best players in the league to Chicago. His first target was Boston's "King of Pitchers," Al Spalding. Hulbert reminded Spalding that he had made his name as a pitcher in his hometown of Rockford, Illinois, before leaving for Boston five years before. "Spalding, you've no business playing in Boston," declared Hulbert. "You're a Western boy, and you belong right here."[3] Hulbert offered Spalding a $500 raise in salary and a 25 percent share of gate receipts to pitch for and manage the White Stockings in 1876, and Spalding eagerly accepted.

As it turned out, Spalding was as disenchanted with the Association as was Hulbert. "I knew that gambling was practiced everywhere," related Spalding many years later, "...[and that players] were being caused to swerve from the legitimate ends of the game, and to serve the illegitimate purposes of the gamesters ... I had made up my mind fully to one thing; that unless a change soon took place in the management of the game, I was done with it at once and forever."[4] Spalding also realized that Boston's perennial domination of the league, which was due in large part to Spalding's own excellence, was killing interest in the game. He was open to the challenge of returning to the Midwest and building another championship team.

Though Spalding was still under contract to Boston for the remainder of the 1875 season, he helped Hulbert round up more players for his future Chicago team. Spalding, on Hulbert's behalf, made generous offers to three of Boston's biggest stars—catcher James (Deacon) White, pitcher and first baseman Cal McVey, and second baseman Ross Barnes. All three men signed contracts to play for the White Stockings in 1876. In late June, probably when Boston played two games in Philadelphia on the 27th and 28th of the month, Spalding obtained similar agreements from the two best players on the Athletics. Third baseman Ezra Sutton and utility man Adrian Anson accepted offers to play in Chicago in the following year. Anson, who had been earning $1,800 per year with the Athletics, signed a $2,000 contract to play first base for the White Stockings in 1876.

The National Association did not recognize contracts that were signed before the conclusion of the previous season, and any of the six players could have changed their minds and repudiated their agreements to play for Chicago. Spalding and Hulbert were not concerned, because they made sure to choose players of good reputations, men who could be trusted to keep their word. All of Hulbert's future stars had already gained reputations for their honesty and fair play. White was called "Deacon" because, unlike many other players of the era, he was a churchgoer, while Anson had impressed Spalding during the overseas trip in 1874, both on a professional and a personal level. Hulbert, too, had kept his eye on Anson, for in early 1875 he approached the Athletics about gaining the young ballplayer's services in a trade. The negotiations went nowhere, but Hulbert wanted a heavy hitter for the cleanup spot in the Chicago lineup, and Anson was the heaviest hitter in the Association.

Hulbert, in turn, earned the admiration of Anson. Hulbert, like Henry Anson, was born in New York State and emigrated to the West in search of opportunities. Anson later described Hulbert as being "as honest as the day is long, and would tolerate nothing that savored of crookedness in any shape or form," and that he "impressed one right from the start as being a self-reliant business man of great natural ability."[5]

Albert Goodwill Spalding, manager of the White Stockings. (Author's collection)

5. WILLIAM HULBERT AND THE WHITE STOCKINGS

Such a description could also be applied to Henry Anson, and Adrian found another role model and mentor in the hard-charging president of the White Stockings.

Hulbert and Spalding tried to keep the signings under wraps, but on July 20 the *Chicago Tribune* published the names of the players who had committed to the White Stockings for the following season. The *Tribune* article listed the Boston quartet, which the newspapers dubbed the "Big Four," and Sutton of the Athletics, but did not mention Anson. Before long, however, Anson's signing hit the papers as well, and the defection to Chicago of six of the biggest stars in the game became the talk of the baseball world.

Some fans and sportswriters might have predicted that the Boston stars would lose interest in performing well for the Red Stockings after signing their contracts with the Chicago ballclub, but the "Big Four" were determined to prove themselves. "It is just as natural for a ball player to play his best to win as it is for a duck to swim," declared Spalding, and the Red Stockings took the field with renewed incentive and won so frequently that Spalding later confessed, "We rather overdid the thing."[6] Boston finished the season with an incredible 71–8 record, winning all 37 of their home games. The .726 winning percentage posted by the Athletics would have been good enough to capture any pennant of the 20th century, but they trailed Boston by a large margin, and halfway through the season it was obvious that the Athletics would have to be content to battle Hartford for second place.

The lack of a pennant race caused fan interest to wane, and attendance declined in almost every major league city, with the Athletics suffering one of the biggest drops of all. The bickering among factions of the money-losing Athletic ballclub intensified, especially after an embarrassing 18–0 loss to Boston and its second-string pitcher, Jack Manning, on September 5. This shutout was the most lopsided loss ever suffered by the Athletics and left the team impossibly far behind in the pennant chase. With fans staying away from the Jefferson Street Grounds in droves, the board of directors searched for ways to trim costs in the last month of the campaign. They gave a tryout to a new pitcher named Lon Knight in September, and Knight performed well enough that the directors decided that they no longer needed their veteran pitcher and field manager, Dick McBride. Despite McBride's 44–14 pitching record, he was expendable, and the directors did not wait until the end of the season to turn him loose. They needed to cut expenses immediately, and fired McBride in one of the most unusual managerial shakeups ever seen in the national game.

On October 9, 1875, McBride faced the Boston club in Philadelphia.

The Red Stockings battered McBride's pitching and took a big lead on the way to a 17–13 win, and the game was barely half over when the team's board of directors decided that it had seen enough. At the end of the fifth inning, the directors stopped the contest, held an impromptu meeting, and fired McBride. They appointed the 24-year-old Adrian Anson as McBride's successor, and in Anson's first decision as manager, he brought Ezra Sutton in to pitch in place of the departing, and no doubt shocked, McBride. After 15 years of service, Dick McBride's career in Philadelphia was over.

Perhaps the directors chose Anson as the new field general because they saw leadership qualities in him, but it is more likely that team politics played a role in his selection. They had known since mid-season that Anson was on his way to Chicago in 1876, so they appointed him instead of a veteran like West Fisler in order to start the next campaign with a clean slate. Besides, Anson's contract with the White Stockings covered only one year, and the Athletic team directors gave Adrian a taste of managing as an incentive to return to Philadelphia for the 1877 season.

Adrian managed the Athletics for the final eight games of the 1875 season. The Red Stockings defeated Anson's charges in Boston two days later by a 15–3 score, and the stunned Athletics then traveled to Hartford and suffered an 18–2 setback. However, despite the absence of McBride and catcher John Clapp, who quit the team shortly after McBride's departure, Anson finished the season on a high note, winning four and tying two of the last six games on the schedule, ending the year with a 9–3 win against the St. Louis Browns. The Athletics finished in third place, as Hartford had won one more game than the Athletics, and though Philadelphia had the higher winning percentage, Hartford was awarded second place in the standings under the rules of the time.

Anson took a risk when he signed with the White Stockings. Hulbert had procured all six men in direct violation of National Association rules, and the leaders of the other ballclubs—those that managed to complete the 1875 season—fumed at Hulbert's coup. Some of the angrier Association members may even have discussed expelling the Chicago ballclub, along with Anson, Sutton, and the "Big Four" of Boston, but Hulbert brushed the danger aside, telling a concerned Spalding, "Why, they can't expel you. They would not dare do it, for in the eyes of the public you six players are stronger than the whole Association." Besides, Hulbert was already hatching the next phase of his plan, the creation of a new league. "Spalding, I have a new scheme," proclaimed Hulbert. "Let us anticipate the Eastern cusses and organize a new association before the March [1876] meeting and then see who will do the expelling."[7]

5. WILLIAM HULBERT AND THE WHITE STOCKINGS

Hulbert's "scheme" was a logical step, given his oft-expressed opinions on the management of the professional game. He was disgusted with the National Association and what he perceived as its eastern bias, especially following the Davy Force case, and he also resented the criticism lobbed his way for pirating Anson and the four Boston stars from eastern teams. Hulbert was aware that professional baseball, if it was to survive, would need much stronger leadership and organization than the National Association of Professional Base Ball Players could provide. On February 2, 1876, he invited eight team owners to Chicago for a meeting at which he laid out his plan for a new circuit, to be called the National League of Professional Base Ball Clubs. The name change was significant, because it indicated that the teams, not the players, would control professional ball at the highest level in the United States.

Hulbert instituted several much-needed reforms. No city could field more than one team, not even New York or Philadelphia, and no city with a population of less than 75,000 would be admitted to the new circuit. The league required each team to post a $100 deposit, a ten-fold increase over the Association's entry fee, and players suspected of gambling or "hippodroming" would be investigated and, if found culpable, expelled from the National League for life. No longer would any team expel a player for dishonesty and see him hired by another club.

To gain support from the eastern clubs, Hulbert persuaded Morgan Bulkeley, the politically well-connected president of the Hartford Dark Blues, to accept the presidency of the new National League, while Washington Olympics team official Nicholas Young became the circuit's first secretary. Hulbert, however, retained almost dictatorial power over the new aggregation. With the assistance of his star pitcher, manager, and right-hand man Al Spalding, this strong-willed man gave life to the first successful professional sports league, one that survives and prospers to this day.

While Hulbert and Spalding formulated the new league, Adrian Anson encountered an unexpected problem in the fall of 1875. He had enthusiastically signed his agreement with Chicago, but his decision drew heated opposition from Virginia Fiegal, his 16-year-old steady girlfriend, almost immediately after he did so. Virginia and Adrian had already begun discussing a future marriage, but she was a Philadelphia native, and did not want to leave her family and friends to live in an unfamiliar city. Adrian, in his autobiography, said only that Virginia "not unnaturally objected to my going so far from home," but the disagreement was, apparently, much more serious than that. Virginia did not want to move to Chicago, and she was so adamant about the matter that Adrian decided to try to free himself from his commitment to the White Stockings.

Anson would gladly have stayed in Philadelphia, especially after he enjoyed a brief term of managing the ballclub, but he had signed a contract to play in Chicago. Many players in the 1870s broke similar agreements, and contract jumping was hardly a cause for shock or dismay in that era. Candy Cummings, for one, signed agreements with three different National Association clubs before the 1872 season began, and it took a special ruling by the Association to compel Cummings to honor one of the three. However, Adrian Anson was not a contract jumper. He desperately wanted to make Virginia happy, but Anson would not go back on his word. He might have simply changed his mind, as did Ezra Sutton, who disappointed the White Stockings when he decided to ignore his agreement and remain with the Athletics in 1876. Anson, in contrast to Sutton, would do his best to find a legal and honorable way out of the agreement and, failing that, would resign himself to playing in Chicago despite the objections of his fiancée.

Adrian found himself in an unenviable position, caught between the expectations of Virginia and those of his new employers. At Virginia's insistence, he wrote a letter to Spalding and Hulbert requesting his release, but the Chicago team executives ignored it. He then made two trips to Chicago in late 1875 to plead with Spalding personally to let him out of his agreement, but Spalding would not budge. The White Stockings had already been stung by the defection of Sutton, and Spalding and Hulbert did not want to lose another powerful bat in the middle of the lineup. In addition, Sutton's return to the Athletics forced Spalding to replace Sutton on the roster with his old Rockford teammate Bob Addy, signed away from the Philadelphia Pearls. Spalding put Addy in right field and moved Anson to third to cover for the departed Sutton, and the manager, understandably, did not want to shuffle the roster again.

On January 8, 1876, Spalding outlined his feelings on the matter in a letter to Anson. "Now Anson," wrote Spalding, "by ... insisting on your fulfillment of contract, can it be said that [Chicago] is demanding anything but what is right and just? You now have a good reputation for honor and integrity and an honorable man can make but one answer to the above question. If players continue to break contracts ... they will certainly kill the hen that lays our golden eggs and thus make the majority of the fraternity suffer at the hands of the dishonorable few."[8] Spalding concluded the letter by threatening to expel Anson from the National League if he did not fulfill his obligations to Chicago in 1876. This warning should have ended the matter, but the Athletics had made a lucrative counteroffer, and Adrian was not a man to give up easily.

The White Stockings played at the 23rd Street Grounds, located at the corner of 23rd and State streets, about 12 blocks north and two blocks east of the present site of U. S. Cellular Field, the former New Comiskey Park. The 23rd Street Grounds had been built in 1874 when the Chicago club reentered professional ball after the two-year hiatus caused by the great fire of 1871. The park seated about 1,500 people, and when crowds exceeded that number, the team made standing room for spectators in the outfield and on the sidelines with ropes. Hulbert and Spalding ordered their players, Adrian Anson and all the rest, to report for practice at the 23rd Street Grounds on April 8.

Anson continued his campaign to convince Spalding and Hulbert to release him from his contract. He did not appear for indoor practice in March, and gave interviews to the Chicago papers in which he insisted that he would not play for the White Stockings in 1876. He hoped to force his new bosses to let him go, but Spalding and Hulbert held firm. Hulbert believed that Anson would skip out on his contract as had Sutton, but Spalding knew that Anson, like his father, was honest to the core and would live up to his agreement if there was no honorable way out of it.

Hulbert suggested that Spalding let the matter drop, but Spalding replied that Anson would stick to his agreement. "What makes you think so?" demanded Hulbert. "Didn't Sutton jump?"

"Yes, but Anson won't," insisted Spalding. "He'll stick until he is released. You may bet all you are worth on that."[9]

Anson virtually begged for his release, but Hulbert, at Spalding's advice, refused to consider it. Adrian was desperate to please Virginia, and decided to try one more time to gain his freedom. In early April he visited Hulbert's office and once again asked out of his agreement. Hulbert turned him down, and Adrian then pulled a large roll of bills out of his pocket. The 24-year-old ballplayer placed the pile of money on Hulbert's desk.

"There's $1,000," said Anson. "I'll give you that for my release."

Hulbert, recalled Spalding many years later, "almost fell out of his chair with astonishment." In an era when players made and broke agreements seemingly at will, Adrian Anson offered to buy his freedom rather than break his word. The offer had the opposite effect of what the ballplayer intended, because Hulbert decided then and there that Anson was the kind of individual that he wanted on the White Stockings. Anson's offer of $1,000 cemented his reputation for integrity, but left the 24-year-old third baseman with no choice but to play for the White Stockings or not play at all.[10]

Adrian tried one final gambit when he reported to the park for the team's first practice. He appeared on the field in a top hat, a vest, striped pants, and a Prince Albert coat. He stood on the sidelines and watched

Spalding and the other White Stockings limber up, all the while knowing that they were also watching him. Spalding ignored him, and after a while Anson began to waver in his resolve. He could not stand the sight of the other men playing ball without him.

Finally, Anson could resist no more. He called to Spalding, "Toss me one, Al."

"What? With those togs on?" asked Spalding. "Not any. Take off your hat and coat and get into the game."

Anson hesitated, but only for a moment. He removed his coat and took his position at third base. He fielded a few balls thrown his way by Spalding, who said, "Now, Anse, come tomorrow in uniform."[11] From that day forward, Spalding and Hulbert heard no more about Anson leaving Chicago. He was now, like it or not, a White Stocking.

Adrian recognized that there was only one way to play in Chicago and keep Virginia Fiegal too. After settling himself in Chicago, he wrote to John Fiegal and asked for permission to marry the 16-year-old Virginia. "I had been a little afraid to do so when at close range, but the farther away I went the bolder I became,"[12] said Anson later. The reply came in the affirmative, and the couple made plans to marry in the fall of 1876.

Still, Adrian expected to spend only one season in the Windy City. "Anson had to play with the Chicagos," stated the *Brooklyn Eagle* three days later, "or forfeit his engagement with the Athletics for 1877 and 1878." Hulbert had signed Adrian to a one-year contract, which was customary at the time, and since the National League did not institute the reserve clause until four years later, Adrian was free to return to Philadelphia at the close of the 1876 season. It appears that Adrian already possessed a verbal commitment to play for, or possibly manage, the Athletics in the following season.

In the meantime, he would honor his contract with the White Stockings, who appeared to be the class of the new league. The team possessed the game's greatest pitcher in Al Spalding, its premier second baseman in Ross Barnes, and its brightest young hitting star in Adrian Anson, along with other hard-hitting performers in catcher Deacon White and first baseman Cal McVey. Hulbert bought himself a virtual All-Star team when he brought Anson and the Big Four to Chicago, and he fully expected his own team to win the first pennant of the league that he created.

The White Stockings opened the season in Louisville on April 25, and the game matched Al Spalding against the second-best pitcher in the game, Jim Devlin of the Grays. Fittingly, the White Stockings "Chicagoed" Louisville by a 4–0 score, with Spalding scattering seven hits. The *Chicago Tribune* described the game:

The ball was the deadest possible to be found. The ground was not in good shape and was moist, sticky, and soft in the outfield, and very soggy all over. The credit for the victory belongs to Spalding more than anyone else, and it is safe to say that better pitching was hardly ever seen.

Third baseman Anson and shortstop Peters faced some stiff hits and fielded them in beautiful style, the throwing of both men being as accurate as rifle shooting. Taken as a whole, the first game of the Chicagos of 1876 was a creditable one and promises well for the score at the end of the season.[13]

This game was the first shutout ever pitched in the National League, and Spalding repeated the performance two days later when he defeated the Grays again by a 10–0 count. The White Stockings then went to Cincinnati, where they defeated the Red Stockings 11–5 and 15–9. They suffered their first loss in St. Louis when George Bradley of the Browns pitched a rare 1–0 shutout, but Spalding's men rebounded with a win in the next game. The White Stockings held first place when they returned to Chicago for the home opener against Cincinnati on May 10.

The papers reported that more than 5,000 and perhaps as many as 6,000 fans crowded the tiny ballpark to see the "coming champions," as the out-of-town sportswriters called the White Stockings. With standing-room only patrons in the outfield and pressing along the foul lines, Al Spalding pitched his third shutout of the season, winning 6–0. With the best pitcher in the league in Spalding and the hardest-hitting lineup in the game, the White Stockings grabbed the league lead in the early part of the season. The only criticism of the team centered on the Chicago uniforms, since Spalding decreed that each player wear a hat of a different color. The *Tribune* complained that the players looked like "a Dutch bed of tulips."

Ross Barnes, the former Rockford Forest City star who became the National League's leading batsman, headed the White Stocking attack. Barnes specialized in the "fair-foul" hit, in which he bunted the ball with a slicing motion so that it bounced once in fair territory and then spun crazily away into foul ground. Such a bunt was still considered a fair ball at the time, as long as it struck fair territory first, and Barnes used this singular skill to lead the league in batting average, slugging percentage, hits, and runs scored in the National League's first season. Barnes also swung away often enough to lead the league in doubles and triples as well.

Adrian Anson could not match Barnes' .429 batting average, but he excelled nonetheless in what he expected to be his only season in a Chicago uniform. Anson batted .356 and drove in 59 runs in the 66 games, missing the league leadership in runs batted in by one (Paul Hines, a holdover from the 1875 Chicago club, led the circuit with 60 RBI that year). Anson added another strong bat to the formidable Chicago lineup and played well at third base, further cementing his position as one of the brightest young stars in the game.

The 1876 campaign was a season of firsts. Ross Barnes hit only one home run in his major league career, but it was the first one in National League history, coming as it did on May 6 in the 15–9 win over the Cincinnati Reds. Al Spalding pitched the first National League shutout, while Boston's Jim O'Rourke stroked the first hit and Tim McGinley scored the first run. Adrian Anson achieved a milestone of his own on May 25 in Hartford, when he wandered off base in the seventh inning after failing to notice a relay throw from the outfield to Hartford third baseman Bob Ferguson. When Ferguson tagged Adrian, Anson became the National League's first victim of the hidden ball trick.

Since the White Stockings led the league in nearly every statistical category, most of the nation's sportswriters conceded the pennant to Chicago only two months into the season. The Chicagos were the "coming champions," said the papers, and other teams used the elite status of the White Stockings to draw fans to their own ballparks. In June, the New York Mutuals put life-sized pictures of Spalding, McVey, Barnes, and other Chicago stars in local shop windows to build excitement for their games with the White Stockings. On June 13, the Chicago club drew a fine crowd to the Union Grounds, where Anson went hitless, but Barnes had four hits and scored three runs as Chicago defeated the Mutuals 5 to 1.

Two days later, a baserunning controversy erupted in the ninth inning of a game between the Mutuals and White Stockings. With the Mutuals ahead 6 to 5 and one out, Anson was on first base when McVey hit a liner that struck Anson in the leg, then dribbled to the outfield. The Mutuals demanded that McVey be called out for Anson's "interference," and they delayed the game for more than ten minutes while they made their case to the umpire. There was no rule covering that particular instance at the time, but the umpire decided that the Mutual second baseman could not have fielded the ball anyway, so he awarded second base to Anson and let the game proceed. The point became moot when the next batter hit into a double play and ended the game, but a rule was devised in the off-season that declared a baserunner out when struck by a batted ball, intentionally or not.[14]

The White Stockings dropped out of first place only once during the season, when they lost two games to the Hartford Dark Blues on July 5th and 6th and fell half a game out of first. The White Stockings always had trouble with the curveball of Candy Cummings, who by 1876 was Hartford's

5. WILLIAM HULBERT AND THE WHITE STOCKINGS 65

The Chicago White Stockings—first pennant winners of the National League. This photograph celebrates the 1876 championship but shows the 1877 team. (National Baseball Hall of Fame Library, Cooperstown, New York)

main hurler, but they pounded all the other teams into submission by lopsided scores. An 11-game winning streak in July put Chicago back in first; among their wins were three against Louisville by scores of 9–5, 18–0, and 30–7, and three shellackings of Boston by scores of 18–7, 11–3, and 15–0. By August 1 Chicago had built a lead of more than six games, and no other team was able to mount a challenge during the rest of the 1876 campaign.

The greatest star of the White Stockings was pitcher and manager Al Spalding. He did not throw a curve ball, as did a growing number of other League pitchers, but led the league in wins with 47 in the 55 games that he pitched in the 1876 campaign. Spalding was not the fastest pitcher in the league, but he used a quick delivery and a frequent change of pace to get the job done; as the *Chicago Tribune* described it, "Clubs come to Chicago and spit on their hands with ferocity and explain that they are going to 'knock the stuffing out of Spalding' because 'anybody can hit him; he is the easiest man in the business.' And then they don't do it all the same."[15]

The White Stockings cruised to the pennant, and Hulbert and Spalding took pride in their team, not only for their fine playing, but for their stellar behavior as well. They had chosen only those players who could be counted on to display modest and temperate habits, and hoped that the deportment of their champions would serve as a model for other teams in the new National League. Stated the *Chicago Evening Journal* at season's end, "Every man on the club has shown himself to be a gentleman as well as a ball player, and there never has been a breath of suspicion against them. They have made friends in and out of the profession, and are a credit to the city of their adoption...."[16]

Some sportswriters, however, singled out Adrian Anson for criticism. The league then allowed only the team captain and one other designated player to coach base runners at first and third, and Anson was the man Spalding assigned to assist him in this task. Though a Louisville paper praised the White Stockings for their "gentlemanly conduct" on the field, it stated that Anson, "standing near third base and yelling ... directions [such as] 'run on, he'll throw wild,' showed very poor judgment and did what we believe will not be tolerated by Manager Spalding in the future."[17]

The Louisville paper was wrong in its assessment. Spalding had already chosen Anson as his assistant on the field, and Adrian used the 1876 season as an opportunity to learn the managerial end of the game from the man who, along with Harry Wright, was its leading practitioner. Spalding was a more aggressive manager than Wright, especially in his relationships with the umpires, and he introduced a more forceful attitude to baseball field management. Many people still considered it unsportsmanlike to argue with the officials as Spalding did, but the gentleman's game of the 1860s was gone forever. In the future, successful managers would question the decisions of umpires with a new belligerence, and Adrian Anson learned his lessons well at the feet of Spalding.

In early October, Spalding showed his appreciation to Anson for his efforts. The White Stockings went on an exhibition tour at the close of the National League season, and on October 3 the team traveled to Marshalltown for a game against Anson's former town team. Adrian had not visited his hometown since he left for Rockford in the spring of 1871, and a large crowd gathered to welcome Marshalltown's most successful ballplayer. No box score exists of the game, but the *Chicago Tribune* reported that Anson played third base for a few innings, moved to catcher, and then took a turn on the mound against his old team.

The White Stockings defeated Marshalltown that day by a score of 35 to 7, but no one in the old hometown seemed to mind. They came to cheer Adrian Anson, Marshalltown's most famous athlete, who was well on his way to a long and distinguished career in baseball.

CHAPTER 6

Manager in Training

> Big Anson, of the Chicagos, who is getting such a cudgeling at the hands of the press, seems to be improving. In the game Saturday with the Bostons he made but one error, but that did not save the boys, for they got most awfully walloped by the champions.
> —*Washington Post*, 1878[1]

Anson, despite his fine performance in Chicago, was ready to leave at the close of the season. In September the papers were still insisting that the 24-year-old third baseman was set to go to Philadelphia as manager for the 1877 campaign, but the future of the Athletics as a National League entity was very much in doubt. Lon Knight and George Zettelein handled the Philadelphia pitching in 1876, but neither could fill the shoes of the deposed Dick McBride, and the Athletics fell to seventh place in the new league. Fan support dropped significantly while the specter of gambling still hovered over the team. The club had difficulty paying its bills and meeting payroll, and in late September the ballclub announced that it would not make its final western trip of the season to Chicago and St. Louis, as it could not attract enough paying customers to meet expenses.

The New York Mutuals, who played at Brooklyn's Union Grounds, were far out of the race as well, losing money during the 1876 season, and within days they, too, decided not to play their final games in the west. The Chicago and St. Louis clubs offered the Mutuals a guarantee of $400 for two games in Chicago and three in St. Louis, but the Mutuals declined the offer, ending their season early. The Athletics, for their part, offered the White Stockings and Browns an 80 percent slice of the gate if they would move their unplayed games to Philadelphia, but both teams turned down the offer, and the Athletics ceased operations for the season.

William Hulbert founded the National League, in part, to rid the professional game of its abuses, and he sincerely believed in the sanctity of contracts and schedules. When the National League held its annual meeting in Cleveland that December, Hulbert assumed the presidency of the circuit and convinced his fellow directors to take a drastic step. At Hulbert's insistence, the board expelled New York and Philadelphia from the league, which left the circuit with only six teams for the upcoming 1877 campaign.

Though this decision left the league without representation in two of the nation's three most populous cities, Hulbert was not unhappy to see the two teams depart, especially the Athletics. Hulbert had bitterly resented the Philadelphia influence in the National Association ever since the Davy Force case and other incidents, and in early 1876 he accepted the Philadelphia team into his new league with great reluctance. In September of that year he wrote to a friend, "I for one should be glad to bid adieu to the Athletics. From my first experience they have always been a double-dealing set of bastards."[2]

The National League gained in stature when it booted Philadelphia and New York from membership, because it demonstrated once and for all that the league, not the clubs, wielded the power in the circuit. Hulbert's White Stockings also profited from the expulsion of the Athletics, as Anson's agreement to return to Philadelphia in 1877 as manager was now invalidated. The Athletics continued in 1877 as an independent team, with a substantially reduced payroll, and could no longer afford to pay Adrian Anson a salary matching the $2,000 that he received from the Chicagos in 1876. No doubt Hulbert would not have kicked the Athletics out of the league merely to secure Anson for another season, but Adrian's continued presence in the Chicago lineup was an excellent side benefit of the expulsion. Hulbert and Spalding enthusiastically welcomed Adrian back to the fold, and he signed again with the White Stockings for the 1877 campaign.

Adrian married Virginia Fiegal in Philadelphia on November 21, 1876, but Hulbert altered the couple's plans when he tossed the Athletics out of the National League. Adrian had expected to build his career in Philadelphia, but the expulsion of the Athletics meant that the newlyweds would have to live in Chicago for at least part of the year if Adrian was to continue his career in baseball. Virginia did not want to leave Philadelphia, so she and Adrian worked out a compromise. They would take an apartment in Chicago in the summer months and spend their winters in Virginia's hometown. Following the wedding, Adrian took Virginia to Marshalltown, Iowa, to introduce her to his family, and then the couple returned to Philadelphia and set up housekeeping. For the next seven years, the Ansons divided their time between Chicago and Philadelphia.

Al Spalding was only 26 years old at the start of the 1877 season, but he had already spent over a decade as a top-flight pitcher and was beginning to wear down physically. He had suffered back problems that kept him out of the Boston lineup late in the 1875 campaign and was worn out at the end of Chicago's successful run for the 1876 pennant. In addition, the curveball was making its presence felt in the game, and though Candy Cummings was nearing the end of his career, almost every other National League pitcher recognized the importance of the curve and worked to master the pitch. Spalding was an old-fashioned "perpendicular" pitcher and had no interest in learning how to throw the curveball.

Spalding believed that he had passed his prime as a pitcher, and proposed to retire from the mound at his peak of his success. He would, instead, play first base for the White Stockings in 1877. To replace himself in the pitching box, Spalding signed George Bradley, a righthander who threw a record 16 shutouts for the St. Louis Browns in 1876. Bradley had verbally agreed to play for Philadelphia in 1877, as had Anson, but the expulsion of the Athletics from the league made Bradley available, and Spalding convinced Hulbert to loosen the team's purse strings to outbid the other National League teams for Bradley.

Spalding may have had a mercenary motive for his switch to first base. In February of 1876, he and his brother Walter opened a sporting goods store on Randolph Street in Chicago, and he planned to use his fame on the baseball diamond to build the business into prominence. Spalding had noticed, during the 1875 season, that a first baseman named Charles Waite of Boston used a thin, fingerless glove to protect his hands from the sting of hard-thrown balls. Waite did not want the fans to notice his glove, so he chose to use one that was flesh-colored. Spalding refined Waite's idea, and created a mitt of dark leather with sufficient padding inside to protect the wearer. The dark glove was immediately noticeable to the faraway fans, and Spalding hoped that his use of such protection could only increase the demand for the product at the Spalding and Brothers store.

Adrian Anson continued at third base for the White Stockings, but the team changed its personnel at several other positions. The "Big Four" broke up after only one season in Chicago when catcher Deacon White returned to Boston in 1877, so first baseman Cal McVey took over for White, Spalding replaced McVey at first, and Bradley became the featured pitcher. Bob Addy moved on to Cincinnati, leaving a hole in right field that caused problems for the club all season long, but on the whole the 1877 season looked promising for the White Stockings.

6. Manager in Training

With Philadelphia and New York gone from the National League, only six teams remained. William Hulbert cited the example of the Athletics and Mutuals to convince his fellow owners that the time was right to publish a schedule of games prior to the start of the season. The league had relied on each team to arrange its own games with its competitors in the past, but in 1877 the league, not the teams, would schedule games for the first time. Hulbert also performed a favor for his player-turned-manager-turned-businessman Spalding when he designated the Spalding baseball as the official ball of the league. Spalding and Brothers provided all the balls used in the league that year for free, in return for publicity and a boost in sales, or so Spalding hoped. Spalding's company subsequently produced the official National League ball for the next 100 years.

Anson in Chicago uniform. (National Baseball Hall of Fame Library, Cooperstown, New York)

Before the new season began, the league rules committee instituted a change that particularly affected the White Stockings. The committee banned Ross Barnes' specialty, the fair-foul hit. Beginning in 1877, a batted ball that struck in fair ground and rolled foul before it got to the first or third base bag was declared foul. No longer would Barnes be able to slice the ball into foul territory while he dashed around the bases. This rule change, which some historians credit with modernizing the game, robbed Barnes of his most dangerous weapon and hastened the end of his career only a few years later.

Spalding, however, developed other weapons. He had learned the fine points of baseball strategy from Harry Wright during his four years with the Boston club, and many now-familiar tactics made their appearance in the earliest days of the National League. For example, some say that the hit-and-run play was not developed until the 1890s, but the *Chicago Tribune* described a very similar maneuver during the middle of the 1877 season:

Some chap stated the following conundrum, professing not to understand it: "Why do batsmen strike a ball when a base-runner is half-way to second base on a clever steal?" The answer was found in Thursday's game, when McVey started to second base, and Anson hit the ball in the exact spot where McGeary had been standing before he ran to his base to catch McVey. It is really a clever batting trick to hit to right field when it lies all open.[3]

Anson was the best hit-and-run man on the team because, according to accounts of the period, he usually did not swing the bat so much as he pushed it at the ball to make contact. He used his outstanding bat control to place the ball virtually wherever he wanted it on the field, and his strength enabled him to propel the ball past the infielders and into the outfield gaps without using a full-bodied swing like most players of the present day. He struck out only three times during the 1877 campaign, while many power hitters of the present day strike out 150 times or more in a season.

Spalding was a great pitcher and an innovative manager, but he proved only average as a first baseman, even with his new glove. Bradley won his first game for Chicago, a 6–5 decision over Hartford at Brooklyn, but lost his next four games as the White Stockings dropped to last place. While Bradley struggled, the Chicago fans begged Spalding to return to the mound, but the manager kept Bradley in the box.

The White Stockings missed the strong bats and fine defensive play of Addy and White, and in mid–May Ross Barnes, the defending league batting champion, came down with a serious illness and left the lineup. Barnes did not return until September, so Spalding put rookie Harry Smith at second base. Smith batted only .202 and fielded poorly, while Spalding proved to be mediocre as an infielder, and defensive lapses plagued the White Stockings during the early months of the season. On May 12 the Chicago team made 21 errors in an 18–9 loss to Boston.

One of the few bright spots for the White Stockings in the 1877 season was Adrian Anson. He led the team in doubles and walks and stood second to McVey in batting average and hits, in addition to his remarkable strikeout record. Anson retained his position as Spalding's assistant and base coach, and his booming voice and undeniable physical presence on the field made him popular with the Chicago fans. With the Athletics out of the league, the fans knew that Adrian's presence on the team was no longer a temporary arrangement, and they heartily cheered their big third baseman. Anson's hitting, along with his enthusiastic coaching and his "kicking" with the umpires, made him one of the most popular men on the team.

6. Manager in Training

Anson was the biggest player in the game, and he learned to use his physical bearing to his advantage, especially on the base paths. In an exhibition game against an International Association team from Pittsburgh, the Alleghenies, Anson was on first when Paul Hines hit a pop-up on the infield. Allegheny infielder Ed Williamson settled under the ball, only to be steamrolled by Anson, who was on his way to second base. The umpire called Anson out for interference, and the *Chicago Inter-Ocean* expressed dismay at Anson's attitude. "It was a very discreditable trick," complained the paper, "and Anson's assertion that he did not see the player makes it even worse, as it is very improbable that such an expert player runs with his eyes closed." The *Brooklyn Eagle* agreed, suggesting that Anson was one of a small number of players "who would rather earn the applause of the roughs and rabble by small meannesses ... than earn the praise of the gentlemen of the crowd by manly efforts to win."[4]

The big third baseman paid little attention to the newspaper criticism. He had learned from Al Spalding that hard, aggressive play wins ball games, and Anson played with the same all-out style whether the game was a league contest or an exhibition tilt that did not count in the standings. "Anything to win" became his unofficial motto, and he did not mind committing a few "small meannesses" to gain the desired results. His attitude offended some of the sportswriters and opposing players, but the Chicago fans appreciated his efforts.

The White Stockings began the month of June in fifth place with a 4–8 record, and Spalding decided to heed the pleas of the fans. He took the mound against Cincinnati in Chicago on June 5, but the Reds pounded his pitches with ease in the first inning. Spalding failed to retire a batter, and when a line drive by Bob Addy struck Spalding in the chest, the Chicago manager was forced to return to first base and hand the pitching load back to Bradley. Though the White Stockings won the game by a 12–5 score, Spalding never made another pitching appearance in the major leagues.

With the team buried in fifth place, Spalding decided to revamp his lineup on July 13. He put Cal McVey in the pitcher's box and moved George Bradley to third base, displacing Adrian Anson, who became the new Chicago catcher. This new lineup won a 6–3 decision over Hartford that day, but the improvement was short-lived, and the White Stockings failed to climb the standings. McVey dropped his next two contests, and Bradley again returned to the mound. Team president William Hulbert grew frustrated with his ballclub, and after an 18–4 loss to Boston on July 18, Hulbert penned an angry letter to outfielder Paul Hines, in which the club president threatened to suspend the player if his performance did not improve. Spalding did not appreciate Hulbert's interference, which made the campaign all the more difficult for the fading White Stockings.

Anson caught most of the rest of the games on the schedule, despite his 22 errors and 28 passed balls in 31 games behind the bat. Barnes was not ready to return to the team and his continued absence compelled Spalding to put himself at second, move outfielder John Glenn to first, and try out a series of prospects in the outfield. The 1877 season turned into a disaster, and only the ineptitude of the Cincinnati Reds kept the White Stockings out of the cellar in the six-team league. The Reds disbanded in July, re-formed a few days later, and continued to play, but some newspapers dropped them from their standings and left Chicago in last place.

Hulbert, still trying to jump-start his team, exploited his position as league president to use the problems in Cincinnati to his advantage. On the day after the Reds disbanded, Hulbert signed two of the best Cincinnati players, Charley Jones and Jimmy Hallinan, to Chicago contracts. The resulting outcry forced Hulbert to give Jones back to Cincinnati when the Reds resumed play, though Hulbert did so only after Jones had helped the White Stockings sweep a three-game series against St. Louis. The Chicago club soon fell back into a losing streak, and the addition of Hallinan failed to give the White Stockings the boost they needed.

William Hulbert, president of the Chicago White Stockings. (Transcendental Graphics)

While Chicago struggled, Harry Wright assembled another outstanding team in Boston. The loss of the "Big Four" dropped the Red Stockings to fourth place in 1876, but curveball specialist Tommy Bond took Spalding's place on the mound and led the league in wins in 1877 with 40. Deacon White returned to Boston after one season in Chicago and led the league in hits, triples, batting average, and runs batted in, while Wright filled a hole at third base with Athletics refugee Ezra Sutton. By August, the White Stockings were making plans for 1878, while Boston battled for the pennant with the Louisville Grays.

The Boston club was known for its sportsmanlike play, but the Louisville Grays were a good team with a poor reputation for integrity. On August 6, the White Stockings played the Grays at Louisville, where the Grays offered to let Chicago captain Cal McVey choose the umpire by selecting one of three names from a hat. McVey chose a slip of paper that contained the name of a local umpire named Devinney, the favorite of the Louisville team, and before the Louisville captain could react, the suspicious McVey snatched the hat away. McVey discovered that all three slips of paper bore Devinney's name, which started an argument that only ended when Louisville agreed to appoint a different umpire. The outraged White Stockings won the game by a 7–2 score.

This incident served as a precursor to the worst scandal in the history of the National League, one that almost destroyed the circuit after only two seasons of play. Louisville followed that disputed game against the White Stockings with four consecutive wins over St. Louis and Chicago, and on August 13 they held first place by four games. The Grays then lost eight and tied one of their next nine contests and fell five and a half games behind Boston in only three weeks. Boston cruised to the pennant, while the Louisville team executives investigated the Grays' collapse. They discovered evidence that four Louisville players, including star pitcher Jim Devlin, accepted bribes from eastern gamblers to throw the pennant race to the Boston club. William Hulbert banned the four players from the National League for life, and over the next several decades the phenomenon of "hippodroming" virtually disappeared.

Adrian Anson defended the honesty of the game in a more physical way. One day, when a man on a streetcar loudly opined that ballplayers "play to win or lose as will best suit their own pockets," Anson demanded an apology. He did not receive one, and Anson belted the man. "I am not ashamed to say," declared Anson more than 20 years later, "that I would do it again under the same circumstances."[5]

The White Stockings exhibited some signs of life late in the season, especially on August 7 in Cincinnati. In that game the Chicago club scored 13 runs in the second inning on the way to a 21–7 win at Cincinnati. The 13 runs set a record, which still stands, for the most tallies by any team in the second inning of a game. Unfortunately, the bad days outnumbered the good ones. On September 4, in Hartford, Adrian Anson made seven errors behind the bat in a 7–1 loss. Anson was a good third baseman, but a poor catcher, and both Hulbert and Spalding realized that Anson's future lay in the infield or outfield.

There were several reasons for the White Stockings' fall in the standings. Ross Barnes, who used his skill at the fair-foul bunt to post a .429 batting average in 1876, suffered when the rules committee outlawed his specialty for the 1877 campaign. He was hampered by the rule change, but was also weakened by his illness and played only 22 of Chicago's 60 games. George Bradley, the pitcher Spalding recruited to replace himself in the box, did not live up to his stellar 1876 performance and wound up with an 18–23 won–lost record. Cal McVey, the second-string pitcher, posted a 4–8 mark, and though he led the team with a .368 average, only Adrian Anson and shortstop Johnny Peters managed to join him in the .300 circle as the defending champions finished the campaign in fifth place with a 28–33 record.

Though Anson posted the fifth-best batting average in the league at .337, the Chicago offense proved anemic all season long. Hitting dropped off throughout the National League, but no team fell farther than the White Stockings, who batted .337 as a team in 1876 but hit only .278 in 1877. Though homers were rare in the circuit that year, mostly because the baseballs manufactured by Spalding and Brothers were deader than any previous ball, the White Stockings set a record when they failed to hit a home run all season. No other major league team has ever played an entire campaign without a single home run to its credit.

Henry Chadwick, the influential baseball editor of the *New York Clipper*, lay some of the blame on the manager. Spalding "had too many irons in the fire," said Chadwick, "and in his attempt to captain the nine, to run the general business of the club, and at the same time to manage his own baseball business and store, he undertook more than any one man could properly attend to, and the results was [sic] a measurable failure."[6] Perhaps Spalding was too distracted to manage well, suggested the *Chicago Tribune*, which cited "[an] utter lack of united effort in the team, and too many captains and managers" as the cause of the problems.[7]

Spalding had retired as a pitcher the year before, and at the close of the 1877 season he opted to give up his position as manager of the White Stockings as well. He could not play, manage, serve as Hulbert's right-hand man, and run his growing sporting goods business all at the same time, so he decided to take a position as business manager of the White Stockings and leave the field management of the team to a hand-picked successor.

Though Adrian Anson had served as Spalding's assistant and had a previous, though brief, term as manager of the Athletics in 1875, Hulbert wanted a more experienced man to succeed Spalding at the head of the ballclub. Fortunately, the man he was looking for had been put out of a job when the Hartford Dark Blues disbanded after the 1877 campaign. Bob Ferguson, a 33-year-old veteran player and manager, was one of the most respected figures in the game in the 1870s, and Hulbert signed him to a one-year contract to manage the White Stockings.

Ferguson began his career in 1865 with the Enterprise club of Brooklyn, his home town, and moved to the Atlantics the next year, becoming one of early baseball's biggest stars. He became the captain of the Atlantics in 1869, and in June of 1870, Ferguson scored the winning run in one of the most famous games in history, the match that ended the undefeated streak of the Cincinnati Red Stockings at 94 games. In 1872 he was elected president of the National Association while still playing for Brooklyn, and was also in demand as an umpire. Ferguson figured out, possibly before anyone else, that right-handed batters hold an advantage over left-handed pitchers, and trained himself to become baseball's first switch-hitter. He managed the Hartford Dark Blues from 1875 to 1877, and led his team to a second-place finish behind Spalding's White Stockings in 1876. Ferguson managed in a hard, aggressive manner, as had Spalding, and Hulbert saw Ferguson as the man to lead the White Stockings back to the top of the league.

Spalding supported the choice of Ferguson for his leadership qualities, but soon grew disenchanted with the selection, for Ferguson also possessed an explosive temper. In 1873, during a game he umpired between the New York Mutuals and the Baltimore Canaries, an argument with Mutuals catcher Nat Hicks became so heated that Ferguson picked up a bat and belted Hicks with it, breaking the catcher's arm in two places. Ferguson was an aggressive competitor like Spalding, but possessed none of Spalding's self-control. "The trouble with Ferguson," wrote Spalding later, "...was not lack of intelligence, courage or integrity; but, rather, a want of diplomacy. He was no master of the arts of finesse. He had no tact. He knew nothing of the subtle science of handling men by strategy rather than by force."[8]

Ferguson had spent almost his entire career at third base, but he installed himself as Chicago's starting shortstop. He did not leave Anson at third; instead, Ferguson signed Frank Hankinson to play the hot corner and put the veteran Joe Start, an old Hartford teammate of Ferguson's, at first base. This left no place for Anson on the infield, so Adrian moved to left field for the 1878 season. Most teams in the 1870s employed one pitcher to throw all or almost all of the team's innings, and Ferguson brought Terry Larkin, an intense right-hander, from Hartford to handle the pitching chores. Al Spalding was now officially retired from the mound, though he played one game at second base in September. Spalding belted two singles but committed four errors in seven chances in that contest, which turned out to be his last major league game. Ross Barnes, still recovering from his illness, sat out the season, and when Cal McVey left the Chicago club and signed with Cincinnati, the "Big Four" were gone for good.

Of the six stars that Hulbert signed, with much fanfare, for the White Stockings in mid–1875, only Adrian Anson remained.

The scandal-plagued Louisville club dropped out of the league in the spring, so the 1878 season began on May 1 with only six teams on the schedule. All of the National League teams lost money in 1877, but Hartford, St. Louis, and Cincinnati could not withstand the flow of red ink and joined Louisville on the sidelines. The circuit, struggling for survival, granted new franchises to Milwaukee, Cleveland, and Indianapolis, which gave the league four teams in the Midwest and only two in the Northeast. The three newer clubs appeared weak, and the pennant chase looked to be a three-way race among Boston, Providence, and the White Stockings, who hoped to return to their 1876 form and snatch the pennant away from Boston once again.

The White Stockings had outgrown the 23rd Street Grounds, and Spalding and Hulbert bought land closer to the downtown area and built Lakefront Park during the early months of 1878. Lakefront Park stood on the same site that housed the National Association ballyard that burned down during the fire of 1871; it stood at the corner of Michigan and Randolph streets, not far from the Illinois Central rail yards, on a site that is now part of Grant Park. It was an oddly shaped ballpark, with a sharply curving outfield fence that stood only 186 feet from the plate down the left field line and 196 feet in right. It was so easy to hit balls over the fence, especially on windy days, that a special ground rule was instituted that counted such hits as doubles, not home runs.

The new facility held more than 3,000 seats, but the players found it disappointing, as it was built on the site of a long-abandoned city dump. Bottles, cans, glass, and other refuse poked through the infield, and each new rainstorm exposed more garbage. The team management improved the playing surface a few years later, but it was difficult to play on in its first few seasons.

Adrian Anson began the new campaign on a high note. With Al Spalding and the rest of the Big Four gone, Anson was now a permanent fixture on the team and one of the two or three brightest new stars of the game. He and Virginia resided during the summer of 1877 in an apartment building on the South Side. In September, Virginia returned to Philadelphia, and in October 1877, shortly after the end of the baseball season, Virginia presented Adrian with their first child, a daughter named Grace.

Adrian was no longer a drinker, but he was a betting man, and enjoyed making wagers with teammates and friends, mostly concerning baseball matters. In one instance, Adrian was mercilessly teased by his teammates when he struck out twice in an exhibition before the 1878 season. Anson angrily declared that he would go through the entire league season without striking out even once, and offered a $500 wager — a large percentage of his annual salary at the time — to back up his boast. His teammates took the bet, and, amazingly, Anson did not strike out for the first few months of the season. Anson finally struck out on a called third strike in midseason, but the other White Stockings agreed that the umpire blew the call and let it slide. In an incredible display of bat control, he completed the 1878 season with only one strikeout to his name, and won his wager.

Anson's feat was perhaps the only bright spot for the White Stockings in 1878. The team opened the season with three consecutive wins, but then lost nine of its next 10 games to drop all the way to last place by the end of May. A nine-game winning streak boosted the Chicago club to second place in late July, but injuries and poor fielding took their toll, and the White Stockings fell out of contention. Anson batted .341 in 1878, but a serious finger infection, which Anson described as "frog felon," interfered with his throwing and forced Ferguson to move him to second base for nine games and to third base and catcher for three games each late in the season. The White Stockings held second place in early August, but lost 15 of their last 19 decisions and finished the season in fourth position with a 30–30 mark, 11 games behind Boston, which captured its second National League pennant.

Ferguson led the team in batting with a .351 mark, but he was mediocre in the field, and alienated most of his charges with his irascible personality. As Anson recalled, Ferguson was "a fair shortstop, [but] by no means a top-notcher, and neither was he a really good manager, he not having the necessary control of the men that he had under him."[9] The manager also resented the interference of Hulbert, whose hands-on management style clashed with Ferguson's desire for total control of the team. Some newspapers complained that Hulbert issued contradictory orders to both Ferguson and Spalding, orders that increased in frequency as the White Stockings fell further behind in the race and frustrated the already irritable Ferguson.

Ferguson threw dramatic temper tantrums on the bench as the losses mounted, and the Chicago papers reported that his tirades led most of the White Stockings to tune him out, especially late in the campaign. Spalding and Hulbert agreed on the manager's negative impact on the team, and shortly after the last game of the season, a 9–6 loss to Cincinnati on September 14, Ferguson received word that his contract would not be renewed for 1879.

Adrian Anson was now 26 years old, and Spalding, who was 26 when he became the manager of the White Stockings, figured that his protégé was now ready to assume the field leadership of the team. On September 18, 1878, Spalding and Hulbert announced that Adrian Anson would lead the Chicago ballclub in 1879. The former "Marshalltown Infant" was now Cap Anson, manager and field captain of the White Stockings. In the words of baseball historian Bill James, "It was the role he was born to play."[10]

CHAPTER 7

Captain of the Chicagos

> Anson is to captain the Chicago nine this season. He has experience, and if allowed to have his way in directing the field will do well, no doubt. But if — as Ferguson was — he is to be subject to contradictory orders from [Hulbert], no improvement over last year's work will be exhibited.
> —New York Clipper, 1879[1]

During the 19th century, long before major league teams employed general managers, personnel experts, and scouting staffs, the manager of a National League ballclub was responsible for evaluating talent and signing players. The winter of 1878–79 found new Chicago field boss Cap Anson working hard to overhaul the Chicago roster. Abner Dalrymple, a fine-fielding outfielder, came from Warren, Illinois, where he worked as a brakeman on the Illinois Central Railroad while starring on the company baseball team. He joined the Milwaukee team in 1876, and when the team moved to the National League in 1878, Dalrymple won the batting title with a .354 mark.[2] Anson convinced Spalding to pay a reported $2,500, a large sum at the time, to Milwaukee for Dalrymple's services.

Dalrymple was a seasoned professional, well versed in the tricks of his trade, and later in life he described how he robbed Boston's Ezra Sutton of a grand slam home run in 1880. Sutton, recalled Dalrymple, "caught the ball a furious wallop and it sailed directly toward me in left field. I had in the blouse of my uniform an extra ball which I had kept there for an emergency. A smoky haze had settled over the field. The ball soared as it neared me back almost against the fence. I seized the concealed ball, stretched my hand upward and leaped, and came down with the ball in my hand. The umpire called the Boston side out."[3]

Dalrymple was a fairly sober and well-mannered individual, in contrast to some of Anson's other acquisitions. George Gore, a speedy 22-year-old center fielder, was dubbed "Piano Legs" due to his thick, muscular calves. Anson discovered him when the White Stockings played an exhibition against a team from New Bedford, Massachusetts, during the 1878 season. William Hulbert, on Anson's recommendation, offered Gore a $1,200 salary for 1879, but Gore demanded $2,500, and the two sides finally settled on a $1,900 contract. Gore was an enthusiastic beer drinker, but Anson was never dissuaded from signing talented players who drank, even though the captain himself had given up alcohol a few years before.

Anson also signed Ed Williamson, who had already experienced a run-in with Anson when he played for the Pittsburgh Alleghenies in 1877; Williamson was the infielder whom Anson was so roundly criticized for trampling during an exhibition game in June of that year. Williamson batted only .232 for Indianapolis in 1878 but displayed good range as well as a strong arm at third base. The 22-year-old Williamson was a drinking man too, as were catcher Frank (Silver) Flint and outfielder George (Orator) Shaffer, who came with Williamson from Indianapolis. They were a talented bunch, but Anson would have his hands full with off-the-field discipline.

Terry Larkin remained as the main pitcher, but the National League schedule increased from 60 to 84 games in 1879, and Anson realized that one man could no longer be expected to pitch all of a team's innings. The captain decided to lighten the load on Larkin by starting Frank Hankinson, a converted infielder, in 26 games, while also using Hankinson as a utility player and frequent substitute in the infield and outfield. The only weaknesses on the ballclub appeared to be at second base and shortstop, where Joe Quest and Johnny Peters were good fielders but light hitters. Anson, who had always resented bouncing from one position to another, completed his lineup by releasing Joe Start and moving himself back to first base, where he would remain for the next 19 seasons.

The White Stockings charged out of the gate in the 1879 season, grabbing the league lead with 14 wins in their first 15 games. By early July they boasted a 23–4 record for their new manager, whose elevation to the captaincy had made him, if possible, more sure of himself on the field than ever before. Anson had always possessed a great deal of confidence in his own physical talent, but, as the Spalding Guide remarked, the captain "combines the quality of alertness with that of absolute self-possession and freedom from anxiety or nervousness to a degree equaled by few ballplayers."[4] He grew a mustache, which eventually reached impressive handlebar proportions and made him look the part of the confident leader all the more.

7. Captain of the Chicagos

He had been waiting for a managerial opportunity for several years, ever since the collapse of the Athletics after the 1876 campaign negated his contract to manage in Philadelphia, and he led the White Stockings with the same aggressive and enthusiastic manner with which he played the game. He mandated tough morning workouts that included infield drills, fielding practice, and the occasional five-mile run with Anson himself setting the pace. He argued with umpires, probably more loudly and frequently than any manager before him, and heaped abuse on rival pitchers from the coaching lines. Anson was able to manage in this fashion because he had the backing of Spalding, and because his own stature as a star player gave him the moral authority to do so. His leadership style proved a success, and within a few seasons most other National League managers followed his lead.

Ed Williamson, shortstop and third baseman. (Author's collection)

Some of his strategic decisions were questionable, as illustrated in a game at Troy on June 14. With Chicago behind by one run in the ninth, Silver Flint walloped a pitch over the left field fence but decided to stop at third. He reasoned that with a runner on third, the catcher would have to play immediately behind the bat instead of several feet behind, and the next batter would have an advantage. We do not know if Anson or Flint thought of this unusual maneuver, but the strategy failed. Flint failed to score, and the White Stockings lost by one run.

The Chicago players responded to Anson's tough leadership style, and they soon learned how far their new field captain would go to protect them. In late June, the White Stockings played an exhibition game in Indianapolis, where both Silver Flint and Orator Shaffer had played the year before. The players left town at the end of the 1878 season with a trail of debt behind them, and their creditors swore out warrants to be served at the ballpark. A policeman attempted to arrest Shaffer and Flint prior to the game, but Anson ordered the officer off the field with his bullhorn voice and aggressive manner. Anson was probably much larger than the cop, who retreated, opting to make his move at game's end.

When the last out was made, Flint and Shaffer made a dash for the carriages, grabbed the reins of one, and galloped away. The policeman enlisted two of his fellow officers and met the team at the train station, only to be confronted by Anson, who "began to cuss," said the *Brooklyn Eagle*, "and he swore with the profanity of a fishwoman until Officer Case collared him for profanity and provoke." A fight ensued, but the officers managed to subdue the captain when they "drew their maces and vowed to make a home run on the first head pitched."[5] They carted Anson to the police station, where he paid a fine and was released, while Shaffer and Flint escaped from Indianapolis by hiding on the train.

Anson took to his new role so heartily that he allowed no one, not even William Hulbert, to interfere with his on-field management. On July 30 the White Stockings played Cleveland in Chicago, and with two on and two out in the seventh inning, Anson came to bat. He hit a lazy grounder to third base, but the Cleveland infielder threw wildly, pulling first baseman Bill Phillips off the bag. Phillips tagged Anson, but dropped the ball, and Anson exploded when the umpire declared him out.

The captain ordered the other two baserunners to hold their places, sent Williamson to the clubhouse for a copy of the rulebook, and argued with the umpire for more than 15 minutes over the play. Williamson finally produced the rulebook, and as Anson flipped through the pages the fans became restless. They began to boo, and Hulbert left the stands and strode onto the field to order Anson to drop the protest and resume the game.

Anson, according to the newspaper game accounts, indignantly refused to obey the team president. The captain angrily denounced Hulbert for interfering in the field management of the team and reminded the umpire that he could call a forfeit if the club president did not remove himself from the field immediately. Hulbert retreated, and before long the umpire found the pertinent rule in the book and reversed his decision in favor of the White Stockings. Chicago won that game, and Hulbert never again tried to overrule Anson on the field of play.[6]

The captain, in turn, put Hulbert's interests before his own popularity. On August 13, rain delayed a game at Cincinnati between the White Stockings and the Reds. The field was too wet for play, but Anson, to the dismay of many present, insisted that Reds manager Cal McVey agree to play at least one inning to save a refunding of the ticket money (the rules then required that the teams play one inning, not five as they do now).

Both McVey and the umpire refused to go along, so Anson appointed his own umpire, a Chicago team executive named Jonathan Brown, and sent his team onto the field while the Reds remained on their bench. Pitcher Terry Larkin threw a few pitches, with no batter present, and then umpire Brown declared the game forfeited to the Chicagos by a score of 9 to 0. Incredibly, at the league meeting that winter, the National League upheld the temporary umpire's ruling and allowed the forfeit to stand as a victory for the White Stockings.

The *Boston Herald* took Anson to task later that week. "Mr. Anson should be made to understand that the spectators at a base ball match do not attend such games for the sole purpose of being swindled. People attend for the sake of seeing the game. If Anson gives such advice as that reported, then the quicker that gentleman goes into other business, the better for the interests of base ball."[7]

The White Stockings held first place until August, when the Providence Grays made a charge and took the lead with a 16–3 record for the month. Anson led his team in batting, but his .317 average was his lowest yet in professional ball. He became ill with chills and fever in July and tried to play through it, but became weaker through the month of August with what the newspapers called a "liver disease." His poor physical condition was the main reason that the White Stockings went 8–9 in August and fell behind Providence in the standings. "[Anson's] liver and its workings," remarked the *Chicago Tribune*, "are the source of intense anxiety to thousands of young men with standing collars who are mildly insane on the subject of baseball."[8]

Anson was seriously ill, but he was not a quitter. He "stubbornly refused to acknowledge himself sick,"[9] said the *Tribune*, and the slumping captain demoted himself to the ninth spot in the lineup during the early weeks of August. He finally benched himself on August 15. Anson tried his best to shake the illness, but he grew progressively sicker as the White Stockings battled the Grays for the pennant. Finally, after the game of August 26, Al Spalding convinced Anson to give up control of the ballclub. Silver Flint took over as manager on an interim basis, while Anson watched a few games from the stands, then left the team for the remainder of the season. Without Anson's bat or his leadership, the White Stockings tumbled out of the race within a matter of weeks. The team went 5–12 under Flint and wound up in fourth place, ten and a half games behind the Providence pennant winners.

Anson's illness was so severe that the *New York Clipper* proclaimed, "It is now said that Anson will never play ball again, his lungs being affected. This, if true, will be sad news to his many friends in Chicago and

Philadelphia."[10] He went to his father's home in Marshalltown to recuperate in the fresh country air of his old hometown. The cure must have worked, as Anson recovered quickly enough to accompany Spalding and the rest of the White Stockings on a post-season exhibition tour of California in October, where the Chicago, Cincinnati, and Rochester teams played local minor-league nines and each other. The crowds were small, mostly because Spalding insisted on charging 50 cents admission in a state where most people paid 25 cents to watch a ballgame, but Anson hit well and battled the umpires with his usual fire. His speedy and complete recovery impressed his teammates and raised expectations for the upcoming 1880 campaign.

At the end of the season, the league office proclaimed Cap Anson the winner of the batting title with a .407 average, but researchers have found a myriad of errors in the statistical records kept by the league. The official tally showed Anson with 90 hits in 221 times at bat in his abbreviated 1879 campaign, but later baseball statisticians combed through the box scores and found that Anson made only 72 hits in 227 trips to the plate to finish at a .317 mark. Paul Hines of Providence, according to those investigators, is the rightful 1879 batting champ with his .357 average. As historian David Nemec has suggested, "The scorekeeper for the Chicago team apparently either failed first-grade math or got a lot of his dinner checks picked up by a certain first baseman."[11] The National League, however, still recognizes Cap Anson, not Paul Hines, as the standard-bearer in batting for 1879.

Anson's first season as manager began auspiciously, and though his illness derailed the team's pennant charge, it also proved that the White Stockings could not win without him. Cap Anson was not only the most valuable player on the team, he was now its acknowledged leader. With a healthy Anson and a more effective pitching, the Chicago fans looked forward to the upcoming 1880 season.

Before that season commenced, the National League instituted a new rule that changed the nature of the game. Beginning in 1880, each team was allowed to "reserve" five of its players for the following year. This empowered the owners to retain the services of their five most important players from one year to the next, forever if they so chose, and those designated players could no longer sell their services to the highest bidder at the end of the season. By the end of the 1880s, the rule was extended to include the entire roster of each team, and from the 1880s to the 1970s every standard player contract included the so-called "Reserve Clause."

The new rule was designed to lessen the competition for star players and bring down salaries, and was successful in that regard. It allowed good teams to hold onto their better players for a longer period of time, and the

Chicago White Stockings took advantage of this unforeseen benefit. The core of the 1879 White Stockings— Anson, Flint, Gore, Dalrymple, and Williamson — remained together and, with a few more important additions in 1880, set out to dominate the National League.

The White Stockings still had a few holes in their lineup, so in the early months of 1880 Anson and Spalding combed the ranks of unreserved National League players. Perhaps their most important acquisition came from Cincinnati, where the Reds neglected to reserve a young catcher and utility man named Mike Kelly. A personable, hard-drinking 22-year-old from Troy, New York,

Mike Kelly, Chicago's "King of Ballplayers." (Author's collection)

Kelly was the son of Irish immigrants, and spoke with a lilting Irish accent. Anson signed him to play right field, but he also backed up Silver Flint at the catching position, and could also play second, short, and third as needed. Cincinnati manager Cal McVey reportedly saw little potential in Kelly, but Anson was deeply impressed with the young man's play on the post-season tour of California in October of 1879. Anson regarded Kelly as "young, green, and ... continually getting tangled in his own legs in an awkward boy fashion. I thought I saw a likely man in him on account of his hitting and base running. These always continued to be his strong points."[12]

Kelly batted .348 for Cincinnati in 1879, and he soon came to be regarded as the best player on the White Stockings, if not the entire league, next to Anson himself. Kelly's personality and wit, along with his excellent play, made him the most popular player of the 1880s. He tried his best not to take the game seriously; he smoked on the bench during games, and one day a reporter asked Kelly if he drank there as well. "It depends on the length of the game," replied Kelly. Anson always forgave his brilliant utility man, because the captain valued talent over good behavior, and Kelly became a star almost immediately upon his appearance in the Chicago lineup.

Anson's White Stockings already possessed a reputation as a forceful bunch, but Kelly introduced his own aggressive style of play to the Chicago team. He hid extra baseballs in his uniform shirt and produced them at opportune times, turning missed fly balls into outs. He knew that the lone umpire could not possibly see everything on the field at any given time, so Kelly often tried to score from second base on a hit to the outfield without touching third at all. Sometimes the umpire caught him, but usually Kelly got away with it. On the road, his baserunning antics drove fans crazy, but Chicago crowds approved of his hijinks and, before long, labeled the popular Kelly the "King of Ballplayers."

Anson also strengthened the pitching staff. Terry Larkin's sore arm, along with Anson's illness, turned September 1879 into a disaster for the White Stockings, and Larkin was also hampered by a head injury he sustained in batting practice from an Anson line drive. To take Larkin's place, Anson signed righthander Larry Corcoran, who played for Springfield and Holyoke during the 1879 season. Corcoran was one of baseball's rising stars, and the *New York Clipper* said of Corcoran, "He has wonderful speed for his strength, and with it a troublesome curve. He also has more than ordinary command of the ball in delivery for so swift a pitcher. He is a good 'headwork' player in the position, and with such a catcher as Snyder or Flint able to support his great pace, it would be difficult to get a base-hit from his pitching."[13]

Corcoran was a fastball pitcher, and Anson decided to sign curveball specialist Fred Goldsmith to complement him. Goldsmith not only made his living throwing curveballs, but also claimed to have invented the pitch. He came from New Haven, Connecticut, the home of Yale University, and he said that in 1866, when he was 14 years old, he demonstrated the curveball for the Yale baseball team. In August 1870, the 18-year-old Goldsmith made national headlines when he gave a public exhibition of curveball pitching at the Capitoline Grounds in Brooklyn. This demonstration prompted many to credit him with inventing the pitch, although evidence shows that Candy Cummings was throwing it in amateur play prior to 1870. Goldsmith posted a 31–5 record for the independent Tecumseh team in Ontario in 1876, beating the Chicago club several times in non-league games that year and deeply impressing Al Spalding. When the Troy team failed to reserve Goldsmith for the 1880 season, Anson signed him for the White Stockings.

Anson retained Joe Quest at second base, but upgraded the shortstop position with Tom Burns, a 23-year-old from Pennsylvania who, unlike most of his teammates, neither smoked nor drank. A dependable young man, Burns batted .262 for Albany of the National Association in 1879, and although he usually played at third base, Anson made Burns his starting shortstop. Anson later stated that Burns "was hardly fast enough to be considered a really good shortstop ... at third base Burns was as good as the best of them; he excelled at the blocking game, which he carried on in a style that was particularly his own and which was calculated to make a baserunner considerable trouble."[14] In future seasons Anson put Williamson at short and Burns on third, but in 1880 Burns played the majority of games at short for the White Stockings, although pitcher Larry Corcoran also saw action there.

The White Stockings set out to capture the pennant they might have won in 1879, had not Cap Anson fallen ill and missed the last six weeks of the season. The Providence Grays beat out Anson's crew for the 1879 pennant, but they started the 1880 campaign without George Wright, their manager and star shortstop. Wright became the first casualty of the reserve clause when the Providence team reserved him but offered him what he deemed an insufficient salary to continue as playing manager. Wright wanted to play for Boston where he could be close to his growing sporting goods business, but Providence held his rights and would not release him. Wright did not return to Providence for two years, and the Grays signed former Chicago shortstop Johnny Peters, who hit only .228 that year, to fill in. The Grays also failed to reserve star outfielder Jim O'Rourke, probably for salary reasons, and the defending champions began the new season at a disadvantage.

The White Stockings opened the season in Cincinnati on May 1 and pulled out a come-from-behind win by a score of 5 to 4. The Reds batted first (in those days the teams flipped a coin to decide which club came to bat first) and scored two runs off Larry Corcoran in the top of the ninth to take a 4–3 lead, but the White Stockings scored twice in the bottom of the inning to win the game. This was the first National League game to be decided by the "sudden death" rule; in previous years, each side was required to complete three outs in the final inning, whether or not the winning run had scored. Chicago had only two outs when the fifth run crossed the plate, and the game was declared over at that point.

The Chicagos won two out of three games in Cincinnati, and then returned to Chicago for the home opener, also against the Reds, on May 7. The White Stockings announced their presence to the rest of the league when they bombed the Reds 20–7 as George Gore belted six hits, all singles, and scored five runs. The White Stockings trounced the Reds by a 15–1 count the next day; that victory was the third of a 13-game winning streak that vaulted the Chicago club past all its competitors and into a comfortable lead in the pennant chase. On May 20 Anson decided to alternate Corcoran and Goldsmith on successive days, at least for a while, and created the first pitching rotation in major league history. This innovation kept both men fresh and helped the White Stockings keep on winning. On May 27, when Fred Goldsmith pitched an 11–0 two-hit win against Buffalo, the White Stockings owned a 14–1 record and a five-game cushion over the second-place Worcester ballclub.

The White Stockings finally tasted defeat on May 29 at Boston. George Wright had not come to terms with the Providence Grays, so he joined the Boston club (managed by his brother Harry) and played his first game that day against Chicago. Anson cried foul, since Wright was still on the Providence reserve list, but the umpire allowed him to play. Wright stroked two singles and played errorless ball at short as the Boston club defeated the White Stockings by a score of 11 to 10. Anson complained to Hulbert about Wright's participation, and the league president (and Chicago club owner) ordered Wright out of uniform. He did not play again for Boston, although Hulbert, whose White Stockings club held a large lead in the pennant race, allowed the result of the game to stand.

Hulbert's dual position as league president and Chicago club owner caused some grumbling in the press. In late 1878 Al Spalding, at Hulbert's direction, signed Orator Shaffer, Silver Flint, and Ed Williamson away from Indianapolis, because Hulbert knew before anyone else that the Indianapolis ballclub was on the verge of collapse. Hulbert wielded so much influence over the Cincinnati club that he represented the Reds at league meetings, and the Reds management barely objected when Anson signed away their best young player, Mike Kelly, before the 1880 season. One critic, when asked about "Hulbert's team," responded, "Which one? He owns eight of them."

Anson, too, came under fire for his methods. By 1880, the captain had already established a solid reputation as the "King of Kickers," ready to argue any point with an umpire if he felt his team was wronged by a decision. Anson had learned from Al Spalding (who was criticized as a manager for "crowding the umpire") and from his four-year association with the always-combative Philadelphia Athletics that arguing with the officials helped the team, especially at Chicago's Lakefront Park. The *Brooklyn Eagle* stated in June that Anson "is achieving a very unenviable notoriety ... by his bullying and bulldozing tactics," and further said that "Anson is disliked in every city outside of Chicago, and every crowd in the other league cities is glad when the Chicago team are defeated,"[15] but Anson did not mind. He was there to win games, not to make friends.

On June 4, Chicago and Providence played the longest game in the history of the National League up to that time, a 16-inning affair that ended in a 1–1 tie when darkness fell. Larry Corcoran and John Ward, said the *Brooklyn Eagle*, "had the batsmen completely at their mercy. The majority

7. Captain of the Chicagos

of the batsmen neither knew how to wait for good balls nor to be ready and in form for hitting when good balls came to them.... The batsmen are too cramped under the rules to hit freely, the pitchers having the best of it altogether."[16] As if to underscore this statement, Worcester's Lee Richmond pitched the National League's first-ever perfect game on June 12, and John Ward of Providence followed with a perfect game of his own only five days later. The pitchers held the upper hand in 1880, and the league wound up with only seven .300 hitters that season. Four of them played for Chicago (Anson, Gore, Dalrymple, and Burns), and the White Stockings employed the league's best hitting attack to extend their lead as the season wore on.

Lee Richmond, the Worcester lefthander, always caused problems for the Chicago White Stockings. In the previous season, when Richmond was a student at Brown University, he pitched an exhibition game for Worcester (before the team entered the National League) against the White Stockings and embarrassed Anson's men with an 11–0 no-hitter. The White Stockings faced Richmond again on June 26 in Chicago, and Anson ordered his left-handed batters, Gore, Dalrymple, and Corcoran, to bat right-handed against the lefty Richmond. The strategy worked, as all three men hit safely and helped Corcoran defeat Worcester, 4–0.

Anson, as a manager, began to build a reputation as an innovator in 1880. His White Stockings were the first professional team to alternate starting pitchers, and the papers praised Anson for shifting players around in the field for different batters and in varied situations. The White Stockings had already developed a primitive form of the hit-and-run play in which a base runner dashed from first to second during the pitcher's windup while expecting the batter, usually Anson himself, to make contact. Anson took this play and refined it with intelligent, fast runners like Gore and Kelly. Anson also showed the benefits of "kicking" to the rest of the league, a strategy that other managers began to emulate, much to the consternation of the umpires. As one sportswriter put it, "One half of Anson's success is his intimate knowledge of close points in the game and an immediate demand for the allowance of his claims."[17]

Another new feature in baseball strategy made its debut in Chicago that season. Larry Corcoran always chewed a large wad of tobacco during games, and catcher Silver Flint suggested that Corcoran keep the chaw on one side of his mouth to signal a fastball, and on the other side to indicate a curve. This was the first successful pitcher-to-catcher signaling system in baseball, and it escaped detection all year by the other teams.

Perhaps Anson's greatest challenge in 1880 lay in enforcing discipline on his raucous crew. The players began to take less interest in their work as their league lead increased, and in mid-June Anson decided to act before problems got out of hand. He fined Mike Kelly five dollars for loafing on the basepaths, and levied a ten-dollar penalty against Ed Williamson, who had cursed at Anson on the field. Anson kept in constant contact with Hulbert and Spalding, both at home and on the road, and with the backing of his bosses, Anson was able to keep a tight rein on his players, though the pennant race was all but over by mid-season.

All the while, Anson kept pounding the ball. He installed himself in the cleanup spot in the lineup, and with fine hitters like Dalrymple, Gore, and Williamson ahead of him, Anson became the leading run producer for the Chicago team. The *Chicago Tribune* introduced a new statistic, called "runs batted in," during the 1880 season, and Cap Anson led the league in that important power-hitting category.

On July 8, the White Stockings defeated Providence for their 21st victory in a row, which set a National League record for consecutive wins that stood until 1916. They finally lost a game on July 8 at Cleveland, when Larry Corcoran took a 0–0 tie into the ninth inning but allowed a two-run, game-winning home run to Fred Dunlap. Still, the loss was only the fourth of the season against 35 wins for Anson's crew, and the White Stockings held a 13-game advantage over second-place challengers Providence and Cleveland. A three-game losing streak in late July, mostly caused by the absence of Goldsmith due to illness, left Chicago 11 and a half games ahead, but the White Stockings rallied behind Corcoran and resumed their winning ways. They did not lose a home game all year until August 12, in a 6–4 defeat by Providence, which was the first loss by the White Stockings in Chicago since August 25 of the previous season.

On August 19, a 6–0 no-hitter by Larry Corcoran against Boston was the first such gem ever pitched in Chicago. That performance put an exclamation point on the season, and Anson's men never looked back. They clinched the pennant on September 15, and on September 30, the last day of the campaign, Anson gave both Corcoran and Goldsmith a rest and sent a local semipro pitcher named Charlie Guth to the pitching box. Guth gave up eight runs and 12 hits to the Buffalo team, though he struck out seven batters, and the White Stockings won the game by a 10–8 score. It was his first, and last, major league game, and the victory gave the team a 67–17 record in Cap Anson's second season as manager of the White Stockings. The .798 winning percentage posted by the 1880 White Stockings still stands as the highest in National League history.

The White Stockings captured the pennant with exemplary hitting and pitching. Corcoran compiled a 43–14 won-lost record, while Goldsmith saw action in 24 games and won 21 of them for an .875 winning percentage, the highest in baseball history until Brooklyn's Elwood (Preacher) Roe surpassed it in 1951 with a 22–3 record. The White Stockings boasted five of the league's top seven batters, with George Gore winning the batting title at .360 and Cap Anson taking runner-up honors with a .337 mark. Abner Dalrymple, the leadoff batter, led the league with 91 runs scored, while Anson's 74 runs batted in placed him first on that list. Newspapers outside of Chicago called the team the "Chicago Bulldozers," not only for Anson's "bulldozing" of the umpires, but also for the way the team trampled all competition in the pennant race.

The White Stockings had collapsed after its first pennant-winning season in 1876, and Anson was determined not to allow that to happen again. Aided by the new reserve clause, which allowed the team to retain its best players, Anson set out to do what his mentor Al Spalding had failed to do in 1877. Anson resolved to capture the flag again in 1881 and become the second National League manager, after Boston's Harry Wright, to win two pennants in a row.

CHAPTER 8

Champions of the National League

> *The Chicagos are nearly a model team, and undoubtedly combine the best base-ball talent in the League. They had a great master, the most wonderful one the fraternity ever knew in the late President Hulbert, and he left a good student in the person of His Mountaincy Anson.*
> —*Cincinnati Enquirer*, 1882[1]

The reserve clause enabled National League teams to retain their best players from one season to the next, and the White Stockings held an advantage over the league in that regard. Cap Anson, baseball's hardest hitter and leading run producer, was so well established as manager and captain of the White Stockings that it is likely that Spalding saw no need to put Anson's name on the Chicago reserve list. This allowed the Chicago club to reserve five other players from among such talented men as Gore, Williamson, Corcoran, and Kelly. In addition, the men whose names did not appear on the list were loath to leave the most successful club in the National League. While other teams altered their personnel as the 1881 season began, the White Stockings kept their entire starting nine and made only one change on their roster, adding Hugh Nicol as a spare outfielder.

For the fifth season in a row, the National League team lineup changed as the new campaign began. In the prior season, the financially unstable Cincinnati Reds angered league president William Hulbert when they rented out their ballpark to semipro teams for Sunday games, which had been anathema to Hulbert since he created the league in 1876. The Reds also permitted other teams to serve beer at their ballpark, and though the Reds did not sell alcohol at their own games, Hulbert was so outraged that

8. Champions of the National League

Cap Anson (front and center) with his 1880 National League champions. (National Baseball Hall of Fame Library, Cooperstown, New York)

he convened a special league meeting in October of 1880. Hulbert proposed an amendment to the league constitution that forbade the teams of the National League from selling "every description of malt, spirituous or vinous liquors upon its grounds, nor in any building owned or occupied by it." When the Reds refused to endorse the change, the other seven clubs expelled Cincinnati from the league, replacing them with a new team from Detroit. Now three of the nation's largest and most baseball-friendly cities—Cincinnati, Philadelphia, and New York—were deprived of representation in the league, mostly due to Hulbert's iron grip on the circuit.

The National League season had traditionally opened on May 1, but as that date fell on a Sunday in 1881, the White Stockings played their first game in Chicago on Saturday, April 30 against Cleveland. The game drew about 1,000 people due to lingering winter weather, but the White Stockings opened with an 8–5 win. Anson's men split their first six games against Cleveland, then won two of three against Troy, finding themselves in fourth place behind Worcester, which won its first eight games and built an early lead in the pennant chase.

The first major controversy of the 1881 season erupted in Chicago in mid–May. President Hulbert owned a dog, a large black retriever, which became a favorite of Anson and his teammates. The ballplayers treated the dog as an unofficial mascot and allowed it to lounge on the roof of the center field clubhouse, where it slept through most of the games. On May 14, when league-leading Worcester played its first game of the year against the defending champions, Chicago's Tommy Burns walloped a liner past the Worcester left fielder, Lew (Buttercup) Dickinson. The ball rolled to the clubhouse, and Dickinson refused to chase the ball, claiming fear of the large black dog. Burns ran around the bases for the game-winning home run while Worcester lodged a protest against the presence of the animal. Hulbert, the dog's owner, understandably refused to overturn the outcome of the game.

Six days later, the Boston Red Stockings arrived in Chicago and immediately demanded the removal of the dog. The Boston club also requested that the clubhouse doors be shut, lest a ball roll through it for a home run. "There's no rule covering dogs and doors," sniffed Hulbert. "But if it will make you any happier, the dog shall be bounced and the door closed."[2]

In that same game, Mike Kelly managed to score all the way from second base on a groundout by Anson. While the umpire watched the play at first, he failed to notice that Kelly did not bother touching third base on his way home; in fact, Kelly never came within 30 feet of the bag. The Red Stockings protested, but the umpire did not see Kelly's shortcut, and the run proved to be the game winner in a 5–4 Chicago victory.

Kelly's deception did not always go undetected. On July 29, in a 6–3 defeat of the White Stockings by Cleveland, Kelly tried the stunt in the third inning. Umpire John Doscher saw Kelly cut across the infield, avoiding third base entirely, and promptly declared the runner out at home. "Kelly needs an admonition," stated one paper, "that this sort of baserunning is too much of a cheap-and-nasty description to give satisfaction."[3]

Kelly personified a new, more aggressive playing style, one that earned the admiration of the Chicago fans, who labeled him the "King of Ballplayers." His charisma helped bring fans to the Lake Front Grounds, and on July 4, 1881, more than 10,000 people jammed the park on a brutally hot day to see the White Stockings play Boston. The crowd spilled out of the stands and into the outfield, and the resulting playing area was so small that the umpire decreed that any balls hit into the standing-room patrons would be good for one base only. Errors by the White Stockings gave the

Bostons several unearned runs and, eventually, a 13–12 victory that broke an 8-game winning streak for the Chicagos.

Kelly, Gore, and the other White Stockings could not have performed in such an aggressive manner without the backing of their captain. If Kelly was the King of Ballplayers, Anson had long since earned the title of "King of Kickers." He was always ready to support his men with his booming voice and physical bearing, and made himself conspicuous on the coaching lines when the White Stockings took their turn at bat. Anson heaped verbal abuse on opposing pitchers, kept up a constant stream of demands upon the umpires, and generally made himself the focal point of all action on the field, at home or on the road. A few years later, one Chicago paper described the captain with a poem:

> He wants to be a kicker,
> And with the kickers stand;
> Find fault with every umpire
> And the way the pitchers stand.
> He kicks about his players,
> And about the scorers, too;
> He thinks the man that never kicks
> A meek and humble fool.
> For he is a kicker from Kickerville,
> And his patron saint's a mule.[4]

Anson's kicking and Kelly's baserunning shenanigans were crucial elements in the success of the White Stockings, as much so as the undeniable talent on the Chicago roster. Such tactics did not make Anson or his White Stockings popular around the league, but their winning ways encouraged other teams to emulate these strategies, and by the mid–1880s almost every team had developed ones that mirrored those employed by the White Stockings, for good or ill. "The Chicagos," stated a Buffalo newspaper, "are teaching all the other clubs how to play the game."[5]

Boston Red Stockings manager Harry Wright, the most successful field boss of professional baseball's first decade, lamented the rowdier, less civilized style of baseball that Cap Anson helped to popularize in the 1880s. "It's hardly right for me to criticize another manager," complained Wright later in the decade, "but Anson's methods are not mine. I don't believe as he does. Anson believes in anything to win—win at all hazards—and does not apparently care whether the game is made an exhibition of scientific ball or not."[6] However, Wright's tenure in Boston ended in 1881 with a sixth-place finish, and he managed in the National League for 12 more seasons without winning another pennant. Wright's style of managing was outdated in the 1880s, and Anson became the prototype for a new breed of field leader.

The league moved the pitching box five feet farther from the plate in 1881 in an attempt to increase offense, and the man who took the greatest advantage of the new 50-foot distance was Cap Anson. The Chicago captain pounded the ball the entire year, leading the league in hits, batting average, and runs batted in. He won his second batting title with a .399 average that stood 66 points higher than the second-place finisher, Buffalo's Jack Rowe. Anson was not only the leading manager in the National League that year, but also its premier hitter, a combination that has (arguably) never been equaled in the history of baseball.[7] If the Manager of the Year and Most Valuable Player awards had been available in 1881, Cap Anson might well have captured both of them.

Anson's men grabbed the league lead in mid–May, when a six-game winning streak vaulted them from fourth place to first in only eight days, and they battled with Worcester and Buffalo over the next month. The White Stockings weathered a rash of injuries in June, with Mike Kelly nursing a swollen hand and Joe Quest suffering a shoulder injury in a fall from a carriage, but Anson kept the team in the hunt, and a streak of 16 wins in 18 games put the White Stockings six and a half games ahead by July 13. A 12–8 win over Providence on June 25 featured seven stolen bases by leadoff man George Gore, who set a record for steals in a game that stands to this day.

Starting pitcher Larry Corcoran complained of arm soreness in July, but Anson managed to keep the righthander in the rotation without overworking him, and the Chicagos pulled away from the rest of the league as Corcoran's arm improved. A 17–0 whitewashing of Detroit on August 11, which featured five hits by Silver Flint and three by Mike Kelly, left the White Stockings seven games in front of the pack. On August 23, Fred Goldsmith injured his arm in the third inning against Detroit, but Anson called upon Corcoran, who was busy counting tickets at the turnstiles. Corcoran pitched nine innings in relief and gained the win in an 8–6 victory in 12 innings.

The White Stockings extended their lead through August, and on August 25, at their final home game of the season, Anson and the team presented William Hulbert with a gold watch and chain. On the chain was a locket containing the pictures of all 12 contributors. The players also brought their mascot, Hulbert's black retriever, out of retirement for the afternoon, though the animal was "carefully conducted to his lair before the game started."[8] The White Stockings coasted to the pennant in September, with the only sour note sounded in a game at Troy on September 27.

8. Champions of the National League

The Trojans and the White Stockings played in a heavy downpour that turned the field into a sea of mud, making the ball almost impossible to catch. Anson loudly objected to the impossible playing conditions, but Troy refused to cancel the game, which was won by Chicago by a 10–8 score. Only 12 fans paid their way into the ballpark that afternoon for the lowest official turnstile count in National League history.

The White Stockings clinched the pennant on September 19 when Troy defeated second-place Buffalo and left Chicago ten games in front with nine games remaining on the schedule. At season's end, the White Stockings traveled to New York for a three-game series against a strong independent team, the Metropolitans, losing the first two contests before a homer by Cap Anson helped the Chicagos defeat the Mets in the third game by an 11 to 2 score. Anson's ballclub capped its impressive season with a five-game sweep of the newly reorganized Philadelphia Athletics, with one of the five wins coming on a no-hitter by Larry Corcoran. The Chicagos then won two out of three from Cleveland, winning the final game on a one-hit shutout by Corcoran, before it disbanded for the winter.

William Hulbert could be proud, not only of his team, but of his greatest creation, the National League. For the first time in its six-year history, the league was able to announce that all eight of its teams would return intact for the following season. Though the league still lacked representation in New York and Philadelphia, it had gained a measure of stability that boded well for its future.

Hulbert, unfortunately, would not live to see the growth of his National League. He was only 49 years old in 1881, but his heart was weak, and his health began to fail during the latter part of the season. He gained reelection as league president in December of that year, but gradually withdrew from league and team matters as the months passed. On April 10, 1882, Hulbert died of a heart attack at his home in Chicago. He was buried at Graceland Cemetery, where his grave was marked with a stone baseball containing the names of the eight National League teams. In a special meeting of the Chicago board of directors a few days later, Al Spalding was named to succeed Hulbert as president of the White Stockings.

The National League instituted a few new rules for the upcoming campaign. The league decided to follow the example of its newest rival, the American Association, and require each player to wear a differently colored silk uniform shirt in 1882, depending on his defensive position. Catchers wore light blue, second basemen wore orange and brown stripes, pitchers dressed in dark blue and white, and so on. The idea probably came from Spalding, whose color-coded hats had earned so much criticism as a

"Dutch bed of tulips" six years earlier. The players hated the new silk shirts, calling them "clown costumes" and demanding to know if two players who switched positions in the middle of a game were required to trade shirts as well. This particular innovation caused so much confusion among fans and players that the regulation was repealed after only one season.

The other new rule was a minor one, but it came into play for the White Stockings during the third game of the season. The league required that base runners run, not walk, back to their bases after a batter hit a foul ball. The new rule was intended to speed up the game, and the league directed its umpires to call a runner out who walked back to a base after a foul. On May 5, in a home game against Cleveland, Cap Anson was on first when Mike Kelly belted a foul ball to the right side. Anson strolled back to first base, prompting Cleveland manager Jim McCormick to demand, successfully, that the umpire declare Anson out. Anson raised a fuss, but the decision stood, and Anson became the first player called out under the new rule.

Though the White Stockings had won the previous two National League pennants, the captain decided to tinker with the lineup. Anson sent the light-hitting second baseman Joe Quest to the bench, moved King Kelly to shortstop and Tommy Burns to second, and installed utility man Hugh Nicol as the starting right fielder. Anson once again alternated Corcoran and Goldsmith on the mound, an innovation that was copied by most of the other teams in the league by 1882. Of the eight National League ballclubs, only Providence and Cleveland entrusted their mound responsibilities to one pitcher.

The new Chicago lineup started the season slowly. By June 15, the White Stockings were settled in fifth place with a 12–14 record, five games behind league-leading Detroit. Anson's men then rode a 14–1 streak all the way to first place, mostly on the hitting of Cap Anson and the pitching of Larry Corcoran. Anson batted .362 in 1882, leading the team in batting average, hits, and runs batted in, while Corcoran pitched the second no-hitter of his career in a 5–0 win over Worcester on September 20. He was the first pitcher in baseball to throw two no-hit shutouts. On June 20, Corcoran achieved another distinction when he belted the first grand slam home run in Chicago team history in a 13–3 win over Worcester.

A loss to Detroit on July 12 broke the streak, but a 23–4 stomping of the Wolverines on the 14th cemented Chicago's hold on first. Ten days later, the Chicago offense took advantage of Cleveland's failure to adopt the pitching rotation. Cleveland starter Jim McCormick had pitched nine of the previous ten games, and manager Fred Dunlap (who had relieved McCormick as field leader in May) decided to give the exhausted hurler a rest and put outfielder Dave Rowe on the mound for one game. Anson's White Stockings pounded the inexperienced Rowe for 29 hits, ten of them doubles, on their way to a 35–4 win. The White Stockings set a record for runs scored in a game that stood for 15 years.

Though the Chicagos led the league in runs scored for the fourth season in a row, the White Stockings failed to gain a firm grip on the league lead, and Anson finally realized that his new defensive alignment did not work. Hugh Nicol batted only .199 for the 1882 season, and while Quest was not much better as a hitter, he was superior to either Tom Burns or King Kelly as an infielder. In August Anson finally relented and benched Nicol. The captain moved Kelly back to right field, put Burns at shortstop, and reinstalled Quest at second base. This move dramatically improved the Chicago defense and set the stage for one of baseball's best pennant races up to that time.

Detroit had dropped out of the race by late August and left Providence and Chicago to battle for the pennant. On September 9, when the White Stockings bombarded the Troy Trojans by a score of 24–1, Chicago trailed the Grays by three games with the most important series of the season, a three-game set against Providence at Chicago, in the offing.

Anson was in an unusually cheerful mood as the Providence series began. "Can't lose today," he said to the writers before the game on September 12. "I've just got a telegram. It's a boy; weighs ten pounds."[9] Virginia had given birth in Philadelphia to a son, whom the couple named Adrian Hulbert Anson. The senior Anson sent Fred Goldsmith to the mound against the Grays that afternoon, and Goldsmith responded with a 6–4 win that left the White Stockings only two games behind.

Chicago won the next day behind Corcoran by a 6–5 count, and when George Wright made a throwing error that cost the Grays two runs on September 14, the White Stockings won the third game by a 6–2 score and leaped into a tie with Providence for the league lead. More than 8,000 people jammed Lakefront Park that day for the largest crowd ever to see a contest in Chicago. Two days later, a 5–1 win over the Worcester Brown Stockings, combined with a Providence loss, gave Anson's men a lead they never relinquished. Chicago won two more contests against Worcester, one of them a no-hitter by Larry Corcoran, to extend their lead to two games. In all, the White Stockings won 15 of their last 16 games to win their third pennant in a row by three games over the Grays.

Perhaps Cap Anson did not enjoy this championship as much as the two that preceded it. Anson had longed for a son, and was filled with joy over the birth of Adrian Hulbert Anson. Sadly, the baby proved frail, and lived for only four days. Since the child was born in Philadelphia and Anson was in Chicago with his ballclub, it is probable that the captain never saw his son alive. Anson later described the baby's death as "the first real grief" that had occurred during his marriage.

On the season's final day, September 30, Anson decided to watch the game from the bench and give a younger man the chance to play first base. Milt Scott, a 16-year-old Chicago semipro player, took the captain's place in the lineup that day, hitting two singles in five trips to the plate against future Hall of Fame honoree Jim Galvin. Scott never again played in a league game for the White Stockings, though he performed for several other teams in the next few years, and he is still the youngest player in the history of the Chicago National League franchise.

The pennant race did not end without controversy. The National League held a meeting in mid–September, immediately after Chicago's three-game sweep of the Brown Stockings, in which it decreed that Troy and Worcester would be dropped from the circuit at the end of the season. Troy and Worcester threatened to shut down immediately and not finish their schedules, which would have thrown the pennant race into disarray, since Providence had yet to play several games against the Brown Stockings. So certain did it appear that Worcester would not play its remaining games that Al Spalding promised to arrange a nine-game post-season series between Chicago and Providence to decide the championship.

Troy and Worcester, to the surprise of many, finished their schedules, which (in Spalding's estimation) made the planned nine-game championship series unnecessary, since both Chicago and Providence would end the season with the same number of games played. However, Providence cried foul when Spalding convinced the Buffalo team management to move three games between Buffalo and the White Stockings to Chicago in the final week of the season. This change gave the White Stockings three extra home games and an undeniable advantage over Providence, which played 15 of its last 17 games on the road. The White Stockings won all three contests from Buffalo and clinched the pennant, but the schedule adjustment caused so much rancor between the Providence and Chicago teams that the Grays demanded that the nine-game series be played.

The 1882 season was the first in which the National League had to cope without the leadership of William Hulbert, and many sportswriters suggested in print that Hulbert would have found a better way to manage the scheduling controversy that turned the pennant race into a fiasco. Spalding tried to renege on his previous agreement to play against Providence, stating that since the Brown Stockings had played all their required games, "I regard the league championship question as settled," but acting league president Arthur Soden pushed Spalding to reinstate the post-season series.

8. CHAMPIONS OF THE NATIONAL LEAGUE

The 1882 Chicago White Stockings, pennant winners for the third season in a row. Front: Nicol and Corcoran. Middle: Quest, Burns, Anson, Dalrymple, Gore. Top: Williamson, Kelly, Flint, Goldsmith. (National Baseball Hall of Fame Library, Cooperstown, New York)

Spalding, faced with the league's most important crisis since the 1877 Louisville gambling scandal, had no choice but to agree. The White Stockings and the Grays arranged for four games to be played in Providence, followed by four more in Chicago and a ninth contest, if necessary, to be played in a neutral city to be agreed upon at a later date.

The Providence–Chicago series was set to begin on October 10, which left a few days available for the White Stockings to play a few exhibition games beforehand. The team traveled to New York, where they played two games at the Polo Grounds against the Metropolitans, an independent ballclub that joined the American Association in the following year. The White Stockings, with Anson on the bench, teenager Milt Scott at first, Larry Corcoran in right field, and Ed Williamson behind the bat, lost to the Mets by a score of 6 to 5 on October 2 as Scott made three errors on dropped throws. Two days later, Anson's men defeated the Mets by an 11 to 5 score and gained a split in the series. The White Stockings then traveled to

Cincinnati for a two-game set against the Red Stockings, champions of the National League's newest rival, the American Association.

Spalding and Anson viewed the games against the Red Stockings as mere schedule fillers, but the Cincinnati players and fans treated the contests as a chance to validate the prowess of the Association. The new circuit had opened for business in 1882 as a direct competitor of the National League, and sought to appeal to the fans with 25-cent admission prices (versus the 50-cent rate in the National) and by making alcohol available at the games, a practice the National did not allow. National League loyalists dismissed the new circuit as "the Beer and Whiskey League," but the Association survived its first season and made plans to move the Metropolitans into New York, which the National had abandoned six years before, in 1883. In the meantime, the Cincinnati Red Stockings looked to spring an upset against the three-time pennant winners from Chicago.

Anson did not appear concerned about the Cincinnati games. He left Mike Kelly behind in New York and put Larry Corcoran at shortstop, a position that the pitcher had not played all year long. With this lineup, Anson and the White Stockings arrived at the Bank Street Grounds in Cincinnati and prepared to do battle with the American Association champions. Some enthusiastic baseball historians have called this meeting the first "World's Series," which it was not, but it marked the first time in baseball history that the pennant winners of two leagues met each other in a postseason matchup.

Anson made a wager before the game, but not on the outcome of the contest. The captain challenged Fred Goldsmith to a footrace from home plate to first base, and the confident pitcher accepted the invitation. Goldsmith was no speedster, but the 29-year-old Anson was one of the National League's slowest runners, and perhaps the captain made the challenge to still the razzing he received from friend and foe alike about his lack of speed. "It is almost unnecessary to say that Anson did not win," reported the *Cincinnati Enquirer*. "The latter can run; so can an ice-wagon or a turtle."[10]

The Reds were managed by Charlie (Pop) Snyder, a former catcher for the Philadelphia Pearls of the National Association who had, by coincidence, been Adrian Anson's rival for the attentions of Virginia Fiegal many years before. Anson stood by disdainfully as the umpire explained the park rules to the opposing captains, and when Cincinnati won the coin toss the White Stockings were obliged to bat first.

Though the White Stockings had scored nearly seven runs per game in the 1882 season, Cincinnati pitcher Will White kept Chicago off the board, and the game remained scoreless as the Red Stockings came to bat in the bottom off the sixth. Chicago's Fred Goldsmith gave up three consecutive singles, which pushed one run across for the Red Stockings, and then rookie second baseman Bid McPhee belted a triple to the gap in right that chased home two more runs. McPhee scored on a wild pitch by Goldsmith to give the Red Stockings a 4–0 lead.

In the ninth, Anson's men finally managed to rally against White. With one out, Dalrymple on third, and Williamson on second, Anson came to bat, determined to break the shutout. The captain swung hard at a high pitch and sent a long fly ball to center, which Jimmy Macullar caught for the second out. Dalrymple tagged up and tried to score, but Macullar threw him out at the plate to end the game. The Chicagos had been "Chicagoed" by a score of 4 to 0, and the Cincinnati fans celebrated their first win over the established National League. As a local newspaper, the *Enquirer*, put it, the Red Stockings had "astonished the Chicagos, the champions of the League, the great, high-toned, and only moral base ball show."[11]

More than 6,000 fans packed the Bank Street Grounds the next day to see if the Red Stockings could sweep the champions, but Anson was determined to leave town with a split. He returned Larry Corcoran to the pitching box, and Corcoran made two unearned Chicago runs in the first inning stand up. He threw a shutout of his own for a 2–0 win and a tie in the two-game series. Most fans would have liked to see a third and deciding contest, but the White Stockings were due to begin their series in Providence against the Grays in only three days, so the teams parted, leaving the question of league superiority unresolved.

Cap Anson, in his usual obstinate manner, believed that his White Stockings had already won the pennant on the field, and saw the postseason series as a mere exhibition. When the White Stockings took the field for the first game in Providence, the fans saw pitcher Larry Corcoran in left field, with Hugh Nicol at shortstop and regular shortstop Tommy Burns at second base. The Chicagos played in "a don't care sort of manner," said the *Tribune*, resulting in a loss to the Grays by a 10–4 score. Anson put Corcoran in the box for the second game and moved Dalrymple back to left and Burns to shortstop, but the White Stockings dropped the next two games before small crowds in chilly Providence.

The scene then shifted to Philadelphia and New York, where Anson's men won two games, and then back to Chicago. The captain, still treating the series as an exhibition, used the occasion to give a tryout to a second baseman named Fred Pfeffer, who had played for Troy during the regular season and became available when the Trojans disbanded. Pfeffer played well as the White Stockings won two of the next three contests to tie the series at four wins each. Some observers wondered aloud if the Grays and White Stockings were trying to prolong the series to maximize the gate receipts, but the baseball public had lost interest in the series, with the attendance shriveling game by game, until only a few hundred Chicagoans bothered to witness the eighth contest. The series mercifully ended in Fort Wayne, Indiana, on October 24 as the White Stockings bombed the Grays by a score of 19 to 7, clinching their third consecutive pennant.

CHAPTER 9

Controversy

> *[Anson's] value as a player and captain cannot be over-estimated ... [he] always plays the game thoroughly, and never flags or loses heart. He is wonderfully agile for a man of his vast magnitude and muscle, standing, as he does, six feet two inches in height and weighing two hundred and fifteen pounds, without any superfluous flesh about him.*
> —New York Clipper, 1881[1]

Cap Anson, at the age of 31, was now the biggest star in baseball. By the end of the 1882 season, he was a two-time batting champion, a three-time pennant winner as a manager, and the National League career leader in hits, batting average, doubles, and slugging percentage. Anson was not the most influential man in the game, since the club owners and executives, especially Al Spalding, held the real decision-making power in the National League. However, Anson was the man whom the fans saw on the field and read about in the dailies. He was the public face of the most successful team in the game.

Its pennant-winning ways and its charismatic stars made the Chicago ballclub the most-watched and most profitable team in the National League. More than 130,000 fans paid to see Anson and his men in the 45 home games played by the Chicagos in 1882. Crowds in Chicago averaged more than 3,000 a game, which dwarfed the attendance figures of all other teams in the league. The White Stockings were also the league's most popular attraction on the road, drawing thousands even in small cities such as Worcester and Troy, where the local ballclubs were hard-pressed to attract fans for other National League teams. The Chicago franchise was so financially successful that Al Spalding decided to invest in an almost complete makeover of Lakefront Park for the 1883 season.

Spalding enlarged the grandstand area behind home plate to fit 2,000 seats, with 6,000 more in uncovered bleachers along the foul lines. With another 2,000 spaces for standing room, the park could comfortably hold 10,000 fans, an unheard-of capacity in those days. The new Chicago president ordered every exposed surface in the park painted, hired a workforce of 41 to serve as ushers and ticket-takers, and introduced baseball's first luxury boxes, a row of 18 high-priced suites along the third-base line. One of those was occupied by Spalding, who kept a telephone and a gong in his suite to conduct business while Anson directed the team on the field below.

One aspect of the park that did not change was the proximity of the outfield fence, which stood six feet high in left field and 37 feet in right. The distance down the foul lines was still the shortest in the league at 180 feet in left and 196 feet in right, and balls whacked over the short fences by Anson, Williamson, and other powerful hitters still counted as doubles in 1883.

The death of William Hulbert, tragic as it was, ended the president's iron grip on league matters and allowed the circuit to regain a foothold in two of the nation's three largest cities. In early 1883, two new teams, the New York Gothams (who would soon after become known as the Giants) and the Philadelphia Quakers (known in some newspaper columns as the Phillies) replaced the failed franchises in Troy and Worcester. Hulbert's almost visceral hatred of New York and Philadelphia had kept those two cities out of the league since 1876, but now, with Hulbert gone, the National League was able to resume its presence in these crucial markets.

Hulbert's passing altered the balance of power in the White Stockings organization as well. Spalding was now president of the club, and as Spalding became more involved in the business end of the team, Anson took more responsibility for player management, both on and off the field. Spalding's elevation to the presidency gave Anson a stronger voice in enforcing rules and tightening player discipline. Anson had served as captain and manager of the White Stockings for four years, but by 1883 he was no longer merely Spalding's assistant, but a power on the club in his own right. Anson was assisted by a new league rule, pushed through by Spalding, which increased the number of players protected by each club under the reserve rule to 11. This development virtually halted player mobility and significantly increased the power wielded by Anson and other managers over their charges.

As the 1883 campaign dawned, Anson decided to keep all but two of the men from his 1882 championship team. Second baseman Joe Quest, who batted only .201 in 1882, was the only weak link in the starting lineup, and Anson replaced him with Fred Pfeffer, who had played for Louisville in 1881 and Troy in 1882. Pfeffer batted only .218 for the Trojans, but he impressed Anson in the post-season series against Providence. Pfeffer was a native of Louisville and spoke both German and English, making him popular with Chicago's growing legion of ethnic fans, who called him "Unser Fritz" ("Our Fritz"). He was a fast runner and a sure-handed fielder whose presence at second base allowed Anson to move Burns back to shortstop and Kelly into right field. Pfeffer's addition to the club completed Chicago's "Stonewall Infield" of Anson, Pfeffer, Burns, and Williamson, a unit that would remain together for the next seven seasons.

Anson also dropped Hugh Nicol, a .199 hitter, and signed a speedy 21-year-old from Iowa named Billy Sunday to serve as the substitute outfielder. Sunday's father had perished in the Civil War mere months after Billy was born, and since Mrs. Sunday was not able to provide for all of her children, Billy spent much of his childhood in orphanages. In his late teenage years, he moved to Marshalltown, where he worked in a furniture factory and drove a hearse for a local undertaker. Sunday gained a position on the Marshalltown baseball team and led the club to its first Iowa state championship since Adrian Anson departed more than ten years before. Billy Sunday's main asset on the field was his sprinter's speed, which he used to cover lots of ground in center field and to beat out bunts at the bat. According to legend, one of Anson's aunts wrote the captain a letter praising the fleet young outfielder, so Anson sent Sunday a telegram inviting him to Chicago for a tryout.[2] It was the first telegram that Sunday had ever received.

In early May of 1883, Billy arrived in Chicago and entered the Spalding store on Michigan Avenue, as directed, to wait for Anson and the rest of the White Stockings to arrive. After a while Anson strolled in, and Sunday, who had never seen a city bigger than Des Moines before that day, nervously introduced himself. "Billy, they tell me that you can run some," said the captain. "Fred Pfeffer is our crack runner. How about putting on a little race this morning?"

Sunday borrowed a uniform from pitcher Larry Corcoran, but he did not yet own a pair of athletic shoes. He raced Pfeffer in his bare feet and won the race by five yards. Anson was impressed, and promptly signed the youngster to a contract. Sunday played his first game for the White Stockings on May 22, and although he could not yet hit major league pitching — he went hitless in his first 13 times at bat — he became Anson's special project. Sunday was Anson's "pet," as the papers called the boy from Marshalltown. Sunday was a raw talent who could "run like a scared deer," in Anson's words, and the captain insisted on keeping the youngster on the roster.

Sunday was an amiable and levelheaded youngster, unlike many of his new teammates. Anson wished that all his men were as well behaved as Sunday, because by 1883 the off-field behavior of the White Stockings had become a constant headache for Anson and Spalding. Several of the Chicago veterans, most notably Mike Kelly, were hard-drinking carousers who did not always show up at game time in condition to play. Anson fined them, with little effect, and his job became all the more difficult as the general level of behavior among the White Stockings grew worse with each passing season.

Other players troubled the club with their financial irresponsibility. In 1883 a Florida man wrote to Spalding and charged that Silver Flint and Ed Williamson had not repaid a loan the man had made to them several months before, and he threatened to take his story to the newspapers if the money was not repaid. Spalding penned a stern letter to Flint in which the club president threatened to boot the catcher out of the National League if he did not repay his debts immediately. The matter was promptly settled, and Spalding's intervention kept the story out of the papers.

Poor team discipline contributed to the end of the three-year reign of the White Stockings. Anson's men won 16 of their first 22 games and held the lead in late May, but a 3–11 skid in June dropped the ballclub into a four-team scramble for the pennant with Cleveland, Boston, and Providence. Cleveland grabbed the lead in July, with the defending champions five games out, but Anson's men played inconsistent baseball all season long and could not mount a sustained charge. An 11-game winning streak in late August and early September put the Chicagos back in the race, but four losses in a row at Boston in mid–September knocked them out of it again.

The Chicago offense was not to blame, as they led the league in runs for the fifth season in a row. In a game at Chicago on July 3, the White Stockings belted 14 doubles, four each by Cap Anson and Abner Dalrymple, in a 31–7 romp over the Buffalo Bisons. Both Anson and Dalrymple tied the National League record for doubles in a game, which has been matched often but never surpassed in the history of the league. On September 6, the White Stockings defeated Detroit by a score of 26–6, setting a record with 18 runs in the seventh inning alone. Tommy Burns came up to bat three times in the seventh and smacked a homer and two doubles for eight bases, a one-inning record total that still stands.

The pitching, on the other hand, was not up to par for the Chicagos in 1883. Larry Corcoran continued to excel, posting a fine 34–20 mark, but Fred Goldsmith was criticized in the papers as having "grown fat and lazy" with a 25–19 record. Cap Anson put himself in to pitch on two occasions, allowing no runs in three innings of work and acquitting himself well, while Ed Williamson and King Kelly also made relief appearances that year. As a whole, both the pitching and the hitting were inconsistent for the White Stockings, resulting in a second-place finish, four games out of the league lead. The Boston team, which had been rebuilt following the departure of longtime manager Harry Wright and was now known as the Beaneaters, won its first pennant since 1878.

One paper took Anson to task for retaining the light-hitting Billy Sunday, who saw action in only 14 games and batted .241 after a terrible start. "Now that the White Stockings have been beaten," a local writer complained, "there are plenty of grumblers who fault management for attempting to go through the season with 10 players, for Billy Sunday, a pet of Anson's, is rated a cipher."[3] Anson ignored the criticism, as he had developed a bond with the earnest young man from Marshalltown. Anson had been Al Spalding's protégé, and in Sunday the captain saw an opportunity to mold one of his own.

As for Anson, he batted only .308 in 1883 for his lowest average yet in the National League. He failed to finish in the top ten of the league in any significant batting category except for doubles and runs batted in, and his fourth-place finish on the RBI list ended his streak of three consecutive seasons in leading the league in that category. However, despite his decline at the plate, the season turned out to be the most pivotal of Cap Anson's career, as far as his reputation was concerned. That year marked the start of the struggle to segregate the national game, a battle in which Cap Anson played an important, if regrettable, role.

On Friday, August 10, 1883, the White Stockings interrupted a trip from Buffalo to Detroit with a stopover in Toledo, Ohio, where they were scheduled to play against the local Northwest League nine, the Toledo Blue Stockings. The Toledo club was one of the best teams in the high minor leagues that year, and was also one of the few ballclubs of the era to employ an African-American player. Toledo's catcher, Moses Walker, was a former Oberlin College student who played ball to earn money to attend the University of Michigan's law school. He and his younger brother Welday had played for Oberlin's first baseball team in 1881, and Moses integrated Michigan's program the following year.

Anson and Spalding had informed the Toledo management that the captain objected to sharing the field with black players, and the locals planned to oblige him. Walker, suffering from a sore hand, had not been penciled into the lineup anyway. The Chicago team arrived at Union Station that Friday morning and was told that Walker would be kept on the bench. However, according to the *Toledo Blade*, "Not content with this, the visitors during their perambulations of the forenoon declared with the swagger for which they are noted" that they would not step onto the field "with no damned nigger." Anson, further inflaming a situation that the Toledo management had thought resolved, loudly reiterated this demand upon arriving at League Park.

Anson's booming voice carried his objections to all corners of the ballpark, and Toledo manager Charles Morton was displeased with the demeanor of the visitors. "The order was given, then and there, to play Walker," reported the *Blade,* "and the beefy bluffer was informed that he could play his team or go, just as he blank pleased."[4] Morton put the sore-handed Walker in right field, and when Anson saw Walker warming up before the contest, he exploded with rage. He declared he would pull his White Stockings off the field without playing the game, but Morton threatened to withhold Chicago's share of the gate receipts. After a spirited argument, Anson unhappily relented. "We'll play this here game," snarled Anson, "but we won't play never no more with the nigger in."[5]

The contest was, according to the *Blade,* "only a fair exhibition of ball playing," with the world champions winning 7 to 6 in ten innings. Anson had given Larry Corcoran the day off, and the Blue Stockings battered Fred Goldsmith for sixteen hits and held Chicago to only ten. The score was tied three times before Toledo took the lead in the top of the tenth, only to see Chicago score twice in the bottom of the inning to win the game.[6] Anson hit a double and a single for Chicago, while Walker was the only Toledo batter without a hit. Walker reached base on an error, scored a run, and played errorless ball in right field.

The Toledo newspaper soundly criticized Anson and his men the following day. "It is not putting it too strongly," said the *Blade,* "to say they were the most untidy looking lot of ball players that have ever graced the City with their presence. Their baggy white uniforms, dirty white stockings, and variegated assortment of caps gave them a slouchy, uncouth appearance which, with their braggadocio manner, was in strange contrast to what most of the audience had expected to see." The *Blade* also stated, "It is likely to prove a very cold day when they again carry a substantial bundle of gate receipts out of Toledo."[7]

The game did not attract much media attention outside of Toledo, and the *Chicago Tribune* did not even mention the controversy in its description of the contest. However, word spread quickly within the baseball world, and the Toledo exhibition helped to crystalize the segregation forces already at work in professional ball. Following Anson's lead, other players and managers became more vocal in their opposition to integration on the field.

Anson was not alone in his aversion to minorities in the professional ranks. The Peoria team of the Northwest League had petitioned the circuit to ban blacks, specifically Toledo's Moses Walker, before the 1883 season began, though Peoria withdrew its request after much "excited discussion." Fred Pfeffer, the new Chicago second baseman, was also a vocal opponent of baseball integration. During the 1881 season, Pfeffer's Louisville team played an exhibition game against a Cleveland semipro club sponsored by the White Sewing Machine Company. Moses Walker was the catcher on that team. When he entered the game in the second inning, Pfeffer and another Louisville player stalked off the field in protest. Pfeffer refused to return so long as Walker remained, but Walker was the Cleveland team's only available catcher so Pfeffer missed the rest of the contest.

Anson's stance struck a nerve, and high-level teams began to release black players and refuse to hire new ones during the next few seasons. A few men, including Walker, held on to minor league jobs, but by 1891 African-Americans had totally disappeared from organized professional baseball. Historian Sol White placed the blame directly on the shoulders of Cap Anson. "[Anson's] repugnant feeling," wrote White in 1907, "shown at every opportunity, toward colored ball players, was a source of comment throughout every league in the country, and his opposition, with his great popularity and power in base ball circles, hastened the exclusion of the black man from white leagues."[8] Perhaps White exaggerated Anson's influence—certainly Al Spalding wielded much more power in league matters than did the captain of the White Stockings—but the bellicose Anson became the public face of the segregation movement within the national game.

Anson mentioned neither the Toledo incident nor his involvement in the expulsion of African-Americans from the game in his later autobiography, so no first-person account explains why Anson believed as he did and expressed himself so forcefully on the issue. Perhaps the answer lies in Anson's view of the world, a limited one in which his values, such as they were, stood out in sharp relief and left little or no room for moderation. Anson apparently believed that the white and black races were best kept separate, and expressed himself in his typical blunt and unequivocal fashion. He used words and phrases that qualify as highly offensive in the present day, because that was the manner in which he expressed himself on almost any topic.

Anson was unquestionably a racist, but his views matched the prevailing mood of the country as a whole in the 1880s. Americans who were born before the Civil War grew up in an era in which slavery was legal, and were raised with the idea that people of African descent were inferior to whites and had no claim on equality in society. The Chicago captain, who taunted the local Indians as a child in Marshalltown, apparently subscribed to this now-discredited notion. Anson conveyed his beliefs on the issue in a manner consistent with his personality, with what baseball historian Robert Smith described as "a grim clinging to prejudice" and "a tendency to express his mind loudly and directly."[9]

Anson worried little about racial matters in early 1884. He was more concerned with the behavior of his team, which was poor in 1883 and would prove troublesome again in the coming season. "There will be no foolishness this year," proclaimed the captain. "No staying out all night and [the] next day telling me they were looking for a lost locket."[10] Anson was now a stockholder in the Chicago ballclub and more closely aligned with management than ever, and was determined to bring his rowdy players under control. He had the full backing of Spalding, who was "thoroughly disgusted by the miserable exhibition made by the club"[11] during the early part of the season. Spalding advised Anson to hire detectives, if necessary, to keep his players from breaking curfew on the road.

The high-scoring White Stockings received an offensive boost for the 1884 campaign. Spalding gained league approval for balls hit over the 180-foot fence in left field at Lakefront Park to count as home runs rather than doubles. The right-field fence was also close to the action, 196 feet away, but it was 37 feet tall, while the left-field barrier was only six feet high and easier to clear, particularly on windy days. The White Stockings had led the league by a wide margin in doubles in 1883, led by Ed Williamson's record-setting total of 49, and looked forward to a large upsurge in runs scored from the expected increase in home runs.

After a second-place finish in 1883, the White Stockings stumbled out of the gate in 1884. They played their first 20 games on the road, and Fred Goldsmith pitched so poorly in the season's first month that Anson dropped him from the rotation and signed George Crosby, a Chicago-born minor leaguer, to fill in. Crosby won only one of his three starts, and by the time the White Stockings returned to Chicago for their home opener on May 29, they were buried in seventh place with a 6–14 record.

The home run barrage began on the White Stockings' first home stand. They battered Detroit with five home runs in the home opener, and on the next day Ed Williamson became the first National Leaguer to hit three round-trippers in a game in a 12–2 rout of the Wolverines. However, other teams belted more homers at Lakefront Park as well, and while most of the Chicago batters enjoyed banner seasons, the pitching failed in game after game. Worst of all, Larry Corcoran was bothered by arm and hand problems in mid-season, which forced Anson to patch together a pitching staff as best he could while struggling to stay in the race.

Providence grabbed the lead in the pennant chase, mostly because they had one reliable hurler who put together perhaps the greatest pitching performance in baseball history. Charley Radbourn shared the pitching load with Charlie Sweeney in the first half of the season, but when Sweeney jumped the team and signed with the rival Union Association in June, Radbourn became the Grays' main starting pitcher. He started nearly every game the rest of the way, at one point starting 28 of 29 Providence games and winning 25 of them, and posted an incredible 60–12 won-lost record. His strong right arm moved Providence into first place while Anson's White Stockings, with their shaky pitching, fell back to the middle of the pack.

Anson contended with his share of newspaper criticism as the White Stockings failed to mount a challenge. The *Washington Post* stated that "the Chicago team has been wretchedly handled by Anson, who has been quite at sea in running the team since he lost the aid and counsel of his friend, President Hulbert."[12] Chicago writers roasted Anson almost daily, though the offense was performing beyond expectations, leading the league once again in runs scored. Pitching woes, caused by the aging of Goldsmith and injuries to Corcoran, were responsible for the fifth-place state of the team, but the captain refused to give up. He kept bringing in pitchers for tryouts, hoping to uncover a replacement for Fred Goldsmith, whom one paper charged had "grown fat and lazy."

Goldsmith's indifferent fielding bothered Anson no end, and after five years with the team Goldsmith was still unable to catch a simple popup despite Anson's coaching. On one afternoon in 1883, with the score tied in the ninth inning and a Cleveland runner on third, Goldsmith dropped a pop fly from Fred Dunlap's bat and let in the winning run. As the White Stockings left the field, Goldsmith remarked to Anson, "I'm getting on, ain't I, Cap?"

"How's that?" replied the angry captain.

"Why, Cap! Didn't you see? I made it hit my glove."[13]

While the Providence Grays built an insurmountable lead in the pennant race, the White Stockings scoured the minor leagues for pitchers, as Goldsmith was rapidly losing his effectiveness and Corcoran, though he posted a 35–23 record in 1884, suffered through a series of nagging injuries. In a 20–9 loss to Buffalo on June 16, Corcoran was forced to take the mound with a painfully infected finger on his pitching hand. Fortunately, he was ambidextrous, and pitched for four innings by throwing both left- and right-handed, alternating his deliveries from one pitch to the next. Finally he could stand it no more, and Anson moved him to shortstop, where he belted two triples and a single later in the game. His finger healed in the next few weeks, and on June 27 he surprised league-leading Providence with a 6–0 no-hitter, the third and last of Corcoran's career. By August, Corcoran's arm had improved, and he volunteered to pitch every day, if necessary, until Anson could find a reliable second starter.

The White Stockings held tryouts for several young pitchers in the latter months of the 1884 campaign. One candidate was Mike Corcoran, Larry's brother, who had gained notice as a semipro star in the New York area. Anson started Mike Corcoran on July 15 against cellar-dwelling Detroit, but Corcoran allowed 14 runs, 16 hits, and seven walks as the Wolverines defeated the White Stockings by a 14–0 score. Mike Corcoran, needless to say, never pitched again in the major leagues.

Anson showed his competitive nature in a game against Boston on June 21. Boston outfielder Jack Manning sprained his ankle in the third inning, but kept playing until he decided that he could not continue. The Boston club wanted to replace Manning with pitcher Charlie Buffinton, but substitutions were only legal at the time with the consent of the opposing team, and Anson refused to grant permission. The White Stockings had lost six of their previous seven games, and the embattled Chicago captain was in no mood to allow the Beaneaters to replace an injured player with a healthy one. Boston finished the game with only eight players on the field as the White Stockings won the game by a score of 11 to 7, though Anson drew a round of criticism in the national press for his poor sportsmanship.

The Cleveland club turned the tables on the captain later in the season, causing Anson to make his second and last pitching appearance in the major leagues. On August 5, Anson gave the starting pitching assignment to Thomas Lynch, a deaf-mute semipro star in the Chicago area, and the captain supported the rookie with two homers as the White Stockings carried a 5–3 lead into the eighth inning. Lynch then complained of arm soreness, and when Anson tried to bring in a relief pitcher, Cleveland manager Charlie Hackett refused to give permission. Anson put Lynch on first base and pitched the rest of the game himself, surrendering five runs and losing the game by an 8–5 count.

The next afternoon, the short fence at Lakefront Park enabled Anson to set a record that he shares to this day. He belted three homers in a 13–4 win, giving him five home runs in two games, a feat that has been tied several times but never surpassed.

Anson's three-homer game was the second in National League history and the first in which the three homers were hit in succession, though the park dimensions certainly played a role in his record-setting performance. Anson, who hit only three homers in 1883, walloped 21 homers in 1884, while the White Stockings hit 142 homers as a team and set a record that stood until 1927. The unusual ground rules at Lakefront Park wrought havoc on the record book, and the main beneficiary of the homer barrage was Ed Williamson. The shortstop whacked 27 four-baggers, all but two of which came at Lakefront Park, and his total set a major league record that stood until Babe Ruth of the Boston Red Sox hit 29 in 1919.

The mood on the ballclub turned sour as the summer wore on. Anson did his best to motivate his men, despite the fact that the team had fallen out of the pennant chase, and the captain levied a steady stream of fines for indifferent play and curfew violations. The players rebelled, especially after Anson hit Silver Flint with $170 in fines in a single day, and in July *Sporting Life* was able to report, "It is no secret that Anson is very unpopular with the Chicago team ... who regard him as a bully and a tyrant."[14]

In July, Ed Williamson and Anson got into a fistfight while playing poker; reports say that Anson produced a hand with four queens, but Williamson claimed the $95 pot with four aces, which led to accusations, threats, and a confrontation in which, according to *Sporting Life* magazine, the enraged Williamson grabbed a water pitcher and tried to break it over Anson's head. Anson and Williamson admired each other's ability, but cared little for each other personally. "Cap's okay as a player," snarled Williamson to a reporter, "but don't count for cornstalks as a man."[15] The strong-armed third baseman gained revenge on Anson by fielding grounders and firing the ball to first base as hard as he could throw it. Anson, who disdained the use of a fielding glove, was forced to stop the hot throws with his bare hands.

Anson had his hands full all season long with the behavior of his players. On the road, he always waited up for his men, planting himself in the hotel lobby with his eyes fixed firmly on the door. He remained there until the last man retired, even if that man did not appear until long after curfew. One night, a group of White Stockings stumbled into the hotel in Cleveland at two in the morning and found Anson asleep at his post. The players tiptoed past him to the stairs, but Fred Goldsmith could not resist a jab at the captain. The pitcher wrote a note that said, "Go to bed, you old fool. They're all in," and left it on Anson's chest.[16]

In Boston, Anson decided to conduct a bed check late one night. The players were housed two to a room, but one room had only one man in it, because the other had stolen out of the hotel after curfew and had not yet returned. Anson pounded on the offending player's door, but his roommate refused to answer. Finally, Anson decided to stand on a chair to peer over the transom into the room. He climbed up, lit a match, and looked through. From somewhere in the darkness, "a clever throw of a pillow extinguished

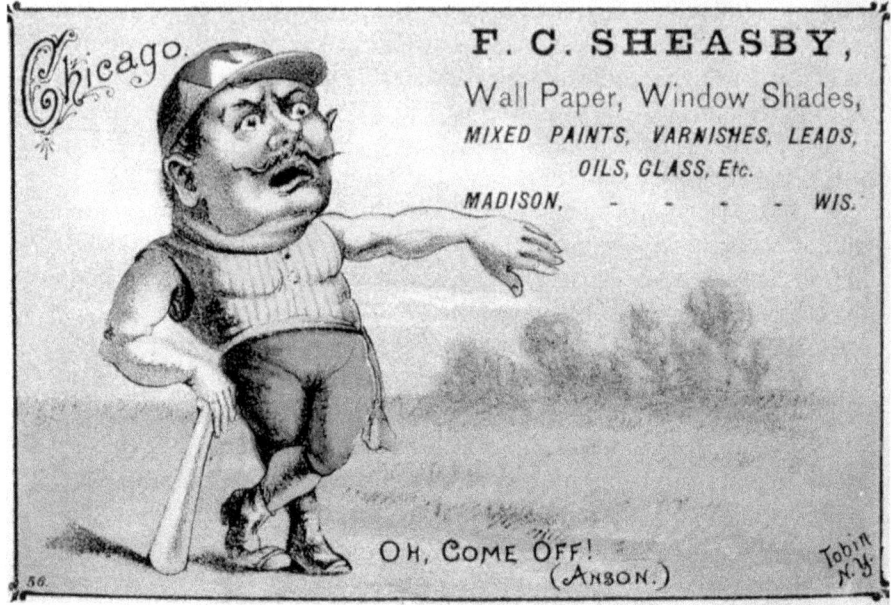

An advertising cartoon featuring Anson, 1887. (Transcendental Graphics)

the match," reported *Sporting Life*, "and before 'Baby' knew what was up his head was outside and the transom closed. It cost the player $100 to throw that pillow."[17]

Fred Goldsmith began to get on Anson's bad side, both for his sore arm and for his increasingly insolent behavior. With home runs flying out of Lakefront Park at a record pace, Goldsmith liked to irritate Anson by whistling a song called "Over the Garden Wall" when an opposing batter belted one. Goldsmith took little interest in his work, and hardly bothered to field his position as the season wore on. Anson sent Goldsmith to the mound in an exhibition game at Toledo in late July, but the badly crippled Toledo ballclub nearly pulled an upset, staging two comebacks before they finally succumbed by a 10–8 score. Anson's home run in the fourth inning provided the winning margin in an unexpectedly close contest.

The 1884 trip to Toledo was much less contentious than that of the year before. Anson did not enjoy his stay in Toledo, but the game was a profitable one, so the White Stockings scheduled another exhibition with the Blue Stockings for the 1884 campaign. However, the Chicago ballclub made certain to avoid a replay of the earlier unpleasant controversy. In April Chicago team secretary Jonathan Brown, no doubt at Spalding's direction, sent a letter to Toledo manager Charles Morton which stated, "no colored man shall play in your nine and if your officers insist on playing him after we are there you forfeit the Guarantee and we refuse to play. Now I think this is fair as we refuse point blank to play colored men."[18] The secretary put the blame on Anson and his players, stating that "the management of the Chicago Ball Club have no personal feeling about the matter ... but the players do most decisively object."[19] On July 25, 1884, Anson and the White Stockings returned to Toledo for another exhibition, but controversy was avoided as Moses Walker remained on the bench.

The American Association, then considered a major league, expanded to 12 teams following the 1883 season, and the Toledo Blue Stockings quit the Northwest League and joined the Association for the 1884 campaign. When Moses Walker caught for Toledo against the Louisville nine on May 1, 1884, he became the first recognized African-American to play in a major league game. The second black major leaguer made his debut for Toledo in July of that year when the injury-riddled ballclub hired Welday Walker, Moses' younger brother, to fill in as an outfielder for three weeks. Welday Walker played in five games and batted .222.

The Walker brothers were the first of their race to play major league ball, but they were also the last to do so in Cap Anson's lifetime. In late September Toledo released Moses Walker, and no other African-American reached the highest level of organized ball until Jackie Robinson joined the Brooklyn Dodgers in 1947. Three years after the second Toledo exhibition game, *Sporting Life* referred to the contest as "the first time in baseball history that the color line had been drawn."[20] Cap Anson, more than anyone else, was the man who wielded the infamous pen.

CHAPTER 10

Back on Top

> *The Philadelphia audience always likes to "guy" Anson, captain of the Chicago nine, because he is such a growler; consequently, when Anson was thrown out at second base yesterday a shout such as has hardly been heard in this city since the war went up.*
> —Philadelphia Star, 1885[1]

The 1884 season was the most difficult yet for Cap Anson as manager of the White Stockings. The club fell far out of the pennant race by late June and struggled to stay above the .500 mark. With no championship to fight for, the players continued to cause headaches for their manager, and the local newspapers filled their pages with vitriolic criticism of Anson and the club management. The *Chicago Tribune* condemned the White Stockings as "cripples, bums, and bigheads" late in the season, and in August the paper charged that the Chicago club was controlled by gamblers, though the *Tribune* offered no proof for this spectacular accusation.

Gambling and game fixing had not emerged as an issue in the National League for several years, not since William Hulbert expelled Jim Devlin and three other Louisville players following the 1877 season, but the problem had not totally disappeared from the baseball scene. Though team president Al Spalding denied that the problem existed ("This evil was got rid of by the League after a hard fight," stated the 1885 *Spalding Guide*) and considered drunkenness "the most conspicuous evil ... connected with professional ball playing," the specter of dishonesty still loomed in the national game.

Anson had faced such a threat late in the 1883 season, when a Boston gambler approached Mike Kelly and offered him a large sum of money to lose four games against the Beaneaters in late September. Kelly, taken aback by the offer, at first suggested that the gambler talk the matter over with Anson, but the man insisted that Kelly, as the catcher, could manage to lose the games on his own without the assistance of Anson or anyone else. Kelly related the story a few years later:

> Anson was in the office. I called him over and told him what the man had said ... I thought Anson would get mad, but he didn't. He said, "My friend, you cannot buy the Chicago club. There isn't enough money in Boston for that. Now, I am going to give you a straight tip. If we can win, we are going to. We're going to make the great fight of our lives. I heard on the very best authority, tonight, that the Bostons were going to do the same thing. One thing I will admit. This week settles whether it will be Chicago and Boston, or Boston and Chicago. Good night, sir. I'll play you a game of billiards, Kel."[2]

A few years earlier, Anson had punched a man on a streetcar who loudly claimed that players win or lose "as best suits their pockets," but by 1883 the captain had learned to handle problems with more finesse. As it turned out, the Chicagos lost all four games in Boston anyway, mostly due to the poor play of Kelly, and fell out of the pennant race. The late-season collapse of 1883 still rankled fans and sportswriters, and, for the first time in his tenure as manager, Anson found himself under pressure from the press and the public. The pennant was lost, but the captain was determined to use the remaining games of the 1884 campaign to prepare his team for another run at the title in the following year.

Fred Goldsmith reached the end of the line in mid-season, and made his final start for the White Stockings on July 23 in a 13–6 loss at Cleveland. He stuck around for a few more weeks, filling in as a spare outfielder, but in mid–August he was released as Anson continued to give tryouts to minor-league pitching prospects. One such young pitcher, Joe Brown, had played for Fort Wayne of the Northwest League and became available when the league collapsed in August of that year. He signed with Chicago in late summer and went 4–2 in six starts, spelling the overworked Larry Corcoran, who had pitched in eight consecutive games before Brown's arrival.

Another Northwest League refugee who joined the club in August ultimately became the greatest pitcher in the history of the White Stockings. John Clarkson was a thin, intense 23-year-old righthander from Cambridge, Massachusetts, where he grew up with four other ballplaying brothers in the hometown of Harvard University. Clarkson's father was a prosperous jewelry manufacturer, and as John learned the jewelry maker's trade, he played for elite amateur teams around Boston until 1882, when he joined the Worcester team of the National League. Clarkson pitched in three games for Worcester, winning only one, before he suffered a sore arm and drew his release. He then joined Saginaw of the Northwest League, and in 1884 he posted a remarkable 34–9 record before the league collapsed and made Clarkson a free agent. The pitcher's father wanted him to sign with the Boston Beaneaters, who played only a few miles from Cambridge, but Clarkson joined the White Stockings instead and pitched his first game on August 27 for his new club. He won 10 of his 13 starts, and batted .262 as an outfielder as well.

Clarkson was a drinking man who became fast friends with catcher King Kelly, but he was also a moody individual who kept to himself much of the time. He threw a good sidearm fastball, but his best pitch was a sweeping curve, which he attained by using his long, thin fingers to impart a great deal of spin on the baseball. Billy Sunday once claimed that Clarkson could toss a billiard ball on a table and make it trace an entire circle. He impressed all who saw him in the last two months of the 1884 campaign, and Anson faced a choice between the two rookies, Clarkson and Brown, for the second-string starter's job in the 1885 season.

Though the team had fallen well out of the pennant chase, Anson remained as competitive as ever. On August 13, before a crowd of 2,000 fans in Chicago, the White Stockings faced Buffalo when George Gore singled to lead off the game. Ordered by Anson to avoid the double play, Gore took off on a grounder by Kelly and tackled Buffalo second baseman Hardy Richardson before he could start the twin killing. The umpire declared both Gore and Kelly out, though the rules at the time stated that only Gore should have been retired on the play, and Anson argued so loudly that, as Richardson later said, "Cap let out a war whoop that could have been heard above the roar of Niagara." Anson refused to back down, and when the White Stockings declined to resume play, the umpire forfeited the game to Buffalo.

The crowd was understandably angry at the abrupt ending of the game, and following an hour of negotiations, the two teams agreed to play off a previous tied contest. One of the White Stockings reached first in the second game, and Anson ordered him to break up the double play as well. When the next batter grounded to second, the runner tried to block the relay, but the throw to first from shortstop Davy Force grazed his ear, and the shaken player returned to the bench and snarled, "Cap, you can stop the doubles yourself."[3]

Anson decided to give his players a baserunning lesson. He reached first base later in the game, and when the next batter grounded to Richardson, Anson ran to second, waved his arms, and tried his best to deflect the throw. He succeeded, but only because Richardson drilled him in the head with the ball, which bounded all the way into the grandstand. The stunned

Anson stumbled to the bench, and when he regained his senses he proclaimed to his players, "I stopped that one, anyway."[4]

John Clarkson pitched his first game on August 27 against league-leading Providence, and the *Chicago Tribune* reported that Mike Kelly was "in no condition to catch" after committing five errors (with three passed balls) in the game. The paper was not referring to drinking; rather, the team was so crippled with injuries that Anson was challenged to put nine reasonably healthy men on the field. Kelly traded positions with third baseman Ed Williamson later in the game, which Clarkson ultimately lost to Charley Radbourn by a 5–3 score. However, the Providence papers reported that several White Stockings appeared to be drunk on the field during a contest in Rhode Island in early September. Anson levied a new series of fines, which caused grumbling among the players, but Clarkson's fine pitching soon started the team on an unexpected winning streak.

Anson's refusal to surrender paid off. The White Stockings posted a 21–4 mark in their last 25 games of the season, ending the campaign with a nine-game winning streak and tying for fourth place. The strong finish convinced Anson and Spalding that the ballclub required only a few minor changes, and not a major overhaul, to compete for the pennant in 1885. The only new man would be curveball specialist John Clarkson, replacing Fred Goldsmith as the number two starting pitcher behind Larry Corcoran. All other positions on the team would remain the same, and Anson looked forward to the 1885 season as a chance to prove that the team that he and Spalding had assembled was still good enough to win a championship.

There would be no replay of the 1884 offensive explosion, as the city of Chicago took back the land on which Lakefront Park stood, and Spalding needed to construct a new park quickly. The club president chose a site on the West Side, at Congress and Loomis streets, and built a park with more standard outfield dimensions. The outfield fences would no longer allow players to hit cheap homers, and Anson believed that the White Stockings could return to a more predictable way of playing the game. Spalding confidently built the new structure with more than 10,000 seats, so sure was he that the White Stockings could fill them with another championship team in 1885.

Cap Anson, too, was interested in a change of environment. He had spent nine years dividing his time between two cities, residing in Chicago during the summer and in Philadelphia in the winter months, but in late 1884 the Anson family decided to move to Chicago on a full-time basis. Anson intended to buy a house with some cash that he had given his father to invest for him back in Marshalltown, so Anson asked the "old gentleman" for the money. Henry Anson told his son to calculate the interest on the investment and give him a bill for the full amount, but the embarrassed ballplayer did not want to tell his father that he did not know how to calculate interest. Even if he had learned how to use fractions and percentages somewhere along the way, at Notre Dame or at Iowa State College, that knowledge was long forgotten.

While Anson fretted over his lack of education, Virginia's brother, Remy Fiegal, made plans to attend business school, with the captain paying his tuition. When Anson took his brother-in-law to Pierce Business College in Philadelphia to register for classes, he was seized with the desire to broaden his horizons. The captain signed up for classes as well, and spent the winter months learning the rudiments of business. Before long, Anson was able to submit a bill to his father, and used the money to buy a house at 160 30th Street on Chicago's South Side. The Anson family (which now included another daughter, Adele, born in April 1884) moved permanently to Chicago in early 1885, and made its home on 30th Street for the next three decades.

The captain was still a billiards fanatic, and was persuaded to make a public exhibition of his skill in March of 1885. Anson played a local expert named Frank Parker at the Central Music Hall in Chicago for $250 per side in a 14-inch balkline game. The captain fell behind early, but caught up as the match progressed, defeating Parker by a score of 500 to 366. One pool expert told the *Chicago Tribune*, "His masse and follow shots show real skill ... I would be willing to back [Anson] against any amateur in the country today."[5]

Many observers agreed that Anson possessed the talent to forge a second career as a billiards expert, but he put his cue stick away after the Parker match. *Sporting Life* magazine had criticized him the season before for "paying more attention to billiards than to baseball, to the disadvantage of the latter,"[6] but baseball was the captain's first priority, and he played no more public matches once the baseball season began. He was determined to regain the pennant and would not allow any distractions.

Anson made it clear to the players that he expected to challenge for the pennant in 1885, and Spalding arranged an April exhibition tour through the Southern states to prepare for the upcoming season. The tour began on April 9 in Cincinnati, three weeks before the start of the National League campaign, and continued on to Nashville, Chattanooga, and Atlanta before the club made its way westward to St. Louis for the season opener on April 30. The White Stockings did not lose a game on the trip, beating most of their opponents by lopsided scores and announcing their presence to the rest of the National League.

The White Stockings lost their first game of the new season at St. Louis by a 3–2 score behind Larry Corcoran, but John Clarkson defeated the Brown Stockings the following day, picking up where he left off at the end of the previous campaign. Spalding's new West Side Park would not be completed until June, and the White Stockings were obliged to spend the first five weeks of the season on the road. Despite this disadvantage, Anson drove the team into first place. By the end of the long road trip in early June, the White Stockings found themselves in a two-team battle with the New York ballclub for the league lead.

New York had tied the Chicagos for fourth place in 1884, but the team received an infusion of talent before the 1885 season commenced. John B. Day owned both the National League Gothams and the Mets of the American Association, and decided that his baseball holdings would prove more profitable if he concentrated his best players on the Gothams. This he did, moving star righthander Tim Keefe and several other Mets to the Gothams for the 1885 season and turning the Gothams into contenders. Early in the 1885 season, manager Jim Mutrie referred to the number of six-footers on his team when he called his men "My big fellows! My Giants!" The papers liked the sound of that, and the franchise (which now plays in San Francisco) has been known as the Giants to the present day.

The new Chicago ballpark sat at the corner of Congress and Loomis streets, and contained seating for about 10,000 people, with 12 private boxes, a cycling track, and courts for lawn tennis. The woodwork was painted a light terra-cotta color, and the entire structure was surrounded by a brick wall 12 feet high. Its fences were 216 feet away down the foul lines, an improvement over the 196-foot distances of the previous facility, and the oval shape of the field made center field much deeper. Spalding instructed the contractors to landscape the field with a gentle slope from the middle to the foul lines for improved drainage on wet days. "Chicago can now be congratulated on having a permanent ball-ground probably superior in many of its appointments to any other in this country," stated one Chicago paper, "and President A. G. Spalding of the Chicago Club is deserving of commendation for the enterprise he has displayed in its completion."[7]

Lakefront Park had been situated in the downtown area, but the new West Side Park was a 15-minute carriage ride from the center of town. Spalding and Anson arranged for the players to dress for each game in a clubhouse downtown, after which the uniformed ballplayers were transported in open carriages to the playing grounds. Crowds followed in their carriages, turning each game day into a parade and whipping up enthusiasm and fan interest for the White Stockings.

West Side Park opened on June 6, and more than 10,000 people paid to see the White Stockings defeat St. Louis that afternoon behind John

Clarkson. Clarkson was now the primary Chicago pitcher, as Larry Corcoran's arm was starting to wear out after six seasons of service. Corcoran pitched seven games for Anson in 1885, winning five, but his sore arm dealt what might have been a fatal blow to the Chicago pennant chances. Corcoran tried his best to pitch through the pain, but in late May he could throw no more. Clarkson pitched seven games in a row at one point, and Anson was so desperate for pitching that he put second baseman Fred Pfeffer in the box in the last game of the long road trip that started the season. Pfeffer beat Detroit that day, but Anson promoted Clarkson to the number one spot in the rotation and searched the league for a new starting pitcher. In early June, Spalding handed Corcoran his outright release.

The White Stockings desperately needed a second reliable pitcher, as the pennant race was one of the closest ever contested in the National League. The Giants kept pace with Chicago through May and June. The White Stockings won 18 games in a row from June 1 to June 24 but could not pull away from the Giants, who reeled off a streak of their own, leaving the New Yorkers only two games behind. On July 1 Chicago capped a four-game sweep of Boston with a 24–10 win that featured a 500-foot home run by Tommy Burns, but Anson's men then traveled to the Polo Grounds in New York and lost three of four to the Giants. On July 5, the White Stockings and Giants were tied for first place.

Two righthanded pitchers, Wash Williams and Ted Kennedy, tried to fill the second rotation slot for the White Stockings, but Spalding may have saved the season when he signed Jim McCormick to complement Clarkson. McCormick was a stocky, Scottish-born righthander who had already won 179 National League games before coming to Chicago. He pitched 74 complete games for Cleveland in 1880, winning 45 of them, and managed the club briefly before giving up the reins to concentrate on his pitching. McCormick won only one of his four decisions for Providence in 1885, but he was a battle-tested veteran who could be counted on to pitch a solid game every other day for his new team.

On August 1, 13,427 fans jammed the Polo Grounds in New York to see the league leaders do battle. The crowd was the largest in major league history up to that time, and witnessed a close game that was marked by one of Anson's famous "kicking" displays. The Giants led by a 6–5 score in the eighth inning when rain delayed the proceedings for more than 15 minutes. The Giants wanted the umpire to end the game, but Anson bellowed that the rain "was not even enough to stop a lawn tennis match" and demanded that the contest continue. The crowd chanted "Kick, Baby, kick!" but Anson got his way when the deluge stopped and the game resumed. The Giants won anyway, breaking a seven-game Chicago winning streak and leaving the Chicagos only two games ahead in the pennant chase.

Cap Anson put together another fine season at the bat, hitting .310 and leading the league in doubles and runs batted in, but John Clarkson was the man who made the difference for the White Stockings. On July 27 he pitched a no-hitter against third-place Providence, and two days later gave up only four hits to the Grays in a 14-inning marathon. The White Stockings finally won the game for their star pitcher in the last inning when Gore singled, went to third on a single by Kelly, and scored the winning run on a sacrifice fly by Anson.

Clarkson was the kind of player that Anson had only rarely encountered. He was quiet and intelligent, but so moody and sensitive to criticism that people called him "Black Jack" Clarkson. Anson usually employed his rough, blunt manner to get the maximum effort from his players, but the captain discovered that if he or anyone else offered any criticism, Clarkson would refuse to pitch for a while. "Many regard him as the greatest [of all Chicago pitchers]," said Cap Anson many years later, "but not many know of his peculiar temperament and the amount of encouragement needed to keep him going. Scold him, find fault with him and he could not pitch at all. Praise him and he was unbeatable."[8]

Clarkson was no roughneck, but he was as competitive as anyone. According to one story, Clarkson once threw a lemon instead of a baseball to the plate to protest the umpire's refusal to call the game on account of approaching darkness. He wore a large silver belt buckle on his uniform pants on sunny afternoons in an attempt to reflect sunlight into the batters' eyes as he pitched. Since he threw the majority of innings for the Chicago club, Clarkson sometimes coasted when holding a lead. "He was peculiar in some things," recalled Anson, "...and in order to get his best work you had to keep spurring him along, otherwise he was apt to let up, this being especially the case when the club was ahead and he saw what he thought was a chance to save himself."[9] Anson learned to adapt his methods to Clarkson's personality, and the young pitcher rewarded the White Stockings with 53 wins, the second-highest total in baseball history.

The low point of the season came on August 10, when the White Stockings closed out a three-game series against the Giants at the Polo Grounds. Anson had boasted to the papers that his men would sweep the upstart Giants, but the Chicagos lost two out of three and closed the series with a 12–0 defeat on a five-hit shutout by New York's Mickey Welch. Anson was disconsolate after the game. "It's bad enough to be beaten three times out of four [counting the previous game on August 1]," remarked the captain, "but to be shut out twice, that's shameful. Just think of it ...

A bottle of "Captain A. C. Anson's Ginger Beer." This was one of Anson's less profitable investments. (Author's collection)

the Chicagos 'Chicagoed!' Didn't score a run in two games."[10] His mood improved when his team embarked on an 11-game winning streak that left them three games ahead in the win column. On September 4, when the White Stockings defeated Buffalo 12–4 behind two homers by Anson, the Chicagos retained a three-game lead over the Giants.

The pennant was decided at the end of September when the Giants traveled to Chicago for four games. More than 10,000 people crowded West Side Park on September 29, spilling over into the outfield, and the umpire decreed that balls hit into the crowd would count for three bases. The Chicagos hit seven triples and defeated the Giants 7–4 behind McCormick for a three-game advantage in the pennant race. Clarkson defeated Tim Keefe the next day by a 2–1 score, and when McCormick pitched Chicago to a third consecutive win on October 1, the White Stockings held a five-game advantage. The Giants were not yet mathematically eliminated, but for all intents and purposes, the pennant race was over.

The Giants played their last game of the season against the White Stockings on October 3 in front of 8,000 people on a cold, wet day at the West Side Grounds. Before the game started, the Giants made a presentation to their opponents. Both teams entered the park preceded by a brass band, and the crowd buzzed in anticipation as the two teams lined up along the first- and third-base lines. John Ward, captain of the Giants, then stepped forward and presented Anson with a gift. It was a satin flag, white and maroon in color, with the inscription, "New York to Chicago, 1885."

"Captain Anson," said Ward, "we came to Chicago hoping and expecting to win this last series of games, but you have beaten us fairly and by good ball playing, and therefore we have no complaints to make. On the contrary, as a souvenir of the season's struggle, and as a token of our friendly feeling, the New York Club presents to the Chicago Ball Club this flag."

Anson was visibly moved by the gesture. "Captain Ward," he said, "when, after an earnest effort, one competitor succeeds, and the other, in a spirit of fairness, kindly presents to the successful party so elegant a souvenir of victory as you have done, in so graceful a manner, it is a pleasant duty to acknowledge, as we do most sincerely, that we found in your club gentlemen and ball players worthy to represent the great city of New York in the national game. Our victory is tempered by regret that we should have won against so generous a foe, while it is especially gratifying that we have won from the 'Giants.' We hope to meet another year, when both of us will do our best to please the public, and give assurance by our conduct, as we have in past years, that each club will do its best to win the championship."[11]

Anson waved his hat in the air and called for three cheers for the Giants. The players on both teams then shook hands and began the game, which the Giants won by a 10–8 score in a game halted after seven innings by darkness and wet grounds. Though the White Stockings closed the season with three losses against the Phillies, Chicago won the pennant by a two-game margin. After three difficult years, Anson had finally regained the championship of the National League.

The season was a profitable one for the White Stockings, with the *Chicago News* reporting that the club took in about $300,000 in gross receipts and spent about $90,000 in player salaries and capital investment. It was also easier on Anson's nerves, for the White Stockings were a better-behaved bunch in 1885. Spalding decided to give each player a bonus of $100, "for having abstained from intoxicating drinks and orgies and for winning the pennant."[12]

However, the season was not yet over. There were now two major leagues, the National League and the American Association, and in October of 1885 the White Stockings and the Association champion St. Louis Browns met in the second "World's Series." The first was held the year before, when Providence of the National League defeated the New York Metropolitans three games to none for the undisputed professional championship, but this series would go seven games. It was scheduled to begin in Chicago on October 14, then move to St. Louis for three games, and go on the road to Pittsburgh and Cincinnati to enable more fans to view the deciding matches.

Anson's men, by all accounts, appeared to be satisfied with the National League pennant, and Anson discovered, to his dismay, that his players cared little about the upcoming series against the Browns. The White Stockings, especially pitchers John Clarkson and Jim McCormick, were tired from the grueling pennant race, and many of Anson's men did not wait to celebrate the pennant. In the first game, which ended in a 5–5 tie, George Gore played sloppily in center field and went hitless, though he scored a run on a walk, and reports surfaced that Gore was intoxicated that day. Anson was so distraught with Gore's performance that he suspended the center fielder for the remainder of the series and put the light-hitting Billy Sunday in his place.

The series nearly ended in the second game, played on October 15 in St. Louis. The White Stockings held a 5–4 lead in the sixth inning when Dalrymple drilled a hit down the line that St. Louis captain Charlie Comiskey thought was a foul ball. Comiskey raised a ruckus, but umpire Dave Sullivan refused to change his ruling. Comiskey then pulled his team off the field, sparking a near-riot among the notoriously rowdy St. Louis fans. Sullivan waited until he was safely ensconced in his hotel room that evening before officially declaring the game as forfeited to Chicago. Comiskey threatened to discontinue the series, but cooler heads prevailed, and the Browns agreed to play the remaining games with a new umpire.

The Browns won the next two games in St. Louis, and the teams traveled to Pittsburgh for the fifth game on October 22. John Clarkson, weary arm and all, pitched the White Stockings to a 9–2 win, and Jim McCormick threw a brilliant two-hitter the next day in Cincinnati for another 9–2 victory. The Browns refused to accept the forfeiture of the second game, however, and considered the series tied at two wins apiece while the White Stockings claimed a 3–2 lead in games. The series might have dragged on for several more games, but both teams were anxious to end the match and start their post-season barnstorming tours, and finally came to an agreement. Most reports state that the teams agreed to throw out the second-game forfeit and that the seventh game, to be played on October 24 at Cincinnati, would decide the championship.

Anson chose Clarkson to start the deciding game, but Clarkson showed up at the ballpark five minutes late, so Anson sent a tired Jim McCormick to the mound instead. The White Stockings scored two runs in the first inning on a double by Kelly, but the Browns responded with four runs in the fourth as the Chicago defense fell apart. The White Stockings committed 17 errors, four by Anson, and the sloppy fielding put the Browns in the lead to stay. The game was called by darkness after the top of the eighth inning, and the Browns walked away with a 13–4 win and, in their minds, the championship of the world.

Following the game, Al Spalding and the embarrassed Chicago team officials declared the series a tie and denied that any agreement had been made to decide the championship by the outcome of the seventh game. "Does anyone suppose," demanded Spalding, "that that if there had been

10. BACK ON TOP 131

The 1885 champion White Stockings. Far left: Corcoran. Top: Gore, Flint, Anson, Kennedy, Kelly, Pfeffer. Bottom: Williamson, Dalrymple, Burns, Clarkson, Sunday. (National Baseball Hall of Fame Library, Cooperstown, New York)

so much as that at stake that I should have consented to the games being played in American Association cities, upon their grounds, and under the authority of their umpires?" This stance contradicted Anson, who had told the press before the deciding contest, "We will not even claim the forfeited game. We each have two victories now and the winner of today's game will be the winner of the series." The captain, who also informed a reporter that the Browns would have had a hard time finishing fifth in the National League, probably wished he had kept his opinions to himself until the series was over.[13]

The 1886 *Reach Guide* disputed Spalding's claim. "When the two teams met for the sixth [leaving out the forfeit] game on the Cincinnati grounds on October 24," stated the *Guide* the following spring, "it was announced by Umpire John Kelly, in the hearing of over one thousand spectators just preceding the beginning of the game, that it had been agreed between the St. Louis and Chicago clubs that that the game of that day would end their series, and as each club had won two games, the result of that contest would decide the series and the question of championship. Captains Anson and Comiskey stood close by while this announcement was being proclaimed, and neither, by word or gesture, affirmed or denied it."

The controversy over the 1885 championship raged for months, with vitriolic barbs lobbed back and forth in the pages of the Chicago and St.

Louis newspapers, but in time the White Stockings and Browns arrived at an uneasy compromise. The participants decided to treat the series as a tie, and the $1,000 pot was split evenly between the two ballclubs. Most of the players on both sides (except for Anson and Comiskey, the first basemen and captains) had agreed before the series to split their winnings anyway, so none of the players except Anson would have walked away without any money.

Anson regarded the outcome of the series as a personal defeat. He, like most National Leaguers, still viewed the American Association as inferior, and he was unhappy with the performance and behavior of his White Stockings. Some reports stated that John Clarkson did not pitch the final game because he was drunk when he arrived at the park five minutes late, and George Gore did the team no favors when his behavior drew a suspension from the captain. The White Stockings did not take the series seriously, but Anson keenly felt the embarrassment of defeat, and was determined to rectify the situation. After a barnstorming trip to the southern states (in which Clarkson declined to participate) Anson and Spalding began making plans to recapture the pennant in 1886 and defeat the Browns in a rematch of the postseason World's Series.

CHAPTER 11

King of Kickers

> *Those old [White Stockings] didn't know much about hitting the ball either; no, I guess they didn't. Only four of us had led the league in batting — Anson, Gore, Dalrymple, and myself. We always wore the best uniforms that money could get, Spalding saw to that.... When we marched on a field with our big six-footers out front it used to be a case of "eat 'em up, Jake." We had most of 'em whipped before we threw a ball. They were scared to death.*
>
> — Mike (King) Kelly, 1888[1]

Anson and his White Stockings gained a small measure of revenge against the Browns after the series. For months Anson had been promoting his "pet," Billy Sunday, as the fastest man in baseball, and the captain publicly challenged the Browns' Arlie Latham to a race against Sunday. Latham, the fastest man in the American Association, was virtually undefeated in footraces within his own circuit, and few Association players believed that anyone could beat him on a 100-yard course. In early November of 1885, Anson and the majority of the White Stockings club arrived in St. Louis for a series of exhibition games, and on November 8 a large crowd gathered at the St. Louis ballpark to watch the long-awaited duel between Latham and Sunday.

The winner's purse was set at $400, but Anson, Gore, and Flint, among others, made large side bets with the St. Louis ballplayers and fans, pushing the total amount at stake into the thousands of dollars. Finally, Sunday and Latham took their positions five yards behind the scratch line for a 100-yard race with a flying start. The starting gun sounded, and Sunday burst to a lead over Latham. They crossed the scratch line with Sunday slightly ahead, but after that the match was no contest. At the 60-yard mark Latham was clearly beaten, and Sunday coasted to a win by more than three yards. Anson was proud of his protégé, but the captain was more interested in avenging the loss to the Browns on the field in 1886. He and Spalding went to work in signing the veterans on the White Stockings to new contracts, hoping that the poor discipline displayed during the World's Series was a passing and not a permanent problem.

The spring of 1886 brought an innovation from the minds of Al Spalding and Cap Anson. Both men had noticed that most ballplayers did not "hit their stride" in the first few weeks of the season; many of them carried extra pounds and required a few weeks of playing before they rounded into shape. Teams played pre-season exhibition games then, but bad weather and travel problems often kept players on the sidelines, and the quality of these games varied from one year to the next. Anson and Spalding proposed to bring their White Stockings to the resort town of Hot Springs, Arkansas, in March, about five weeks before the start of the season, and whip the players into shape with a regimen of exercise and practice.

The idea was not entirely new. Harry Wright took his Philadelphia Phillies to Charleston, South Carolina, for spring practice at the same time, and some baseball historians state that the Boston club made a similar training trip two years earlier. The captain himself had suggested such an idea during the 1884 campaign, when *Sporting Life* magazine reported, "Anson talks of taking his men to Hot Sulphur Springs next year ... he hopes to relieve the men of all stiffness, soreness, and rheumatism, and start off with a physically strong team."[2] Anson and Spalding may not have invented "spring training," but they made the concept a viable one, and all other major league teams followed their lead in subsequent years.

The need for spring training camp became evident when several of the players showed up with plenty of excess weight on their frames, though Anson, as usual, was perfectly fit. "The Captain himself is in fine trim," stated a new periodical, *The Sporting News*, in its first-ever issue that March, "the exercise obtained in walking around a billiard table every day having kept his weight down to the proper figures."[3]

The White Stockings retained all their starters from the 1885 campaign, but Anson and Spalding added several new faces to the roster. The club had managed with an eight-man regular lineup, two main starting pitchers, and a reserve or two for several years, but when the National League expanded its schedule to 124 games for the 1886 season Anson recognized that he needed more men as insurance against injury. A two-man pitching rotation would no longer suffice in a longer season, and Anson's main focus in the winter months of 1885-86 lay in hiring a third reliable starter to complement Clarkson and McCormick.

The captain found his man in John (Jocko) Flynn, a righthander from Lawrence, Massachusetts. At five feet six inches and 145 pounds, Flynn was not an impressive physical specimen, but he could pitch, hit, and play the outfield. "On the street he looks like one of your lawn-tennis dudes," remarked one newspaper. "On the field he is, to quote everybody, a perfect terror."[4] He was a terror off the field as well, fitting in nicely with the hard-drinking crew, but Anson saw promise in the young pitcher. To ease Flynn's adjustment to the National League, Anson signed a third catcher, George (Prunes) Moolic, also from Lawrence, Massachusetts, who had caught the deliveries of Flynn in the minor leagues the year before. Since catchers suffered more injuries than any other player on the field, Lew Hardie, a New Yorker who had caught three games for the Phillies in 1884, signed on as the fourth catcher.

The other main acquisition impressed Anson when he batted .462 in three games for Chicago in October of the previous season. Jimmy Ryan was a blond, 23-year-old outfielder who had made a name for himself at the College of the Holy Cross in Worcester, Massachusetts. He was a good hitter, a fast runner, and could also play shortstop and pitch in an emergency. Ryan, who went on to enjoy an 18-year career, was one of the few position players in baseball history to bat from the right side and throw from the left.

Ryan's presence allowed Anson to introduce a new concept in baseball strategy. Anson had noticed that Abner Dalrymple, a lefthanded batter, did not hit lefthanded pitchers well, so Anson instituted what may have been the first platooning arrangement in major league history. There were only three regular lefty starting pitchers in the National League at the time, but whenever a lefthander took the mound against Chicago, Anson placed Dalrymple on the bench, put Ryan in left, and moved either King Kelly or Jocko Flynn to right field. With a righthanded starter on the mound, Dalrymple returned to left and Ryan to right. In addition, the righthanded Silver Flint usually batted in the ninth spot, but Anson moved him to the first or third positions against lefties.[5]

Anson's lineup maneuvers would not have been possible to execute in previous seasons, as National League teams carried as few men as possible to save on salaries. The White Stockings were able to add personnel to their roster mainly because the franchise was, by far, the most profitable in the league during the middle 1880s. Spalding was a thrifty club president, but with the league schedule expanding to 124 games (from 98 games the season before) and no appreciable increase in player salaries, the White Stockings could well afford the extra men. Besides, the National League expanded its reserve rule to allow each team to retain 12 men and to roll over from year to year, forever if the team so chose. Each ballclub was now able to wield nearly complete control over more players than in previous years.

The White Stockings faced a new challenger for the pennant in 1886. The Detroit Wolverines had struggled since entering the National League in 1881, but in late 1885 the Buffalo Bisons folded and sold their four biggest stars to Detroit. First baseman Dan Brouthers, third baseman Deacon White, catcher Jack Rowe, and second baseman Hardy Richardson comprised a new "Big Four"—the first had been Chicago's quartet of stars in 1876, which included White—and turned the Wolverines into instant contenders. Since Detroit's main starting pitcher was a lefthander, Charles (Lady) Baldwin, Anson hoped that his new platooning system would give the champions an advantage over their foes.

The White Stockings left Hot Springs and traveled to Kansas City to open the 1886 season against the National League's newest team, the Cowboys, on April 30. Clarkson won the opener by a 6–5 score in 13 innings, and Jocko Flynn followed with a 17–8 win the next afternoon. The first home game was played on May 6 against the Wolverines, and Anson used his platoon lineup for the first time against Detroit lefthander Lady Baldwin. The Chicagos came away with a 5–1 win behind Clarkson.

Anson's men tore through the National League in the first two months, but the Wolverines kept pace as the 1886 pennant chase became another two-team fight. By June 5 the White Stockings boasted a 22–5 record, but the Wolverines, at 23–5, held first place by half a game. Anson was frustrated, not only because the Wolverines stubbornly refused to fold, but also because his players were causing problems off the field. Despite the team's fine play, the 1886 season presented Anson with some of the worst off-the-field controversies that he had ever encountered.

The veteran players on the Chicago team had made manager Anson's life difficult for several years. In 1882, before the team left on a trip to Boston, Gore and Williamson kept Mike Kelly out late one night and got him so drunk that they approached Anson the next morning and asked if Kelly could be left behind in Chicago to recover. "Forget it," replied the captain. Williamson then suggested to Kelly that he might want to disguise himself to escape the notice of the hostile Boston fans. Kelly agreed and visited a barber, who shaved his head completely bald, and the players no doubt had a laugh at Anson's stunned reaction to Kelly's change in appearance. The crowds in Boston recognized him anyway, and the incident served as yet another distraction that Anson did not appreciate in the middle of a pennant race.

Some of the pranks centered around money. The rowdier White Stockings were always short of cash and constantly asking for advances on their salaries, which Anson was understandably reluctant to grant, but the players found another way to squeeze money out of their captain. The men were well aware of Anson's fondness for wagering, and used that knowledge to their advantage. Abner Dalrymple described an incident that took place in the early 1880s:

> We always worked Anson when we were hard up and wanted money. It was in 1883, when the Chicago team was in Cincinnati. We were on our way home and the boys didn't have any money. We came across Kittelman, who was the champion of the hundred-yard run in the United States at the time. Most of the team knew Kittelman, but Anson didn't. We made it up between us that we would get Ans into a bet. Some of the boys went to him and offered to bet that there was a man in Cincinnati who would beat Billy Sunday in a hundred-yard race.
> Ans thought Sunday could beat anybody living. "You're on," he said. The crowd went out to the ball ground and measured off 100 yards and put them on the line and started them with a pistol, and Kittelman beat Sunday about a yard. The laugh was on Ans when we told him that that was Kittelman, the champion of the United States, but we got the $50. Sunday didn't know, any more than Ans, that he was up against the champion.

A short time later, the players sized up Anson as "still gamey," so they worked a ploy to get more money out of their captain. They made another $50 bet that Fred Pfeffer could beat Sunday at 100 yards. Sunday had already defeated Pfeffer at that distance, but the captain did not know that the players had arranged for Anson's "pet" to fall down before he hit the finish line. Sunday and Pfeffer started the race, Sunday stumbled and fell as ordered, and the players split another $50 from Anson.[6]

No one was immune from the practical jokes played by the Chicago club, not even the president of the United States. Late in the 1886 season, a Chicago congressman made arrangements for Anson, Spalding, and the White Stockings to meet President Grover Cleveland at the White House. Anson, a lifelong Democrat, was thrilled to meet the chief executive, for he saw in Cleveland the same unflinching honesty and rectitude that he admired in William Hulbert and in his own father. The captain of the Chicagos had come a long way from his birth in an Iowa frontier town to an audience with the president.

President Cleveland was a baseball fan who had followed the game when he served as sheriff of Erie County, New York, and mayor of Buffalo prior to his election to the nation's highest office. The president, whom Mike Kelly later described as being "as affable and courteous as it was possible for a man to be," greeted Anson and his team cordially. "I'm happy to meet you, Captain Anson," said the president. "You have the champion ball club, I believe."

Kelly described what happened next:

> Anson gripped his hand. Then I was the second man to be introduced. The President's hand was fat and soft. I squeezed it so hard that the President winced. Then George Gore did the same. Burns gave the President another warm grip, and Dalrymple did likewise. When it came to McCormick, the President's good right hand was almost doubled up. McCormick shook his hand warmly; so warmly, in fact, that President Cleveland looked glad and happy when it was all over. He would rather shake hands with one thousand people than two ball nines, after that day.[7]

Disciplinary matters came to a head in July of 1886, when Spalding began to receive disturbing letters from prominent Chicagoans, local fans, and other sources. All of the missives, related Spalding, "told stories of drunkenness and debauchery, in which members of the White Stockings were implicated. These recounted scenes of revelry and carousing that were altogether reprehensible and disgusting." Local reporters soon got wind of the story and began criticizing the players in their newspapers. Spalding confronted Kelly about the "scenes of revelry and carousing," but the King of Ballplayers denied the charges. "What are you running here?" demanded Kelly. "A Sunday School or a base ball club?"

Anson levied fines, but drinking was out of control among the veteran White Stockings, and Spalding decided that he could no longer ignore the issue. "I knew that some of the men were drinking to excess," recalled the team president years later. "...I was aware that these were keeping late hours; it was a notorious fact that their habits were altogether improper." Spalding further determined that he, not Anson, would deal with the matter, so he hired a Pinkerton detective to trail the men and document their activities. Within two weeks a detailed report arrived, and Spalding then ordered Anson to call his men together for a meeting.

The report was nearly an inch thick, and Spalding delegated one of the players to read it aloud. The first few pages dealt with the activities of Anson, and one of the White Stockings whispered, "Here's where the old man gets off." Predictably, the detective found nothing incriminating in Anson's behavior, nor did he discover anything untoward in the doings of his next subject, Billy Sunday. However, the rest of the report dealt with other team members and recounted incidents of drunkenness, carousing, and other matters that Spalding later described as "too awful for patient consideration." Seven of the White Stockings were implicated, and they listened with rapt attention as their lives were laid bare for their teammates.

When the reading ended, Kelly broke the silence. "I have to offer only one amendment," stated Kelly. "In that place where the detective reports me as taking lemonade at 3 A.M., he's off. It was straight whiskey. I never drank a lemonade at that hour in my life."

Spalding was not amused. "What's to be the penalty?" demanded Spalding.

"That's up to you, sir," replied the players.

Spalding turned to the captain. "Anson, what's to be the punishment? Do you want to fine these men?"

"No," said Anson, "we don't want their money."

One of the players then asked how much Spalding had paid the detective. The amount was $175, and the unidentified player then suggested that the seven guilty men pay $25 each to repay the cost of the investigation. Spalding and Anson agreed, and the matter was settled, at least temporarily.[8]

Billy Sunday was never a disciplinary problem, though he liked to drink with his teammates, but an incident happened in 1886 that changed his life. He and several of the White Stockings were barhopping in Chicago one day. They sat down on a curb at the corner of State and Madison streets and watched as a company of musicians from a nearby rescue mission played gospel hymns, songs that Sunday recognized from his childhood in Iowa. One of the musicians noticed Sunday's apparent interest and invited him to come to the mission to hear men and women tell how they were saved from alcohol, prostitution, and other forms of vice.

The gesture struck a chord in Sunday. His eyes filled with tears as he turned and told his teammates, "I'm through. I am going to Jesus Christ. We have come to a parting of the ways." Some of his teammates laughed, while others paid little attention, but the young outfielder from Marshalltown meant what he said. The next morning at practice, Sunday was surprised to find all of his teammates ready to shake his hand and congratulate him on his stand. "Bill, I'm proud of you," said Kelly, the wildest carouser on the ballclub. "Religion is not my long suit, but I'll help you all I can."[9]

Billy Sunday was a changed man from that moment on. He never drank again, and he immersed himself in religious mission work in Chicago, where he met a fellow missionary who became his wife a few years later. As the months passed, Billy Sunday became more interested in religion than in baseball, much to the dismay and confusion of his mentor Cap Anson. Sunday's newfound zeal drove a wedge between the captain and his baseball protégé, and in September 1888, when Sunday was married in a Chicago church, Cap Anson did not attend the wedding.

An 11–3 victory against St. Louis on June 17 gave the White Stockings a 26–7 record but left the team two and a half games behind the Wolverines with a three-game set at Detroit in the offing. On June 19, more than 10,000 people jammed the small Detroit ballpark, spilling into the outfield to see their first-place club battle the defending champions. Jim McCormick won his 12th game without a loss as the White Stockings defeated Baldwin and the Wolverines by a 5–4 score. The teams did not play on Sunday, but the Detroits scored a 4–1 win over John Clarkson on Monday that restored their two and a half game bulge in the standings.

Anson staged at least one major blow-up with an umpire every season, and the explosion of 1886 occurred in the third and final game of the series against the Wolverines. "Honest John" Gaffney was one of the newest National League umpires, but had already experienced several run-ins with Anson and the White Stockings during the season. Early in the game, Gaffney ruled a Detroit runner safe at second base on a pickoff attempt, and the captain was still seething later in the contest. Gaffney knew that a controversy was coming; as he told the papers later, "I had not been umpiring long and had been repeatedly warned about Anson. I was told that the big captain would sit on me at the least provocation." The provocation came in the late innings when Gaffney called a Detroit runner safe in another close play at second. Gaffney described the situation two years later for a Philadelphia newspaper:

> "Not out!" cried I.
> "What?" exclaimed Anson, walking toward me, boiling with rage.
> "Anson, this will cost you $10."
> "Yes, and it will cost you your position, you ____."
> "Fifty dollars more! That makes it $60."
> "Why, you insignificant little Irish ____, what do you mean?"
> "Fifty more!" cried I; "that makes it $110 and I'll stay with you a week. If you can stand it I can."[10]

The game ended with a 5–4 Detroit win, leaving the White Stockings three and a half games out of the lead, but Anson was not finished. "Will I pay [the fines]?" he replied to a question from a reporter. "Not I, not a dollar, not a penny. If Gaffney does not remit the fines I'll have him fired, or my name's not Anson." Even the taciturn John Clarkson complained to the papers, "Every time Gaffney came on the [Detroit] grounds the crowd cheered him until the windows rattled a half-mile away. He's for them every time and they know it, too."[11]

Despite the captain's threats, league president Nick Young supported Gaffney in the controversy. "Anson is a hard worker and a good fellow," said Young, "but I suppose ... he has walked a hundred miles up and down the first base path in mild deprecation of the umpire's decisions."[12] Anson, despite his protests, paid the fine, and it appears that Gaffney earned Anson's admiration with his uncompromising stand. Anson was an inveterate bullier of umpires, but those who stood up to him, like Gaffney, earned the respect of the King of Kickers. "That ended the matter there," said Gaffney later. "Anson went back to his base, and I have not had any trouble with him since."

The White Stockings blasted the tail-end teams in 1886, with

Captain Anson in 1887, a season in which both the Detroit and Pittsburgh clubs offered to buy his services from Chicago. (Author's collection)

Chicago winning 34 of 36 contests against Kansas City and Washington, but their head-to-head performance against Detroit eventually decided the pennant race. Anson's men closed to within one and a half games in July with a 15–1 run and, while Detroit won only one of eight games in early August, Chicago took the lead later in the month with a 14-game winning streak. The White Stockings made the race interesting when they lost five in a row in late September and found themselves in the lead by only one game on October 8, but the next day Detroit ended its season with a doubleheader loss at Philadelphia. Anson's club defeated Boston by a 12–3 score, clinching its second consecutive pennant and fifth in seven years.

Once again, the White Stockings met the St. Louis Browns of the American Association in a best-of-seven post-season showdown. The Browns entered the series on a roll, having swept the National League St. Louis Maroons for the championship of the Mound City, while the White Stockings were exhausted from their pennant race with the Detroit Wolverines. All three Chicago pitchers, Clarkson, McCormick, and Flynn, complained to Anson of sore arms, and the White Stockings entered the "World's Series" at a distinct disadvantage. For the Browns, star pitcher

Bob Caruthers hurt his knee against the Maroons and was questionable for the Series, but all their other players were healthy, rested, and anxious to score an undisputed win over the National League champs.

Anson, with Spalding's approval, agreed to the seven-game match on one condition. He demanded that the prize money (a healthy $15,000 as compared to only $1,000 the year before) be awarded on a winner-take-all basis. This move made the series, in the words of baseball historian Robert Smith, "the talk of every ball fan between the Mississippi and the Atlantic Coast." Though most of the White Stockings and Browns paired off and agreed to split their winnings no matter the outcome, Anson and Charlie Comiskey, the rival first basemen and managers, were determined to play on an all-or-nothing basis.

The two teams agreed to hold the first three games in Chicago, with the next three at St. Louis and the location of a possible seventh game undetermined for the moment. The series began on October 18, 1886, with Dave Foutz on the mound for the Browns in place of Caruthers, and the White Stockings took the lead in the first inning when Anson lined a triple that scored Kelly and Pfeffer chased Anson across the plate with a single. The Chicagos never looked back as John Clarkson pitched a masterful 6–0 shutout. Caruthers evened the series the next day, beating McCormick by a 12–0 score, and Charlie Comiskey sent Caruthers back to the hill in the third game to face Clarkson. Anson went hitless, but Kelly belted three hits as the White Stockings beat Caruthers 11 to 4, for a two games to one lead as the series moved to St. Louis.

McCormick and Flynn, however, were in no condition to pitch, and McCormick was reportedly so inebriated that Anson sent him back to Chicago. With Flynn on the shelf with a sore arm, Clarkson went to the box for the third time in four days and lost to Foutz by an 8–5 count. Chicago had tied the score in the top of the sixth, but Fred Pfeffer dropped a pop-up with the bases loaded, and then made a poor throw that prevented the White Stockings from completing a force-out that might have led to a double play. That evening, according to reports, none of the Chicagos except for Anson appeared to be troubled by the loss, and rumors circulated that the White Stockings had placed bets against themselves with local bookmakers. While Anson raged at a St. Louis reporter ("Didn't you see it yourself? Wasn't you there?" exploded the captain) his charges were smoking cigars, drinking champagne, and telling stories in the hotel lobby. The word "hippodroming" made its appearance once again in the nation's sports pages.

Anson began to scramble at this point, and brought in Ed Williamson to pitch the ninth inning of the fourth game in an attempt to save the arm of his only available pitcher. The one inning of rest did not help. Clarkson was unable to pitch in the fifth game, and Williamson drew the starting assignment. The shortstop-turned-pitcher did not make it through the second inning, so Anson sent outfielder Jimmy Ryan in to pitch the rest of the game, which the Browns won by a 10–3 score behind their third-string starter, Nat Hudson, who pitched a three-hitter. Now the Chicago papers roasted Anson for his use of Williamson as a starter, as the *Chicago News* complained, "the game was given away yesterday in St. Louis.... The hippodrome was so artistically played that there really was no inclination to cry out against it."

Anson with the 1886 National League championship. (Author's collection)

The sixth game of the series, played at St. Louis on October 23, was one of the greatest of the 19th century. Clarkson, as dominating as ever, took a 3–0 lead into the bottom of the eighth inning, and it looked as if Anson's men would stay alive for another day. Unfortunately for the White Stockings, left fielder Abner Dalrymple dropped a fly ball, igniting a St. Louis rally that tied the score at 3. The game went into extra innings, and the Chicagos failed to score in the top of the tenth.

Clarkson, pitching in his fourth game in six days, finally faltered in the bottom of the inning. He hit Curt Welch with his first pitch, but when umpire Dickey Pearce waved Welch down to first, Anson stormed to the plate, bellowing that Welch purposely got in the way of the ball. For once, Anson's kicking worked, and Pearce changed his mind and ordered Welch back to the plate. On the next pitch, Welch drilled a single into center field and soon moved to third on an infield hit and a sacrifice. With Doc Bushong at the plate, the exhausted Clarkson heaved a wild pitch past the reach of catcher King Kelly. As the ball rolled away, Welch slid happily across the plate to win the game and the championship. The sportswriters called it the "$15,000 slide" for the amount of winner-take-all prize money won by the Browns.

Some confusion exists over whether the errant toss should be charged as a wild pitch or a passed ball. "I signaled Clarkson for a low ball on one side," explained Kelly after the game, "and when it came it was high upon the other. It struck my hand as I tried to get it and I would say it was a passed ball. You can give it to me if you want to. Clarkson told me that it slipped from his hands."[13]

The Browns played well, but to most observers it seemed obvious that the White Stockings were not "on their game." Spalding complained to the reporters that Jim McCormick was "so thoroughly soused, he could not have struck out the batboy" in the second game, and some writers suggested that several other members of the White Stockings were drunk on the field. For the second year in a row, the White Stockings ended their season with an embarrassing defeat, and Spalding was so outraged that he refused to pay train fare for his players to return to Chicago.

Anson, in his autobiography, was diplomatic about the loss. "We were beaten and fairly beaten," wrote Anson many years later, "but had some of the players taken as good care of themselves prior to these games as they were in the habit of doing when the league season was in full swim, I am inclined to believe that there might have been a different tale to tell."[14] At the time, however, the captain was crestfallen that his ballclub was undone in the post-season series by the indifference of its own star players. Anson was also financially affected by the defeat. Since all the White Stockings besides Anson had reportedly made arrangements to split their winnings with members of the Browns, the captain was the only player on either team who went home without any money.

CHAPTER 12

A New Beginning

> Anson was six feet two, an erect, square-shouldered, lop-eared man, tightly muscled, of a slightly dour countenance. His eyes were deep and his gaze level and clear. His mouth was firm, his nose curved and badly proportioned, like something a child might draw. There was a fierceness in his nature which took the form of a stubborn honesty and independence, a grim clinging to prejudice, a tendency to express his mind loudly and directly, and a desire to go his own way — and to have his own way.
> — Robert Smith, 1947[1]

The 1886 season was a trying one for both Anson and Spalding. The men at the core of the White Stockings, including Anson, Gore, Dalrymple, Flint, and Williamson, had played together since 1879, with Kelly and Burns joining in 1880. All of these men were either past their 30th birthday or nearing it, and several posed discipline problems that worsened with each passing year. Neither Spalding nor Anson looked forward to another season full of fines, suspensions, and arguments, and both men believed that the Chicago team was too poorly disciplined to win another pennant in 1887.

Spalding, probably at Anson's urging, attacked the problem in a manner that outraged the Chicago fans. At the end of November 1886 he released two of the most popular White Stockings, George Gore (to New York) and Abner Dalrymple (to Pittsburgh). Dalrymple had slipped badly, batting only .233 in 1886 after experiencing eye problems during the season, but Gore was still an important part of the Chicago offense, batting .304 with 150 runs scored in 112 games. Gore was angry when he learned of his release, and reportedly told Anson, "I'll go if I have to, but if I do, I promise you'll never win another pennant."[2] In early December, Spalding threatened to dump Jim McCormick, a fine pitcher whose talent was increasingly negated by his unreliability, and catcher Silver Flint, unless the two veterans promised to behave in 1887.

The biggest move of the off-season took place after the first of the year. King Kelly was the most talented and troublesome player on the ballclub, and refused to sign a contract for 1887 with the White Stockings after Gore and Dalrymple were released. "I have determined not to play with the Chicagos any longer," said Kelly in December. "President Spalding and Captain Anson have not treated me properly, and for that reason I have made up my mind to sever my connection with the champions."

Kelly proclaimed that he was tired of the constant stream of fines levied by Anson and Spalding for his nighttime activities. "The officials of the Chicago Club never fail to take advantage of any opportunity to impose a fine upon a player. McCormick, Gore, Flint, myself, and several other members of he team were fined for no cause whatever. They say that we were guilty of intoxication. As for McCormick and myself, I will say that there is no truth in this charge. It was simply drummed up in order to lessen the salary list of the club."

Kelly expressed a desire to join the New York Giants and play once again with his friend George Gore. "One thing is certain," said Kelly, "I will never play ball again as a member of the Chicago Club, and if Mr. Spalding refuses to give me an honorable release, I will retire from the profession."[3]

Spalding insisted to the papers that Kelly's name was on the Chicago reserve list for 1887 and that he had no choice but to play for the White Stockings. However, other teams inquired about the King's availability, and Spalding decided to entertain offers from all National League teams except the Giants. The Boston Beaneaters entered into negotiations with Spalding in the early weeks of January and offered $5,000 for Kelly's release, to which Spalding replied, "We wouldn't think of letting Kelly go at the figure you offer, but for double that amount we would consider it."[4] Boston upped the offer to $7,500, but Spalding played a waiting game. By early February the Boston owners were ready to meet Spalding's price of $10,000, an unprecedented sum at the time for the services of a single player. On February 14, 1887, the two teams completed the sale, and the stunning transaction filled the headlines on the nation's sporting pages.

Kelly was happy to leave Chicago, and voiced his doubts that the White Stockings could contend in the coming season. "When two good batters and base runners are taken out of a team," said Kelly, "their absence will make a strong aggregation weak. Anson has claimed right along that it was due to his work that Chicago won the championship. Next season he will have to prove it."[5]

Anson gave his own explanation for the sale of Kelly to the Beaneaters. He claimed, not too convincingly, that an urgency to maintain competitive balance in the league was an overriding concern. "We let him go to Boston because a good price was offered at a time when the Chicago club had been too successful and when it was good policy to slightly weaken the club," Anson explained.[6] This statement was highly suspicious, coming from a competitive man like Anson. Kelly was sent packing because his off-field behavior had become intolerable to Spalding and Anson.

The White Stockings also lost two of their three starting pitchers from the 1886 season. Jim McCormick refused to sign a contract with the Chicago club, so Spalding traded him to Pittsburgh in late March in exchange for George Van Haltren, a 21-year-old pitcher from California who had performed well against a major league barnstorming team in the winter months. Jocko Flynn, who sat out the series against the Browns with a sore arm, showed no improvement over the winter, and by spring it was clear that his pitching career was over. He played one game in the outfield for the White Stockings in 1887 and then left the major leagues.

An Allen & Ginter baseball card of Anson, 1888. Allen & Ginter produced the first series of sporting cards. (Author's collection)

The departures of Flynn and McCormick forced Anson to build a new supporting cast for staff ace John Clarkson, and the captain's task was further complicated when Van Haltren failed to report for duty. The young pitcher remained in California, tending to his seriously ill mother, and refused to come east despite Spalding's threat to blackball him from the professional leagues. In Van Haltren's absence, Anson signed Mark Baldwin, a 24-year-old righthander who had pitched Duluth to the Northwest

League pennant the year before. Anson had tried to use Baldwin in the series against St. Louis the previous fall, but Browns manager Charlie Comiskey objected, since Baldwin had not played any games in the regular season. His presence on the post-season roster might have given Anson an opportunity to rest the overworked John Clarkson and possibly changed the outcome of the series.

The Stonewall Infield of Anson, Pfeffer, Williamson, and Burns remained intact, but the White Stockings displayed a new outfield in 1887. Anson promoted Billy Sunday to a starting position in center, moved Jimmy Ryan to right as a full-time replacement for Kelly, and signed Marty Sullivan to play left. Catcher George Moolic, who caught almost all of Flynn's starts in 1886, was not retained, but Tom Daly and Dell Darling arrived to support Silver Flint. In all, five of the mainstays of the 1886 pennant-winning team were gone, all replaced by younger and more temperate men, or so Anson hoped.

Spalding, who had become almost as much of a temperance crusader as the late William Hulbert, was not one to stand back and hope for the best. In the 1880s, drunkenness was one of the leading evils of baseball. Spalding decided to attack the problem head-on before this new team, like the previous one, could spiral out of control. Before the season began, Spalding demanded that each player promise to refrain from alcohol. Spalding called it the "cold water principle," and suggested that every team compel its players to take a similar pledge.

The National League rules committee was busy again before the 1887 season began, with some of their decisions directly affecting Cap Anson. The committee members decided that it would take four strikes, not three, to strike a batter out in 1887, and that a walk would consist of five balls. They further decreed that a batter should receive credit for a hit if he coaxed a walk from the pitcher, a development that promised to raise batting averages across the board, and that a pitcher should deliver a ball with one foot on the back line of the pitcher's box. This standardized the pitching distance, for the first time, at 55 feet and six inches.

The most important rules change, as far as Anson was concerned, removed the right of the batter to call for a high (above the belt) or a low (below the belt) pitch, and set the strike zone as the entire area over the plate between the knees and the shoulder of the batter. Anson had always been a high-ball hitter, and had invariably called for pitches above his belt. Now, for the first time, he would be required to swing at low pitches or risk having them called as strikes. Anson's swing was designed for high pitches, and many observers believed that Anson would be the player affected most by the new regulations. In February, the newspapers reported

12. A New Beginning 149

that the captain was spending several hours a day in intense batting practice, doing nothing but swinging at low pitches.[7]

The Chicago fans were incensed at the departure of their favorite stars, and lashed out at both Spalding and Anson when the team started the 1887 season with one win in its first six games. On May 6, the White Stockings lost their home opener to Pittsburgh by a score of 6 to 3, and the fans cheered the former Chicago star Abner Dalrymple while booing Anson. One Chicago paper reported, "never in Chicago's base ball history has the season opened so dismally and disastrously as to-day. The general feeling that the club management has sold out Chicago's chances for the league championship found expression in the most taunting remarks from the big crowd present. When Anson made a claim on the umpire such calls could be heard as 'Sit down, you big duffer!' 'You slave driver!' 'Sell some more men!' ... President Spalding was terribly mortified and industriously kept out of sight. The new talent gave a wretched exhibition and the only ball playing was that done by the old timers."[8]

The papers criticized the team and its captain harshly as the season wore on. Chicago fans had been accustomed to success after the White Stockings captured five pennants in the preceding seven seasons, and reporters showed little patience for the rebuilding process. The fans may have been more understanding if the team had simply grown old, but Spalding let men like Kelly, McCormick, and Gore go when they were still productive. Since Anson fully supported Spalding's restructuring of the team, and was the public face of the Chicago ballclub, he withstood more criticism in 1887 then he had experienced since his arrival in Chicago 11 years earlier.

Spalding viewed newspaper criticism as merely one more form of advertising. "Good, liberal roasts in newspapers of wide circulation," said Spalding, "are much more effective than fulsome praise." Many years later, Spalding claimed that he used a courier to provide information to one of the team's most vociferous critics, Harmony White of the *Chicago News*, on a weekly basis. "I could not afford to be neglected in his paper," explained the club president, "for since he had let up in his attacks our attendance was dropping off."[9]

Anson concurred with his boss. When one Chicago writer commiserated with the captain about his treatment at the hands of the sportswriters, Anson told him not to worry. "It does not bother me a bit," proclaimed Anson. "I have got used to being hauled over the coals, and rather like it, because it is a good 'ad' for me. If the public can stand it I am sure I can."[10] The bad press continued as the White Stockings dropped four in a row to Detroit and Washington in mid–May, but Anson, ever the optimist, put on a brave face for the papers. "Do not worry about the Chicago chances, my friend," he told *The Sporting News*. "We will get there later as sure as I live."[11]

The new White Stockings took some time to jell. They won their next four games against Indianapolis and Detroit, then dropped five in a row, and by May 18 they were buried in seventh place in the eight-team National League. With Mark Baldwin inconsistent and George Van Haltren remaining in California, Spalding offered Pittsburgh $5,000 for their star pitcher, Jim (Pud) Galvin, who had defeated the White Stockings twice in the early days of the season. Pittsburgh declined the offer. After the Senators bombed Baldwin by a 14–6 count on May 17, Anson grew so disgusted that he sat out the next day, putting Tom Daly on first in his stead. The captain's self-imposed exile yielded no improvement, as the White Stockings lost again to the Senators in a game that featured five errors by left fielder Marty Sullivan.

However, to Anson's satisfaction, the team was better behaved than its predecessors, and he derived more pleasure in managing the club in 1887. "Since the men gave me their promise that they would not drink any more, at least till the close of the season, it has not been necessary to have any rules," said the captain. "There are no more night carousals, no more headaches in the morning and no more unsteady nerves in the afternoon; no more surliness or jealousy."[12] Aside from an incident in which Jimmy Ryan cursed Anson when the captain criticized him for not running out a grounder, these White Stockings were practically angelic compared to the departed Gore, Kelly, and others.

One former player was already displaying the effects of his hard-partying ways. Pitcher Larry Corcoran began the 1887 season at Nashville, but the Indianapolis Hoosiers of the National League signed him on May 9 and put him into action against the White Stockings two days later. Anson's men blasted their former teammate all over the lot in an 11–6 win, and it was evident that, at age 27, Corcoran was finished with baseball. The Giants knocked Corcoran out of the box four days later in what proved to be his last major league game, and the Hoosiers released the sore-armed pitcher shortly thereafter. Corcoran was only 31 years old when he died four years later of kidney failure.

George Van Haltren finally reported to the White Stockings on June 26, after the death of his mother in California, and pitched his first game against Boston the following day. Before the game, Anson performed a ritual designed to introduce each new player to the Chicago fans. The White Stockings paraded across the field, with Anson and Van Haltren in the lead, and when the two men reached home plate, Van Haltren waved his cap to the cheers of the crowd. The nervous young pitcher walked a record 16 batters, losing to Boston by a 17–11 score, but Anson decided to give him another chance. Three days later he settled down and nearly beat the Senators, losing 4–3 in a game that featured four errors by Cap Anson. Van Haltren broke into the win column on July 2, pitching a five-hitter and belting two singles and a homer in a 10–2 victory. The young pitcher performed so well at bat that Anson put him in right field on days that he didn't pitch, moving Jimmy Ryan to center and Billy Sunday back to the bench. By mid–July Anson had installed the versatile Van Haltren as leadoff man for the White Stockings, an unusual role for a rookie pitcher.

Van Haltren's bat cooled down after a week or two, but he provided Anson with a reliable third starter behind Clarkson and Baldwin, and the White Stockings sailed over the .500 mark in late June with nine wins in ten games. Two of those came against the league-leading Detroit Wolverines, who had employed the league's best offensive attack to hold first place all year long. As Clarkson put together another outstanding season, leading the league in every positive pitching category, the White Stockings rallied behind him. Chicago took second place with an eight-game winning streak in early July, and moved into position to challenge the Wolverines for the pennant.

With Al Spalding busier than ever in the business end of the team, the responsibility for trades, player discipline, and spring training fell to Anson more than ever. As *Sporting Life* stated in July of that year, "Al Spalding holds Anson personally responsible for the general management of the team, and Anson holds the players individually responsible to him."[13] Spalding still found time to chew out his players every now and then — as late as 1889 he stormed into the locker room after a game and tore into Anson for popping up with runners on base — but for the most part, Anson held full control of the ball club from 1887 forward.

It can be said that 1887 was the year in which the baseball world began to recognize the White Stockings as Anson's team. The captain had personally scouted and signed most of the young players that dotted the Chicago roster, and the national press referred to those first-year men as "Anson's Colts." With most of the more troublesome souls gone to other teams, Anson tightened the reins of leadership, though older players such as Clarkson and Williamson chafed under the captain's strict rules.

Anson, by now one of the ten oldest players in the game, enforced his leadership by example, leading the league in batting average throughout the 1887 campaign. In a year in which walks counted as base hits, Anson's average rose over the .400 mark in June and remained there for the duration of the season. At age 35, Anson was still an efficient cleanup batter and

John Clarkson, Chicago pitching star whom Al Spalding sold to Boston for $10,000 in April 1888. (Author's collection)

the leading run producer in the Chicago lineup. He was also in the best physical shape of anyone on the team, and set the pace in pregame practice and the occasional five-mile run on off days.

A game against Washington on July 13 featured one of Anson's most bizarre strategic maneuvers, one that recalled a similar play by Silver Flint eight years before. The White Stockings were losing by a 3–0 score in the ninth inning when Anson, with one out, walloped a ball far over the left field fence for a home run. Anson, however, stopped at third, and the umpire decided to leave him there, since there was then no rule requiring a batter to cross the plate on a home run.

Anson later explained that his presence on third base would force Washington catcher Connie Mack to play close behind the batter, increasing the chances for a wild pitch or a passed ball, and putting more pressure on the pitcher with Pfeffer and Williamson coming up. Mack crossed up Anson by playing his usual position several steps behind the plate, ignoring the runner on base, and Pfeffer grounded out and Williamson struck out to end the game with Anson still on third.

Anson's standing as a player and manager had never been higher, but the 1887 campaign also saw Anson damage to his posthumous reputation when he again took center stage in the fight against integration. On Wednesday, July 13, the White Stockings played in Washington and then stopped in Newark, New Jersey, for an exhibition game against the local International League squad. The International circuit was something of a haven for African-American players in 1887, with Moses Walker catching for Newark, pitcher George Stovey winning 33 games for the same ballclub, and Buffalo second baseman Frank Grant leading the league in home runs.

Walker was injured and not in the lineup for the exhibition match, but Newark manager Charles Hackett intended to use his best pitcher,

12. A NEW BEGINNING 153

Stovey, against the Chicago. Anson, however, had other ideas, and expressed them in his usual blunt way. "Take him [Stovey] out," demanded Anson, "or I get off." The Newark management complied, telling the newspapers that Stovey was ill, and replaced him with their second-string pitcher. The game proceeded without further incident, with Newark defeating Chicago by a score of 9 to 4. The only point of interest in the contest occurred in the fourth inning when a group of fans interrupted the game to present Chicago's Tom Daly, who had played in Newark the year before, with a gold watch.

Anson, once again, stood resolutely in favor of a baseball color line, and his stance may have emboldened other players in their refusal to play against African-Americans. In September of that season, the St. Louis Browns of the American Association scheduled a game against the New York Cuban Giants, one of the leading black teams of the era. The game never took place, as eight Browns players signed a petition and presented it to team owner Chris von der Ahe the night before the contest. The petition read:

> Philadelphia, Penn., Sept. 10.
> To Chris Von Der Ahe, Esq.:
>
> DEAR SIR: We, the undersigned members of the St. Louis Baseball Club, do not agree to play against negroes tomorrow. We will cheerfully play against white people at any time, and think, by refusing to play, we are only doing what is right, taking everything into consideration and the shape the team is in at present.
>
> W. A. Latham, John Boyle, J. E. O'Neill, R. L. Caruthers, W. E. Gleason, W. H. Robinson, Charles King, Curt Welch.[14]

Team captain Charlie Comiskey offered the opinion that "some of the boys wanted a day to themselves" and expressed puzzlement at the protest, since the Browns had played several previous contests against black teams without incident. In addition, petition signer Curt Welch was a teammate of Moses Walker in Toledo in 1884, and had not previously complained about playing with or against men of African descent. In the interests of team harmony, von der Ahe cancelled the game, handing another victory to the segregation forces.

The directors of the International League passed a rule during its July league meeting, one that barred its teams from signing any more black players, and at the end of the 1887 season, Newark dropped both George Stovey, its leading pitcher, and Moses Walker, the starting catcher. Walker played for Syracuse in the following season, and when the White Stockings arrived for an exhibition game in September 1888, Anson once again refused to play against Walker. The main local newspapers did not even mention Anson's demand that Walker remain on the bench, so ingrained was the idea that blacks and whites should not mix on the field of play. A black paper, on the other hand, described the controversy and stated that "the big baby [Anson] was satisfied" when the Syracuse management held Walker out of the lineup that day.[15]

Working conditions for African-American players deteriorated swiftly in the late 1880s. White pitchers hurled fastballs at their heads, while white fielders attempted to trip them as they rounded the bases. Star infielder Bud Fowler wore shin guards, the first in baseball history, under his uniform pants to protect himself from the spikes of white baserunners. Several teams omitted their black players from team pictures since white players refused to be photographed with them. Moses Walker left Syracuse at the close of the 1888 season, and before long there were no more black players in organized ball. In 1891, *Sporting Life* magazine was able to report that the era of baseball segregation was firmly established. "Probably in no other business in America," stated the magazine, "is the color line so finely drawn as in base ball. An African who attempts to put on a uniform and go in among a lot of white players is taking his life in his hands."[16]

Though Anson lent his booming voice to the anti-integration forces, it is naïve to think that Anson alone was responsible for barring African-American players from the game. Robert Peterson, in *Only the Ball Was White*, stated that Sol White and other historians have exaggerated Anson's role in the establishment of the color line. To suggest "that [Anson] had the power and popularity to force Negroes out of organized baseball almost single-handedly," wrote Peterson, "...is to credit him with more influence than he had, or for that matter, than he needed. For it seems clear that a majority of professional baseball players in 1887, both Northerners and Southerners, opposed integration in the game."[17]

Still, the fact remains that Adrian Anson stood, loudly and proudly, on the wrong side of history. He willingly involved himself prominently in a crusade that most likely would have occurred anyway. even if Anson had never played professional baseball. However, his legacy is forever tainted by the virulence with which he opposed the presence of minority players in the national game.

The White Stockings chipped away all summer at Detroit's lead, and on July 20 a 7–6 win at Boston put Anson's men only two games behind. Chicago stayed within two games of the lead until a series at home against Detroit in mid–August. The White Stockings won the first two games, 8–2 and 6–4, and pulled into a tie for the league lead for the first time that season.

12. A NEW BEGINNING   155

While the White Stockings mounted a challenge, Spalding boasted to the local reporters about his well-behaved younger team. "We have young men in the club," said Spalding, "mere boys, some of them, who take as much pride in their temperance record as they do in their ball playing record. That is saying a good deal, but it is only the truth and I know what I am talking about. When I asked the boys not to drink anything until the close of the season, and they promised me that they wouldn't, I said we should adopt any plan we thought best to discover whether they were keeping their pledges or not. It gives me a good deal of satisfaction to say that no man has violated his pledge.

"There is a rivalry among them not only to keep liquor away but to so conduct themselves that there shall not be the slightest grounds on which to rest a suspicion."[18]

Anson's Colts, many of whom were playing in their first pennant race, began to tire in late August. They alternated wins and losses on an Eastern swing to Pittsburgh, New York, and Washington, and the Wolverines began to pull away from the rest of the league. When the White Stockings dropped a doubleheader at Detroit on September 7 and fell seven games behind, their pennant hopes were dashed. Detroit cruised to its first and only National League title as Anson gave playing time to eager rookies in the last few weeks of the 1887 campaign. Chicago held second place through the end of September, but was passed in early October by Harry Wright's Philadelphia Phillies, finishing in third place with a 71–50 record.

Anson caused some grumbling among the players when he demanded tighter discipline as the team fell out of the race. He fined Fred Pfeffer $40 for two misplays in New York, and Pfeffer angrily wrote to Spalding, demanding that the fines be rescinded. Pfeffer claimed that Anson abused him "shamefully," and the matter caused lingering resentment in the last few weeks of the season.[19] The *Chicago News* reported that Spalding, too, upset the White Stockings when he made an offer of $5,000 to be split among the players if they won the pennant. Spalding did not make the offer until the club was too far behind to mount a challenge, and the team showed its "gratitude" by losing its next three games.[20]

The new rule that counted walks as hits in 1887 sent averages rising all across the National League, with the main beneficiary of the rule being the captain of the Chicagos. Anson's batting average would have been .347, fourth best in the league, if walks were not entered in the hit column, but his 60 bases on balls pushed his average to .421, giving him his third batting championship. Years later, Anson expressed pride at his league-leading mark. "In 1884," said Anson in 1918, "they removed practically all the restrictions from the pitchers. Yet three years later, under conditions which would now be considered much more unfavorable to the batsmen, I batted the highest of my career, .421. That was 16 years after I first joined a major league."[21]

The White Stockings failed to repeat as champions, but baseball observers gave Anson the lion's share of the credit for assembling a new team on the fly and challenging for the pennant without an extended rebuilding period. Anson's reputation as a manager and leader had never been greater, and other teams took note of his accomplishments. Surprisingly, the owner of the Detroit Wolverines, Frederick Stearnes, was not impressed with his manager, Bill Watkins, though the Wolverines won the pennant that year, and he openly coveted the Chicago field boss. In mid–September, Stearnes sent a letter to Spalding in which he made an offer for Anson:

> FIFTH AVENUE HOTEL, NEW YORK, Sept. 14
> A. G. Spalding, Chicago:
>
> DEAR SIR: I have recently noticed severe, and what seemed to me unjust, criticisms of Anson. The papers seem to desire a change of management. Recognizing the ability of Anson, both as a ball player and manager, I would ask as a special personal favor that if any change is contemplated you will notify me immediately. I am not only willing but anxious to pay more for his release than any other club would. With Anson in charge the present Detroit club could hold the pennant for years to come.
>
> Kindly wire on receipt of this what my chances are of securing him. Fraternally yours,
>
> F. K. STEARNES.
> P. S.—Would an offer of $10,000 be entertained.

Stearnes already owned a slow, power-hitting first baseman in Dan Brouthers, who batted .419 (counting walks as hits) in 1887, but having two similar players on his team did not trouble the Detroit owner. "Of course I would not think of letting Brouthers go," said Stearnes. "I could play one of the two men in the outfield."

Spalding was not surprised by the offer. "Very many times we have received inquiries from other club managements asking whether we would entertain a proposition for Anson's release," explained Spalding. "To all such queries I have invariably replied in the negative."

"What has Anson to say about it himself?" asked a reporter.

"Anson. Well according to the best of my recollection, Anson just smiled. He has a very expressive smile, you know."[22]

A month later, the Pittsburgh Alleghenies became convinced that

Anson was the answer to their problems too, and they made an offer to Spalding for the captain's services. The Alleghenies offered Chicago $15,000 for Anson, and the deal, if consummated, would have been the most expensive player transaction up to that time. Once again, Spalding turned the money down, and Anson was flattered by, but not interested in, the Pittsburgh offer. "It's a poor year when I cannot make $15,000 where I am now," said the captain, "and it would take more money than that to purchase my release. That much is certain. I am well satisfied where I am, and it is probable that I shall spend the remainder of my baseball days in Chicago. I am satisfied with the city and the club."[23]

CHAPTER 13

Second Place

[Anson's] reputation as a "kicker" is familiar not only to all attendants at the games but to many who have never even seen him.
— John M. Ward, 1888[1]

Cap Anson and his family were now permanent residents of Chicago, and during the late 1880s he pursued several ventures in the business world. One such opportunity came his way as a result of a premature innovation from the mind of Al Spalding. The team president believed that baseball games could be played at night, and in 1883 he wrote a letter to the new National League president, A. G. Mills, in which he offered to have his White Stockings play a "picked nine" of stars from the other league teams under the lights. It would have been baseball's first All-Star contest as well as the first night game, but Mills was unconvinced and refused to grant permission. Spalding shelved his plan, and nearly 50 years passed before either the All-Star Game or the first night baseball game were played in the major leagues.

Spalding did not let the idea drop, and at the end of the 1886 season he installed temporary light towers at West Side Park. He then constructed a skating rink and a gigantic ice slide there and hired Anson as superintendent of his new winter playground. For 25 cents, one could ride on a 700-foot toboggan course that twisted and turned all over the infield and outfield, or skate along the sidelines where the club had played mere months before. The attraction proved popular in Chicago's colder-than-usual winter of 1886-87, and both Anson (who, most likely, invested some of his own money in the project) and Spalding profited from the enterprise.

Some of Anson's other business ventures proved less successful. An enthusiastic handball player, Anson opened a multiple court handball arena in downtown Chicago in the late 1880s. It was a money loser, as was a partial ownership in a poolroom. His most spectacular commercial failure came when a friend convinced the captain to invest $500 in a company that bottled ginger beer, using Anson's name as a selling point. Anson soon put another $1,000 or so into the struggling operation before the ginger beer finally went into production. The project looked promising until customers discovered that "Captain A. C. Anson's Ginger Beer" had too much carbonation in it, causing the bottles to explode on their shelves. Anson doled out even more money to extricate himself from this disaster.

Cap Anson on a playing card, 1888. (Transcendental Graphics)

The captain was obviously disappointed in his financial setbacks, but a personal tragedy proved even more devastating for the Ansons. In September of 1887 Virginia gave birth to a son, whom the couple named Adrian Constantine Anson Junior. Anson was thrilled by the arrival of a long-awaited son, but the captain was filled with grief when the baby died on January 18, 1888. Sixteen months later Virginia presented Anson with another daughter, named Dorothy, who grew into a healthy child. Cap Anson doted on his three daughters, but longed for a son to complete his family, and the death of Adrian Junior was his second such sorrow in a five-year period.

As Anson grieved, Spalding planned more changes to the Chicago roster as the new season approached. The team president had made it clear to the other National League teams that Cap Anson was not for sale, but any other member of the White Stockings could be bought for a price. As Spalding explained to *The Sporting News* in September 1887, "I will sell Clarkson, Williamson, Pfeffer or any man in the team for $10,000, and consider it a good investment. The fact is, no ball player is worth that much to a club. There is no player so good but that his equal can be found."[2] For proof, one needed to look no farther than the Boston nine, which added baseball's most popular player in King Kelly and improved by only a few games in the win column. The Beaneaters finished the 1887 season in fifth place, the same position they held at the end of the 1886 campaign before Kelly arrived.

Spalding was still concerned about the behavior of his star players, and by early 1888 was ready to unload John Clarkson, the temperamental pitching ace, who wanted out of Chicago. Clarkson led the league in wins, complete games, innings pitched, and strikeouts again in 1887, but missed playing with his friend King Kelly. Clarkson spent most of the season in a dark mood, and quarreled with Anson all year long. "Many regard him as the greatest [of all Chicago pitchers]," said Anson many years later, "but not many know of his peculiar temperament and the amount of encouragement needed to keep him going. Scold him, find fault with him and he could not pitch at all. Praise him and he was unbeatable."[3]

Anson probably should have known that teasing the mercurial pitcher was not the wisest strategy, but after the White Stockings sold Kelly to Boston, the captain could not resist a good-natured jab. "John," said the captain early in the 1887 season, "perhaps you will be seasoned well enough next year to bring a good round price in the market. How much do you suppose we could realize on you?"[4] Clarkson, taken aback by the remark, replied that he was happy in Chicago, but as the season wore on he began to pine for his home in Boston. The pitcher lived in a boarding house in Chicago during the season, and longed to return to Boston and set up a year-round household. "I am anxious to have a home of my own and to fit it up as a permanent residence," said the pitcher in October of that year. "In Chicago I am obliged to board, and no boarding house will ever seem to me like home."[5]

In December 1887 Clarkson told *Sporting Life*, "I want to play here [in Boston] because all my family live here, and here are most of my dearest friends. I think it's about time that I should have something to say about where I shall play. Chicago won't release me. Very well, then, I shall not play ball at all next season. I will remain in Boston and work at my trade. I mean just what I say. I shall not play in Chicago under any circumstances."[6] His trade was jewelry making, and Clarkson swore that if he could not get himself released to Boston, he would return to his hometown of Cambridge, Massachusetts, and join his father in the family business.

Two other White Stockings had tired of playing in Chicago, and they, too, proclaimed their desire to leave. Second baseman Fred Pfeffer and shortstop Ed Williamson resented Anson's strict management, and wanted to follow the example of Mike Kelly and earn more money elsewhere.

Williamson may have been influenced by newspaper reports from Philadelphia that called him "the king bee of the league short stops" and stated that he was "the $10,000 beauty that the Philadelphia Club should buy." The shortstop had tangled often with Anson since joining the team in 1879, and now wanted to ply his trade for another club. Pfeffer, however, was the man whom the Phillies coveted most, and Philadelphia co-owner Al Reach (a former teammate of Anson on the Athletics) offered Spalding a hefty sum for the veteran second baseman.

Pfeffer, who hit .278 with 89 runs batted in for the White Stockings in 1887, demanded a higher salary for 1888 than Spalding was willing to pay. He threatened to sign elsewhere if he was not satisfied, but Spalding placed Pfeffer on the Chicago reserve list, which severely limited the player's options. Spalding declared to *The Sporting News* that Pfeffer's threats were hollow and that "he will play here or nowhere," though Pfeffer may have figured that Spalding would cave in and sell him away as he had done with Mike Kelly the previous winter. Spalding did not budge, and Pfeffer realized that the team president meant business. The second baseman held fast for a while, but signed his contract in late January.

By February 19, 1888, the White Stockings had all their men under contract except for Clarkson, who proved to be the toughest negotiator of the lot. Unlike other Chicago players, Clarkson could well afford to leave baseball, and his threat to quit the game and enter the business world was not an idle one. Reports reached the papers as early as December that the Boston club, which bought Kelly from Chicago the year before, was interested in Clarkson as well, but Spalding refused all overtures throughout the winter months. Spalding believed that Clarkson's price, like that of Kelly the year before, would reach the $10,000 mark if he waited long enough.

The Boston club increased its interest in Clarkson as the weeks passed, and in late March Boston gave Spalding a firm offer of $7,500 for the pitcher's release. Once again Spalding played a waiting game, and on April 4, a few days before the start of the season, Boston upped the price to $10,000. Spalding accepted, and Clarkson happily reported to the Beaneaters to pitch to his favorite catcher, King Kelly. The Boston owners considered the money well spent, as they gained reams of publicity for their "$20,000 battery," the most expensive pitcher-catcher combination in baseball history up to that time.

Chicago fans were stunned at the loss of Clarkson, but Anson moved quickly to fill the void with Gus Krock, a 21-year-old lefthander from Milwaukee who pitched for the pennant-winning Oshkosh team in the Northwest League in 1887. Anson liked big players, and Krock fit the mold. He stood six feet and two inches tall and weighed a little more than 200 pounds, and some called him the strongest man in baseball. Four other teams, including Detroit and Pittsburgh, had bid for Krock's services, but he wanted to pitch close to home, and signed with the White Stockings that winter.

As Gus Krock joined the team, another mainstay left in the spring of 1888. Pittsburgh club owner W. W. Nimick met with Spalding and made an offer for outfielder Jimmy Ryan, which Spalding rejected. Nimick then expressed an interest in Billy Sunday, and Spalding was more receptive to this proposition. Sunday had always been a favorite of Anson, but he had no power, and the captain wanted to improve an offense that finished fifth in the eight-team league in runs scored. Anson had benched Sunday in mid-season of 1887 in favor of Van Haltren, and Anson may have already been planning to move Van Haltren to the outfield permanently. The relationship between Sunday and Anson had cooled due to Sunday's immersion in religious missionary work, but Anson wished Sunday well, and the two men parted on relatively good terms.

Sunday played baseball for three more years, but in the spring of 1891 he turned down a generous contract offer in favor of a position as a secretary of a YMCA chapter in Pittsburgh. Sunday had always been an outgoing and likeable young man, and soon discovered that he enjoyed preaching the Gospel even more than he loved playing baseball. He had, literally, found his calling as a preacher, and within fifteen years Billy Sunday became America's most famous and popular evangelist. He preached his Christian message to tens of thousands, using baseball stories and terminology to drive home his points, and always spoke of his mentor, Cap Anson, in the most admiring terms. Anson, in turn, was always proud of the young man from Iowa who used the White Stockings as a stepping-stone to national fame.

The Stonewall Infield remained intact, with the outfield now consisting of Marty Sullivan in left, Jimmy Ryan in center, and George Van Haltren (on non-pitching days) and Bob Pettit sharing right field. Anson also signed a young catcher and outfielder from Marlborough, Massachusetts named Charles Farrell, whom everyone called "Duke," who saw service in right field as well. With a strong-looking pitching rotation of Krock, Baldwin, and Van Haltren, the White Stockings appeared ready to challenge for the flag once again.

Anson enjoyed making wagers with rival players and managers, and was such an enthusiastic bettor that he developed his own verbal betting shorthand. In the spring of 1888, Anson spotted New York Giants manager Jim Mutrie at the National League meetings. "Suit of clothes, Jim?" inquired Anson.

"Certainly," came Mutrie's reply.

"Series or championship?"

"Championship, of course," said Mutrie. A short time later, Anson crossed paths with Giants captain Buck Ewing and wagered another suit of clothes on the outcome of the season series between Chicago and New York. Anson made bets for hats, steak dinners, and suits, partly because he enjoyed the betting action, but mostly to demonstrate his confidence in his White Stockings. By the end of the spring, Anson had made bets totaling in the hundreds of dollars, so certain was he that his ballclub would recapture the pennant after a one-year hiatus.

Virginia Anson made her own contribution to the team in 1888. She was invited, either by Spalding or her husband, to design a new uniform for the new season, and her design was notable for its absence of white stockings. Mrs. Anson's uniform provided for black stockings, and the ballclub instantly became the "Black Stockings" or the "Blacks" in the newspapers.

The most important news of the preseason came, not from Anson, but from Spalding. On March 24, the team president announced that the White Stockings and a "picked nine" from the rest of the National League would try once again to spread the American national pastime to other parts of the globe. Spalding proposed to lead two teams of ballplayers on an exhibition tour of Australia, New Zealand, and the "Sandwich Islands," or Hawaii, immediately following the conclusion of the 1888 campaign.

Spalding's motives were not altogether altruistic. He called the tour a "base-ball missionary effort" that would "[give] the masses everywhere an opportunity to witness a pastime particularly American, and [show] to all the world that one may be at the same time a professional ball player and a gentleman."[7] At the same time, as he told a reporter, he wanted to go to Australia "for the purpose of extending [his] sporting goods business to that quarter of the globe and to create a market for goods there."[8] Should baseball bloom into an international phenomenon, reasoned Spalding, then people all around the globe would buy their bats, balls, and gloves from A. G. Spalding and Brothers.

Anson, who so enjoyed his trip to England 14 years before, became one of the most enthusiastic promoters of the Australia excursion. Spalding was the primary financial backer, but Cap Anson paid $3,750 for a partial interest in the enterprise. This was no small sum to Anson, as it represented about one and a half year's worth of the captain's salary, but he put his faith in Spalding's ability to attract enough curious Australian fans to recoup the investment.

The 1888 season began with an altercation, as did so many games involving Anson's team in that era. The "Black Stockings" opened the season on April 20 in Indianapolis, with the Hoosiers taking a lead in the first inning. As the Hoosiers' Paul Hines crossed the plate with the game's first run, Chicago catcher Dell Darling whacked him across the back of the head with his fist in what the Associated Press called "a disgraceful scene." This act outraged the Indianapolis players and fans, and bad blood flowed again in the fifth inning when Marty Sullivan flied out and tangled with Indianapolis third baseman Dude Esterbrook as he ran off the field. Esterbrook punched Sullivan, and Anson charged from the coaching box and pushed Sullivan forward, shouting, "Slug him! Slug him!" The resulting battle brought the local police onto the field, but the cops were met by Anson, who did not stop yelling and arguing until threatened with arrest for inciting a riot. Sullivan and Esterbrook were taken to the police station and released on $25 bail apiece, and though Chicago won the game, Anson received his share of criticism in the papers for days afterward.[9]

The Chicagos played some of the tail-end teams in the first few weeks of the season and won 12 of their first 14 contests. By early May they held first place, until a 20–9 loss to Boston's John Clarkson on May 15 put the Beaneaters and the White Stockings into a tie for the lead. Anson's men then reeled off three wins against the Beaneaters to take first place by three games. Boston dropped out of contention by June, but the defending champion Detroit club and the New York Giants made the pennant race a three-way affair.

The race brought out Cap Anson's superstitious nature, which appeared to go hand-in-hand with his well-documented racism. He believed, as many did then, in jinxes, the "evil eye," and good and bad luck. Baseball, in particular, was rife with such beliefs, perhaps as a result of the pressure to win or from the difficult playing and traveling conditions of the time.

Anson's team, like most National League clubs in that era, employed mascots to bring good luck or to ward off the "hoodoo," or bad luck. "At one time," explained the *St. Louis Globe-Democrat* in 1898, "a team that did not have a mascot was not in it. Captain Comiskey of the old St. Louis Browns and Captain Anson of the old Chicago White Stockings were enthusiasts on the subject. They were firm believers in the ability of a mascot to down a hoodoo. In the halcyon days of both these clubs, each had a mascot who during his regime was looked upon as an omen of good luck and commanded respect of players, managers, and the public."[10]

Mascots were either human or animal in nature. A particular breed, or color, of dog was considered to bring fortune and wins to a ballclub, and the Brooklyn team in 1893 employed a yellow Labrador retriever as its good luck charm. The 1889 Columbus Solons kept a wildcat, while a New

Jersey semipro team carted around a four-foot long alligator for a brief time in the late 1880s. Other teams used human mascots, and red-haired girls and small boys in uniform were considered to be good luck. Brooklyn, in the late 1880s, employed both a red-haired girl and a white horse for luck, and the more superstitious fans believed that team mascots helped the ballclub in their pennant-winning seasons in 1889 and 1890.

In the mid–1880s, Anson's White Stockings kept a boy of about five or six years of age around as a mascot. His name was Willie Hahn, and he caught Anson's notice when he came to the park one day dressed in a miniature uniform. Anson allowed him to mingle with the players during pregame practice, where he charmed Ed Williamson so thoroughly that the tough-as-nails shortstop became the little boy's friend and protector. Willie attended nearly every home game, since his family lived not far from the park, and the White Stockings won their 1886 National League pennant with Willie Hahn as their mascot.

Major league teams utilized mascots as good luck charms well into the 20th century. In the 1920s, Babe Ruth of the Yankees chose a little boy named Ray Kelly as a personal mascot, but the club also employed a hunchback named Eddie Bennett, who let the players touch his hump for luck before they went to bat. Bill Veeck, who worked for the Chicago Cubs in the 1930s, later recalled how team owner Philip Wrigley hired a man to sit in the stands and give the "evil eye" to opposing players. Some teams continued to use small children as their mascots, though other clubs thought that more exotic characters, such as cross-eyed children, midgets, and the like, exerted a greater force against the "hoodoo."

Cap Anson firmly believed in hoodoos, and was in need of a mascot to ward off bad luck during the 1888 season. In early June, the league-leading White Stockings arrived in New York for a four-game series against the third-place Giants, and the superstitious Anson decided to change his luck with a new mascot. He looked over the usual candidates and, despite his oft-expressed contempt for minorities of all stripes, chose one Clarence Duval, an African-American who appears from photographic evidence to have been in his late teens or early twenties. "Clarence was a little darkey that I had met some time before while in Philadelphia," explained Anson in his autobiography. Anson described him as "a singer and dancer of no mean ability, and a little coon whose skill in handling the baton would have put to the blush many a bandmaster of national reputation. I had togged him out in a suit of navy blue with brass buttons, at my own expense, and had engaged him as a mascot."[11]

Anson wanted to impress the Polo Grounds crowd with his first-place ballclub, so he attired his ballplayers in long coats and marched them around the field before the first game of the series against the Giants, with Clarence Duval at the head of the parade. "Like a regular street parading company they came on the field," related the *Brooklyn Eagle* the next day, "attired in their show clothes, the feature of which was black cloth swallow tail coats, and marched abreast, appropriately, by a little uniformed darkey mascot, forsooth, who wielded a drum major's baton in high style; and this is the way the Chicago Club has lowered its crack team of ball players down to the level of a street circus show."[12]

The new mascot did not bring any luck to Anson that day. The White Stockings lost the first game of the series by a 19–2 score, and the loss dropped their lead to two games over Detroit and three games over the Giants. Chicago won the next three games, however, and opened up some breathing room in the league race. Anson began to think that perhaps Duval was a good luck charm after all. He made plans to take Duval to Boston, the next stop on the month-long road trip.

Duval had other ideas. "He was an ungrateful little rascal, however," stated Anson years later, "and deserted me for Mlle. Jarbeau, the actress, at New York, stage life evidently holding out more attractions for him than life on the diamond."[13] Perhaps theatrical people, like ballplayers, needed mascots to ward off jinxes and hoodoos. It was considered especially poor luck for a mascot to desert his team, and the White Stockings lost three of their next five games against Boston and Pittsburgh.

With strong but inconsistent hitting, and mediocre starting pitching, the White Stockings fell out of first place in late June and never managed to regain the lead. A skid of eight losses in nine games dropped the Chicagos to third place behind Detroit and New York. The only Chicago win in this streak was a wild 21–17 affair against the Wolverines, in which Jimmy Ryan belted two triples and two singles and pitched the last seven innings in relief of Mark Baldwin. Ryan developed into a star in 1888, but with Pfeffer, Burns, Williamson, and Sullivan all hitting at .250 or below, Ryan and Anson were the only consistent performers in the Chicago lineup.

Anson might have improved the Chicago hitting attack with a future Hall of Famer sitting on his own bench. Hugh Duffy was a 22-year-old Irishman from Rhode Island who batted .380 for Lowell in the New England League in 1887. The Boston Beaneaters of the National League had offered him a contract for $2,600 a year, but Duffy so admired Cap Anson that he told *Boston Globe* sports editor Tim Murnane, an old Philadelphia teammate of Anson, that he would play for Chicago for $600 less. Murnane arranged the deal, and Duffy reported to spring training with the White Stockings.

Duffy was a strong young man with broad shoulders, but stood only five feet and seven inches tall. Anson expressed disappointment when he finally met his new recruit. "Duffy," intoned the captain, "you fall about five inches and 25 pounds short of the major league size."[14]

"Signing with Chicago and playing with Chicago were two different things, I discovered," said Duffy many years later. "This has been found out by many a player since. Anson liked big men. I wasn't big."[15] Duffy made the team, possibly at Spalding's insistence, but Anson kept him on the bench for more than two months. Duffy did not get into a game until June 23, when he played right field and hit two singles in a 10–1 win over Pittsburgh, but he played sporadically for several weeks thereafter while Sullivan, Pettit, and Farrell shared left and right field.

The Giants took over first place on July 31, and strengthened their lead in August as Anson's frustration grew with what the *Sporting News* called his "slightly spavined Colts." During one game against Detroit, he pulled Mark Baldwin out in the middle of an inning, his anger at the pitcher so noticeable that it elicited boos from the Chicago fans. The papers criticized the Chicago hitting attack, despite the fact that the team led the National League once again in runs scored. One paper charged that the batters swung too wildly at the ball, "producing a series of atmospheric waves that will undoubtedly have a marked effect upon the weather." Jimmy Ryan led the league with a batting average in the .330s, but Anson still struggled below the .300 mark in late August, putting his streak of 16 consecutive .300 seasons in jeopardy.

When the White Stockings traveled to New York to battle the Giants, the games at the Polo Grounds attracted a sizeable contingent of actors, singers, and musicians. Baseball held an appeal for the denizens of the show business world, since ballplayers plied their trade in the afternoon and entertainers performed at night. During the 1880s, many stage actors and other performers became well acquainted with baseball figures, including Cap Anson. The captain found that he enjoyed dressing in formal wear, hobnobbing in a world different than his own, and during this time he established numerous friendships among theater folk.

Digby Bell and DeWolf Hopper, two popular young actor-comedians with the McCaull Opera Company, were friends of Cap Anson who counted themselves among the most rabid baseball fans in the New York theater community. In August of 1888, when the White Stockings came to New York for a series, they persuaded opera manager John McCaull to sponsor a day at the ballpark for the members of the company, followed by a special performance that evening for the New York and Chicago teams. The opera people attended the game between the White Stockings and the Giants at the Polo Grounds on August 14, which was won by Anson's men by a score of 4 to 2. The game brought Chicago one game closer to the league lead, and ended the record-setting 19-game winning streak of Giants pitcher Tim Keefe.

That evening, Anson and his White Stockings decked themselves out in black tie and arrived at the Warrick Theater shortly before the Giants, led by captain John Ward, made their entrance to the applause of the crowd. As the White Stockings and Giants took their seats on opposite sides of the theater, DeWolf Hopper searched for a baseball-related monologue to perform for the assembled players. He found what he was looking for when his friend, novelist William Gunter, handed Hopper a clipping from a San Francisco newspaper. It was a poem, 13 stanzas in length, titled "Casey at the Bat."[16] Related Hopper years later, "I looked at it and I nearly fainted. If 'Casey' is anything, it is a mile long."

Hopper committed the poem to memory in only one hour. A prompter stood close by in the wings, but the young actor did not require assistance. Hopper commanded attention from the first line of his recitation, and acted out the story of Mighty Casey at the plate with the bases loaded and his Mudville team down by one in front of a rapt crowd. Hopper, in his memoirs, described the scene. "When I dropped my voice to B flat, below low C, at 'but one scornful look from Casey, and the audience was awed,' I remember seeing [Giants catcher] Buck Ewing's gallant mustachios give a single nervous twitch."

All expected Mighty Casey to deliver the game-winning hit, but author Ernest Lawrence Thayer had other ideas. The final words of the poem, "Mighty Casey has struck out," stunned Anson and the rest of the crowd. "And as the house, after a moment of startled silence, grasped the anticlimactic denouement," said Hopper, "it shouted its glee. They had expected, as any one does on hearing Casey for the first time, that the mighty batsman would slam the ball out of the lot, and a lesser bard would have had him do so."[17] By coincidence, the final score of the Mudville game was 4 to 2, the same as that of the White Stockings–Giants contest that had concluded a few hours before.

"Casey at the Bat" became an unforgettable part of baseball lore and made DeWolf Hopper a star. Hopper recited the piece more than 10,000 times during his long stage career, but no audience ever reacted as enthusiastically as did Cap Anson and the other ballplayers who were the first to hear the now-famous poem.

The White Stockings departed New York four games behind the Giants and fading fast. Al Spalding, who wanted to bill his ballclub as the champions of the National League on the upcoming overseas tour, increased pressure on Anson and the team, but some of the older players resented the stress. Ed Williamson was sidelined in late August with a boil on his elbow that left him unable to throw, but Anson, fighting desperately to climb back into the race, demanded that the shortstop play anyway. He had tried to fill Williamson's place with Duffy, who made three errors in two losses to Pittsburgh, and the captain ordered Williamson back into the lineup despite the injury. On August 30 the resentful Williamson arrived late for a game at Indianapolis, drawing a $25 fine from his angry captain. Anson was "as cross as a bear with a sore head," stated *The Sporting News*, and his mood darkened as the Chicago club fell further out of the race.

Anson refused to concede, and offered tryouts to several new pitchers as the season wound down. One was Addison (Ad) Gumbert, who joined the team after posting a 27–9 record at Zanesville of the Tri-State League. He was a finesse pitcher, with good control and a mediocre fastball, but showed enough talent to earn an invitation to spring training in 1889. Another new man was the Irish-born John Tener, a righthanded pitcher from the college ranks who overcame a disastrous debut (a 14–0 thrashing by the Indianapolis Hoosiers) and compiled a 7–5 record in the late stages of the season. Tener had worked in the business world as a bookkeeper, and his intelligence impressed Anson and Spalding, who offered him a position as pitcher and treasurer of the overseas tour.

The most important signing came in mid–September when Anson landed the most sought-after player in the nation. Bill Hutchison, a 28-year-old righthander, was a Yale graduate who used his remarkable fastball to pitch the Elis to the national college title in 1880. He then gave up baseball for an executive position in the lumber business. For the next several years he declined all offers to pitch in the professional ranks, save for a two-game stint with the Kansas City team in the Union Association in 1884. Hutchison pitched amateur ball on the weekends until he finally relented and joined the Des Moines club of the Western League, posting a 26–10 record in 1887 and a 23–10 mark in 1888. Anson had been trying to land the fastballer for years, as had every other major league manager, and Hutchison's signing represented a major victory for Anson and the White Stockings.

The Giants, who coasted to the pennant in September, received a taste of Anson's win-at-all-costs spirit when they arrived in Chicago for a four-game series. In the second game, the White Stockings led by an 8–2 score in the fifth inning when Giants catcher Buck Ewing declared that he was injured and unable to continue. The Giants wanted to replace Ewing behind the bat, but Anson, as usual, refused to give permission for a substitution. "That won't do, sir; that won't do," bellowed Anson to the umpire.

"I can't stand that." The Giants had been belting the pitches of Tim Keefe all day, and Anson suspected that Ewing wanted to replace himself at catcher and then move his replacement to the mound in relief of Keefe. The captain also thought that Ewing wanted to save himself for the next two games of the series, so Anson loudly refused to let Ewing leave the game. The Giants then angrily stalked from the field, giving the game to the White Stockings by forfeit. The Chicago fans booed lustily, but since the White Stockings received credit for a win, Anson regarded the day as a success.

The White Stockings ended the 1888 season in second place, nine games behind the pennant-winning Giants, and the campaign closed ignominiously with a forfeit loss. On October 13, a rainy Saturday in Philadelphia, Anson gazed out of his hotel room window early in the afternoon and decided that there was no chance his team would be required to play that day. The rain came down steadily for an hour, but when the skies cleared at 3:30 that afternoon, more than 1,500 people showed up at the Philadelphia ballpark expecting to see the final game of the season. Harry Wright brought his Phillies to the park, but Anson and his White Stockings were nowhere to be found. The umpire forfeited the game to the Phillies, who took sole possession of third place in the standings with the win.

Anson blamed his team's second-place finish on "inexperienced pitchers," and he was probably correct in his assessment. The 1886 White Stockings used only three starting pitchers all season long, but the 1888 ballclub gave starting assignments to 11 different men, which indicated that the absence of John Clarkson may have been the single biggest factor in the failure of Anson's crew to win the pennant. Gus Krock did his part, winning 25 games and completing all of his 39 starts, but Mark Baldwin fell to a 13–15 record and George Van Haltren stood at 13–13 despite a 6-inning no-hitter against Pittsburgh on June 21. However, the Chicago starting rotation looked promising for 1889. With Hutchison, Baldwin, Gumbert, Krock, and Tener competing for berths on the pitching staff, Anson could move the hard-hitting George Van Haltren to the outfield on a permanent basis.

On an individual level, Cap Anson enjoyed a fine season in 1888. He went on a hitting tear in the last five weeks of the season, pushing his batting average up to .344 and winning his fourth batting title over his young outfielder Jimmy Ryan, who finished at .332. Anson also led the league in runs batted in for the seventh time and nipped Detroit's Dan Brouthers for the best on-base percentage in the National League. Though Anson's defensive play at first base was sometimes ridiculed, he led the league for the first time since 1881 in fielding percentage at his position. The captain was now one of the ten oldest players in the National League, but was still one of its most reliable performers at the age of 36.

The White Stockings were disappointed in their second-place finish, but had little time to dwell on the matter. Immediately after the close of the season, Anson and his players returned to Chicago to prepare for the post-season trip to Australia. On October 20, 1888, a special train consisting of two Pullman sleepers and a dining car carried Anson and his men on the first leg of a journey that Henry Chadwick called "the greatest historical event recorded in the annals of the national game."[18]

CHAPTER 14

Around the World

On the field [Anson] is always the most conspicuous figure. Active and alert, gruff in his commands, something of a bully towards his men, a chronic objector and browbeater of the umpire, crowds everywhere guy him unmercifully for his tactics, which are, in fact, often harsh and offensive. But these things are all part of his peculiar generalship.
— Harry Palmer, 1888[1]

The White Stockings would be challenged on the Australia trip by the "All Americas," an all-star aggregation of players who mostly came from the other seven National League teams. There were many interested candidates for the 10 slots on the All America team, but, as Spalding later stated, "it was absolutely essential that all ... should be men of clean habits and attractive personality, men who would reflect credit upon the country and the game." Spalding handpicked the players, rather than ask for volunteers, as he wanted to avoid "a deluge of applications from undesirable players in the fraternity."

Anson and Spalding selected ten Chicago White Stockings and ten All Americas to make the trip, with each team carrying a starting nine and one extra pitcher. The Chicago squad consisted of catcher Tom Daly, pitchers Mark Baldwin and John Tener (with Tener serving extra duty as treasurer of the tour), the entire Stonewall Infield of Anson, Pfeffer, Williamson, and Burns, and an outfield consisting of Marty Sullivan, Jimmy Ryan, and Bob Pettit.

The All America roster, captained by New York Giants shortstop John Ward, was much more unsettled, with men coming and going as the months passed, but by October Ward's lineup was complete. It consisted of John Healy of Indianapolis and Ed Crane of New York on the mound, and an infield that included George Wood of Philadelphia, Fred Carroll of Pittsburgh, Ward, and Jim Manning of Kansas City. Billy Sunday, the perfect example of "clean habits and attractive personality" as far as Spalding was concerned, suffered a leg injury late in the 1888 season and declined Spalding's offer, while Mike Kelly agreed to join the tour but changed his mind at the last moment. Spalding signed Kelly's Boston teammate Tom Brown to play right field, with Ned Hanlon of Pittsburgh in center and Jim Fogerty of the Phillies in left, and extracted a promise from Kelly to join the All Americas later that month.

In late September, while the White Stockings played a series at Washington, Chicago congressman Frank Lawler arranged for Anson's ballclub to visit President Grover Cleveland at the White House. The President was locked in a close re-election race against the Republican presidential nominee Benjamin Harrison, but agreed to take a few minutes out of his schedule to greet Anson and his men. No doubt Anson passed the word to his charges that he would tolerate no shenanigans, such as the painfully firm handshakes given to the President by Mike Kelly and others during their last visit to the White House two years earlier. Fortunately, most of the troublemakers from the 1886 team were long gone from the White Stockings, and the players were all on their best behavior.

Congressman Lawler, like Cleveland a Democrat, introduced the ballplayers. "Mr. President," he said, "allow me to introduce to you the members of the Chicago baseball club, which will shortly sail for Australia to introduce the game of baseball in that country. They have won the pennant six times out of twelve, and New York being a doubtful State, and the New York team in doubt as to winning the pennant, they dropped a game to them just to make sure."

The President laughed. "Captain Anson, don't do that way in Australia," he said.

The Chicago players meet President Grover Cleveland. (Transcendental Graphics)

Anson introduced each of his men, and then addressed the chief executive. "Mr. President," said the captain, "we will shortly sail for Australia for the purpose of introducing the national game in that country, and we will have a team to be known as the All-America team, composed as a representative from each of the League teams in America. I would like to ask as a favor that you will give us a letter indorsing the game of baseball as the national sport of this country. Such a letter would give us standing in Australia and would be of great benefit to us."

President Cleveland replied that he would look into the matter and draft the letter if he found it the proper thing to do. As the teams left the White House, the congressman said, "By the way, Mr. President, all these boys are good Democrats."

"Then they can't be beaten," replied President Cleveland, and the meeting was over.[2]

A gaggle of relatives and friends accompanied the party. Cap Anson did not want his wife to miss the traveling experience of a lifetime, so Virginia left 11-year-old Grace and four-year-old Adele in the care of relatives and accompanied her husband on the trip. Spalding's wife stayed home, but the club president's elderly mother joined the travelers, as did Ed Williamson's wife. Three reporters, two from New York and one from Chicago, accompanied the ballplayers, as did former shortstop George Wright, a veteran of the 1874 trip to England, who served as umpire for most of the contests. Digby Bell, DeWolf Hopper, and several of Anson's other friends from the New York theater community made plans to travel with the ballplayers until the tour reached California.

The two teams were due to arrive in San Francisco on November 18, when they would board a steamship for the Hawaiian Islands. During the preceding four weeks, the teams played 23 exhibition games, 17 between each other and six with local minor league teams, on the trip west. Spalding planned these contests as a way to take in some money early in the trip to defray the expenses involved in overseas travel, and as a hedge against a lukewarm reception in Hawaii and Australia. He also hired a daredevil balloonist named Professor Bartholomew as an added attraction. The Professor caused a sensation everywhere he went as he ascended to the skies in his hot-air balloon and then leaped from it, landing safely on earth using a primitive parachute of his own design. If people could not be induced to pay to watch baseball, reasoned Spalding, perhaps they would pay to see the death-defying feats of Professor Bartholomew.

President Cleveland did not send the letter of introduction that Anson requested, much to the captain's disappointment, but Spalding expressed confidence in the venture. "It was known that many baseball lovers lived in the Hawaiian Islands," wrote Spalding in 1911, and that the British colonies "were nearly all devotees of field sports, for they had a racial love of outdoor games and enjoyed a climate that made their playing possible nearly the entire year."[3]

The first game of the tour took place in Chicago on October 20, and although John Ward was not yet present (he was due to join the party a week later), more than 5,000 Chicago fans saw Al Spalding take the mound for the first time in almost ten years. He faced Bill Hutchison, the recently signed fireballer whom Anson lent to the All Americas for the occasion, and Spalding pitched the White Stockings to an 11–6 win. Following the game, the teams decamped to the train station, boarded a banner-decked Chicago, Burlington, and Quincy train, and left Chicago for the first leg of the trip. The next stop was St. Paul, Minnesota, where Spalding owned a branch store of his growing sporting goods empire. Mike Kelly was expected to catch for John Ward's ballclub, but when he failed to appear, Anson pressed Silver Flint into service behind the plate. Chicago defeated the All Americas, but lost to the local minor league team later that same afternoon. The next day, Anson's men lost to the All Americas before polishing off St. Paul with a 1–0 shutout win by Mark Baldwin.

Cap Anson had invited his father Henry to travel abroad with him, but the 62-year-old patriarch of Marshalltown decided that he was unable to spare the time away from his business interests. The "old gentleman," however, boarded the train when it passed through Marshalltown on its way west, and Henry remained with the travelers for the American leg of the trip. He played cards with the ballplayers, who found the captain's father a genial and engaging soul, and Henry Anson thoroughly enjoyed himself in the company of his son's charges. Another familiar face on the train was that of Hiram Waldo, the Rockford businessman who had served as president of the Forest Citys back in 1871 when the teenaged Anson played for them. "Uncle Hi" was an important influence in the lives of Anson and Spalding, both of whom began their baseball careers in Rockford, and Spalding was pleased to host his old friend and mentor.

The train took on one more unexpected passenger as it passed through Nebraska. Anson had not planned to bring a mascot on the trip, but the captain's former good-luck charm, Clarence Duval, caught up with the group in Omaha on October 25. When the teams played in Hastings, Nebraska, the following afternoon, Duval assumed his place at the head of the parade of players and gave a show for the crowd. Though Anson ordered Duval to leave ("we had no use for deserters in our business," said the captain), the players wanted to keep him around. They convinced Anson and Spalding to bring the mascot along to Australia, and Anson made Duval prom-

Actors and ballplayers on the American leg of the world tour. Mascot Clarence Duval, in a drum major's hat, sits in front of Anson. (Author's collection)

ise not to desert the team as he had in New York several months before. "To my astonishment," recalled Anson years later, "he kept his word, remaining with us all through the trip and returning with us to Chicago. Outside of his dancing and his power of mimicry he was, however, a 'no account nigger,' and more than once did I wish that he had been left behind."[4] Anson's view of minorities in general, and Duval in particular, wavered not a bit throughout his life.

John Ward and Ed Crane joined the tour at Oxford, Nebraska, after the pennant-winning Giants defeated the St. Louis Browns in the World's Series, and when Mike Kelly failed to appear in Denver as promised, Anson signed catcher-outfielder Billy Earle of the Cincinnati Reds as his replacement. The rosters were now set, though a few extra men (including Chicago's Bill Hutchison and George Van Haltren) were available to play for the All Americas during the exhibition tour of the western states. The teams split two games before good crowds in Denver, and played their way through Colorado Springs and Salt Lake City before arriving in San Francisco on November 4 for a two-week stay.

Anson was eager to show the world to Virginia, and was determined to take in all of the sights of San Francisco, good and bad. The Ansons were

14. AROUND THE WORLD

both repelled and fascinated by Chinatown, where they experienced the "squalor and misery" of the opium dens in the company of a local tour guide. Chinatown was "a blot on the fair name of San Francisco," judged the captain, and the couple spent the remainder of their time in the city in search of less exotic points of interest. Ward enjoyed Chinatown even less, suggesting that those who visited the place would eagerly favor the exclusion of the Chinese from America.

Some players discovered their own entertainment in San Francisco, much to the detriment of their ballplaying. John Ward and Ned Hanlon arrived an hour late for one game; they had been out bird hunting that morning, where they found the game "as thick as crickets," explained Ward, and they simply could not pass on such an opportunity. A few of the All Americas may have been drinking too much as well, since Ward later wrote of the players and their "Order of the Howling Wolves," which were led by unidentified "untamed spirits" best left to the reader's imagination. After the All Americas lost two games to local minor league clubs, one San Francisco paper complained, "Spalding and his players have not done much for baseball on their visit to this city; the two clubs have played several games, and in but one have they put up the variety of ball they are capable of doing.... Ball-players cannot train on late hours and alcohol and win."[5]

The All Americas played poorly in California, and Spalding worried about their lack of enthusiasm. Spalding had offered a $1,000 bonus to the team that won the most games on the tour, but he and Anson feared that the members of both ballclubs had paired off and arranged to split their winnings, following a common practice of the time. Reportedly, all the White Stockings except Anson had made such agreements with the St. Louis Browns during the 1885 and 1886 post-season championship matches, and the quality of play suffered noticeably. Spalding soon modified the terms of the bonus and gave each winning team $55 immediately upon the conclusion of each contest. This payment, hoped the team president, would provide an incentive for each side to play its best.

Anson made sure that his White Stockings played as hard as ever, but all was not well with the captain of the Chicagos. Ward, an educated and literate sort, had written an article for the October 1888 issue of *Cosmopolitan* magazine that criticized Anson for his on-field tactics. Stated Ward:

> [Anson] is not one of your senseless kickers who finds fault merely because he is being beaten ... it is true, however, that he will go to the outside limit of the rule every time, and, while his claims may be legitimate so far as the rule is concerned, they are not always in accord with a

sense of fair play [and] he will occasionally stoop to certain questionable tricks upon the field and encourage these in his men.[6]

Anson was certainly aware of the article, and it undoubtedly caused some tension between the two captains. Ward also remarked several times during the trip that he could take his All America aggregation and beat any team in the National League with it, including Anson's White Stocking club. Anson, still smarting from his second-place finish in the 1888 pennant race, replied forcefully that his Chicago ballclub would beat all comers, including the pennant-winning Giants, in 1889. Ward's boasting and Anson's angry retorts put a chill in their relationship.

Anson also developed a strong dislike for Jim Hart, the former Louisville manager whom Spalding hired as business manager for the American leg of the tour. Hart, an open and gregarious sort (a "first-class talker," according to *The Sporting News*), had gained the trust and friendship of Spalding, to the dismay of Anson, who dismissed Hart as an incompetent back-slapper. Hart had finished in fifth and fourth place in his two seasons as Louisville skipper while Anson was winning pennants, and the captain failed to understand why Spalding would place his confidence in such a man. Nonetheless, Spalding was impressed with Hart's work, and reports state that the gate receipts for the American exhibition games totaled $17,000, a sum that was $7,000 more than Spalding had anticipated.

When Spalding took up a collection among the players to buy Hart a pair of diamond cufflinks as a thank-you gift for his efforts, only Anson declined to make a contribution. "Just why Mr. Hart should be made the recipient of a valuable gift under such circumstances was more than I could fathom," remarked Anson years later. Anson's refusal became "the little acorn" that grew into "the oak of disagreement between James Hart and myself," stated the captain, and that disagreement would prove to have serious ramifications for Anson in the future.

As the date of departure for Hawaii neared, Spalding made a stunning announcement to the players on both teams. His advance man, a theatrical promoter named Leigh S. Lynch, had been busily making arrangements for baseball and cricket contests in Australia, but also had orders from Spalding to seek opportunities in other lands. On November 16, two days before their embarkation from San Francisco, Spalding informed the travelers that the tour might not merely visit Down Under and sail for home. It was possible, said Spalding, that the tour might proceed from Australia to Ceylon, to India, to the Pyramids of Egypt, and then to Italy, France, and England. Nothing was yet official, but the proposed extension of the tour met with unanimous approval from Anson, Ward, and their charges.

They were excited by the opportunity to be the first group of professional ballplayers to take the game of baseball around the world. On November 18, the players boarded the steamship *Alameda* and set off on their round-the-world adventure.

The first disappointment of the tour occurred in Hawaii. A game had been scheduled in Honolulu on Saturday, November 24, but the ship failed to make good time, and sailed into the harbor on Sunday morning. The Hawaiian ruler, King Kalakaua (Hawaii was an independent nation at that time) gave a feast for the players, but since Hawaii's blue laws were every bit as strict as those in the United States, the teams were not allowed to play on Sunday. Spalding agreed to abide by the local laws, though he lamented the loss of income that a game would have provided. The Hawaiians had raised a guarantee of $1,000 for the contest, which Spalding reluctantly forfeited.

The King, whom Anson claimed had "drunk himself into a stupor" when the teams failed to arrive on Saturday, nonetheless rolled out the red carpet for his visitors. The two teams presented themselves to the King, with Clarence Duval at the head of the line, and the ruler was fascinated by the dark-skinned mascot. King Kalakaua gave Duval a $10 gold piece for his dancing prowess, which was the only money that the Spalding tour managed to earn in the Hawaiian Islands.

The Americans would have preferred to spend another day in Hawaii, but the schedule was tight, and the ship left Honolulu that Monday morning, bound for New Zealand. Fourteen days later, the travelers landed in Auckland, where the All Americas won a sloppily played game by a 22–13 score in front of 4,500 people. Another four-day cruise carried the travelers to Sydney, Australia on the evening of December 14.

The Australians gave their visitors a rousing welcome. Large crowds lined the streets, cheering the ballplayers as they left the ship and proceeded to their hotel. The next afternoon, the first baseball game played in Australia by professional teams drew more than 5,500 curious fans, though many of them were probably more interested in seeing Professor Bartholomew jump from his balloon. The only disappointment for Anson came when the All Americas won all three contests held in Sydney. The all-star aggregation also trounced Anson's men in a cricket match by a score of 67–33. It was a one-inning game in which Anson, in his only turn at bat, popped out on the first pitch and scored no runs.

The Australian newspapers could not help but remark upon the impressive physical appearance of the Americans, in direct contrast to Australia's stout and weighty cricketers. "Right worthy of welcome did those visitors appear," stated the *Melbourne Argus*, "stalwarts every man, lumps of muscle showing beneath their tight fitting jersey garments, and a springiness in every movement which denoted grand animal vigor and the perfection of condition. We could not pick eighteen such men from the ranks of all our cricketers, and it is doubtful if we could beat them by a draft from the foot ballers. If base ball has anything to do with building up such physique we ought to encourage it, for it must evidently be above and beyond all other exercises in one at least of the essentials of true athletics."[7]

"If this is the result of cricket and that of base ball," remarked one spectator, "it is time we burned our bats and stumps and got out a consignment of clubs and bases."

The Americans were less successful on the cricket field. On December 18 they played a one-inning match against a team from Sydney, with 18 Americans battling a group of 11 Aussies. The match started well when Cap Anson, the leadoff striker for the Americans, tallied 15 runs. Fred Pfeffer, Jim Manning, and George Wright also reached double figures, but nine other Americans, including Al Spalding, were shut out as the visitors posted a score of 81 runs. The Australians then came to bat with Billy Earle bowling for the Americans.

Earle retired the first batter and was then replaced by Anson, who gave up 44 runs to the next three strikers before yielding the bowler's position to Earle and, later, to Wright. Only seven strikers went to bat for the home team, but their superiority resulted in a 115–81 victory, a score that would have been much greater if all 11 Australians had taken their turn at the wicket.

A crowd of more than 10,000 watched Anson's Chicago club defeat the All Americas at Melbourne, though Professor Bartholomew certainly helped swell the size of the crowd, and the All Americas returned the favor two days later with a 15–13 win on Christmas Eve. The Americans then took a train to Adelaide for three games, where Chicago won two of three before enthusiastic crowds. The *Adelaide Advertiser* remarked, "Not a single possible catch was missed.... The throwing too, was brilliant and in these two points the visitors set a lesson for the majority of cricketers. It was a treat to see the ball sent swiftly and unerringly from man to man as the occasion required."

In Ballarat, an inland gold-mining center, Professor Bartholomew met with near disaster. He jumped from his balloon, but the parachute did not open completely, and he slammed into the cornice of a building and injured himself seriously enough to land in a hospital for a month. The Professor's tour of Australia was over, but the ballplayers played on, returning to Melbourne for a New Year's Day doubleheader that was swept by the Chicagos. On January 5, more than 11,000 people saw the tourists' last game in Australia, a four-inning 5–0 shutout by Mark Baldwin that gave Anson's team a split of the 12 games played in Australia. Three days later, the teams boarded the German steamship *Salier*, bound for Colombo, the capital of Ceylon (now called Sri Lanka).

The voyage across the Indian Ocean was no picnic. The crew spoke only German, which suited second baseman Fred Pfeffer but proved frustrating for the rest of the party. High waves induced seasickness for almost all of the passengers. The ballplayers amused themselves by playing cards, shooting dice, and tormenting Clarence Duval. After one difficult night at sea, the men put Duval on trial and sentenced him to take a bath, despite the mascot's loud objections. "A madder little coon than he was when released," remarked Anson later, "it would be difficult to find." It appears that the ballplayers treated Duval in the same manner that Cap Anson treated the local Indians during his childhood in Marshalltown.

The ship docked in Colombo on January 25, and a five-inning game took place that afternoon on the local cricket grounds before 4,500 Englishmen and Ceylonese. Spalding had hoped to travel next to Calcutta, but reports of disease reached the tour and canceled the planned visit. Instead, the *Salier* left port the next morning and headed for Egypt. The most interesting feature of Colombo, at least to Spalding, was the sight of rickshaw drivers ferrying passengers around the city. Spalding was so fascinated by the vehicles that he wondered aloud if such a conveyance would work on the streets of New York and Chicago.

Fortunately, the trip from Colombo to the Arabian Peninsula took place in better weather and calm seas, but tour promoter Leigh Lynch and outfielder Jim Fogarty managed to pull a practical joke that frightened the other passengers, especially Anson. On the second day out of Colombo, the crew of the *Salier* discharged several guns in the early morning hours as a birthday salute to the German emperor, Kaiser Wilhelm II. Fogarty and Lynch then screamed "Pirates! Chinese pirates!" at the top of their lungs and threw the entire ship into a panic. Pitcher John Tener, the tour treasurer, gathered the moneybags and locked himself in his room, while Anson, so the story goes, picked up a bat and made ready for the pirate invasion.

"They say that I filled my mouth with Mrs. Anson's diamonds," said Anson years later, "grabbed a baseball bat and stood guard at the doorway, ordering my wife to crawl under the bunk, but that statement is a libel and one that I have been waiting for years to deny. I only got up to see what a Chinese pirate looked like, that's all."[8] Before long, the travelers realized that they had been fooled, and, as Anson said, "I would have been willing myself, that morning, to have been one of a party to help hang Fogarty at the yardarm."

The *Salier* journeyed up the Red Sea, landing in Suez ("the dirtiest place on God's green footstool," sniffed Anson), and the party then boarded a train for Cairo, where crowds of natives swarmed around the Americans, much to Anson's displeasure. He even managed to find fault with the women in the "motley crowds." They were "veiled to the eyes," remarked Anson, "a fact for which we probably had reason to be devoutly grateful, if we but knew it, as there was nothing in their shapeless figures to indicate any hidden beauty."[9] African-Americans were not the only minority who found disfavor in the captain's eyes.

The players alighted from the train and fought their way through the crowds to their hotel, and on the following afternoon rode camels and donkeys to Giza, where George Wright laid out a baseball diamond in the hard sand near the Sphinx and the pyramids. The travelers played on this field in front of a crowd of uncomprehending natives, with the All Americas taking a 10–6 win, "for which I apologized to the Sphinx on behalf of my team after the game was over," said Anson. The players then took turns throwing baseballs at the eyes of the 4,200-year-old sacred statue, after which the entire party climbed onto the Sphinx for a photograph, much to the horror of the natives. Neither Anson nor Spalding appeared concerned about offending the sensibilities of the Egyptians, though perhaps most Western tourists in that era would have behaved in a similar fashion. Nonetheless, the Egyptian leg of the trip represented a low point in cultural relations between the American tourists and their foreign hosts.

After a rough steamship ride across the Mediterranean to Italy, the tourists played a single game in Naples on February 19, which drew a large crowd but ended badly when Anson instigated the biggest argument of the tour. The fans swarmed the field after a foul ball knocked a small boy unconscious, and in the fifth inning, with the All-Americas leading by a score of 8 to 2, Anson demanded the cancellation of the contest. John Tener, who served as umpire that day, denied Anson's request, so the captain stormed off the field and ordered his men to return to their hotel. Tener forfeited the game to the All-Americas, who were the "maddest lot of players that ever left a field," according to Ward, who declared that he would not play another game on the trip. Spalding acted quickly to smooth over the controversy and save the remainder of the tour, but the incident heightened the tension between Anson and Ward.

Rome was a major disappointment. Spalding tried, and failed, to gain an audience with Pope Leo XIII, and when he asked for permission to play a game in the 1,800-year-old Colosseum, the Italian authorities turned him down. Even an offer of $5,000 in cash did not sway the local officials, and some of the Americans chose to view the incident as a "gratuitous insult."

Had Spalding bothered to check into the matter, he might have discovered that the elliptical Colosseum arena measured only 246 feet long and 144 feet wide, which would have been much too small to hold a baseball, or even a softball, field. Also, the floor of the arena was a wooden platform that stood above an underground level of dressing rooms and holding pens, and was ravaged by nearly two millennia of war, neglect, and earthquakes. In 1889, the debris-strewn floor of the Colosseum was in no condition to host a game of any kind. The travelers changed plans and played at the Villa Borghese outside of Rome, where Chicago won by a 3–2 score before King Umberto and many other dignitaries.

Anson, Spalding, and the baseball tourists on the Sphinx, February 1889. (Transcendental Graphics)

After a game in Florence, in which Anson caught, the tour passed through Nice and Monte Carlo before arriving in Paris on March 3. The French were singularly indifferent to the game, and although the players and their wives were charmed by the capital, Spalding regarded the country as a poor potential market for sporting goods from Spalding and Brothers. "The Frenchman," stated the *New York Herald*, "is as unlikely as the Italian to become interested in baseball. He is too impatient and impulsive to ever undertake that study of the game that is necessary." The game attracted fans from the American expatriate community, but, as Spalding later recalled, "the Parisians did not seem to catch on to any appreciable extent."

Anson, who appreciated "the many kindnesses that were showered on us during the time that we remained in the French capital," was likewise unimpressed with the French. Recalled Anson in his autobiography:

> As a business man the Parisian is not a decided success when viewed from the American standpoint, but as a butterfly in pursuit of pleasure he cannot be beaten. He is polite and courteous at all times, however, but is not to be trusted when making a trade, he having learned to look upon all Americans with money as his natural and legitimate prey, and so is prepared to take advantage of you and yours whenever the opportunity is given him.[10]

The game in Paris, played at the Parc Aristotique on March 8, was the scene of the worst injury of the tour. Ed Williamson slid into second base on a steal attempt in the second inning and tore up his knee on the cinder infield. He did not play again on the trip, and the knee became so badly infected that when the tourists crossed the Channel and arrived in England on March 10, Williamson went directly to a hospital, remaining there for nearly a month. Anson replaced Williamson, whom he described as being "always a tower of strength to us," by moving Ryan to shortstop and pitcher Mark Baldwin to first, with Anson behind the plate. This multiple shifting weakened the Chicago defense and helped the All-Americas to a 6–2 win.

The travelers had looked forward to an easy trip across the English Channel after their previous misadventures on the Indian Ocean, but the passage to England was one of the roughest parts of the tour. A violent storm, the worst on the Channel in years, tossed the boat around like a cork on the water. "Up and down, down and up," recalled Anson, "all night long ... as helpless as logs we lay in our staterooms, not much caring whether the next plunge made by the ship was to be the last or not." One wave carried away the bridge of the ship, but the craft managed to limp into New Haven the next morning, with the seasick ballplayers and tourists grateful for a safe landing. The players were scheduled to play their first contest at Bristol on the day of their arrival, but the storm flooded the grounds, causing the match to be postponed. That was fine with Anson, who remarked, "There was not one of the party who could have hit a balloon after the experience of the night before."[11]

With the Bristol match on hold, the tourists played their first game in London, at the Kensington Oval on Lord's Grounds, on March 13. This was the scene of the famous cricket match of 14 years earlier, where Spalding led the Americans to a win over the British. Now, the baseball players would have the field all to themselves, and, in an added coup, the Prince of Wales made arrangements to attend the match. Though John Ward left the tour and set sail for home immediately upon landing in England, Spalding was determined to put on a first-class game for the heir to the British throne.

The game was played in a typical British chill and fog, but more than 5,000 Londoners came to see the match. When the Prince appeared and took his seat in the royal box, the umpire stopped the game and Anson led the American ballplayers in three cheers for the royal visitor. The Prince bowed to the crowd and the game resumed.

The people of London were polite, but their opinion of America's national game had changed not a bit in the 14 years since the previous tour. The press praised the fielding and throwing skill of the Americans, but complained about the dominance of the pitcher and the difficulty involved in hitting the ball fairly. "The pitcher seems to have it all his own way," complained one paper, noting that "there is an extraordinary amount of 'work' on the ball. The result is that the unfortunate batsman, be he ever so skillful, makes but a lame and feeble display ... the odds against him are so great that our English love of fair play is offended.... For this reason, baseball will never be popular in England."[12]

The Prince of Wales shared that view. Spalding sat with him during the game at Kensington Oval, patiently explaining the finer points of strategy and the rules of the game, and the prince appeared quite interested in the sport. Spalding later recalled that the prince let out an enthusiastic cheer when Anson belted a triple and slid into third base early in the contest. At game's end, a reporter asked the prince for his impressions of the American sport, which the heir wrote on a card and showed to Spalding. "I consider Base Ball an excellent game," wrote the future King Edward VII, "but Cricket [is] a better one."[13]

The tour left London (after a stopover in Bristol to play the delayed match) and proceeded through Birmingham, Sheffield, and Bradford before arriving in Glasgow, Scotland. With both shortstops out of action, some of the contests played in the British Isles featured Anson at catcher, pitcher Ed Crane at short, and catcher Tom Daly as pitcher, to the confusion of the British press. "It will be observed by those who have read the accounts of the matches already played in this country," said the *Bristol Times and Mirror*, "that several important alterations were made in the posts assigned to the various players. The most celebrated pitcher of each side was given a rest, and Daly, the great catcher of the Chicago team stood at short slip [sic], his usual position being occupied by Anson."[14]

The players were growing tired, and when Daly complained of a sore arm, Anson and Spalding juggled their lineups even more. Fortunately, the trip was nearly over, and after games in Liverpool, Belfast, and Dublin, the travelers boarded a steamer for home. The Atlantic crossing was relatively peaceful, and the ballplayers arrived in New York on the afternoon of April 6 to a tumultuous welcome and a steady series of banquets. The most impressive took place at Delmonico's restaurant in New York, where DeWolf Hopper recited "Casey at the Bat" while Spalding, Ward, Anson, and humorist Mark Twain gave speeches and toasts until the wee hours.

The group had been gone for six months and played more than 50 games on four continents. The tour lost money, with Anson recouping only about $2,200 of his $3,750 investment, but it spread the name of Spalding all over the globe, giving international exposure to A. G. Spalding and Brothers.[15] Spalding already operated stores in Chicago and New York, with distributors all over the United States and Canada, and the trip helped Spalding and Brothers gained a foothold in Europe, Australia, New Zealand, the Hawaiian Islands, and other far-flung outposts. The publicity generated by the "Spalding Tour" helped to make the former pitcher a millionaire, and he considered the money he lost as a worthwhile investment.

Cap Anson, who regarded the round-the-world excursion as the defining experience of his life, devoted nearly half of his autobiography, 142 pages in all, to the events of the trip. However, it appears that the 36-year-old captain looked upon the opportunity to visit other lands not as a way to expand his horizons, but to ratify his existing opinions and prejudices. Anson's accounts are full of cringe-inducing references to Clarence Duval as a "chocolate-colored coon" and worse, and he evinced little interest or sympathy for the "beggars" and "motley crowds" that he encountered in his travels. Anson enjoyed his sojourn around the world, but returned to America unchanged by the experience.

Duval went on his way at journey's end, and little information about him survives. The Chicago Players League club engaged him as their mascot for the 1890 season, but in August of that year he was arrested in Chicago for his involvement in an illegal dice game. The outcome of his case is unknown. Duval popped up again in the nation's newspapers in March of 1898 when he was performing as a drum major in St. Louis under the name "Lord Barnie." The spring baseball meetings were being held in that city at the time, and Duval went to the hotel to see some of the people he had met years before in the baseball world. A reporter informed Duval that Anson was not there, having been fired by the Chicago club a few weeks before, and the former mascot expressed sympathy for his old boss. "Cap and I used to make things pretty lively," said Duval, as quoted in the

Washington Post. He then disappeared from the public eye, and no one knows what happened to him after the spring of 1898.

Anson probably paid no attention to Duval and his whereabouts at the conclusion of the six-month tour. The 1889 season was slated to begin on April 24, only 16 days after the ship docked in New York, and there was much work to be done if the White Stockings were to recapture the National League pennant.

CHAPTER 15

The Brotherhood War

> Any man who signs a contract to play ball with the Chicago club wants to understand two very important rules of the club. One is that he shall play ball from the moment he goes upon the field until he leaves it, and the other is that he must, at all times, whether in uniform or out of it, have a wholesome regard for the wishes of old Anson.
> —Al Spalding, 1888[1]

The beginning of the 1889 season was less than three weeks away when the travelers arrived in New York on April 6, but the tour was not yet finished. Spalding arranged for a series of contests to be played in New York, Brooklyn, Washington, and seven other cities, culminating in a final exhibition game to be played in Chicago on April 20, four days before the official start of the National League season.

The two teams spent the next two weeks playing ball by day and filling their evenings with banquets, toasts, and speeches. Anson gained valuable experience in public speaking on this final leg of the trip, as the *Chicago News* reported. "Captain Anson's late success as an after dinner speaker," remarked the paper, "show what a deserving young man can accomplish by long years of conscientious talking back when the umpire's decisions do not suit him."[2] Anson, whose fame had been enhanced by the world tour, found pleasure in the spotlight. He grew to enjoy giving speeches and the attention that came with his status as baseball's biggest celebrity.

On April 15, the teams arrived in Washington for a visit to the White House. They were to meet the new Republican President, Benjamin Harrison, who had defeated Grover Cleveland the previous November. Harrison, to Anson's dismay, was not the gracious host his predecessor had been. The new chief executive kept his hand inside his coat during the visit to avoid making contact with anyone, and curtly declined an invitation to watch the game that afternoon. The visit lasted only a few minutes, and John Ward (who had rejoined the All America club in New York) remarked that the meeting with Harrison was the coldest snap the tourists had experienced in their travels around the world.

On the evening of April 19, the entourage returned to Chicago for a welcome-home parade, the likes of which had never been seen before. The players rode in open carriages escorted by representatives of 130 business and sporting organizations, with 1,000 bicyclists leading the way to the Palmer House for the final banquet of the tour. More than 150,000 people lined the streets for a glimpse of Spalding, Anson, and the players who carried the American national game around the world. The revelry lasted well into the night, with the final game taking place the next day at the West Side Park. This contest ended badly for Anson's men, as the All Americas reached Mark Baldwin for 21 hits and took a 22–9 win that gave the all-star aggregation a 28–22 edge (with three ties) over the Chicagos in the 53 games played on the tour.

Though the captain would have preferred to win more games, Spalding showed his appreciation by rewarding the captain in a manner unprecedented in baseball. In March of 1889, Spalding signed Anson to a 10-year contract as manager of the White Stockings, an agreement that promised to keep Anson at the head of the team until the end of the 1898 season. Anson was also a stockholder in the ballclub, having either bought shares in the franchise or received them as bonuses from team president Spalding. By 1889 Cap Anson, who harbored dreams of becoming a magnate like his friend Spalding, owned 13 percent of the Chicago club.

Anson and his men spent the next several days reacquainting themselves with their families and catching up on the news of the baseball world. Most of them were stunned when they heard what had transpired in their absence. The National League magnates had pushed through a new salary classification plan. They proposed to rate all players in the league in five categories, labeled A through E, fixing the salaries according to their category. An A player, the highest level of the five, would receive $2,500 a year, an E player would get $1,500, and the other levels would receive compensation between these two figures. This was the first salary cap in professional sports, and it touched off the first great player rebellion.

The controversy had been simmering for several years. The players' right to sell their services had been increasingly restricted through the 1880s as the National League owners expanded the five-man reserve rule of 1880 to include virtually the entire roster of each team. This restriction acted as a drag on salary growth, which was the impetus for the rule in the first place, but the founding of the American Association in 1882 provided players with another market for their skills. In 1883, however, the Association and the National League reached an agreement to coexist and respect each other's reserve arrangements, which closed the marketplace and bound players to their teams for life if the team so chose. A player had no ability to move from one team to another, but owners could sell players away for large sums with no recompense to the athlete. In the words of John Ward, "Players have been bought, sold, or exchanged as though they were sheep instead of American citizens."[3]

Ward found himself in such a position in 1889. While he was in Europe, the Giants and the Washington Senators agreed to a deal in which Ward was to be sold to the team in the nation's capital for $12,000, a record-setting sum that surpassed the sales of Clarkson and Kelly to Boston two and three years earlier. News of the proposed deal reached the shortstop in Italy, and was most likely the reason that Ward left the tour upon his arrival in England and hurried home to America. The deal died when Ward, whose salary under the classification plan would be set at one-fifth of his purchase price, declared that he would retire rather than play in Washington.

The imposition of the reserve rule in 1880 and its expansion during the next several seasons increased tension between labor and management in baseball. In October of 1885 several members of the New York Giants, led by Ward, created a "protective organization" of players called the Brotherhood of Professional Base Ball Players. Chapters sprang up in other major league cities during the following baseball season, and in May of 1886 Fred Pfeffer, Ed Williamson, and Silver Flint joined the organization, followed by King Kelly and Jim McCormick later in the season. Cap Anson, the captain of the White Stockings, did not join; whether or not he was asked to do so is not known, but he was closely allied with Spalding, whom the Brotherhood men saw as their greatest adversary.

Ward, the leader of the Brotherhood, spent the winter months of 1888 and 1889 traveling the world with Anson and Spalding. Because of his absence, the Brotherhood could do nothing about the salary classification plan, and when Ward returned to America, the plan was presented to him as a *fait accompli*. Ward stoutly protested the salary plan, demanding a meeting with the National League magnates, but Spalding, the head of the player relations committee, replied that he would be unavailable until fall. The outraged Ward favored an immediate strike by the players over the matter, but his fellow Brotherhood members demurred. They agreed to play under the salary plan during 1889, but threatened to secede from the National League and form their own circuit, called the Players League, for 1890.

15. THE BROTHERHOOD WAR

The upcoming player revolt cast a shadow over the 1889 campaign, but Anson ignored the controversy and set to work assembling his team. He had six starting pitchers from which to choose (Baldwin, Hutchison, Gumbert, Krock, Tener, and newcomer Frank Dwyer), a surplus of outfielders, and four catchers battling for three spots on the team. Three of the four infield spots were set, but Ed Williamson's knee injury would keep him out of action for several months. Anson signed Charlie Bastian, a weak hitter and good fielder who had spent the last four seasons with the Philadelphia Phillies, to play short until Williamson's return.

The captain, who by this time wielded full control over the Chicago roster, decided to present an infield of himself, Fred Pfeffer, Bastian, and Tom Burns, with an outfield consisting of Van Haltren in left, Jimmy Ryan in center, and Duffy in right. Shortly after the last game of the world tour, Anson made his final roster decisions and stunned all observers when he released four of the travelers. The captain cast adrift pitcher Mark Baldwin, catcher Tom Daly, and outfielders Bob Pettit and Marty Sullivan mere days before the beginning of the 1889 season.

Rumors abounded that the four players were released for drinking and general misbehavior overseas, but the Chicago captain may have had a plausible reason for dropping each man. Baldwin was Anson's main starting pitcher on the trip, but lost out in a competition among five other pitchers. Baldwin's final defeat on the tour, the 22–9 embarrassment in Chicago on April 20, might have sealed his fate. George Van Haltren's permanent move to the outfield and the emergence of Hugh Duffy left no room for Sullivan and Pettit, while the sore-armed Daly gave way to the better-hitting Duke Farrell, with Dell Darling and Silver Flint in reserve. Still, the foursome gave yeoman service on the round-the-world trip, and their release (after all other teams had already set their rosters for the coming season) was widely regarded as an unnecessarily heartless decision.

The plight of shortstop Ed Williamson also elicited sympathy. Williamson remained in London, recovering from his knee injury, for nearly a month before he was finally well enough to board a ship for home in early April. While his knee healed, word spread that Spalding had left the shortstop to fend for himself in Europe, a charge that the club president hotly denied. Spalding claimed that he made arrangements to supply Williamson with funds and "see that he wanted for nothing," adding later, "Chicago has cared for him liberally thus far and would continue to do so."

Anson, too, dismissed the reports of ill treatment. Williamson, said Anson, was receiving "a fixed sum every week. It's no concern of the public what this sum is, but it is sufficient for all his current expenses." Several years later, the captain told a reporter that the rumors were exaggerated.

"He wasn't hurt very badly," claimed Anson, "and had all his expenses paid at that. If he had been ill treated I would have been the first to protest."[4]

However, Williamson told *The Sporting News* in June that he received no weekly payment from the club. His teammates and other league players raised money and held benefits for the injured shortstop, which seemed to indicate that Williamson did, indeed, need money. Perhaps the controversy was blown out of proportion by the bickering between the players and owners, but the alleged poor treatment of Williamson became a rallying point for the Brotherhood in its battle with Spalding and the other National League magnates.

Anson made his usual series of pre-season wagers to display confidence in the ballclub. He bet a hat with Jim Hart, who became the manager of the Boston Beaneaters in early 1889, that Chicago would finish ahead of Boston in the pennant race, and wagered a suit of clothes with New York manager Jim Mutrie that the White Stockings would beat out the Giants. However, the captain soon found that his confidence was misplaced. The White Stockings stumbled in the early part of the season, and a 1–7 skid in late May and early June left Chicago in sixth place, six games below the .500 mark.

The captain was certain that his pitching was the strongest in the National League, but Bill Hutchison struggled with control while Tener and Gumbert fought inconsistency. Gus Krock, a 25-game winner in 1888, suffered from a sore arm and was traded to Indianapolis after posting a 3–3 record. Perhaps Anson regretted the dismissal of Mark Baldwin, who went to Columbus and led the American Association in games, innings pitched, and strikeouts, and won 27 games for a poor team.

Charlie Bastian batted only .136 in relief of Ed Williamson, so Anson tried both Hugh Duffy and Jimmy Ryan at short with little success. Williamson returned to the lineup in August, but could not run, and other teams refused to allow the White Stockings to use a pinch runner for the injured shortstop, since Anson routinely denied his opponents the same privilege. The White Stockings finished the season in third place, far behind New York and Boston, causing Anson to lose most of his pre-season wagers.

Anson's personality irritated his men as the club fell out of the pennant race. Several of his charges were proud of their Irish ancestry, including Duffy, Ryan, and Tener (who was born there), but the opinionated Anson freely expressed his disdain for Irish ballplayers. He "had no use for the players who had Irish blood in their veins," complained Duffy to the *Chicago Tribune*, "and never lost an opportunity to insult those men who have played with him in the past."[5] Anson no doubt remembered his

15. THE BROTHERHOOD WAR

disciplinary headaches with Mike Kelly, Jim McCormick, and Larry Corcoran, among others, but his blanket condemnation of the Irish angered his men and prompted Hugh Duffy to despise the leader that he had once so admired.

Jimmy Ryan, the talented young outfielder, also came to detest Cap Anson. Ryan was an emotional ballplayer who sometimes failed to run out grounders and pop-ups, and when Anson snapped at him for his laziness, Ryan argued back to the man he called the "big stiff." The newspapers reported that Anson and Ryan clashed so often during the round-the-world tour that Anson tried to trade Ryan almost immediately after

Anson on a Goodwin round trading card, 1889. (Author's collection)

returning to America. "Jimmy has given the big captain a good deal of trouble," said the *New York Star* in April 1889. "He does not care what Anson says, he gets right back at him. This does not please Ans, who told [John] Ward on the trip abroad that he believed nothing but a good thrashing would do Ryan. Ward advised [Anson] not to do that, and suggested that he sell or trade him."[6] Ryan was perhaps the best young outfielder in the game, but his moodiness caused a never-ending series of clashes with his brusque captain.

The summer of 1889 was a difficult one for the White Stockings. Though Van Haltren, Ryan, and Anson batted over .300 while Duffy hit .295 and scored 144 runs, the Chicago hitting attack was inconsistent as Pfeffer hit only .228 and Williamson .237. Bill Hutchison, the most sought-after pitcher in baseball a year before, finished with a 16–17 record and won his last four games to avoid a 20-loss season. John Tener went 15–15, while Frank Dwyer and Ad Gumbert posted identical 16–13 marks. Meanwhile, former Chicago righthander John Clarkson won 49 games for Boston and nearly pitched Jim Hart's Beaneaters to the pennant all by himself. Had the White Stockings held onto Clarkson, the 1889 pennant race might have ended differently. As it was, Anson's men finished only two games above the .500 mark, and only the ineptitude of the teams below them kept the Chicagos in third place.

As the 1889 season drew to a close, rumors abounded that the Brotherhood players would quit the National League *en masse* and create their own Players League. Anson heard the rumblings, and said later that "I used what influence I possessed in trying to dissuade such of my players as was possible from taking what I then regarded as a foolish step."[7] He did not succeed in his arguments, and in November of 1889, the Brotherhood set up its own eight-team circuit and persuaded the majority of the National League's best players to jump to the new league.

Anson dismissed the threat. "They will never hit a ball," sneered the captain, "and we will have all the men we want back before the championship season commences." He was wrong. The Players League found sufficient financial backing to create eight teams, six of them in National League cities. In a direct challenge to Al Spalding, who wielded most of the behind-the-scenes power in the National League, Ward installed St. Louis Browns captain Charles Comiskey as manager of the new Chicago ballclub in the Players League. Comiskey had grown up in Chicago, where his father had served as an alderman, and he leaped at the chance to return to his hometown and compete with Anson and Spalding.

A few National League stars remained loyal to the established circuit, including Boston pitcher John Clarkson, who was involved in some of the Players League's early meetings and was branded as a traitor when he returned to the Beaneaters. However, Mike Kelly turned down a reported salary of $10,000—four times as much as an A player received under the salary plan—and cast his lot with the Brotherhood. New York Giants slugger Roger Connor, asked by club owner John B. Day to "name your price" to remain in the National League, also passed on the large payday and moved to the new circuit, as did almost every star except for Clarkson, Giants shortstop Jack Glasscock, and Cap Anson.

The National League appointed a "war committee" headed by Chicago team president Al Spalding, who set to work strengthening the league for the coming battle. In one of the committee's first acts, it dropped the league's two weakest ballclubs, those in Indianapolis and Washington, and persuaded the American Association teams in Brooklyn and Cincinnati to join the National for the 1890 season. Both clubs had signed most of their key players before they could desert to the new circuit, so the National League would begin the season with at least two competitive ballclubs. All the other National League nines, including Anson's Chicago team, embarked on a wild scramble for talent.

15. THE BROTHERHOOD WAR

By January, Williamson, Pfeffer, Ryan, Duffy, and almost all of the other stars of the 1889 White Stockings signed with Comiskey's new ballclub. Anson's pitching staff was torn apart, with only Bill Hutchison (who signed a multi-year contract when he joined the team in 1889) remaining with the Chicagos. Among position players, only third baseman Tom Burns and Anson himself stayed loyal to the National League. The "Stonewall Infield" was now history after seven seasons, and the White Stockings faced a major rebuilding job. The only solace for Anson lay in the fact that almost every other league team — except for Brooklyn and Cincinnati, which arrived nearly intact from the Association — faced the same uphill struggle.

Anson's portrait in the *New York Clipper*, November 10, 1888. (Author's collection)

The Brotherhood attempted to capture all of the National League's best players, and in early 1890 John Ward approached Cap Anson about casting his lot with the new league. Ward certainly realized that the probability of the captain's defection from the White Stockings was slim, since Anson held stock in the ballclub, but Ward made the effort anyway.

"I was invited to join; Ward came to me and invited me to cooperate with the boys," said Anson later that season, "and I said 'What's the object?' and he told me it was to be a sort of protective organization to watch over the players and see that there were no wrongs committed. Well, I didn't join. I replied, 'I've been playing ball in the National League for a good many years now, and I have yet to hear of a wrong they failed to right. When you can give me one instance to the contrary I'll be with you, heart and soul.'

"Well, they didn't bother me after that with invitations. Maybe they were afraid of me; but if I had joined — I don't say that I would have done so, mind you — but if I had I would not have betrayed them as they betrayed their old employers."[8]

Anson would not have to look beyond own team for evidence of poor treatment of players by management. The release of four world travelers in 1889, the alleged abandonment of Ed Williamson in Europe during the world tour, and the sales of John Clarkson and Mike Kelly for amounts far greater than their yearly salaries angered the members of the Brotherhood, but appeared to have no effect on Anson. In his twentieth year of major league baseball and fifteenth season in the National League, Anson was a company man through and through.

Chicago emerged as a key battleground in the war between the leagues, and Anson entered the conflict at a distinct disadvantage. Comiskey, who brought several of his veterans from St. Louis with him, assembled a team with himself, Fred Pfeffer, Ed Williamson, and Arlie Latham on the infield, with Hugh Duffy, Jimmy Ryan, and former batting champion Tip O'Neill in the outfield. His top pitcher was Mark Baldwin, who was still seething over his release after the round-the-world tour, and declared that he wanted nothing better than to beat Anson. John Tener, Frank Dwyer, and Ad Gumbert completed Comiskey's rotation. While the new ballclub emerged as the favorite in the first Players League pennant race, Anson faced the daunting task of assembling a competitive team, with himself, Burns, Hutchison, and a cast of youngsters and unknowns. He and Spalding scoured the professional leagues for prospects. Outfielder Walt Wilmot came from the disbanded Washington ballclub, where he played inconsistently but showed promise when he led the league with 19 triples in 1889. A catcher named Malachi Jedidiah Kittridge joined the Colts from Quincy in the Central Interstate League; he never hit much, but played in the majors for 15 seasons on the strength of his defense. Outfielder Cliff Carroll had played for the Providence pennant winners in 1884 but had been out of the majors for two years, while the switch-hitting Jimmy Cooney came from Rhode Island and succeeded Ed Williamson at shortstop. Second base and right field proved to be problem areas for Anson's team all year long, but the captain was able to find a suitable player for every other position.

With pitching at a premium, Anson was forced to abandon the four-man rotation. Bill Hutchison made 36 starts and pitched in 318 innings in 1889, but when Anson designated the righthander as the staff ace, Hutchison's workload nearly doubled. Hutchison wound up making 66 starts in 1890 and relieving in five other games, and his 603 innings pitched led the league. To support Hutchison, Anson brought in Pat Luby, a South Carolinian who made 31 starts, and searched the country for more pitching talent. "I have drag nets out all over," proclaimed Anson. "I mark promising men, find chances to watch them play, get to know them, and if they have the right spirit and sand I give them a show with us."[9]

Anson, at least publicly, waxed enthusiastic about his new players. On February 26 he wrote to Al Spalding:

> Dear Sir:
> Replying to yours of Feb. 20, as to my opinion of the new players we have under contract, would say that upon the whole I am very much pleased with them. I think we have been exceedingly fortunate in nearly all our selections. We have great men in Cooney, Nagle, Wilmot and Carroll. I am very much pleased with O'Brian and Andrews and feel sure that they are going to please their Chicago friends by the showing they will make this season. I believe we have an excellent pitcher in Coughlin and a great little catcher in Kittredge.... Just at present I do not think we want to sign any more players, and unless I am much mistaken our old players will be little missed.[10]

Spalding made sure that this letter found its way to the Chicago newspapers. A few weeks later, Anson used an exhibition game in Houston to demonstrate his dedication to winning, even in the pre-season. Behind by two runs with the bases loaded, Anson thought of a new way to get the runs home. He instigated a loud argument with the umpire, and shouted "so fierce and long that he held the attention of the Houston players until all three Chicago baserunners had slipped home, the umpire having neglected to call time."[11]

Anson worked diligently to turn his young players into major leaguers. "It was hard work and plenty of it," said Anson, "and though some of the players objected to the amount of practice forced upon them, and the strict discipline that was enforced, yet they had to put up with it, as that was the only manner in which the necessary playing strength could be developed."[12] He pushed himself harder than anybody, and, in his 20th year of professional ball, still appeared to be in the best physical shape of anyone on the ballclub.

With the removal of most of his veterans, the age difference between Anson and his charges grew, and the papers started calling the veteran captain "Pop" Anson. The writers referred to the youngsters as the Colts or the Cubs, and before long the Chicago ballclub dropped the name White Stockings and became "Anson's Colts." The Cubs appellation faded away but resurfaced in the early 1900s, several years after Anson left the ballclub. Comiskey's Players League club opportunistically adopted the name White Stockings, but the press called them the Pirates because they stole away so many of the established National League stars from Anson's club. Comiskey struck another blow when he convinced Clarence Duval, Anson's former mascot, to join them, though Anson probably did not lose any sleep over Duval's defection.

While Anson whipped his Colts into shape, Spalding battled the Players League with every weapon at his disposal. A series of lawsuits, mostly over broken contracts, failed to keep any of the Brotherhood men from jumping to the new league, so Spalding shifted his focus to the playing field. The Players League issued its season schedule in March, so Spalding arranged for the National League to play on the same dates in the same cities, fighting the upstart circuit head-on for the patronage of the fans. The club president declared many promotional days and gave away countless tickets, prompting a Players League official to complain that in Chicago, free passes were "more plentiful than water." Spalding knew that both leagues would lose large amounts of money in 1890. He planned to turn the battle with the Players League into a war of attrition, believing that the established circuit could better withstand the inevitable losses. He declared that the established league would "spend all the money necessary to win this fight. From this point out it will simply be a case of dog eat dog."[13]

Spalding carried the struggle to the newspapers, reporting inflated attendance figures in a bid to boost the popularity of his ballclub. In June, a reporter asked Chicago team secretary Jonathan Brown for the official attendance of the day's game. "Twenty-four eighteen," chirped the secretary, though there were probably fewer than 100 people in the stands. When the reporter left, Spalding asked Brown how he could make such a statement.

"There are twenty-four on one side of the grounds and eighteen on the other," replied Brown. "If he reports twenty-four hundred and eighteen, that's a matter for his conscience, not mine."[14]

Since the Players League employed most of the biggest stars of the game, the upstart circuit took an early lead in the attendance battle. The reporters knew that both leagues routinely over-reported their turnstile counts, so the *Chicago Tribune* sent a reporter to count the actual number of people in the stands in May at both the National League and Players League parks. The reporter found that Anson's Colts averaged only 828 fans per game in its first nine home dates, while Comiskey's club averaged 1,654 in its first five contests. The results were the same in New York, Philadelphia, and other cities, as the Players League outdrew the established circuit all season long.

A more serious issue for the National League came into focus in mid-season. The New York Giants were hard hit by Players League defections, with almost all of their stars from the pennant-winning 1889 Giants team deserting to the new circuit, and in July club owner John B. Day informed Spalding that his ballclub could no longer pay its bills. The collapse of the

National League team in the nation's largest city would hand an important public relations victory to the Players League, so Al Spalding arranged an immediate infusion of $80,000 in cash as a bailout for the Giants. Spalding accomplished this by purchasing $20,000 worth of Giants stock and convincing the owners of Boston, Indianapolis, and Philadelphia to do the same.

Spalding divided $15,000 worth of stock between himself and two other investors, and then sold the remaining $5,000 worth to Cap Anson, who, most likely, borrowed the amount of purchase against his existing share of the Chicago franchise. This move made Anson, the would-be magnate, a part owner of two National League teams. The captain had always been the National League's biggest booster in the war against the Brotherhood, but now he held an even larger financial stake in its outcome.

While Spalding fought behind the scenes, Cap Anson stepped forward as the most vociferous booster of the National League. The captain had made his loyalties public as early as spring training, when the Colts played an exhibition contest in St. Louis and found themselves sharing a hotel with Comiskey's Brotherhood team. Anson decided to use the occasion to make a statement to his former players. He signed "A. C. Anson and wife" on the guest register, then placed the names of all his new Colts in brackets underneath. He then wrote "The Chicago Base Ball Club" in large letters above the names, and underlined "The" four times in bold strokes.[15]

Anson took the defections of Pfeffer, Williamson, and the others as a personal affront, since he had scouted and signed those players and set them on the road to stardom, and he harshly criticized the Players League at every opportunity. "I have better pitchers, better fielders, better base runners and better all-around men than any other base ball aggregation that has ever represented Chicago," declared Anson. "The Brotherhood club is made up of stars whose reputation has long since been established and who are today playing on that reputation."[16] In May he challenged Comiskey's Pirates to a winner-take-all match at the end of the season, and in July he went on the attack again. "The Brotherhood is making a wonderful bluff," said Anson, "but it can't last ... I don't believe [the Pirates] made enough profit to pay half the lumber bills for the grand stand. When the crash comes, you can hear it a mile off."[17] Hardly a week went by without another public blast from Anson against the Brotherhood.

While the captain insulted the Players League in the papers, the Colts battled to keep from dropping out of the pennant race. Brooklyn and Cincinnati, the two most complete ballclubs, fought for the early lead, with Harry Wright's Philadelphia Phillies close behind and Anson's Colts in the middle of the pack. Anson spent all season holding tryouts for second basemen and right fielders; he used six different men, including himself, at second, and six more in right as the season progressed. The strength of the team lay in the pitching staff, where Bill Hutchison and Pat Luby started nearly three-fourths of the games and kept the Colts in the race.

Anson started the year poorly at the bat, but he and the rest of the team began to improve by mid-season. The Colts stood at the .500 mark on July 19, but an 18–9 record in August lifted them into a battle for second place with Boston, Philadelphia, and Cincinnati. A 19–1 streak gave the Colts a hold on third position by mid–September, and a five-game winning streak at the end of the campaign put the Colts in second place to stay. If Anson could have filled the second base and right field holes, the Colts might have beaten Brooklyn for the pennant.

All the National League teams were desperate for talent and auditioned new players all summer long. In August, a young pitcher for the Cleveland Spiders made his first major league appearance against Chicago. Denton (Cy) Young was a 23-year-old from rural Ohio who had compiled an unimpressive 15–15 mark with Canton of the Tri-State League, though he had pitched a no-hitter against McKeesport (with 18 strikeouts) the week before his major league debut. Though Anson and the other Colts rode Young mercilessly during the game, calling him "hick" and "farmer" and mocking his too-small uniform, Young beat Chicago by an 8–1 score in the first game of a doubleheader. Young allowed only three hits, none to Anson, and after the game the captain, according to legend, offered the Spiders $1,000 for the "big rube."

Cleveland elected to keep Young, who won a record 511 games in his 22-year career that lasted until 1911. Some sources claim that Anson saw Young pitch in 1889 and was not impressed, calling Young "just another farmer" and passing on the chance to sign him. If the story is true, then Anson failed to see the potential in the man who became the winningest pitcher of all time. A year later, during the pennant race of 1891, Anson grumbled to a reporter, "If I had Young, I'd win the championship in a walk."[18]

Some of the captain's new men performed well, including pitcher Pat Luby, who went 20–9 and won a team record 17 games in a row, but not all of Anson's Colts lasted long. One oft-quoted story concerns a young player named Ed Lytle, who played his first major league game for the Colts at Pittsburgh on August 11, 1890. Anson put Lytle in left field, and the captain became distraught at Lytle's propensity to throw the ball to second baseman Bob Glenalvin anytime he fielded it. No matter what the situation, even with a Pittsburgh baserunner rounding third and heading for home, Lylte threw the ball to Glanalvin.

Finally, Anson confronted Lytle on the bench. "Lytle, why do you always throw to second?" demanded the irate captain. "Can't you throw anywhere else? Why do you always give the ball to Glenalvin?"

"Because, Captain Anson," responded the young man politely, "Glanalvin is the only man on the nine to whom I've been introduced." Anson released Lytle that evening, and his career as a Colt was finished after one game.[19]

The Brooklyn ballclub won the pennant by six games over Anson's Colts, but Anson may have delivered the best managing performance of his career that year. Brooklyn had lost almost no men to the Players League, having left the American Association and joined the National League as a unit in the spring, while Anson was required to build a new Chicago club almost from scratch. Bill Hutchison, who started nearly half of the Chicago games and led the league in wins with 42, deserved a great deal of credit for the Colts' second place finish, but Anson's ability to build a competitive team on the fly kept the Colts in the race to the end. Though the Chicago Players League team drew more fans, Anson's Colts won the on-field battle as Comiskey's star-studded team finished a disappointing fourth.

Anson also compiled a fine season at the plate following a slow start. He batted .312 and led the league in on-base percentage in his twentieth year in professional ball, and also set a new major league record with 113 walks in 139 games. At 38, Anson was still one of the most feared hitters and run producers in the major leagues.

The captain remained an unyielding foe of the Brotherhood, and when the Players League teetered on the brink of financial collapse, Anson urged Spalding and the other National League magnates to fight to the finish. "Compromise?" asked Anson. "No sir, this is not the time to talk compromise.... Just as long as the League and the Brotherhood exists there is bound to be a fight. One of them has got to go ... there won't be any compromise with my consent."[20] In August, the captain engaged in some cloak-and-dagger work at Spalding's direction in an attempt to induce defections from the Brotherhood. While Spalding offered Mike Kelly $10,000 to jump back to the National, Anson negotiated in secret with New York catcher Buck Ewing, holding out an $8,000 salary and the manager's position at Cincinnati as an inducement to leave the Players League. Both men rejected the overtures, but Ewing was harshly criticized for meeting with Anson and fought charges of disloyalty to the movement for the rest of his career. The incident convinced many Brotherhood members that Cap Anson was as much an enemy to their cause as Al Spalding.

Anson told the papers that he would be happy to keep his 1890 team intact for 1891, but the Players League fell apart in November when some of the new organization's financial backers decided to sell out rather than lose money for one more season. The Players League was "deader than the proverbial door-nail," proclaimed Spalding, and the National League victory was due in no small measure to Cap Anson. He kept the heat on the Brotherhood all through the 1890 season, fiercely defending the National League cause and allowing Spalding the latitude to work behind the scenes towards the demise of the upstart circuit. Some later writers called Anson "the man who saved the National League," and while this might be an exaggeration, Anson justly received a large measure of credit for the victory. However, many of the Brotherhood players would never forgive Anson for his insulting personal attacks on the Players League. The players had long memories, and Anson's constant criticism would cause innumerable problems for the captain in the years to come.

CHAPTER 16

A Disputed Pennant Race

> To hear ball players talk of [Anson], one would think they all hated him, and yet they all think the world of him. His opponents are always making vows to spike him at their first opportunity, but for all that you never hear of him being spiked. Only a few days ago a ball player who was passing through the city made me a short call, and in talking about the great captain he said, "The more I swear at Anson the more I admire him."
> — A. G. Spalding, 1892[1]

With the demise of the Players League, the peace agreement between the Brotherhood and the National League specified that all former League players would rejoin their former teams. Cap Anson expected to regain the services of all of his defectors, but by early March it was apparent that not every former Chicago player intended to return. One who declined was Ed Williamson, who never fully recovered from his knee injury and batted only .195 for Comiskey's Pirates in 1890. He opted for retirement and opened a saloon on Chicago's South Side. Hugh Duffy, the Players League leader in hits and runs scored, also rejected an invitation to return to the fold. "The Chicago club treated not only myself but several other men unfairly [in 1889]," said Duffy, "and I have no earthly use for them."[2] When the Boston Players League team remained intact and moved to the American Association for the 1891 season, Duffy went with it, depriving the Colts of one of the game's brightest young stars.

George Van Haltren passed on the opportunity to play for Anson once again, accepting an offer instead from Baltimore's American Association club. "I am not playing ball for love," said Van Haltren, "and the club that can pay me the most money can get my services."[3] That club was clearly not

Cap Anson at first base, probably in the late 1880s (as evidenced by the black stockings). (Transcendental Graphics)

the Colts, since Spalding was intent on limiting the payroll, so the prized pitcher-turned-outfielder signed with the Orioles. Duke Farrell also abandoned the National League and joined the Association, but Jimmy Ryan rejoined the Colts after expressing his disillusionment at the Players League adventure. "Let the men who put up the capital manage the game," suggested Ryan, "and let the men who do the playing get paid for it and keep still. This is all any ballplayer should ask. There is one thing certain and that is that I will not play again under the same conditions."[4]

Ad Gumbert came back to assist Bill Hutchison and Pat Luby on the pitching staff, and second baseman Fred Pfeffer signed on to play second base. Though Pfeffer returned, another part of the Stonewall Infield was sidelined as Tom Burns, the only position player besides Anson who had remained with the Colts in 1890, suffered a serious elbow injury. To replace him, Anson signed a 21-year-old third baseman named Bill Dahlen, who batted .342 at Cobleskill, New York the year before.

Dahlen would become one of Anson's most talented but difficult players. He was a sure-handed infielder and possessed a strong arm. However, he was hot-tempered and enjoyed gambling and carousing almost as much as King Kelly had several years before. Dahlen was careless with money, and sparked controversy almost immediately when word reached the papers that he had signed an earlier contract with Milwaukee and kept $500 in advance money before inking his deal with the Colts. The Milwaukee management wanted its money back, and the dispute simmered for nearly a year before Dahlen managed to return the funds and settle the matter. He was always asking Anson for advances on his salary, most of which the captain denied, and Dahlen's turbulent relationship with Anson would become one of the continuing storylines that defined the Colts throughout the 1890s.

Anson planned to take the Colts to Fort Lauderdale for spring training, but the Denver team of the Western League offered to stage a series of exhibition games with the Colts if the Chicago team would hold its spring camp in Colorado. Anson accepted, but soon wished that he had not, as it

Anson bobbles a throw at first. (Transcendental Graphics)

snowed in Denver almost every day of the trip. Bad weather prompted the cancellation of most of the scheduled exhibition contests, and the Colts returned east to start the season with only limited practice time behind them.

Anson and the Colts crossed paths with one of the future legends of the sport when they stopped in Cedar Rapids, Iowa, for an exhibition match against the local Three-I League team. The Cedar Rapids third baseman was a feisty 18-year-old from New York State named John McGraw, and the teenaged infielder did his best to catch Anson's eye. McGraw singled off Bill Hutchison in the first inning and then said to Anson, "Say, old timer, so that's what you call big league pitching, eh? We'll murder that fellow."

McGraw was aware that the Chicago captain liked competitive personalities, so he instigated three heated arguments. The captain spent the afternoon jawing back and forth with the youngster, but after the third set-to "he saw the humor in it and smiled at me encouragingly," recalled McGraw. "I'll never forget how good that smile made me feel."[5] After the game Anson complimented McGraw on his playing and, according to McGraw, asked if the teenager would like to play for the Colts someday. However, Anson liked big men, and McGraw only weighed about 120 pounds at the time. The Baltimore Orioles bought McGraw's contract instead a few months later, and he led the Orioles to three pennants in the mid–1890s. In 1902, McGraw began a 30-year career as manager of the New York Giants, with whom he won ten pennants, eclipsing Anson's record of five league championships.

The Colts were still a young team, and Anson moved quickly to establish discipline in the ranks. When outfielder Elmer Foster began to dissipate during spring training in Denver, Anson bought him a train ticket and ordered him back to Chicago. Foster pleaded for another chance, which the captain granted, but when Anson spotted him and pitcher Pat Luby drinking in the hotel bar in Pittsburgh, he levied a $25 fine on each man. Foster became belligerent with Anson, and the captain suspended him immediately.

Anson was not ready to give up on the erratic outfielder, but Foster had already decided that he hated Anson. On one spring evening, according to a story told by Chicago sportswriter Hugh Fullerton, Foster and several other players smuggled a beer keg into their hotel room. They drank and played poker while Anson, keeping guard on the sidewalk outside the hotel, congratulated himself that none of his players had slipped out to carouse. The captain was also pleased to see no Colts in the hotel bar, little realizing that they were getting drunk upstairs behind locked doors.

When the keg was nearly empty, Foster looked out the window, only to see Anson camped on the sidewalk below. Foster let out a shriek of glee, then pitched the keg through the window. It made a loud clang when it hit the sidewalk about 20 feet from Anson, bounced, and fell again as the startled captain ran for cover.

"I know it was Ryan, Daly, or Foster," said Anson later, "but which one I'm not certain."[6] Later in the season, still steaming about the incident, he cornered outfielder Jimmy Ryan one day and said, "Jim, I think it was you. I can't prove it yet, but I'm going to, and when I do, I'm going to give you the worst licking you ever took."[7]

At the end of the trip, Foster approached Anson to ask for a favor. Feigning contrition, Foster explained that he was "a bit short" and asked the captain to pay his laundry bill.

"Certainly, Foster, certainly," proclaimed Anson, who made his way

16. A Disputed Pennant Race

to the registration desk as Foster hurried out of sight. The bill totaled $42.55, a huge sum at the time. Foster had charged meals and drinks to his room and listed them as laundry. When the team returned to Chicago, Anson decided that enough was enough. He waived Foster out of the league and released him to Kansas City, and Foster never played another major league game.

Dahlen, Pfeffer, Ryan, and Gumbert constituted an infusion of talent to the nucleus of the 1890 team, and Anson believed that his Colts could once again win the pennant after a five-year hiatus. They would have to do so while playing in two different home parks. Spalding, in an effort to reach out to fans of Charlie Comiskey's defunct Chicago Pirates club, bought an interest in the old Players League park at 35th and Wentworth. Spalding wanted to draw fans from the South Side as well as the West Side of Chicago, and made plans to play on Mondays, Wednesdays, and Fridays at West Side Park, and on other days of the week at the South Side Grounds.

This decision was one of Spalding's final official acts as president of the ballclub. In mid–April he shocked the baseball world by submitting his resignation to the team board of directors. Spalding explained that, with his sporting goods concern having grown into a nationwide success story, he wished to move to New York and oversee his business operations from the largest city in the nation. Spalding was gratified when the board followed his recommendation and named Jim Hart, the former manager of the Boston Beaneaters, as his successor.

Anson may have been surprised by Spalding's retirement, but he was dismayed with the appointment of Hart. Anson had known Spalding for more than 20 years and served him faithfully, first as assistant and then, for the last 12 years, as captain and field manager, and it seems that Anson believed that he deserved a promotion to the front office. The captain had always worked closely with Spalding, as Spalding had done with William Hulbert, and Anson believed that when his playing days were over — an instance the 39-year-old first baseman knew was in the near future — he would leave the field and join the front office, as Spalding had done more than a decade before. Anson was astute enough to recognize that Hart's assumption of the presidency weakened his own future position in the management end of the ballclub.

Though Hart was a friend and confidant of Spalding, Anson and Hart had never gotten along. The relationship between the two had been strained since the round-the-world excursion, when Anson refused to contribute to a fund to buy Hart a set of diamond cufflinks for his work on the tour. Anson also held Hart's managing skills in low regard, since Hart had been fired by Boston as manager following the 1889 season after overworking pitcher John Clarkson in a bid to win the pennant with a mediocre team. Anson and others saw Hart as a mere stooge of Spalding, who still held the majority of stock in the club. It did not bode well for Anson to have such a poor relationship with the man who was now his boss.

Spalding, sharp businessman that he was, realized that Anson's feelings had been hurt by Hart's appointment, and wrote a conciliatory letter in which he tried to paint Hart as a mere figurehead. However, Spalding apparently did not believe that Anson was qualified to become president of a baseball team. The Chicago ballclub had grown into a highly profitable enterprise, returning a 20 percent dividend to its stockholders after the 1887 season and clearing a profit of $60,000 for the 1888 campaign. The team needed a president well versed in the nuances of finance, contract and property law, and other facets of business administration. Anson, less than ten years earlier, did not even know how to figure interest on an investment, and some of his private business ventures had failed miserably. Spalding needed only to remind himself of Anson's ginger-beer fiasco for proof that the captain was a baseball man, not a businessman.

No longer was the club merely an entity that put on baseball games; it was also heavily involved in real estate. The organization owned tracts of land, ripe for development, in Chicago and its environs, and hoped to use one of those in the near future to build a new ballpark. It also owned land in Hot Springs, Arkansas, where development might be stimulated by the spring training trips of the Colts and other teams. Anson knew baseball strategy, but knew nothing about real estate and commercial development. Spalding understood, even if Anson did not, that the captain's skills were best suited to the playing field.

The Colts appeared to be the class of the National League, even without Williamson, Duffy, Farrell, and Van Haltren. Anson replaced them with holdovers from the 1890 Colts, including Jimmy Cooney at shortstop, Cliff Carroll and Walt Wilmot in the outfield, and Mal Kittridge at catcher. Rookie Bill Dahlen started the season at third base, moved to the outfield when Tom Burns recovered from his injury, and played well enough to mark himself as a future star. Once again Anson relied on Bill Hutchison for most of the pitching, since the fastballer appeared to thrive on a heavy workload. For the second season in a row, the tireless righthander started nearly half of the scheduled contests and led the league in appearances, starts, innings, wins, and complete games. Holdover Pat Luby and Players League refugee Ad Gumbert rounded out the rotation, which Anson operated as if it were a four-man starting corps with Hutchison pulling double duty.

16. A Disputed Pennant Race

For most of the season, Anson's Colts controlled the pennant race. With 18 wins in their first 25 games, the team held first place on May 21 with a four-game bulge over Pittsburgh. The Alleghenies (who were not yet known as the Pirates) dropped back as the New York Giants and Boston Beaneaters mounted challenges. The Colts lost seven in a row in June, giving up their lead to the Giants, but a seven-game winning streak moved Anson's men into a virtual tie with the New Yorkers in July. By August 1 the Colts held the undisputed lead, and an 11-game winning streak in late August, which included a 28–5 victory over Cleveland, left the Colts five full games ahead of the Beaneaters.

Anson was unusually feisty during his 21st season of professional ball. On August 6 the Colts and the Beaneaters engaged in a battle in which Chicago's Pat Luby and Boston's young pitching star Kid Nichols fought to a 6–6 draw through 12 innings. In the 13th, the Colts put two men on base, bringing the 39-year-old Anson to the plate. The captain figured that the 21-year-old Nichols could be rattled with the game on the line, so he chose this moment to test the young pitcher's nerve. Anson set up in his usual righthanded batting stance, and then, as Nichols prepared to pitch, jumped over to the opposite box, switching to a lefty stance. The captain repeated the move several more times as Nichols started to throw, stopped, started again, and stopped again.

The flustered pitcher demanded that the umpire order Anson to stop, but there was no rule against this move at the time, so Anson kept hopping back and forth over the plate. The umpire ordered Nichols to throw, but the pitcher complained that Anson's body was in the way. Finally, Nichols simply refused to pitch, and the umpire sent Anson to first and loaded the bases. Thoroughly exasperated, Nichols hit the next batter, Cliff Carroll, forcing in the winning run.

Chicago's lead over Boston increased in early September, and with the pennant race apparently over Anson decided to put on a show for the fans. The local papers had been making fun of his advanced age, much to Anson's displeasure, so on September 3 he surprised some 3,500 Chicago fans when he appeared on the field wearing long gray whiskers. The 39-year-old captain took fielding practice before the game while sporting the false beard, as the crowd laughed and called upon Anson to "Take 'em off!" Anson, however, surprised the fans even further when he decided to play the contest while wearing the beard. For nine innings Anson's false whiskers flapped in the breeze, "hurling defiance into the teeth of age by aping its appearance," in the words of the *Chicago Tribune*.

Anson soon discovered that the beard could work to his advantage. He informed umpire Thomas Lynch that if one of Boston hurler Kid Nichols' pitches grazed even a hair of his head, real or not, Anson would be entitled to take first base. He did not get a chance to test his theory, since Nichols did not throw an inside pitch to Anson all day. Despite the sideshow atmosphere, the Colts defeated Nichols and the Bostons by a 10–1 score and extended their lead in the pennant chase to seven games.

The Colts then traveled to Brooklyn and absorbed their worst loss of the season when Anson overslept on the morning of a doubleheader. The papers claimed that the hotel porter forgot to wake the captain, and the first game began without Anson. Pitcher Tom Vickery ran into immediate trouble, and when the score reached 9 to 0 in Brooklyn's favor Jimmy Ryan came in from center field to pitch. Anson finally appeared at the park in the fifth inning, but the game was out of hand by then, and Brooklyn marched away with a 21–3 win. A hard-fought 9–8 victory in the second game somewhat mollified the embarrassed Anson, who belted a home run, and the doubleheader split maintained the Colts' six-game advantage in the pennant chase.

Two wins at Boston on September 14 and 15 gave the Colts a six and a half game lead with slightly more than two weeks to go, and most observers deemed the pennant race all but over. *The Sporting News* stated that the Boston club "might as well give up all hope of flying the flag," but the Beaneaters would not go down quietly. They defeated the Colts on September 16 behind Kid Nichols to drop the lead to five and a half, and the suddenly vulnerable Colts fell into a slump, losing three in a row at New York.

At the same time, the Beaneaters, led by Nichols and former Chicago mainstay John Clarkson, began one of baseball's most incredible winning streaks. Starting with the September 16 win against the Colts, Boston won 18 and tied one of its next 19 games, chipping steadily away at the lead. The Chicago lead fell to two and a half games after the three losses at the Polo Grounds. The Colts then won five in a row against Cincinnati and Pittsburgh but still lost another half game, as the Beaneaters won six games against Brooklyn and Philadelphia. By September 26, when the Colts tied the Alleghenies and the Beaneaters defeated the Phillies, Chicago's lead stood at one and a half games.

The Beaneaters won so easily, scoring double digits in many of their games, that some Chicago boosters raised suspicions about their good fortune. The Giants defeated the Colts three days in a row from September 17 to 19, but when they met Boston later that month, they held star pitchers Amos Rusie and John Ewing and cleanup hitter Roger Connor out of the lineup. Without its best players, New York dropped five games in a row to the surging Beaneaters by lopsided scores. The Dodgers and Phillies also performed poorly against Boston, while Chicago's opponents battled tooth and nail against the Colts. The scenario looked suspicious, and before long the newspapers began to suggest the unthinkable — that the eastern teams lay down to help Boston win the pennant.

Anson held his tongue, at least for a while. "No, I do not believe the eastern clubs are throwing games to Boston," said the captain in Cleveland. "I would rather lose the pennant; I would rather finish second after all the work of the past month, than believe that Boston is winning games by having them thrown to her by other clubs."[8] Privately, however, Anson fumed with indignation. His temper erupted when a Brooklyn fan sent him a telegram, asking if the Colts' 21–3 loss to the Dodgers on September 7 was played "on the square." The captain replied, "I will not insult my players by showing them your telegram nor degrade myself by answering your questions."[9]

On September 28, the Colts began a three-game series at Cleveland. Patsy Tebeau, the Spiders manager who had played briefly for Anson's White Stockings in 1887, told Anson before the first game that it "looked like a throw-down" in the eastern cities, but that his Spiders were not involved. Tebeau promised that his club would play its hardest against Chicago, and proved it by winning two of three against Anson's men. During that series, Chicago pitcher Ad Gumbert visited the Cleveland locker room and overheard a Spider player say that unidentified eastern baseball boosters had offered $1,000 to the Cleveland team for each win against the Colts. No one knows if Tebeau's men received any money, but Anson was now convinced that the Beaneaters were stealing the pennant from his Colts.

The captain unaccountably chose this time to upset his players with his still-simmering hatred of the Brotherhood. In late September, with the pennant slipping away, Anson and Fred Pfeffer ate breakfast in a Cleveland hotel with a reporter from the *Chicago Tribune*. The seething manager blamed the former members of the Players League for throwing the race to Boston, and could hold his feelings in check no longer. "If I had my way about it," boomed the captain, "every leader of the Brotherhood movement would have been barred forever from the national game." Anson went on to explain that John Ward manipulated the ballplayers in early 1890 for his own purposes, and Pfeffer and the others joined the Players League ignorant of Ward's true motives. Pfeffer angrily rose from the table and stalked off without touching his breakfast. The incident caused bitterness between Anson and his Colts in the last week of the season, and "has reopened the breach between [Anson] and Pfeffer perhaps for all time," said the *Tribune*.[10]

Two losses in three games in Cleveland left the Colts one and a half games behind Boston with three to play. Boston defeated the Phillies twice on the first two days of October while the Colts lost two contests to Cincinnati by scores of 6–1 and 17–16, and Boston clinched its first pennant since 1883. Anson fumed, but *The Sporting News* took a surprisingly benign view of the controversy. "To the victors belong the spoils is [the fans'] motto," stated the Bible of Baseball, "no matter how the spoils are won. So to-day the people of Boston are shouting Hosanna, while Anson's champions of a week ago find no one so humble as to do them honor. Such is life in the base ball world and so will it always be."[11]

If the Giants and other teams did indeed throw the pennant to Boston, there are a few possible reasons. One oft-told story claimed that Anson, as captain of the likely Chicago pennant winners, entered into talks in August with the league-leading Boston Reds of the American Association about a possible post-season "World's Series." The Reds had recently obtained King Kelly from the collapsed Cincinnati Association franchise, and a showdown between Anson's Colts and Kelly's Reds might have proved popular at the box office. The National League moguls, horrified that Anson might lose the series and give legitimacy to the other circuit, decided to throw the race to the Beaneaters, who had no intention of meeting their cross-town rivals in any post-season matchup.[12]

The Sporting News proposed that Anson's unpopularity with the rank-and-file National League players was to blame. "There is no denying that Anson has few friends among the Eastern ball-players," stated the paper in early October. "Most of them got more pay than the Chicago players and the fact that with the lowest paid team in the League Anson has made such a record has created considerable ill-feeling toward him. There are other reasons why Anson is unpopular on the diamond, and for these the players would prefer seeing the championship go to Boston."[13]

Another oft-cited possibility suggests that the players of other National League teams threw the race because of lingering animosity from the Brotherhood year, and that the object of their antipathy was Spalding, not Anson. Anson was not the most popular man in the National League, but he was a stockholder in the Chicago ballclub, and no one could have reasonably expected him to join the Brotherhood revolt in 1890. Spalding, however, was the man who sank the Players League and brought salaries tumbling sharply downward in the process, and some believed that the former Brotherhood men threw the race to Boston to repay Spalding for his actions. Though Spalding had resigned the presidency of the Colts earlier in the year, he still held the majority of stock in the club, and the players, as the story goes, wrought revenge on the man who proudly proclaimed, "The Players League is as dead as the proverbial doornail."

16. A Disputed Pennant Race

Of course, the Colts could have made the whole issue moot if they had not lost four straight games to Boston and New York in mid– September, and if they had not dropped five and tied one of their last seven games of the 1891 season. The Colts won six, lost nine, and tied one of their last 16 games, while Boston went 18–1–1 in their last 20 contests. One could say that the Colts simply went into a slump at the worst possible time. However, Anson remained convinced for the rest of his life that his Colts lost the pennant unjustly. In his autobiography Anson claimed, "a conspiracy was entered into whereby New York lost enough games to Boston to give the Beaneaters the pennant."[14] Though the league turned aside the Chicago protest after a cursory investigation, Anson firmly believed that the Giants and other rival teams cheated him out of his sixth league championship.

There were three major leagues in operation during the 1890 season, but only one would exist in 1892. The American Association lasted one year longer than the Players League, and in the winter months of 1891–1892 the Association also bit the dust. Four of their teams (Baltimore, Louisville, Washington, and St. Louis) were folded into the National League, which was transformed into a clumsy twelve-team circuit. Most importantly, the number of major league teams dropped from 24 in 1890 to 16 in 1891 to 12 in 1892, and the resulting distillation of playing talent raised the level of play in the National League. Cap Anson's Colts could not afford to stagnate. They, and every other National League team, would be required to improve markedly in order to challenge for the pennant in 1892.

CHAPTER 17

The Grand Old Man

> *A ballplayer who leads a temperate life should be good for actual service till his 40th year. I will say, however, that the players these days take care of themselves better than they used to do, and nine out of ten save their money.*
> — Cap Anson, 1896[1]

At the start of the 1892 season, Cap Anson was the second-oldest player in the game behind the 42-year-old Giants outfielder Jim O'Rourke, and was one of a handful of men who remained from the National League's inaugural season of 1876. When James (Deacon) White retired at the end of the 1890 campaign, that left Cap Anson as the last of the 117 players who were present at the birth of the National Association in 1871. Anson's statistical record was the most impressive in the game's history up to that time, as he was the all-time leader in games played, times at bat, hits, doubles, total bases, and runs batted in. By 1892 Anson was universally known as "The Grand Old Man of the Game," a living symbol of the sport's history.

As he approached his 40th birthday, it was inevitable that Anson would slow down as a player. Though he led the league for the eighth time in 1891 with 120 runs batted in, his batting average dropped below the .300 mark for the first time in his 21-year career. Some of the newspapers suggested that the captain might have retired from the playing field had his Colts won the pennant in 1891, but the controversial pennant race made Anson more determined than ever to bring the flag back to Chicago. He probably never considered ending his playing career on such a low note, and reported to training camp at Hot Springs in his usual excellent physical condition. Fred Pfeffer, still smarting over Anson's criticism of the

Brotherhood late in the previous season, remarked to *The Sporting News* that the captain would never leave the diamond until he was dragged off.[2]

Not every member of the 1891 Colts returned to the fold in 1892. The angry Pfeffer declared that he would never play for Anson again and threatened to quit the game and go into the saloon business if he were not traded to Louisville, his hometown. Anson hoped that he and his longtime second baseman could resolve their differences, but Pfeffer remained adamant, and in early April Jim Hart traded Pfeffer to Louisville for infielder Jim Canavan and $1,000. Twelve-year veteran Tom Burns also left the Colts for Pittsburgh, where he became the manager of the team now known as the Pirates, and his departure left Anson as the lone remaining member of the Stonewall Infield.

The National League, which was now officially called the "National League and American Association of Base Ball Clubs" with the demise of the rival Association, gave its fans a new kind of pennant race in 1892. The league used a spilt-season format in which the schedule was divided into halves and the winner of each half-season would meet in a post-season series for the pennant. This setup gave each team two chances to win the title and, the magnates hoped, would keep the tail-enders from losing fan support in the latter months of the season.

Some of the other National League teams, most notably Boston, rushed to sign the stars of the American Association when that circuit collapsed in late 1891, but Chicago was unable to improve itself. The Colts had demanded the return of Hugh Duffy, Duke Farrell, and George Van Haltren, all of whom played for Anson in 1889 and then decamped for the Players League, but the commission that negotiated the surrender of the Association awarded Farrell to Pittsburgh and Duffy to Boston. Van Haltren was allowed to stay with the Baltimore club that joined the National League, along with three other former Association teams (St. Louis, Washington, and Louisville), for the 1892 season. Anson and the Colts hotly objected to losing three of the best young players in the game, men they had discovered and nurtured, but the decision stood.

Those three might have boosted Chicago into contention, but Anson was still confident that his Colts would return to the top after barely missing the pennant the year before. Not everyone was convinced, especially *The Sporting News*, which remarked, "There's new and swifter blood in the League teams of this season."[3] Sam Dungan, a promising hitter from California, claimed the left field position, but Chicago fans were concerned with the rest of the team. Cap Anson was slowing down at bat and in the field, while second baseman Jim Canavan and shortstop Jimmy Cooney were weak hitters. "The town isn't stuck on Anson's outfit," said *The Sport-*

ing News, "and he needs a championship to get back into popularity. Anson is respected, but so is Christopher Columbus."[4]

The captain had high hopes for his ballclub in 1892, but the early part of the season was once again darkened by personal tragedy. On May 7, Virginia Anson gave birth to another son, who was named John Henry Anson after his grandfathers John Fiegal and Henry Anson. Cap Anson joyously celebrated the arrival of a long-awaited son, but sadly, his happiness turned to grief again. John Henry Anson died four days later, casting the Anson household into mourning for the third time.

The 1892 season was a roller-coaster ride for Anson and his men. The Colts opened the season with wins at St. Louis and Louisville and then lost nine games in a row, falling all the way to tenth place in the 12-team league. In May a 13-game winning streak and a 19–3 record for the month put the Colts in second place, but a 1–10 skid dropped the team to eighth position by June 24. The Colts finished the first half of the season in eighth place with a disappointing 31–39 record. Perhaps their most interesting contest took place on June 30, when Chicago's Ad Gumbert and Cincinnati's Tony Mullane battled to a 7–7, 20-inning tie, the longest game ever played in the National League up to that time.

The Boston Beaneaters, in the meantime, received a pass into the post-season series when they won the first half of the split season. King Kelly and the Beaneaters clinched the half-pennant in early July, and decided to enjoy themselves in the remaining days of the first half of the season. On July 11, in a game at Chicago, the Boston players showed up for the game in "calico and gingham suits of loud pattern and color," according to the *New York Times*, sporting false beards and mustaches as well. They played in this strange garb, and Kid Nichols defeated Bill Hutchison and the Colts by a score of 3 to 2.

The players reacted poorly to the constant losing, and Jimmy Ryan once more became a thorn in Anson's side. The center fielder injured his leg in a game in Boston in June and left the lineup. Anson ordered Ryan to report to the park during his recovery, but Ryan saw no reason to do so and stayed away. When Ryan finally showed up at South Side Park, Anson informed him of his suspension without pay. Ryan told the papers that he would never play for Anson again, and the Chicago players sided with Ryan in the dispute. The Colts "roasted Anson from supper to breakfast and called him names under their teeth that were very unladylike," said the *Chicago Times*, though Anson, as usual, refused to back down.[5]

The second half of the pennant race began on July 15, but the Colts fell out of contention almost immediately, in part due to Jimmy Canavan's failure to replace Fred Pfeffer at second base. Canavan batted only .166 in

1892 and compiled the lowest batting average in major league history for any player with 400 times at bat or more. Anson searched for a replacement, a task that should have been easier after the National League limited each team to 13 players in a mid-season salary-cutting move. Star players like John Clarkson found themselves released by their teams, but no second basemen became available, and Anson was stuck with Canavan for the remainder of the season. With shortstop Jimmy Cooney also batting well under the .200 mark, Anson was saddled with the worst-hitting team in the league. The situation improved somewhat when Anson benched Cooney, moved Bill Dahlen to short, and inserted newcomer Jiggs Parrott at third, but the Colts still trailed the rest of the league in runs scored.

Though Ryan threatened to quit baseball rather than play for Anson, he returned to the lineup in early July and immediately started a 29-game hitting streak, the longest of the season in the National

Jimmy Ryan, Chicago's talented and hot-tempered outfielder. (Author's collection)

League. Despite his fine hitting, the Colts lost their first four games in the second half, falling all the way to tenth place before an eight-game winning streak pushed them back up to sixth by the end of August. The Colts never threatened to enter the pennant race, and the team finished the second half well behind Cleveland, managed by former White Stocking Patsy Tebeau. The Colts ended the 1892 campaign with a 70–76 record and gave Anson his first sub-.500 mark in his 17-year career as manager.

In September, Anson made apologies for his team. "Chicago cranks amuse me a great deal," said the captain. "When we had that winning streak, taking thirteen consecutive games, the people thought we were a strong club, but we weren't. I never saw a team play a luckier game than we did for a while there. Why, we won on our luck and nothing else. On the other hand, for the last month we have been putting up rotten ball in the eyes of most of our patrons, while in reality we've been outplaying our visitors day after day, although, until the recent turn of the tide, we have been losing steadily."[6] Despite the captain's attitude, Chicago fans let Anson know that they were unhappy. They booed Anson so severely during August and September that the captain stayed off the coaching lines when the Colts were at bat.

Statistically, the Colts were a disaster, finishing last in the league in runs scored. The team batting average, weighted down by Canavan's .166 mark and Cooney's .179, fell to .235, the lowest in the National League. Anson stubbornly played every inning of every game at first base, but suffered through his worst season at the plate, batting .272 with only 65 runs scored in 146 games. His 74 runs batted in led the Colts, but too few batters (aside from Dahlen, who hit for a solid .291 average) managed to reach base for him to drive in. On the pitching side of the ledger, Bill Hutchison led the league once again in wins, starts (70) and complete games (67). Hutchison might have won 50 games with a good team behind him, but poor hitting support from his teammates left the fastballer with a 36–36 record. Ad Gumbert posted a 22–19 log, while Pat Luby, disciplined during the season by Anson for drunkenness, fell to an 11–16 mark.

Most teams would have considered firing their manager after such a poor season, but Anson was protected by a 10-year contract that he signed in early 1889. However, rumors reached the papers late in the 1892 campaign that Jim Hart wanted to ease Anson out of the picture by sending him to the New York Giants, a team in which Walter Spalding, Al's brother, and Anson himself were stockholders. Nothing came of that speculation, and the Giants hired the former Brotherhood leader John Ward as their manager for the 1893 season.

Nonetheless, Hart managed to find a way to shorten the captain's contract, or so Anson claimed in later years. In December of 1892 Hart, with the approval of Spalding, reorganized the Chicago franchise into a stock company. The new corporation issued 1,000 shares of stock, with 320 going to Al Spalding, 320 to local banker John Walsh, 130 to Cap Anson, and smaller amounts to Hart and other investors. Anson, who retained his 13 percent ownership in the ballclub, was required to sign a fresh contract with the new organization. He did so in early February 1893, but when he returned home that night and read the document aloud to Mrs. Anson, the captain noticed that the term of the contract ran for five years, not the six that remained on the old agreement. The previous contract ended in February of 1899, but the new one concluded on February 1, 1898.

Anson, in a move he later regretted, decided to say nothing about the missing year. He believed that his friend Spalding would "set things right" five years hence, so he kept his reservations to himself and began to work on improving the Colts for the 1893 campaign. However, the captain never trusted Hart again, if indeed he had trusted Hart before, and the relationship between the team president and his manager continued to deteriorate as the 1890s progressed.

Team discipline was one issue that divided the two men. Spalding had trusted Anson to handle disciplinary matters since the mid–1880s, but Hart created problems when he intervened on behalf of the players. In 1891, when Anson benched catcher Mal Kittridge and put Pop Schriver behind the plate in a home game, Kittridge became so verbally abusive that the captain fined him $50 and left him behind when the Colts departed Chicago on a road trip. Hart met with Kittridge, reinstated him, and sent him off to rejoin the ballclub. In 1893, Jimmy Ryan became enraged when a $10 fine, which Anson levied for poor behavior in a Cincinnati hotel, was withheld from his paycheck. Ryan threatened to quit the team if the money was not returned, so Hart decided to rescind the fine.

Many observers believed that Anson was too strict with his men, and the *Chicago Post* referred to the captain in early 1892 as "Capt. Adrian-Iron-Hand-at-the-Wrong-Time Anson."[7] The captain tried to rule his Colts with the same iron-fisted treatment he employed during the 1880s, but many of the young players proved as resistant to discipline as Mike Kelly, Ed Williamson, and Silver Flint had been a decade before. Hart's interference in behavioral matters, however, did nothing to improve the situation.

Salary disputes proved another source of annoyance for the Colts. Player compensation rose sharply during the Players League war, when some stars earned as much as $5,000 to $8,000 per season. The deaths of the Players League in 1890 and the American Association in 1891 gave the National League a monopoly over professional baseball in America, and in 1893 the league magnates slashed player salaries to the bone. The Colts, with a relatively young team aside from Anson, cut many of its men to the $1,000 to $1,500 range, with the predictable cries of outrage from the players.

Anson, ever the company man, dismissed the complaints. "I know at least fifty players in the league," remarked Anson, "who would play ball for nothing in preference to being paid a salary in another occupation. They have been playing ball since their early boyhood. They know the game and nothing else, and they love it."[8] Jimmy Ryan, Walt Wilmot, Ad Gumbert, and Pop Schriver did not feel the same. They refused to sign at reduced salaries, and none of the four reported to Chattanooga in March to begin spring training.

Ad Gumbert may have been the most bitter of the four holdouts. A workhorse on the mound and a good hitter as well, he was struck in the head with a fastball from Pittsburgh's Mark Baldwin in May of 1892. Gumbert lay unconscious for nearly six hours, and some papers reported that he had been killed. He recovered well enough to regain his spot in the rotation, but his hitting prowess decreased markedly. Though Gumbert pitched well as the number two starter behind Hutchison in 1892, Anson offered him a contract with a $900 pay cut, mostly due to his decline at the plate. Gumbert turned down Anson's offer, but the captain refused to trade him, so Gumbert remained at home while the rest of the Colts played ball down south.

The Colts entered spring training without two of their main starting pitchers from the 1892 season. Ad Gumbert refused to play again for Anson, and the captain released Pat Luby after a string of disciplinary problems. To fill their spots, Anson signed righthander Hal Mauck and lefthander Willie McGill. Mauck was a 24-year-old minor leaguer from Indiana, while McGill had gone 13–7 for Cleveland of the Players League in 1890, when he was only 16 years old. McGill had struggled since then, reportedly due to alcohol problems, but he was still a teenager with a world of potential.

Second base had been a problem position for the Colts in 1892, but Anson found the man to fill the void. Bill Lange, a 22-year-old from the California League, was exactly the kind of big, strong athlete that Cap Anson liked. He was six feet and one inch tall, weighed a muscular 190 pounds, and was one of the fastest men in the National League from the day he joined it. Many years later, A.H. Spink of *The Sporting News* described Lange as "Ty Cobb enlarged, fully as great in speed, batting skill and base running." He was a hell-raiser, as were so many of Anson's best players, but Anson was never hesitant about signing a talented player, no matter what he did off the field. The captain also retained George Decker, a 24-year-old utility man who played well for the Colts in the last half of the previous season. Decker was a much better fielder than Anson, and many fans hoped that their 41-year-old captain would hand first base to Decker before long.

Anson, when asked by a reporter which team would win the 1893 pennant, chirped back, "Why, Chicago, of course. Who else?" Few observers believed him, because, except for Lange and two pitchers, the Colts would start the new season with the same personnel that finished in ninth place in 1892.

The Colts, like every other team, would have to adapt to one of the most far-reaching rule changes in the game's history. Before 1893, a pitcher stood in a rectangular box and was required to start his delivery with one foot on the back line, which was 55 feet and six inches from home plate. For the new season, the league mandated that a pitcher throw the ball with one foot on a rubber plate situated 60 feet and six inches from home plate. Fastball pitchers, such as Cy Young and Bill Hutchison, had overpowered hitters at the previous pitching distance, but the new configuration promised to increase batting averages and produce more high-scoring contests.[9]

Cap Anson had seen many changes in the game during his long career, but his heart and mind were set firmly in the past. He had always disdained the use of the fielding glove, and still played barehanded in the early 1890s long after most major league infielders had made the switch. Anson himself received criticism for his refusal to wear a glove after the 1887 season. "A pair of gloves cost Chicago the pennant this year," stated one Chicago writer. "Anson was too pig headed to wear gloves, and I find that he has made at least thirty-five errors by muffing thrown balls and lost about seven games in this way."[10]

By 1892, Cap Anson was the only remaining barehanded major league first baseman. He stubbornly resisted using a glove, even though A. G. Spalding and Company was the nation's largest manufacturer of baseball equipment and profited handsomely from the sale of fielding gloves. However, even Anson finally realized that he could no longer avoid injury from a thrown ball without protection on his hands. In September of 1892 the 40-year-old Anson appeared on the field with a glove for the first time. As the *Brooklyn Eagle* commented, "It is not known whether the patriarch's hands are getting tender or not, but certain it was that the glove was scarcely smaller than a pillow. It was big and thick and looked as if it might stop cannonballs without injury to the wearer. Anson got everything that came his way, however, and was able to carry the mitt on his left hand without a balance weight on the other."[11]

Team president Jim Hart, concerned about the declining fortunes of the team as well as competition from the 1893 Chicago World's Fair, decided to make a bold departure from past practice and introduce Sunday baseball to Chicago. Construction of a new, modern ballpark, the West Side Grounds, had been completed at the corner of Congress and Loomis streets, and during the 1893 season the Colts played 14 games there on Sundays when the fair was closed. The Colts moved permanently to the new facility the following season, but played weekday games at South Side Park for the remainder of the 1893 campaign.

William Hulbert had vociferously opposed Sunday ball when he founded the National League in 1876, and Al Spalding echoed his president's opinion. "So long as I have anything to do with base ball," said Spalding in 1885, "I shall do all in my power to prevent Sunday games ... and kindred disgraces."[12] Anson had also publicly objected to Sunday ball, but times were changing, and the captain's opposition to the practice had weakened in subsequent seasons. The St. Louis and Cincinnati ballclubs had attracted large Sunday crowds for years, and the Colts decided to follow suit. On May 14, 1893, the Colts played their first Sunday home game, losing to the Reds by a score of 13–12 before a crowd of 13,232.

Holdouts, bad luck, and assorted injuries doomed the Colts in 1893. In contrast to 1892, when Anson's men alternated between winning and losing streaks, the 1893 edition of the Colts fell to the second division and remained there all season long. They won only four of their first 15 games, settling in 11th place in mid–May, until a 14–11 streak pushed the Colts up to ninth position, where they stayed for most of the year. Jimmy Ryan returned in April, while Walt Wilmot rejoined the club in mid–May, but Ad Gumbert remained on the sidelines. In July Anson traded him to Pittsburgh, and in August Gumbert sued the Colts for breach of contract.

The new pitching distance had little effect on some of baseball's young stars, such as Cleveland's Cy Young and Boston's Kid Nichols, but the older National League pitchers struggled to adapt. Bill Hutchison, the 34-year-old Chicago workhorse, discovered that the added distance made his fastball less effective, and since he did not throw a curveball, National League batters found his pitches easier to hit. Hutchison won only five of his first 14 decisions before a sore arm sent him to the sidelines in June. Mauck and McGill failed to pick up the slack, and by mid-season Anson was forced to bring in minor league pitchers for tryouts.

In all, 12 pitchers started games for Anson in 1893, but only one made an impression. Clark Griffith was a 23-year-old righthander from Missouri who used intelligence and control to win games. He went 30–18 in the California League in 1893 before signing with the Colts, and made his first start for Chicago on September 7. He lost a 7–3 decision to the Phillies, but defeated the same club a week later by a score of 12–5. Griffith was not the kind of pitcher that Anson usually coveted. He stood only five feet and six inches tall and threw a mediocre fastball, but performed well enough to earn an invitation to spring practice in 1894.

The Chicago pennant hopes, such as they were, evaporated in August. Jimmy Ryan, who despite his behavioral problems was still the best player on the team, was injured in a train accident on August 6 and was lost for the season. Bill Dahlen fell ill that same month, forcing Anson to move Bill Lange to shortstop, while the captain suffered a charley horse and sat out for a week. Anson batted .314 in 1893 and led the team in runs batted in once again, but was slowing down noticeably in the field and on the bases. Many fans and sportswriters believed that Anson was nearing the end of the line, and, as *The Sporting News* put it, "Anson, [Jim] O'Rourke, and [Mike] Kelly would do well to retire from the game before they get the bounce."[13]

The Colts stumbled through August and September, and on August 23, when Amos Rusie of the Giants shut out the weak-hitting Colts on three singles, *The New York Times* expressed its amazement at the ineptitude of Anson's ballclub. "Cook County, Ill., has had some good ball teams in its day," stated the *Times*, "but the team now representing the aforesaid county is not calculated to add to its renown. Where Capt. Adrian Constantine Anson got his nine of misfits is a mystery. They can't play, bat, run bases, or throw a ball; in fact, they are not capable of doing anything but to ride in parlor cars, put up at good hotels, and draw their salaries."[14]

The captain was so demoralized by his losing ballclub that he hardly bothered to argue with the umpires as the Colts sank deeper into the second division. The Chicago papers criticized him for his seeming indifference, but Anson may have been distracted by personal problems. His wife was ill, and Anson took time off from the ballclub in September to tend to family matters. He appointed Walt Wilmot acting captain and assigned George Decker to play first base, and the Colts went on a modest winning streak in their captain's absence. The smooth-fielding Decker played so well that the voices in the bleachers urging Anson to retire from active play grew louder.

The 1893 season mercifully ended on October 4, as the ninth-place Colts finished at 56–71, compiling their worst won-lost record in Anson's term as manager. Bill Hutchison, a 40-game winner in 1890 and 1891 and a 36-game winner in 1892, fell to a 16–24 log, while Willie McGill finished at 17–18 and Hal Mauck at 8–10. Bill Lange performed well in his inaugural season with a .281 average and 47 stolen bases, while Bill Dahlen took a major leap toward stardom with 113 runs scored in 116 games. In contrast, Anson batted .314 but saw his power numbers drop, as his slugging percentage was only the fifth-best on the Colts. Anson had never been a fast runner, but was now so slow that nearly 80 percent of his hits were singles. He managed only two triples, and no homers, all year. In a final insulting gesture, the minor league team from Galesburg challenged the Colts to play for the "Illinois State Championship." Anson declined the offer, stating that the Colts would play no exhibitions after the conclusion of the National League season.

The captain was frustrated with his team, which had finished under the .500 mark for the second year in a row and showed few signs of challenging for a pennant any time soon. Team president Jim Hart was also unhappy, because Anson showed no interest in retiring. *The Sporting News, Sporting Life*, and the Chicago newspapers all suggested, subtly or otherwise, that Anson would be well advised to end his career after 23 years in the game, but the captain often boasted that he never read the papers and had no idea what the sportswriters were saying about him. Cap Anson was, by 1893, a mediocre hitter, a poor fielder, and an increasingly inflexible manager, but he owned an unbreakable contract, and Hart was stuck with him for four more years.

CHAPTER 18

Anson and His Colts

Oh captain, my captain!
Why lag you in the rear?
Is this old Anse that used to prance
And whom the foeman fear?
Is this the Viking gaunt and gray
That taught the youngsters how to play
And showed the Colts the winning way,
The yeoman of the year?
— The Sporting News, 1894[1]

The captain attended the league meetings in New York in February of 1894, where he waxed optimistically about his Colts to reporters. He made his annual pennant prediction, proudly proclaiming that this team was his best since his 1886 champions. "Poor Anson has an attack of this kind every year,"[2] complained *The New York Times*, but Anson, as usual, believed every word of his boast. He backed up his optimism by betting $500 and a suit of clothes with Eddie Talcott, the treasurer of the Giants, that his Colts would finish ahead of the New Yorkers in 1894.

On February 28, Anson visited Wall Street and received the strangest reception ever seen at the New York Stock Exchange. He watched the frenzied action on the trading floor for some time without being recognized, but before long several New York Giants fans shouted out their greetings. One trader slipped out of the hall, bought a bag of oranges at a nearby fruit stand, and distributed them to his fellow traders with the suggestion that they test the fielding skill of the famous ballplayer. With that, a flurry of oranges whizzed by Anson's head, and the captain decided to take up the challenge. He stopped most of the missiles, departing the exchange with his pockets full of oranges.

"The New York Stock Exchange is a nice place," proclaimed Anson, "but the next time I go there I'll bring a mask and a chest protector along."[3]

The Colts, in a cost-saving move, did not make a spring training trip to the South that year, so Anson attended to some personal business in March. He traveled to Washington in an attempt to gain an appointment as postmaster of Marshalltown for his aging father. Cap Anson was a celebrity and a strong Democrat, but there were more than 20 other applicants for the post, and the Postmaster General bypassed Henry Anson once again for the coveted position. The disappointed captain, perhaps eyeing a future career in Chicago politics, attended a meeting of the Democratic National Committee as an observer, then returned to Chicago and took over his ballclub.

The 1894 Colts faced many of the same pitching problems as the 1893 edition. Willie McGill grew increasingly unreliable, reportedly due to drinking and late hours, while Bill Hutchison still struggled to adapt to the increased pitching distance. On the positive side, Clark Griffith showed promise as a starter, and Anson bolstered the rotation with the signing of Bill "Adonis" Terry. The handsome Terry, a righthander, was a 20-game winner for Brooklyn earlier in the decade until arm problems forced him to the sidelines. Terry's arm was now sound, and Anson penciled him in as the fourth starter on the ballclub.

Anson moved Lange away from second base and put him in center field, where he could make the best use of his speed, and shifted Jiggs Parrott from third to second. Charlie Irwin joined the Colts and shared third base and shortstop with Bill Dahlen, while Anson held down the first base bag in his 24th major league season. Lange's move to center field pushed the now-recovered Jimmy Ryan to right, with Walt Wilmot in left and Schriver and Kittridge sharing the catching chores once again. Anson believed that this group could challenge for the pennant, or so he told the press at the league meetings in February, when he labeled this newest group of Colts as "the best team on earth."

The Colts failed to live up to their captain's prediction. The 1894 season disappointed Chicago fans once again, as the Colts lost eight of their first nine games and dropped to the basement of the National League. The lack of adequate spring training was probably a factor, and although Anson began the season with a hot bat, the other Colts could not find their collective stroke. On June 1 they managed only one hit in a 5–0 loss at Brooklyn, and the Dodgers' Ed Stein, a former Colt, pitched a seven-inning no-hitter the next day, defeating the Colts by a 1–0 score. The 1894 season marked the greatest offensive explosion in baseball history (the league as a whole, pitchers included, batted .314 that year) but the Colts struggled at the plate in the early part of the campaign.

Anson still played in the old-fashioned, take-no-prisoners style. Fred Clarke, a future Hall of Famer who made his major league debut for Louisville that year, later recalled his first game against the Colts. "I made a hit apparently good for two bases," Clarke said. "As I rounded first Anson tripped me, and I had to scramble back to first. I didn't say a word, but the next time I deliberately hit an infield out and as I got to first I landed on his shoe with my spikes and ripped the shoe open.

"He was a rough man, with a good punch, but I knew he could never catch me. Anson was slow, and had to hit for his reputation. He let me alone after that incident."[4]

On July 15, a game against Brooklyn led to a change in the rulebooks. In the eighth inning of a close game at Chicago, Brooklyn manager Dave Foutz ordered his pitcher, Charlie Gastright, to walk Anson intentionally with two men on. Anson watched three balls sail wide of the plate, but when the fourth came, the captain jumped across the plate to the other side of the batter's box and drove the pitch down the right field line for a triple. The Dodgers argued for more than ten minutes, but umpire McQuade let the hit stand, since there was then no rule that prohibited a batter from stepping over the plate to swing. After a few other players performed the same feat that year, the league amended the playing rules to require that the batter remain in the box while swinging.

Bill Dahlen started the season slowly, but showed improvement as the weather warmed up. On June 20 he hit a single against Cleveland's John Clarkson, beginning the longest hitting streak ever seen in the major leagues up to that time. Dahlen connected safely in 42 consecutive games and did not go hitless again until August 7, after which he hit in another 28 games until Brooklyn stopped him again on September 15. He batted .397 in that 71-game stretch, with 96 runs scored, and his 42-game hitting streak is still the third longest in National League history.

Anson, too, battered the ball all year long. He went 5 for 7 in a 26–8 win over St. Louis on August 1, and his average hovered above the .380 mark for most of the season. His average was not high enough to challenge for his fifth batting title, since three other National Leaguers were hitting well above the .400 mark, but the 42-year-old captain led his team in batting. He also led the league in fielding percentage at first base, though some people claimed that Anson covered so little ground by 1894 that he fielded fewer balls than any other man at his position. Regardless, Anson's performance in 1894 has rarely, if ever, been matched by any other player of the same age.

A controversy in Louisville that August led to a forfeit. The home team, throughout baseball history, has always supplied the baseballs to the umpires for each game. Anson had long suspected Billy Barnie, manager of the weak-hitting Louisville ballclub, of freezing or soaking the balls to deaden them whenever the Colts came to town for a series. On August 2, Anson became alarmed when two different baseballs split apart during play, so he smuggled a newer ball into the game. The Colts battered this ball for a 9–3 win, which the Louisville club protested, and Anson stewed after the game over Barnie's apparent shenanigans.

This gave the Chicago players an opportunity to create some mischief. With the assistance of *Chicago Inter-Ocean* sportswriter Hugh Fullerton, they composed a fake telegram and sent it to Anson at the hotel. The message read: A. C. ANSON, CHICAGO BASEBALL CLUB. LOUISVILLE HOTEL, LOUISVILLE, KENTUCKY. DON'T PLAY WITH BARNIE'S BALLS. (Signed) JAMES A. HART.

The next day, Anson arrived at the park with a box of new, official National League baseballs, and vigorously tried to persuade umpire Tom Lynch to use them instead of the Louisville supply. An argument naturally ensued as the Colts egged on their manager, but the debate ended when Anson pulled the fake telegram out of his pocket. "Get in the carriages, boys," shouted Anson, waving the telegram. "Hart upholds me!" None of the players dared to reveal the prank to Anson, so they left the field, forfeiting the game to Louisville by a score of 9 to 0. The forfeit cost the Chicago club a $1,000 fine from the league, and only months later did Fullerton confess his role in the joke to Hart. Anson, according to Fullerton, never found out that he had forfeited a game on the basis of a false telegram.[5]

Two days later, the Colts returned to Chicago for a homestand that began with a near-tragedy. On August 5, Anson had just struck out in the seventh inning against Cincinnati when a discarded cigar ignited some rubbish underneath the right field bleachers at the West Side Grounds. Team president Jim Hart had installed a barbed-wire fence in the outfield to keep rowdy fans off the field, and the 1,600 people in the bleachers were immediately trapped between the flames and the fence. The scene turned chaotic, and as one eyewitness reported, "Men began to clamber up [the] wires like rats in a cage.... The first got through easily. Others tried to slip between the wires and hung there, entangled fast in the barbs."[6]

Jimmy Ryan and Walt Wilmot ran to the outfield and attempted to pry the wire fence loose from its posts with their bats. They were able to free some of the fans, but others were injured when they fell or jumped from the bleachers. Fortunately, the weight of the crowd pulled the fence down and allowed the fans to escape. No one was killed, but dozens suffered injuries, and the fire caused about $20,000 in damage to the new ballpark.

The Colts arrived in New York on August 20, but faced the Giants that afternoon without Cap Anson. The captain had received a telegram from Marshalltown that morning, advising him that his father was deathly ill and not expected to recover. With the team buried in ninth place, well out of the pennant race, Anson boarded a train for Iowa.

Team discipline disintegrated almost immediately upon Anson's departure. On August 22, during the last game of a three-game series at the Polo Grounds in New York, a theatrical friend of Anson's presented the team with a huge bat, nearly six feet long, which was intended as a satire of the previous controversy involving the forfeited game against the Colonels. It was inscribed, "The bat Anson used at Louisville," and in Anson's absence the bat was given to acting captain George Decker. In the ninth inning, with the Colts trailing by six runs, Bill Lange took the gigantic bat to the plate. Neither the Giants nor the umpire offered an objection; Lange managed to swing the club and dribble the ball to first base, where the Giants' Jack Doyle bobbled the ball for an error. Lange's grounder started a three-run rally, but the Giants won by a score of 8 to 5.

The Colts, without Anson, lost all three games at the Polo Grounds and then traveled to Washington for a three-game set against the Senators. This trip renewed an ongoing debate about catching a ball thrown from the top of the capital's tallest building, the Washington Monument.

The primary work on the monument was completed in 1884, though it was not finished and opened to the public until 1888. Since its completion, baseball players and sportswriters disagreed on whether or not a baseball could be caught if tossed from the top of the obelisk. In 1885, shortly before its dedication, Washington infielder Paul Hines volunteered to catch a baseball thrown from the summit, but called off the attempt after seeing the speed of the falling sphere. Another man, not a ballplayer, tried to catch a ball and failed, breaking several of his knuckles in the process. Others tried, but none succeeded, and most believed the feat to be impossible.

Anson, in his usual opinionated manner, took the opposite viewpoint. The Chicago club stayed at the Arlington Hotel whenever it traveled to Washington, and on each visit, he and the hotel's chief clerk, H. P. Burney, engaged in spirited conversation about catching a baseball from that height. The top window of the monument stood some 504 feet above the ground, and Burney tried to convince Anson that the force of a falling baseball from that great height might seriously injure, or even kill, anyone foolish enough to try and catch it. Anson hotly disagreed, though he never offered to make the attempt himself, and by 1894 the debate between Anson and Burney had been raging for nine years.

When Anson left the team in mid–August, the Colts proceeded to Washington without him, and the topic arose once again in the Arlington Hotel lobby after dinner one night. Catcher Pop Schriver, playing his fourth season for the Colts, offered his opinion that a ball dropped from 504 feet up could not be any more difficult to handle than a fastball from the arm of Amos Rusie or Bill Hutchison. Schriver was convinced that Anson was right, and volunteered to put his captain's theory to the test.

Anson almost certainly would not have allowed one of his men to expose himself to injury in this manner, but he was a thousand miles away in Iowa, and the Colts were determined to find out, once and for all, if the feat was possible. In an attempt to vindicate Anson — and, perhaps, to get the captain to stop talking about the subject on every future trip to Washington — a delegation of Colts made its way to the monument on the morning of August 25, 1894. No one knows if acting captain George Decker gave his permission or even knew about the stunt before it happened.

While Bill Hutchison and Clark Griffith rode the elevator to the top of the obelisk, Schriver and the other Colts made small talk with Burney, hotel manager Frank Bennett, and a few spectators, all the while trying not to draw the notice of the park police. Finally, Griffith and Hutchison waved from the top window of the monument. Schriver waved back, and then Griffith flung a baseball out of the window. The pitcher had figured, correctly, that merely tossing the ball out the window would make it bounce against the side of the sloping monument, so he gave the ball a healthy heave into space.

Schriver tried to pick up the flight of the ball, but after some indecision he stood aside and let it drop to earth. It did not burrow ten feet into the ground as many expected; instead, the ball merely dented the ground and bounced away like a fly ball to the outfield. This encouraged the catcher, who waved again to Griffith. Moments later, a second ball came sailing out the window. Schriver positioned himself under this ball, catching it cleanly to the applause of the spectators and, no doubt, to the chagrin of all who had wagered against him at 2–1 odds. A park policeman then arrived and threatened to arrest the ballplayers for creating a disturbance, but some quick talking put the officer in a better mood, and Schriver's feat became the talk of the baseball world. The joyous Colts then went out and defeated the Senators that afternoon by a 10–5 score.

Anson's reaction to the news of Schriver's catch was not recorded, though he certainly disapproved of a stunt that could easily have gone awry. He must have been pleased, however, that his fiercely argued opinion was proven correct after all, though he probably wished that he had been present to win a few wagers on the outcome.

Schriver's catch was the only excitement the Colts enjoyed during the captain's absence. The win in Washington was the lone victory in a 1–7 skid that began when Anson left the team in New York. The Colts rallied to win three in a row from the Phillies and Dodgers, but then dropped eight more in succession, culminating in a 25–8 home loss to Boston. *The Sporting News* complained that without Anson, the Colts played "like a ship at sea without a rudder." There was good news, however; Henry Anson recovered from his illness, and the captain returned on September 15 and led his team to a much-needed win against Brooklyn. The rest of the season passed uneventfully, and the Colts finished in eighth position with a 57–75 record, 34 games behind the pennant-winning Orioles.

Anson played in only 83 of his team's 137 games in 1894, but his .388 batting average proved that he could still hold his own at the age of 42. Ironically, Hugh Duffy, the former White Stocking whom Anson had nearly released six years before, won the batting title for Boston with a record-setting .438 mark. Duffy and his Beaneater ballclub represented a new style of play in the National League, one that emphasized brains and intelligence over brawn and muscle. Anson, in contrast, still showed a bias to big, strong ballplayers, and signed men similar to himself whenever possible. He valued hitting, and because he was not a gifted fielder, he minimized the importance of fielding skill. "I don't care if they can't field a little bit," he said to the *New York Clipper* in 1892. "In my experience I have found that a man can be taught to almost stop cannon balls, but it is a very difficult task to teach them to line 'em out."[7]

The Boston club won three pennants in a row from 1891 to 1893 while the Colts finished under the .500 mark in each of those seasons. The game of baseball was evolving, but it appeared that Anson was not interested in changing with it. While other teams divided their starting pitching assignments evenly among three or four hurlers, Anson sent Bill Hutchison out to pitch 603 innings in 1890, 527 in 1891, and 627 in 1892, with a staggering 75 starts in the 1892 campaign. Hutchison was the last pitcher to throw 600, or even 500, innings in a season, and by 1894 his arm was as burned out as was Larry Corcoran's ten years before. Hutchison never posted another winning record after 1892, and his 6.06 earned run average in 1894 spelled the end of his career soon after.

Politically, Anson had grown into a staunch conservative, and his traditionalist strain of thought influenced his view of the baseball world as well. He disdained the sacrifice bunt and other newer strategic maneuvers, though Boston and Baltimore won pennants with them. Most of the National League teams used more sophisticated signal systems than the Colts, and sharp players on other teams could read the Chicago signals with ease. In one series against the Colts in 1894, Baltimore stole bases almost at will by getting good jumps on the Chicago pitchers, while Anson did not make any in-game adjustments. "Anson makes his team play by formula," complained the *Chicago Tribune*, while other teams had learned to alter their strategies immediately according to game situations.

His conservatism extended to his refusal to touch alcohol or tobacco. "I have not drank and I have not smoked since I was convinced that it was not well for me to do so," said Anson to *The Sporting News*. "I broke them both off short, the smoking especially, for I was never much of a drinking man.

"I haven't had tobacco in any form for ten years. I did smoke a great deal, ten or twelve cigars a day. My doctor told me to cut it down to three. I told him I'd rather quit. I haven't put a cigar in my mouth since. A while ago, when I was over in Marshalltown, the same doctor fished out a couple of cigars and asked me to have a smoke. I told him I didn't smoke. 'Why not,' he asked. 'Because you told me not to,' I answered.

"Tobacco has taken many a young player off the diamond, and some of them off the earth, I believe. Smoking doesn't help a man to play ball."[8]

The captain was a virtual teetotaler, having drunk only a few glasses of champagne since his Philadelphia days, and could point to the examples of several of his old teammates for evidence of the negative effect of alcohol. Larry Corcoran died of kidney failure in 1891, and in 1894 three more hard-drinking Chicago players from the championship years passed from the scene. Ed Williamson, Silver Flint, and Mike Kelly, the "King of Ballplayers," all fell on hard times after their playing careers ended, and all succumbed to alcohol-related illnesses. Of the 13 men who played at least five games for Anson's 1885 pennant winning ballclub, five were already dead before their 38th birthdays. The captain used their stories to preach moderation, if not outright temperance, to his men, but few of the younger Colts paid much attention.

Anson's abstention from these vices set him apart from his younger charges, many of whom were hell-raisers of the first class. Off the field, Anson reacted to behavior problems by tightening the level of discipline, which resulted in more frustration for himself and the players. The captain became more quarrelsome, on the field and off, as the 1890s progressed, and managed to keep simultaneous feuds going with sportswriters, players, umpires, the National League, and his boss, Jim Hart. One sunny day, as the story goes, an unidentified Chicago player pointed to the dark image on the ground next to Anson. "That ain't no shadow," said the player. "That's an argument. Everywhere Cap goes, the argument goes."

Before the 1895 season began, Anson illustrated his confidence in the

Colts in his usual way. He made a string of bets with rival managers, club officials, and almost anyone else who cared to wager against his ballclub. The papers reported that Anson bet several team officials and fans of the New York club, including new owner Andrew Freedman, a total of $1,500 that the Colts would beat the Giants in the standings in 1895. He bet $50 and a suit of clothes with Cincinnati team owner John T. Brush that Chicago would finish ahead of the Reds, and reportedly made similar wagers with Boston manager Frank Selee and several Pittsburgh officials. In all, Anson was in for several thousands of dollars in wagers, not to mention his many side bets of hats, dinners, and suits.

Anson had always loved to make wagers, a habit that he picked up in the many billiard parlors that he had frequented since his teenage years. However, his betting increased in frequency during the mid–1890s, if reports in papers such as *The Sporting News* and *Sporting Life* are accurate. He even placed a wager with one of his teammates, outfielder Walt Wilmot, who believed that the Cleveland Spiders would finish ahead of the Colts in 1896. Anson bet him $100 on the spot, and paid off at the end of the season.

A Mayo Cut Plug Tobacco card of Anson, 1895. (Author's collection)

Unlike another famous baseball betting enthusiast, Pete Rose, Anson bet against his own team at least once. In 1895, when Clark Griffith was mired in a slump, Anson used a well-placed wager to jolt his young hurler back into the win column. "I'll bet you $20 that we lose the game today," said the captain. Griffith took the bet and won the game, and Anson, for once, did not mind losing.

The captain was such an enthusiastic gambler that he accepted wagers from strangers. In the spring of 1892, a Cleveland fan spotted Anson in a

St. Louis hotel lobby and declared that the Spiders would finish ahead of the Colts in the standings. Anson pulled a $100 bill out of his pocket and proclaimed, "You can win this if they do!"[9] Anson lost that wager and many others that year, due to the ninth-place finish of the Colts. In January of 1895, Anson told *The Sporting News*, "I want to bet any man in the world $100 that the Chicago Club beats out any six clubs in the league next year. By this I mean that I will bet that much against each of the six clubs the other fellow picks out to beat us."[10]

The captain was also deeply involved in wagering on other activities, including the sport of trapshooting, at which he was an expert and was good enough to win prize money in tournaments. He also enjoyed playing as well as betting on billiards, putting his own money on the line while serving as his own principal backer. In January 1894 he challenged the Iowa state billiards champion, George Hersh, to a 400-point match in Marshalltown. Anson lost, and *The New York Times* reported, "[Anson has] lost several large wagers this year on billiard games."[11] Presidential politics, too, caught his eye, and during the national campaign of 1896 Anson publicly offered a wager of $5,000 against $3,000 that the Republican nominee, William McKinley, would win the election in November over Democratic candidate William Jennings Bryan. McKinley won, though it is not known if anyone took the captain up on his bet.

One particular betting scheme, which Anson instituted to monitor the gambling habits of his players, backfired in a spectacular way. Many of the Chicago players were horse racing fans, and skipped practice to go to the track so often that the captain volunteered to book all their bets himself and pay off any winnings at the posted odds, using the race results that appeared in the afternoon papers later that day. This setup, figured the captain, would keep his charges from sneaking off to the track and allow them to focus on their work. Anson might have profited from the scheme, had not Clark Griffith discovered a way to receive the results soon after each race, several hours before Anson knew the outcome. Griffith and the other Colts parlayed this knowledge into a two-week winning streak that ended only when the exasperated captain grew tired of losing money.[12]

Anson was an optimist, but he was no millionaire, and did not have an unlimited amount of money at his disposal. While the Colts struggled during the 1895 campaign, the *Washington Post* reported that Anson "stands to lose more than $3,000 in wagers this season." Such an amount was greater than his annual salary, and it appears that Anson took out loans from the ballclub to cover his betting losses, using his 130 shares of stock in the franchise as collateral. Later in the decade, when a dispute arose concerning the payment of dividends to stockholders, Anson complained to the

18. ANSON AND HIS COLTS

The 1895 Chicago Colts. In numerical order: Moran, Terry, Abbey, Lange, Stratton, Everitt, Stewart, Dahlen, Decker, Anson, Hutchison, Wilmot, Ryan, Kittridge, Irwin, Griffith, Donahue. (National Baseball Hall of Fame Library, Cooperstown, New York)

papers that the Chicago club had paid no dividends. Jim Hart replied that Anson's 130 shares were so heavily encumbered that any profits he made were applied to the balances of his loans.[13] Anson was a great ballplayer, but a poor gambler, and although a strong finish by the Colts in 1895 helped him avoid a huge loss, it appears that the captain's betting habit was beginning to put his financial future at risk.

The Colts established their spring training camp in Galveston, Texas, where Anson introduced several new faces to the lineup for the 1895 season. Bill Everitt took over for Charlie Irwin at third base, a move that allowed the captain to place Bill Dahlen permanently at shortstop, while Ace Stewart won the second base position from the weak-hitting Jiggs Parrott. Willie McGill, who posted a 7–19 record in 1894, drew his release, leaving Bill Hutchison, Clark Griffith, and Adonis Terry in the starting rotation. Tim Donahue won the backup catching job from Pop Schriver, and although many Chicago fans preferred to see George Decker at first base, Cap Anson remained in the lineup and continued to bat in the cleanup spot.

Sunday ball proved to be the biggest controversy of the 1895 campaign.

William Hulbert had outlawed Sunday games when he founded the National League in 1876, but the Chicago ballclub's traditional opposition to playing on the Christian Sabbath weakened in 1892 when the league dropped its ban on the practice. In 1893 the Colts began playing on Sundays at the West Side Grounds, drawing huge crowds despite the complaints of the homeowners who lived near the ballpark. The *Chicago Post* stated that local families objected "to having Anson's colts beaten so often on Sunday within their sight and hearing." In 1895 the matter came to a head when a citizen swore out a complaint against the ballclub for disturbing the peace, and when the Colts and Cleveland Spiders played at the West Side Grounds on Sunday, June 23, policemen appeared at the park to arrest the participants.

The authorities handled the situation with civility. In the third inning, the umpire announced a five-minute delay while the Chicago players reported to the clubhouse, where they were formally arrested and released on bail. They completed the game, which was won by the Colts, and two weeks later a judge found Anson and the rest of the Colts guilty and fined them $3 apiece. Hart appealed the verdict, and the case was continued until the following January.

Anson used an old trick to win a game against the Giants in Chicago on June 8. The Colts were batting with the game tied at 4 in the bottom of the ninth. There were men on first and second with two out, with Walt Wilmot at bat and Anson coaching at third. The captain loudly complained that the cover of the ball was torn, and demanded that Giants pitcher Dad Clarke allow him to inspect it. Anson's bellicose ranting so angered Clarke that he wheeled around and shouted, "Here, you check it!" and threw the ball at Anson's head. The captain stepped aside, the ball flew by, and the runners each moved up a base.

Clarke and the Giants raged at the umpire, who correctly pointed out that Clarke was not obligated to let Anson check the ball, and after a few tense minutes the game resumed. Wilmot hit a grounder to the shortstop, who fumbled the ball, and the game ended as the winning run scored from third.

Clarke seethed about the play all evening long, and accosted the umpire at the park the following day. The confrontation soon escalated into a shoving match, which brought a ballpark security guard into the fray. The guard was John Fiegal, Anson's father-in-law, who had retired from his Philadelphia bar and restaurant business and moved to Chicago several years before. Fiegal was in his mid-sixties, but was a tough character like his son-in-law. He punched Clarke in the face several times, forcing the pitcher to flee.

The Colts fell out of the pennant race early in the season, and were in a sour mood by the end of July when Anson was required to quell a mutiny on his team. On July 31, in a game against the Pirates at Chicago, Anson turned his ankle while stealing second in the fifth inning. In the sixth, he decided to take himself out of the game, sending a new pitcher, Walter Thornton, to play first base. The other Colts, especially Griffith, Dahlen, and Kittridge, wanted the better-fielding Tim Donohue at first, and sent Donohue out to relieve Anson. Donohue arrived at first just as Anson was handing his glove to Thornton, and the captain demanded to know what Donohue was doing there.

"I'm going to play first," said Donohue, with the backing of Griffith, Dahlen, and Kittridge.

Anson turned on his players and "shouted loud enough to be heard three squares," according to *The Sporting News.* "You go back to the bench as fast as you can, Mr. Donohue," said Anson, "and you other fellows go ahead and play ball. I'm running this club."

Griffith slammed his glove down on the mound, and when he finally began pitching again he merely tossed the ball to the plate with nothing on it. In the meantime, the other infielders tried their best to throw the ball past Thornton at every opportunity for the remainder of the game. Incredibly, the Pirates could not hit Griffith's lazy pitches, and Thornton held on and helped keep the game close. In the ninth inning, Thornton hit a two-run double that won the game for the Colts. Anson had not only asserted his authority, but also won the game in the process.[14]

It may have been a coincidence, but that contest started the Colts on a four-game winning streak that pushed the team up three places in the standings. Six teams—Chicago, Philadelphia, Boston, New York, Brooklyn, and Cincinnati—were fighting for fourth place, all bunched together less than 10 games behind the league-leading Cleveland Spiders. By August 4, the Colts held fourth position and remained only three games out of the league lead. A disastrous road trip, in which they lost seven in a row at Philadelphia, Brooklyn, and Boston, knocked the Colts all the way down to ninth, but Anson was not in the mood to surrender. "What? Give it up?" exploded Anson to a reporter in late August. "Give up nothing! ... The Chicago ballclub does not yield a point to anybody. I don't care who is tired and wants to quit. We won't."[15]

The captain kept his team playing hard, despite a few personnel setbacks. Jimmy Ryan was lost for a week when he cut his thumb while shaving, and Ace Stewart became upset when Anson signed Jack Truby, a new second baseman from Rockford. Stewart refused to report to the park for several days, and Anson left him in Chicago on the team's last eastern trip of the season. Still, the Colts finished the 1895 in fourth place, their best showing since the disappointment of 1891, and gave the Chicago fans some basis for optimism.

Anson usually spent the fall months hunting, playing billiards, and appearing in post-season exhibition games, but in the fall of 1895 he decided to try his hand at an entirely new endeavor. The captain had cultivated many friendships with actors in the preceding years, and was convinced that he, too, could find success on the stage. At the conclusion of the 1895 season, Anson and his wife packed their bags and boarded a train for New York. Cap Anson, the "Grand Old Man" of baseball, was headed for Broadway.

CHAPTER 19

Cap Anson on Broadway

> My dear little woman, baseball is mighty uncertain. The best must lose sometimes. But I'll play today as I never played before, and if I don't hit the ball, then the old man has lost his "good eye." Go in there, smile at your sweetheart, and don't lose hope till the last man is out.
> — A snippet of Anson's dialogue from "A Runaway Colt," 1895[1]

Charles Hoyt, one of the most popular light comedy writers of the time, was both a baseball fanatic and a friend of Cap Anson. Hoyt was constantly looking for new ideas, and the captain suggested on many occasions that Hoyt write a play about baseball. In May of 1895 Hoyt approached Anson with a proposal for a play in which Anson would portray himself as the manager of the Colts. The captain liked the concept, and Hoyt set to work, returning in two months with a script. The full title of the play was "A Runaway Colt: A dalliance with facts, folks, and other things pertaining to the noble game of baseball."[2]

The play concerned a handsome young man named Manley Manners, a minister's son and college baseball player who receives an invitation to pitch for Chicago, but runs into opposition from his parents, who view baseball as a low-class sport and an unfit calling for the son of a reverend. The local bishop, however, is a baseball fan, and invites a "Mr. Adrian" to dinner to meet the Manners family, who do not know that their guest is actually Cap Anson, manager of the Colts. The captain extols the merits of baseball life, impresses Manley's parents with his manners (especially when he turns down a glass of wine), and ultimately succeeds in changing the father's opinion of the game.

Later in the four-act melodrama, a rival suitor devises a scheme to steal Manley's fiancée, Mercy Given. He convinces Manley's brother, a bank teller, to wager $2,000 of bank funds on the Colts to win an upcoming game against Baltimore, all the while planning to bribe Anson to throw the contest and bring shame to the Manley family. The villain would then demand Mercy's hand in marriage as his price for getting the Manley family out of its jam. Anson, of course, is too honest to lose a game for money, and decides to trust the youngster to pitch the big game. "You mustn't worry," he tells Manners. "He can't do anything to you, and if he tries, I'll stand by you."

Manley replies, in the typically stilted dialogue of 1890s melodrama, "Thank you, Captain. In a case of trouble, I'd rather have you for a friend than any man on Earth! I won't worry and I'll pitch pennant ball for you as long as my arm lasts."[3]

The final act takes place with the audience behind the grandstand at the West Side Grounds, with slapsticks creating the sound of ball on bat and on-stage characters describing the action on the field. In the final scene, the Colts are down by a run in the bottom of the ninth inning against the Orioles, but Bill Dahlen (actually, the actor playing him) singles, bringing Anson to the plate. The captain saves the day with a home run, ending the play on a happy note.

Hoyt was known for his witty dialogue, and the script includes several examples of his style of humor. When Manley's sister suggests to the bishop that they pray for victory with Anson at bat and the game on the line, the bishop replies, "My dear, it is too late to pray. Make all the noise you can and rattle the pitcher." Hoyt also make a joke at the expense of the weak-hitting New York Giants. Anson, concealing the nature of his vocation, explains to the Manners family that he wants to hire Manley "to handle leather goods and in certain cities to deal with strikers."

"There are no strikers in New York, are there?" asks Mrs. Manners. Anson replies, "There haven't been any this year in my business."[4]

Another inside baseball joke occurs in the third act, set at the Colts' spring training in Florida. A love-struck hotel maid follows Anson around all day, and the captain orders Manley not to leave his side. "Don't leave me alone with her," commands Anson. "If you do, I'll expel you — or worse yet, trade you to Louisville."[5]

The captain busied himself with the Colts during the summer months of 1895 while Hoyt hired a cast and crew. Anson had not yet seen the completed script, but discussed his future role with good humor. "I shall rehearse the piece for some weeks, of course, but I expect to be a very bad actor," he said in July. "I do not know who will be the other members of the company, but I have not tried to get any other ball-players. I will star and Hoyt will take the chances."

"Do you intend playing 'Hamlet?'" asked a reporter.

"No, I think I will stick to first base. I'm more used to it."

"What do you think of the elevation of the stage?"

Anson smiled at the reporter. "Well," he said, "I think it could stand to be raised a little, especially in some theaters, where the orchestra gets between the actors and the audience."[6]

Other ballplayers had trod the boards, including Mike Kelly, who played a small role in a Hoyt play in the late 1880s and spent his off-seasons reciting "Casey at the Bat" in vaudeville houses. Another man who knew his way around a theater was John Ward, who was married to Helen Deauvray, a famous actress of the time. Ward suggested that Anson would find

A poster for Anson's play, "A Runaway Colt." (Transcendental Graphics)

a Broadway audience much different than the crowd at a baseball game. "When [the fans] were on the bleachers," said Ward, "they were too far away from Anson for the old man to hear the bon mots they cracked at his expense. But up in the gloaming next to the roof they are within ear shot of him, and he can hear every word."[7]

Bill Joyce of the Giants offered another reaction. Joyce, who lived in St. Louis, remarked that John Healy, who pitched for the All Americas on the world tour in 1888–89, was now working in a grocery store in the Mound City. "The gang will buy their retired eggs from [Healy] when Anson comes to St. Louis with his show," promised Joyce.[8]

Anson entered into an intense rehearsal schedule immediately following the conclusion of the 1895 season, but his stage career almost ended before it began. The captain had taken up the sport of bicycling, which enjoyed a rage in Chicago in the mid–1890s, and Anson attacked the new pastime with his usual enthusiasm. On October 21, he accepted a challenge from his daughter Grace to race down Michigan Avenue. While riding over a set of railroad tracks, he lost control of his pedals, and when he tried to find them again he put his foot into the spokes of his back wheel. He fell to the pavement and struck his head on the curb, a blow which left him unconscious for more than an hour and a half.

He was taken to a nearby drug store, where a doctor determined that his skull was not fractured, and then a cab took him home. "I was riding without toe clips," explained the captain, "and that explains how I came to fall ... I was riding quite close to the curbstone, and the front wheel lurched into it. Then I went down. After that I did not know much of what was going on around me until I was in the drug store."[9] The next morning, with his head encased in bandages, Anson boarded a train for New York to begin rehearsals. The play would not arrive on Broadway until December, but would open out of town in less than four weeks.

The show opened in Syracuse, New York, on November 12, 1895 at the Wieting Opera House. Anson was understandably nervous, and when he stepped onto the stage for the first time, he stood stiffly as the packed house applauded his entrance. When the cheering died down, the actress on stage with him delivered her line, but Anson did not reply. She gave it several times before the captain managed to stammer out his response. It appears that even Cap Anson was subject to attacks of stage fright. After a few awkward moments, Anson continued the play, and the engagement turned out well. Despite a few rough spots, most people considered the work to be at least a qualified success. "Anson acquitted himself very well," allowed the Syracuse correspondent to *The New York Times*. "He is scarcely an actor, but he was thoroughly in earnest."[10]

The company then went to Troy and Buffalo before arriving in Brooklyn at the Montauk Theatre in late November for a one-week engagement prior to its Broadway debut. Virginia Anson handled the captain's makeup, because early in the tour she saw the makeup man work on her husband and decided that she could do a better job. She also convinced Hoyt to drop a kissing scene involving her husband. "There was a little bit of that early in the play," said Virginia to a Brooklyn newspaperman, "but when the girls learned that I was with him, they stopped."

"Stage kisses don't count," suggested the reporter.

"Do you hear that, Ma?" protested the captain, but Virginia got her way.

The reporter asked Anson about his new line of work. "How do I like acting?" said Anson. "Well, I don't dislike it. You see I'm not in the business from choice. I don't profess to be an actor, but then Mr. Hoyt made me a good offer and I took it. I've had only about two weeks' experience and less than that to learn my part. I appear in every act and make six changes, so I have my hands pretty full."

He disputed reports from Syracuse that said he suffered from stage fright. "Well, I must confess I felt a little nervous at the start," he said. "We opened at Syracuse. I had very little preparation and while I was somewhat raw I think I did first rate. My reception was very encouraging. In fact, the applause was so great that I had to wait several minutes before I could begin my part. Some of the reporters said I forgot my lines, but that isn't so. Every actor must wait for his cue and that's what I did."

Anson also suggested that the actors who portrayed Bill Lange, Jimmy Ryan, Bill Dahlen, and other Colts were "a little too fat," but on the whole he trusted Hoyt's judgment in casting and direction. He made no grand claims of his own acting prowess, telling the reporter, "What my ability as an actor is you can judge from the front."[11]

The Brooklyn critics were more discriminating than the ones in Syracuse and Buffalo, and gave the play a thoroughly negative review. "The comedy is not up to the Hoyt level," complained the *Brooklyn Eagle*. "It goes by fits and starts, ending with a bump at the end of every act; that is, after the first, which is flat from start to finish. Pop Anson is lumbering and good natured throughout, but his ability to make a hit is now, and must for some time to come, be confined to the ball field." The paper also criticized the rest of the cast for "natural inability or insufficient training," and gave Anson some faint praise by saying, "Pop at times rose to the level of several of his alleged support."[12]

The seats were filled at the Montauk at the beginning of the week, but the bad reviews caused business to drop off until the house was no better than half full by the end of the run. Hoyt, disappointed with the pans from the Brooklyn critics, did some frantic rewriting, with the major change involving the final scene. The original script called for the audience to hear the action on the field from behind the grandstand, but Hoyt now opened up the stage and set the scene on the field itself, complete with "Colts," "Orioles," and an umpire. These changes increased the size of the cast and the cost of the production, but Hoyt wanted the play to succeed in New York, so he made the changes and hoped for the best. After a few rehearsals of the revamped final act, the play was ready for its opening night on Broadway. On December 3, 1895, "A Runaway Colt" began a three-week run at the American Theatre.

The New York critics, surprisingly, treated the novice actor Anson gently. *The New York Times* gave the production a good, though not a rave, review and stated that Anson "made a home run at the American Theater last night." The *Times* praised Anson's presence, both in the on-field and off-field scenes, and said, "Mr. Hoyt knew Mr. Anson when he wrote the piece, Mr. Anson knows what Mr. Hoyt wrote, and somebody has taught him what to do when he is not on the diamond."[13]

"He speaks his lines with the directness of an artillery officer, no matter whether he is accepting an invitation to dinner or defending the good cause of professional base ball," the *New York Dramatic Mirror* wrote. "He is quite as good as most of the people on stage with him." The *Herald* was less enthusiastic, suggesting that Anson was "prone to imitate an Illinois Methodist preacher giving out the long meter doxology."[14]

On the third night of the show, several members of the Baltimore Orioles attended, greeted Anson backstage beforehand, and were enlisted to play themselves in the climactic ballgame. They donned uniforms and took their positions on the "field" as Anson hit the home run that ended the play. Of course, the Orioles could not allow this opportunity for mischief go by without playing a joke on their longtime rival. As Anson rounded third base, one of the Orioles tripped him on the way home. Anson's unexpected fall mirrored the box-office performance of the show, which drew smaller audiences as the engagement continued. The American Theater was half-full on good days, and Hoyt soon realized that he had a money-losing proposition on his hands.

After the New York run, the company moved to Chicago, where the play opened at the Grand Opera House on December 23. Though Anson was the longtime star of the local team and one of the best-known men in Chicago, attendance was small, though some of the notices were good. "The audience took about a minute upon his first appearance to let [Anson] know that he still had hosts of admirers," said one paper, "...'A Runaway Colt' is a hit, if last night's auditors were fair umpires."[15]

Not all the local critics were amused. "Week before last," stated the *Tribune* in its "Drama and its Devotees" column, "Charles H. Hoyt presented to the patrons of that theater a drama (may heaven forgive us for calling it thus!) designed solely to exploit a dull and uneducated professional athlete. Its language was slangy, its fun was the fun of the tavern, its plot was preposterous, its actors were mostly 'variety' performers. Mr. Hoyt has put together some entertainments that were really clever, but 'A Runaway Colt' was driveling stupidity."[16]

Hoyt pulled the plug after only a week in Chicago, and after the last performance on December 29, cast and crew hit the road for Milwaukee, Minneapolis, and other Midwestern cities. The people of Wisconsin and Minnesota were unimpressed with Anson as an actor, and on January 8 word reached the papers that "A Runaway Colt" would cease production. Anson and the rest of the cast were dismissed. "As an actor, Anson is a failure," proclaimed the *Washington Post*.

Frank McKee, Hoyt's producing partner, blamed the failure on Anson's lack of personality on stage. "Anson was such a frappe that every time he entered the theater the steam pipes perspired ice water," complained McKee. "He's such a chill that he could put on a linen duster and golf hat and discover the North Pole."[17] Anson replied that Hoyt and McKee should have booked the play into larger cities after New York instead of the smaller Midwestern towns in which the show appeared. If the play had been seen in National League cities, where people knew baseball, reasoned Anson, it might have found success on the road for months. In February Anson, ever the optimist, announced that he intended to buy the rights from Hoyt and McKee and produce it himself, but nothing came of the offer, and "A Runaway Colt" never again saw the light of day.

Sadly, the failure of the play caused a rift between Anson and Hoyt, who only two months earlier had told the papers that he wanted to buy the Louisville ballclub and sign Anson, "a personal friend of mine," as its manager. Hoyt, who was an excitable character, called the play "a fiasco" and blamed the captain. "Anson wanted me to write a play for him," said Hoyt, "and I did, I'm sorry to say. It was killed by Anson, and I gave it a burial without flowers. I called it 'A Runaway Colt.' It was a case, b'gosh, of a runaway audience after the first night.

"Anson used to boast to me what a magnetic chap he was; how he could draw thousands to see him play ball, and he was sure he could draw in the theater. Why, to tell you the truth ... every time Anson walked on the stage it began to snow. I was thinking of having a snow scene painted, to be used when Anson was acting, but he objected. He said it would destroy his magnetism."[18]

Anson, despite the failure of the venture, was proud of his brief stage career. In his later years, he wrote his letters on personal stationery that bore the inscription:

A Better Actor Than Any Ball Player

A Better Ball Player Than Any Actor

However, when Anson produced his autobiography a mere four years after his Broadway experience, he made no mention of "A Runaway Colt" at all. Clearly, Anson was disappointed by the experience, and grew defensive about the subject whenever the sportswriters brought it up. Far worse was the razzing that he received from opposing players, who found enough verbal ammunition to use against Anson for the rest of his career. Bill Joyce, manager of the Giants, teased Anson about it one day. "I notice, Anson, that when you were playing last winter you didn't use any signals at all."

"How's that?" asked the captain.

"Why, when you played in 'A Runaway Colt,' no one was on the coach line to signal you when to act."[19]

Nick Young, the league president, also weighed in on Anson's prowess as a thespian. "I don't think it's policy for ballplayers to force themselves into the theatrical business," said Young to the *Washington Post*. "They don't add to the dignity of the game and they encroach on the field of people who obtain a legitimate livelihood from the stage. Mr. Anson was a failure. So was Mike Kelly."[20]

Early the following spring, when Anson was out of the lineup with a sore arm, he used powerful magnets to speed the healing process at the suggestion of a Chicago doctor. "Anson could use some magnetism," said one player. "He found that out in 'A Runaway Colt.'"

After a while, Anson grew tired of the constant kidding about his acting abilities. "I may be a rotten thespian," boomed Anson one day, "but there are others!" With that statement, Anson put his stage experience behind him and focused once again on his baseball career. The 1895 season marked the ninth consecutive season that the Chicago club had finished the year without winning the pennant, and Anson proposed to end that long losing streak. "We'll win next year," he promised the Chicago sportswriters at the end of the 1895 season, and he set out to make good on his boast.

For the first time in several years, the Colts started the season well. They played their 1896 home opener on May 3 in front of a record crowd of 17,231 at the West Side Grounds, with thousands of fans behind ropes in the outfield. Their presence made the playing field so small that the umpire decreed that balls batted into the crowd would count for three bases. The Colts hit nine triples that day, three by Bill Dahlen, and defeated the Browns by a score of 16 to 9. Anson, bothered by a chest cold that lasted for more than two weeks, took a seat on the bench and put George Decker on first, a move which improved the Chicago defense and helped the team stay above the .500 mark in the season's first six weeks.

Clark Griffith was a smart pitcher, and used quick thinking to win a game from the Phillies on May 8. In the ninth inning, with the Colts ahead by two, the Phillies had one out and a runner on first with their captain, Billy Nash, at the plate. When Nash disagreed with a strike call and turned around to argue with umpire Tim Keefe, Griffith noticed that Keefe had not called time. While Nash stood at the plate with his bat in his hand, talking to the umpire, Griffith got the ball back from the catcher and threw a pitch to the plate. The ball struck the bat and dribbled to Griffith, who threw to second to start a double play that ended the game.

The Colts held third place until mid–May, but injuries and poor pitching caused them to sink in the standings until they bottomed out on June 2, when a 6–2 loss in New York dropped them to ninth place with a record of 18–21. Anson had re-entered the lineup, shifting Decker to left field, and second base became a problem area for the team once again when Baltimore's George Van Haltren spiked Jack Truby, whom Anson insisted would be "the best second baseman in the league" before long. The spike wound put Truby in the hospital and forced Anson to put the 36-year-old Fred Pfeffer, recently released by the Giants, at second. Pfeffer had slowed down noticeably, and since Anson's range was also severely limited, the right side of the infield became a weak point in the Chicago defense.

While Baltimore, Cleveland, and Cincinnati battled for the league lead, Anson's Colts struggled to escape the second division. A 19–3 loss to Cleveland on July 1 put the Spiders in first place, dropping Chicago to ninth with a 32–32 record. The season appeared lost once again, and *The Sporting News* remarked, "Anson is almost as much a success with the Colts this season as he was with 'A Runaway Colt' last winter." The paper did not intend the remark as a compliment. More voices in the newspapers, and in the bleachers, called for Anson to step aside as a player, but the Grand Old Man was having none of it. "When do I intend to retire from the diamond?" asked Anson. "As long as I can hit that ball I will be in the game! Good hitters are gold and precious stones to a club, and it strikes me they are growing scarcer and scarcer every day."[21]

One could tell that Anson had no intention of retiring by the way he cared for his bats. As the *Cincinnati Enquirer* explained:

> There are more loose timbers around the Chicago ball park and Spalding's store than it would take to start a good-sized lumberyard. In odd nooks and corners at the ball yard especially you will run into an old log, a wagon tongue, or an old cart shaft.
> Anson has either taken them there himself or had them hauled in. They are timber for his bats. He never overlooks a good piece of wood, no matter where he is.
> If he sees a well-seasoned and solid piece of wood in Galveston, New York, or San Francisco, he will ship it to Chicago. Someday, when he thinks of it again, he will haul it out and have it turned into a bat.
> It has been stated that he has 276 bats in the basement of his home, but there are some who put the figure closer to five hundred. He has them hung up like hams. His locker is always full of bats. He never permits anybody else to use any stick in his private stock.[22]

An 8–7 win against Cy Young and the Spiders on July 2 started the Colts on their best streak of the season. They won 25 of their next 33 games and pushed all the way up into fourth place. One of the most unusual wins came on July 13 against Philadelphia in Chicago. Ed Delahanty, the slugging outfielder of the Phillies, belted four home runs against Adonis Terry, one of which sailed over the scoreboard in right center for the longest ball hit all year in Chicago. Delahanty became the second man to hit four round-trippers in a game, but the first to do so in a losing cause, as the Colts scratched out a 9–8 victory.

The Colts started to fade in mid–August, and as they fell out of the pennant race the locker room bickering grew worse. Clark Griffith, the radical pitcher, nearly came to blows one day with his catcher, the politically conservative Mal Kittridge, over the respective chances of Bryan and McKinley in the upcoming presidential election. Lange, Ryan, and others began to stay out late, often showing up at the park in no condition to play. Anson issued fines, which Jim Hart refused to collect, and team discipline collapsed again, as it had in each of the previous several seasons.

Selfish play was a problem for the Colts, and Bill Lange was one man who infuriated Anson when he played for his statistics and not for the team. Lange was locked in a battle with Boston's Billy Hamilton for the league stolen-base title in 1896, and tried to steal as many bases as possible, regardless of the score or the game situation. One day late in the season, Lange stood on second in a close game with Anson at bat. The captain laid down a perfect sacrifice bunt and lumbered down to first. He turned to third base, expecting to see Lange there, but the bag was unoccupied. Lange, not willing to lose an opportunity for a stolen base, remained on second, making Anson's sacrifice meaningless. Anson was further incensed when Lange stole third cleanly on the next pitch. "Cap had a narrow escape from apoplexy," remarked sportswriter Hugh Fullerton, but the episode was only one of many such incidents that season.

By September, few players bothered to participate in pre-game practices, and the Colts' lack of discipline was a poorly kept secret around the league. "The indifference of the Colts and their aversion to practice," said the *Washington Post*, "is due to the fact that they are on the whole a low-salaried lot of players. Underpay and overwork is as discouraging to a ballplayer as to an employee in any other trade or profession."[23] The paper stated that only four Colts, including Anson, earned the league maximum salary of $2,400, while Cleveland was said to have nine men at that level and most of the other clubs had six or more.

Anson, who received the highest salary on the team and also owned 13 percent of the stock, paid little attention to the monetary concerns of his teammates. He boasted to the papers about the first-class traveling accommodations that the Chicago management always provided, though the low salaries were responsible for at least some of the behavioral problems on the ballclub. As one paper put it, "While Uncle Anson and his stable of Colts knock knees under the mahoganies of swagger hotels and are bowled to and from the ball parks in décolleté hacks, there are those among the Colts who would prefer higher salaries and less style."[24] Salary differences and behavior issues caused the gulf between the young players and the old captain to grow wider with each passing season.

In addition, it appears that by 1896 the Colts had lost faith in their 44-year-old captain as a player. Anson batted .331 for the season, but his power was nearly gone, with his slugging percentage dipping below the league average for the first time in his career. He stole 24 bases but scored only 72 runs, fifth-most on the Colts, though he drove in 90 and missed the team leadership by two. His lack of speed clogged the base paths, crippling the Chicago offensive attack, though Anson stubbornly kept himself in the cleanup spot in the lineup. At first base, Anson's range, which was never more than adequate, had fallen well below the league average. The combination of the slow Pfeffer at second and the lumbering Anson at first put pressure on the pitching staff to keep batted balls away from the right side of the infield.

The captain sensed that his days as an infielder were coming to an end, so he inserted himself into the lineup at catcher for 10 games with middling results. Anson might have been able to hang on for another year or two if the designated hitter rule had been in effect in the 1890s, but the DH would not become a part of the game for another 75 years. Hitters were required to play in the field in Anson's day, and Cap Anson was running out of positions to play.

At the very least, the slow-as-molasses Anson should have dropped himself to the sixth or seventh spot in the lineup, though most fans and writers believed that Anson, after 26 seasons of professional play, should retire from the diamond with dignity. The captain, as usual, brushed off such concerns. In 1895, a reporter asked Anson, "Like the opera singer [Adelita] Patti, will you proclaim this your last season?" Anson exploded, "Farewell season? Well, I'll be playing ball when I'm 70! I started out to play ball as long as Spalding made them."[25]

In the last week of September, Anson ordered his men to appear for morning practices, but the club was out of the pennant chase by then. The Colts, to their captain's dismay, were more concerned with ending the season and going home than in winning games. On many mornings, Anson practiced by himself at the West Side Grounds. The players were staying out later and drinking more, and in late September pitcher Clark Griffith decided to end his season early. He went home to Missouri without obtaining permission from the captain or Jim Hart. He did not miss any games, because the last two series of the season were rained out in Chicago and Cincinnati, but Anson was, in the words of *The Sporting News*, "more or less out of humor with the men" as team discipline collapsed.

On September 26, the *Chicago Tribune* carried an interview with Anson in which the captain blasted his players for their attitudes. "I want to go on record," said the captain, "as saying that the majority of the players of the Chicago team have not been acting fairly with the management or with the baseball public which supports them. I do not believe any set of men can play good ball after a week of absence from the field without exercise or practice ... I ordered the men to meet here every day for light practice work, with the idea of keeping in perfect training. My orders have been ignored. Only three men have appeared here, and only one has practiced regularly. They have attended the races and had a good time at balls and parties.

"I can fine them for such conduct and cut off their salaries, and I may decide to do it. I see no reason why these men should be paid when they do no work nor even report for duty."

Anson then exacerbated the situation with an argument that deepened the rift between the captain and his erratic but brilliant shortstop, Bill Dahlen. In late September the Colts played three games in Louisville and returned to Chicago, where a series against Cleveland was rained out, and then boarded a train to Cincinnati for the final games of the season. Each player had a ticket to board the train, while Anson held a separate ticket for the sleeping car for each man. Anson required that each player come to him for his sleeping car ticket before turning in, because he closely monitored the late-night habits of his players; this arrangement gave him a chance to see if any Colts were either out past curfew or drinking. Late one night, Dahlen turned into his berth for the evening, only to be awakened by the porter, who demanded to see Dahlen's ticket for the sleeping car. Dahlen spit out a few epithets, telling the porter to go and see Anson.

The porter reminded Anson that anyone without a sleeping car ticket would be put off the train at the next stop, as per the rules of the railroad. Anson, upset with Dahlen for turning in without getting his ticket, suspected that the shortstop had been drinking and did not want to be fined or suspended. He told the porter to put Dahlen off the train if he was so inclined. At the next stop, somewhere in rural Indiana, the porter ejected Dahlen from the train. The Colts arrived in Cincinnati the next morning without a shortstop, and the club immediately suspended Dahlen.

The players were surprised by the harshness of Anson's discipline, and *The Sporting News* reported that the Colts were "considerably worked up over the incident, and their sympathy seems to be strongly with Dahlen. They do not discuss it, however, in the presence of Anson."

Anson, as usual, made no apologies for his actions:

> It was my right to demand of Dahlen that he come to me for his ticket. When we start upon a trip I expected all of them to report to me, and then I can furnish them with tickets or other accommodations that they need. I am also able thereby to note their condition and make sure that they are all on hand. Mr. Dahlen did not do this, and in taking the action I did I was merely insisting on my rights and duties as manager of the team.[26]

Anson picked the wrong time to pull a stunt like this, especially when his relationship with Dahlen was always touch-and-go at best. The shortstop had quarreled with the captain in Cleveland in early September, when Anson fined Dahlen for skipping practice. Dahlen, after six seasons in Chicago, was only earning $1,500 in salary by 1896, and every dollar subtracted from his paycheck cut deeply. He was always asking Anson or Hart for advances, but Anson (if not Hart) always turned him down, which only served to intensify his resentment. Dahlen had not spoken to Anson in more than two weeks at the time of the train incident, which probably occurred because Dahlen found communications with his captain so distasteful that he would rather risk expulsion from the train than ask for his ticket.

Dahlen did not miss any games, as the series in Cincinnati was rained out, but the rift between the two was not mended for several months. Eventually, Jim Hart announced that Anson and Dahlen had smoothed over their differences, and perhaps Hart returned the money that the club withheld from Dahlen's paycheck while he was suspended. The Colts had finished the 1896 season in the first division, but since the team roster would not change for the following year, Anson could look forward to another season of disciplinary problems and tense relations with his players.

Cap Anson had been building his team since the Brotherhood year of 1890, but his Colts were not getting any younger, and had not been a factor in the National League pennant chase since 1891. The Chicago fans were growing restless, and although the captain made his annual springtime pennant prediction for the coming year, fans and management were running out of patience. If the team did not challenge in 1897, Anson's 19th season at the helm, he might not be around to celebrate his 20th.

CHAPTER 20

The Final Season

> How old is Anson? When the ark
> First found once more a resting place
> Old Noah, groping in the dark,
> Discovered Anson on first base —
> The grand old man had held it down
> In spite of floods that came to drown.
> — *The Sporting News*, 1897[1]

The 1897 season began with a management decision that provoked outraged responses from the players. The National League magnates unilaterally decided that the six-month player contract would run from April 15 to October 15, not from April 1 to October 1 as it had previously. The owners made this change for two reasons. The players received their first paychecks two weeks after the beginning of the season, so the owners would not be required to pay their men until April 30. The new contractual timeframe also delayed off-season barnstorming trips by reserving the first two weeks in October for the major league clubs.

The magnates rationalized making the switch because the weather was better in October than in April, but the players seethed, especially the Colts. The *Brooklyn Eagle* reported that the Chicago players "have been for three days discussing the matter and making threats of open rebellion."[2] The players were powerless to do anything, as usual, but they vented their feelings against Al Spalding and, indirectly, towards Anson, who told the papers that he did not see any problem with the arrangement, since the players received their usual salary in the same amount of time. Since Spalding was the main mover and shaker behind most of the National League's policies, the Colts blamed him for this latest contract amendment.

20. THE FINAL SEASON

The Colts appeared to be in good shape when they left Hot Springs, but began the season by losing three one-run games in a row at Cincinnati. Two wins in three games against the helpless Browns in St. Louis followed, but the Colts lost two and tied one at Louisville before arriving in Chicago for their home opener against the Browns on May 3. They brought a 2–6 record back home with them, and although it was too early to panic, the Colts were already entrenched in the second division. Pitcher Clark Griffith, a 25-game winner in 1896, was holding out for more money, and the Colts desperately needed him to return to the rotation before the season got away from them.

Cap Anson in the late 1890s. (National Baseball Hall of Fame Library, Cooperstown, New York)

Since Anson had announced that 1897 would be his final year as a player, the club arranged a tribute to their long-time captain. The home opener was designated as "Anson Day," with a ceremony planned to honor the 27-year veteran for his contribution to Chicago baseball. Anson, speaking to reporters on the train carrying the team from Louisville to Chicago, looked at pictures of his younger self in the *Chicago Tribune* and insisted "I am just as young now as I was then.... Don't feel a day older than I did then."

"Then he jumped off the train at Forty-Second street and jogged homeward," said the *Tribune*, "where it is always Anson day."[3]

Anson played in only three of the nine games on the road trip, and was still hitless on the season. He was not even sure if he would play in the game on his day. "I don't know," said Anson. "If the people want to see me I'll go in, but I want to see what the feeling is." He wanted to start Clark Griffith in the home opener, but Griffith and Jim Hart could not reach an agreement; the *Tribune* said that the two sides were only $100 apart, but both men were stubborn, and Griffith left Hart's office without signing a contract. Rain washed out the contest, as well as the Anson Day festivities, which were rescheduled for the next day. Anson tapped right-hander Jimmy Callahan to pitch in Griffith's place.

The weather improved on May 4, and more than 14,000 people filled the West Side Grounds to honor Cap Anson. Among the celebrants were vaudeville star Eddie Foy and actor Maurice Barrymore, who brought his teenaged daughter Ethel, an aspiring actress, to view the celebration. Anson, who had recently shaved off his mustache ("Let it grow again, Uncle Adrian," pleaded the *Chicago Tribune*) approached home plate, where a table filled with trophies and other mementoes was set up for the occasion. As the players from both teams lined up on the first and third base lines, a band played John Philip Sousa's "El Capitan March."

The master of ceremonies presented Anson with the day's most impressive gift, an engraved silver tea service purchased by his friends and admirers. He then turned the podium over to Anson. The captain thanked the fans for their support, and while only an approximate transcript of his off-the-cuff speech appeared in the newspapers, the captain began his remarks with the statement, "This is the proudest day of my life."

He continued:

> Both for the good will that prompted it and for the beauty of the gift itself, I value the offering made to be by my friends and well-wishers beyond anything I can express in words. I really don't know in what words to put my appreciation of the offering. I can only say that I am deeply thankful to every person that has remembered me and especially to the committee which had the matter in charge. It is a pleasure to know that I have such friends. The gift will always be a reminder to me of the generosity and kindness of the Chicago people.[4]

Anson decided to play after all, putting himself in at catcher and batting last in the lineup. The Browns had planned to start Bill Hutchison, the former Colt, but manager Tommy Dowd decided to send Duke Esper to the mound instead. It was the wrong decision; Esper retired the Colts in the first inning, but allowed four runs in the second, and the Colts cruised to a 5–2 win behind Jimmy Callahan.

Cap Anson singled in the second inning for his first hit of the season and, despite his noticeable lack of speed, surprised the Browns when he attempted to steal second base. The *Tribune* called it "the mistake of his life" and continued, "Like an agile hippopotamus the Cap'n was moving in a series of undulating contortions toward second base. The ball was waiting for him when he got there, but the Cap'n made a conscientious effort to give a spectacular effect to the performance and slid. He soiled and smeared his new white suit irretrievably."[5]

Still, the fans appreciated the effort and cheered the 45-year-old captain as he jogged off the field. They also enjoyed a good laugh in the sixth inning when a group of admirers presented outfielder Jimmy Ryan with a bouquet of roses when he went up to bat. "How much did they cost, Jimmy?" shouted someone in the crowd.

The celebration was a success, and although the win gave the Colts only their third victory in the season's first 10 games, Anson promised to use his new silver service at a banquet for the players at season's end. The banquet, announced the captain to his men, would be held after the Colts clinched the 1897 championship. The team had also constructed a new flagpole at the ballpark, and Anson promised the fans that the pennant would fly there at season's end.

Anson Day was the high point of the 1897 campaign for the Colts. The club fell to the Browns the next day, then traveled to Cleveland and lost three in a row to the Spiders. By May 10 the Colts found themselves buried in last place with a 4–11 record, already seven and a half games behind the leaders with the season only three weeks old. The same fans who cheered Anson and his team so heartily on May 4 turned surly, and before long Anson could not appear on the field without a chorus of boos echoing from the stands.

Opposing players showed little respect for the Grand Old Man of the Game. In mid–May, Anson slid hard into the Senators' Gene DeMontreville in a play at second base. DeMontreville turned on the much older Anson. "Why, you red-headed old yap," snarled DeMontreville, "if it weren't for your age I'd get after you. It's a wonder you wouldn't apply to a home for the aged and give a young man a chance."

"Young man," remonstrated Anson, "you ought to be ashamed of yourself. The idea of talking like that to me. I'm old enough to be your father."

"Stronger than that, Ans," replied DeMontreville. "Make it your grandfather."[6]

Anson knew how to give it back. In August he rode Pirate pitcher Emerson "Pink" Hawley from the coaching box, and Hawley called out, "If I had your money I would be riding in cushion-tiered carriages."

"Yes," replied Anson, "and if I had the money you think I have I would buy your release from Pittsburgh, trade you for a yellow dog, and shoot the dog."[7]

Tom Brown of the Senators, a veteran of the 1888-89 Spalding tour, criticized Anson's fielding to the newspapers. "Never in my life," said Brown in 1897, "did I regard Anson as a first-class first baseman. Anson always was slow in stooping for a low-thrown ball, and he covered about enough ground to bury himself in."[8] The captain was almost immobile around the bag, so in May he placed the more nimble George Decker at first base. Anson did not want to sit on the bench, so he put himself in at catcher, much to the dismay of Jim Hart and the other Colts.

Anson, who valued a strong offense, inserted himself behind the plate because regular backstops Mal Kittridge and Tim Donahue did not hit much (Donahue batted .209 and Kittridge .202 in 1897). However, both Donahue and Kittridge were far superior to Anson defensively, and the Chicago hurlers shuddered at the prospect of pitching to their superannuated captain. Their fears were soon realized, as Anson proved himself as inept behind the plate as he had been in the infield. Some of the Chicago pitchers resented Anson's stubbornness. In May, Anson misplayed a pop-up behind the plate, and the ball fell harmlessly to earth. Pitcher Buttons Briggs shouted, "Say there, Cap, you know if you catch those on the fly they're out. They used to be when I was a boy."[9]

The captain's tenure behind the plate ended abruptly on May 20 in a game against Washington. In a 16–14 Chicago loss, the Senators stole bases at will as Anson made one wild throw after another to second and third bases. In the ninth inning, in what one paper called "the final straw that rent the camel's spinal column," Anson let a throw from the outfield get by him as the winning run scored. The home fans taunted him mercilessly — one suggested that "if you were as funny on the stage, that play of Hoyt's would be playing to the capacity yet"— and the embarrassed captain angrily threatened to retire from active play.

On the same day, the St. Louis Browns waived veteran first baseman Roger Connor, baseball's all-time home run leader at the time, and Jim Hart realized that if he could convince Anson to hang up his spikes, he could put in a claim for Connor. Hart knew that Anson's usefulness as a player was long over, and offered a curiously half-hearted defense of his manager. "Anson realizes that there are stronger first basemen and catchers than himself," Hart told the papers that evening. "Our patrons didn't fancy his fielding as a first baseman, so they set up a howl. But he figured that he ought to be in the game for his hitting, and so he went behind the bat. Now they are up in arms against his catching."[10] However, Anson calmed down and opted to remain on the playing roster, causing Hart to reluctantly pass on Roger Connor.

Anson clashed with Hart over personnel issues in the early months of the 1897 campaign. Second baseman Fred Pfeffer, the last remaining active member of the 1885-86 championship team (besides Jimmy Ryan and Anson himself), was now 38 years old and barely hanging on. Pfeffer played poorly in spring training, but Anson still held a soft spot in his heart for his old teammate. "[Pfeffer's] head is as level as ever," said Anson to the papers, "and he could make many a play in that infield if Dahlen would only

20. THE FINAL SEASON

work with him."[11] Hart, however, knew that Pfeffer had reached the end of his career, and signed Jim Connor, who played well in the Western League in 1896. Anson resented Hart's interference and handed Connor his release, but Hart kept Connor on the team over the captain's objections. Anson started the season with Pfeffer on second, but after 32 games the captain finally gave up and gave the spot to Connor.

The Colts also had a hole in left field, which Anson tried to fill with Walter Thornton, who had failed in a trial as a pitcher the year before. Thornton hit well but fielded atrociously, with 23 errors in only 59 games, and in late May Anson returned to first base and moved George Decker to left. Hart wanted to fill the spot with a young outfielder from Bedford, Ohio, named Elmer Flick, but, as the team president told the *Chicago Tribune*, "I did not want to force a man on Anson ... and Anson did not want any more experiments, so we lost the chance to get Flick."[12] Flick went instead to the Phillies, where he started a career that landed him in the Hall of Fame.

In late May, Anson put pitcher Jimmy Callahan in left field, a move that proved beneficial and gave the team a needed boost. This assignment took Callahan out of the pitching rotation, but he hit well and improved the outfield defense. Callahan fielded so well, in fact, that Anson outsmarted himself. The captain then defied Hart when he benched Connor and moved Callahan to second base, a position that Callahan had never played, and returned Decker to left. Callahan's inexperience at second base showed, and his presence there further weakened the struggling infield defense. Callahan's difficulties and Anson's immobility rendered the team almost helpless on balls hit to the right side, which discouraged the Colt pitchers as the season wore on. An injury to shortstop Bill Dahlen exacerbated matters as the Chicago defense failed in game after game.

Off the field, the rowdy Colts ignored Anson's curfews and flouted his rules. They were a wild bunch, a "joy club" in the parlance of the era, and the strict disciplinarian Anson found himself unable to handle his charges, many of whom were young enough to be his sons. "The Colts," said the *Washington Post*, "are the most slipshod lot in point of discipline of any team in the major league, and Anson has no one to blame but himself for it."[13] Anson stated a few years later that "[a] lack of discipline and insubordination began to show from the start" of the 1897 season, but he attributed the problem to Jim Hart's failure to collect fines from the players. The behavior deteriorated as the season progressed, but Hart looked the other way as the Colts sank in the standings.

The players took a special delight in tormenting their manager. The Colts, like all ballclubs in that era, traveled by train, and on one particular trip the Pullman company tried out a new kind of mattress in the sleeping cars, an air-filled pad held in place by screws. Bill Dahlen loosened all the screws in Anson's berth, and when the captain tossed his 230-pound frame into bed that evening he dropped through the mattress with a loud whooshing noise, tumbling to the floor with a thud. The players roared, but Anson refused to acknowledge their ridicule. He slept on the hard floor and seethed the entire night. He wanted to get rid of Dahlen, but the Baltimore Orioles turned down a Dahlen-for-Hugh Jennings swap, and Anson was stuck with his talented but rowdy shortstop.

John McGraw, captain of the pennant-winning Orioles, blasted the Colts for their attitude. "I never saw such an indifferent lot of ballplayers," complained McGraw. "Dahlen and Bill Lange are brilliant players, but they are inclined to be rebellious, and they have no respect whatever for Anson, who is a perfect gentleman and an ornament to the team. Ryan and that blasé gent, Dahlen, abuse the old man shamefully, though I suppose it is his own fault to stand for it."[14] The younger Colts learned to follow the example of veterans like Ryan and Dahlen, making the environment hardly conducive to winning and team play.

The Colts played poor, disinterested baseball, and it became clear by midseason that Anson had totally lost control of his team. An embarrassing 19–7 loss to Boston on June 19 left the Colts in tenth place, 17 games behind the league leaders. The road trip ended with a 6–5 loss to Pittsburgh on June 23 that dropped the Colts to 11th position. That night, at the Pittsburgh train station, Anson became infuriated at the sight of his players joking and roughhousing on the platform. The fuming captain set his sights on Hugh Fullerton, a young sportswriter, who was waiting for the train along with the jovial ballplayers.

"Fullerton, you're a damned coward!" bellowed Anson. "Why don't you write the truth?"

Fullerton, taken aback, asked Anson what he meant.

"Why don't you tell the people of Chicago," demanded the red-faced captain, "that the Chicago club is a bunch of loafers and drunkards, throwing Anson down?"

"They might make me prove it," replied Fullerton. "A reporter can't write that sort of thing."

"You're afraid to write it," said Anson. "You're protecting them."

Bill Lange punched Fullerton playfully on the arm. "Go on and write it, Hughie," Lange said. He was joking, but Anson was deadly serious.

"Say that Anson says it," shouted the captain. "Put it in blackface type that Anson says the Chicago ball club is a bunch of drunkards and loafers who are throwing him down."

20. The Final Season

Fullerton gave Anson what he wanted. He left the platform and wrote the story immediately, returning to Chicago on a later train. Fullerton's column the next day began with this statement:

> Captain A. C. Anson desires me to announce in blackface type at the head of this column that the Chicago ball club is composed of drunkards and loafers who are throwing him down.

Fullerton's train beat the Colts back to Chicago, and the reporter went to Jim Hart's office the next morning. The morning papers had hit the streets, and Hart was livid with rage. "Did Anson say what you wrote?" demanded Hart. Fullerton answered in the affirmative, and a few moments later Anson strolled into the office.

Hart turned toward his manager. "Anson, did you say what Fullerton wrote?"

"Yes," bellowed Anson, "and the damned coward didn't make it half strong enough!"[15]

This contretemps sealed Anson's fate with the Colts. His contract ran until February 1, 1898, but for all practical purposes Anson's managerial tenure in Chicago ended that day in Hart's office. Shortly after, Hart sent Fullerton to see John Walsh, the banker and railroad magnate who held a large portion of stock in the team. Walsh, off the record, told Fullerton, "There hasn't been a minute since you wrote that story that the blanked old Swede could have stayed with the club if he hadn't had a contract."[16]

Anson's tantrum at the Pittsburgh railroad station may have energized the Colts, if only temporarily. Six days later, an injury-ravaged Louisville Colonels team came to Chicago, and the Colts bombed the visitors by a score of 36 to 7. The Colts walloped Louisville pitching for 32 hits, with Jimmy Callahan getting five and Lange, Connor, and substitute infielder Barry McCormick (who was so thin that the papers called him Exclamation Point) four each. Ten walks and nine Louisville errors helped the Colts set a new all-time record for runs scored in a game, a mark that still stands. In early July the Colts beat league-leading Boston three games in a row and starting clawing their way back up the standings.

The Colts tried their best to turn the season around, but another of Anson's rejects came back to haunt them. Jack Powell, a righthanded pitcher in the fast Chicago semipro leagues, regularly pitched batting practice for the Colts in the mid–1890s. Powell desperately wanted Anson to sign him, but he was a control pitcher with a merely ordinary fastball. Anson liked hard-throwing hurlers, and turned down Powell with the comment, "He hasn't anything." In 1896 Powell signed with the Fort Wayne minor league team, which was owned by Cleveland Spiders magnate Frank Robison, and in June of 1897 joined the Cleveland rotation. On June 26, in his second major league start, Powell shut out the Colts by a 5–0 score and allowed only six hits, three by Anson. Powell went on to win 246 games in a major league career that lasted until 1912.

The teams in sixth through tenth position were tightly bunched that year, and the Colts battled the Pirates, Senators, Phillies, and Dodgers for the coveted sixth spot and a slice of the first division. An embarrassing 20–2 home defeat to Baltimore represented a setback, but by July 27 the Colts grabbed eighth place, and another modest winning streak drove Anson's men to sixth after a 16–6 win over Louisville on August 10. Anson was the star of the game on August 8 in a win over Cleveland as the 45-year-old captain banged out five hits and scored the winning run.

The Colts got to within two games of the .500 mark, but a quirk of scheduling put them on the road for the rest of the season (except for two games) after August 8. The team did not respond well to the extended road trip, and Anson's mood soured during a disastrous swing through Washington, Baltimore, and New York. The Colts won only one of their 16 games on the trip, dropping permanently out of the first division.

That victory, against the Giants on August 30, put Anson's quick temper on display for the fans at the Polo Grounds. The Colts led 7–5 after eight innings when darkness began to fall, so Anson demanded that umpire Bob Emslie call the game. Emslie refused, and Anson cursed the umpire, drawing an ejection and a $25 fine for his trouble. The captain refused to allow anyone to bat in his place leading off the top of the ninth, so the Colts started the inning with one out. Despite this handicap, the Colts scored three times and widened their lead.

When the Giants came to bat in the bottom of the inning, they saw George Decker on first base in place of Anson and pitcher Danny Friend in left field, wearing a bathrobe over his uniform with a Chicago cap perched on his head on Anson's orders. The Giants protested that Friend was not in a regulation uniform, wasting more time in the dwindling sunlight, and after two Giants went out, the whole controversy flared anew. With daylight almost gone and the Giants arguing, the exasperated Emslie finally called the game, with the score reverting to the 7–5 count which stood at the end of the eighth. Anson had made his point, though he made a farce of the game in the process and elicited more criticism from the Chicago papers.

The Colts slid down the standings in September, and four losses in a row to the Orioles in Baltimore dropped them to ninth place, where they remained for the balance of the season. The Colts ended the 1897 campaign in St. Louis, where Cap Anson played what turned out to be the last games of his major league career. On October 3, the 45-year-old first baseman belted two home runs in the first game of a season-ending doubleheader, though the Colts lost the game by a 10–9 score. In the second game, Anson made one hit, a single, and stole a base as the Colts finished their season with a 7–1 victory.

It was apparent to all, except maybe to the captain himself, that Anson's age had finally caught up with him. He batted .285, a respectable mark today, but the entire National League, pitchers included, hit .313 that season. His batting average fell below the league average for the first and only time in his major league career, while his slugging average trailed the league standard for the second year in a row. Despite his obvious decline at bat, Anson still batted in the fourth spot in the lineup, which left the Colts at a disadvantage against ballclubs with harder-hitting cleanup batters.

The captain was also spectacularly immobile in the field. Jake Stenzel of the Browns explained his batting success against the Colts by saying, "When I'm up there with men on the bases and get the pitcher in the hole, I never let him even up. I kill the first ball he puts up or bunt it towards Anson, which is as good as a hit."[17] The *Chicago Tribune* reported that the Orioles laughed openly at Anson and the Colts in their September series in Baltimore, and Jack Doyle shouted to the Oriole batters from the coaching lines, "Bunt it down to the old man. He can't get anybody." By August, the Chicago papers were demanding, almost pleading, that Anson retire as a player and hand first base to either Bill Everitt or George Decker.

Most significantly, Anson was no longer effective as a manager. The team was simply too undisciplined to challenge for the pennant, and most of the players either hated their manager or ignored him. Anson blamed team management, especially Jim Hart, for failing to support him, but any team with talented players like Griffith, Callahan, and Lange, among others, should have finished higher than ninth place, 34 games out of first. Philadelphia Phillies manager George Stallings spoke for many when he remarked, "I will only say this much: I wish I had that Chicago team."[18] Attendance was stagnant at the West Side Grounds, and the 1897 campaign represented the 11th season in a row that Anson's club had failed to win the pennant.

In terms of baseball strategy, Anson was hopelessly behind the times. Boston and Baltimore won pennants with the sacrifice bunt, the hit-and-run, and the trap play, but Anson tried to reverse the decline of the Colts by increasing team discipline, not by adopting new strategies. The captain still relied on big, muscular hitters and minimized the importance of defense, an approach that worked in the 1880s but not in the 1890s. Baseball had changed, and Anson had failed to change with it. "Captain Anson says that the game has not improved scientifically in twelve years," reported *The Sporting News*. "Certainly not with the Chicagos."[19]

Anson's tenure in Chicago was over, but he appeared to be the only person who failed to realize it. No doubt Hart hoped that Anson would make it easier on everyone involved and announce his retirement, but no word came from the captain in the weeks immediately following the end of the 1897 season. Rumors, many of them no doubt planted by Hart, appeared in the Chicago papers almost every day, some of them stating that Anson would manage in the Western League in 1898, others connecting him to possible vacancies in St. Louis or Philadelphia. However, Anson declared in late October that he fully expected to lead the Colts to the pennant in 1898, and that he might even return to first base for his 28th major league season.

Hart did not want Anson to return, and the relationship between the captain and the team president grew even worse in November. The two men took separate trains to the league meetings in Philadelphia, and officials from other teams remarked that they never saw Hart and Anson together during the three-day event. Anson tried to make trades, which Hart ignored, and the captain's frustration boiled over when he received word of remarks Hart made at a banquet. Philadelphia Phillies owner John Rogers gave a speech in which he offered the opinion that the sport of baseball would last longer than the Olympic Games of ancient Greece, and Hart replied that he hoped so, for by then the Chicago club might win another pennant.

Anson confronted Hart about the statement the following afternoon, but the team president dismissed his manager's concerns. "Am I not the President of the Chicago club," replied Hart, "and as such was it not as much a reflection on me as it was on you, if it was a reflection. You are too sensitive, Captain."[20] Hart further irritated Anson when he spent much of his time at the meetings with Tom Burns, the former Chicago third baseman and longtime member of the "Stonewall Infield." It was no secret in the baseball world that Hart wanted to dump Anson and hire Burns as the new field boss, and the papers all but confirmed that Burns was ready to take over the Colts in 1898.

The Chicago fans were more than ready to say goodbye to their longtime captain, and many owners and team officials felt the same way. One unidentified National League manager, whom the *Chicago Tribune* described as "probably the most successful manager of the present day," spoke for many when he praised Anson as a person but questioned his effectiveness as a leader. "I have no doubt Anson was once the greatest of managers, but he is ten years behind the times," stated the man. "He is trying to run a baseball club on the same lines that prevailed ten years ago. You know what that will come to. Personally, Anson is a splendid fellow, dignified and honest, and a great credit to the game."[21]

The Sporting News also got into the act. The paper issued weekly bulletins on Anson's impending dismissal, predicting that Hart would sign Tom Burns as Anson's successor and claiming that Anson was wealthy enough to "want for nothing" if and when he left the Chicagos. In early December, the paper published an article about the surprising popularity of baseball in Japan. The item was titled, "Send Anson There."[22]

Al Spalding decided to speed the process along. He invited the Ansons to accompany him on a trip to Europe in the fall of 1897,

Another view of Anson in the late 1890s, around the time of his dismissal from the Chicago ballclub. (National Baseball Hall of Fame Library, Cooperstown, New York)

though his motives involved more than sightseeing with his old friend and teammate. Spalding hoped to convince Anson to step down as manager of the Colts, but he knew that the task would have to be handled delicately. Anson accepted the invitation, and the party left New York on the steamship *Saale* in late November for a four-week journey to England.

Spalding and Anson discussed team matters on the ship and during their excursions, with Spalding dropping his share of subtle hints regarding Anson's departure. Anson, however, was not a man to pick up on subtlety in any form. Anson suggested that he and Spalding pool their resources and buy the club, forcing out Jim Hart and John Walsh while putting Anson more firmly in control. He suggested a series of trades and other moves to make a success of the 1898 season. Spalding realized that the captain was not catching on to the true reason for their discussions.

While Anson and Spalding toured the British Isles, Jim Hart was hard at work in Chicago. He let the papers know that Tom Burns was his choice to manage the Colts in 1898, but that no official announcement would come until February. Hart also told the papers that no player signings, trades, or other personnel moves would be made for several months, and that he had not even decided where the Colts would train in the spring. It was obvious to fans and sportswriters that Hart did not want to make any plans for 1898 until Anson had departed the organization.

The traveling party returned in late December, and though Spalding told reporters that no decisions had been made, Anson later recalled that Spalding informed him upon their return to America that his career in Chicago was over. "It was then," said Anson, "that I was advised by Mr. Spalding to resign, which I refused to do, preferring to take my medicine like a man, bitter as the dose might be."[23] Stubborn to the last, the captain would not make the transition an easy one. Though he knew that he was a goner in Chicago, Anson did not seek out another job in baseball. He busied himself with other pursuits, serving as referee for a billiard match at the Grand Opera House in Chicago and waiting for the inevitable public announcement of his dismissal.

The next six weeks passed too slowly for Spalding and Hart, who hoped that Anson would relieve them of their onerous duty and resign of his own volition. The stubborn captain, predictably, did not let them off easily, and as the February 1 deadline approached, Spalding and Hart decided to go on the offensive. On January 29, 1898, the Associated Press asked Spalding to confirm or deny the rumors that Anson would be dropped from the Colts. "I have taken pains as a mediator," replied Spalding, "to find out from Chicagoans how they feel about a change of management. There is a decided undercurrent in favor.... Lovers of baseball think that Anson has been in power too long."[24]

Spalding's statement indicated that the rumors, which had filled the sports pages of the Chicago newspapers all winter, were true. Cap Anson's career in Chicago, after 22 seasons as a player and 19 as a manager, was finished.

CHAPTER 21

An Unemployed Manager

> *Anson's retirement from the Chicago Club pleased the cranks in that city and caused regret in the other eleven cities. The grand old man of baseball, despite his steady decline as a player, has always been a drawing card and his absence will be greatly felt. But in the march of progress, sentiment carries no weight, and Anson had to be dropped in order to strengthen the Colts.*
>
> —*Brooklyn Eagle*[1]

On February 1, 1898, Chicago team president Jim Hart released a statement that read, in part:

> The press and the public seem to have taken it for granted that A. C. Anson will not be manager or captain of the Chicago Baseball Club [in] the coming season. This case is one which has been practically left to the press and the public for decision. The stockholders of the club have endeavored to be guided wholly by these factors in the disposition of this case. It is the desire of the club to do exactly that which the public desires and the opinion of the majority of the stockholders is that the patrons of baseball in Chicago desire a change of management of the team; and because of that belief the directors have decided to not renew the contract with Mr. Anson which has just terminated.
> Mr. Anson has served the club long and faithfully, and it is with feeling of the deepest regret that circumstances are such that he will sever his connection with the club. Personally, I have the highest regard for him.... There is not now, and never has been, friction between Captain Anson and myself. I have conducted my end of the business without interference from him, and he has conducted his end of the business without interference from me.[2]

A reporter from the *Chicago Tribune* showed Anson the statement from

Hart. Anson read it thoughtfully, then said to the reporter, "I have nothing to say in connection with the letter nor am I yet prepared to make any statement in regard to my future. I am, in truth, undecided myself."

One enterprising newspaperman contacted Henry Anson in Marshalltown for his reaction. Henry was now past 70 years of age, but busier than ever, managing his many business interests with the assistance of Adrian's brother Sturgis. Henry told the *Tribune* that he knew his son would not return as manager of the Colts, and that he wanted Adrian to move back to Iowa. "As far as I am concerned," said the captain's father, "I do not regret his retirement from the Chicago club and would prefer to see him retire from baseball altogether. Not because he can't play ball, for he can as well or better than ever. His muscles and his brain are as active, if not more so, than ever, and everybody knows it takes both to play ball nowadays. But I want him to leave Chicago and come back to Marshalltown, the land of his birth, and assist me in the upbuilding of the city."[3]

A more unusual tribute came from St. Louis. Clarence Duval, Anson's former mascot, was performing there as a drum major in what the papers labeled a "coon show" at Hopkins' Grand Opera House, and expressed his regret over the dismissal of his old boss. "Well, well, well! So the old man's on the shelf. I'm sorry to hear it. I went around the world with the Chicago–All American team with Cap Anson and had a glorious old time. We lived on the fat of the land and many funny sights we saw. The ole man was a whole show in himself and as I could do several different turns the Cap and I used to make things pretty lively."[4]

Adrian Anson was too proud to pull up stakes in Chicago and return to his hometown in Iowa, though no suitable positions in the baseball world were available for him to fill. A proposal was made to appoint Anson as chief of umpires of the National League, a position that had been used in recent years as a sinecure for retired managers. Harry Wright held the post after he retired as manager of the Phillies in 1893, and when he died two years later the job was awarded to John B. Day, the former New York Giants owner fallen on hard times. Anson declined to be considered, partly because it smacked of charity, but mostly because he did not want to strip Day of his only means of income. Anson may have been the "Grand Old Man," but he was not yet 50 years old, and believed that he could still find employment in baseball.

Al Spalding felt badly for Anson, a man he had known for nearly 30 years, though he never wavered from his belief that Anson's dismissal was necessary. Spalding also knew that the fans, who booed Anson mercilessly during the 1897 season, nonetheless expected their longtime captain to be treated to a proper send-off, in recognition for his 22 years of playing service and 19 years of managerial tenure. Since admirers of the famous English cricket player, Dr. W. G. Grace, had awarded their hero a considerable amount of money as a testimonial upon his retirement a few years earlier, Spalding decided that Anson should receive a similar public tribute.

Three days after Hart's announcement, Spalding sent a telegram to more than 30 leading baseball men and business leaders:

> Chicago, Ill., February 4—Do you favor Anson testimonial? Will you help public meeting here Saturday?
> A.G. Spalding.

The response was immediate. Virtually everyone who received the telegram answered in the affirmative, and Spalding arranged for a discussion of the matter at the Chicago Athletic Association on Saturday, February 5. Spalding hoped to use the meeting to set specific plans in motion for the event.

The meeting took place as scheduled, but ended quickly when Spalding read a letter that he received that morning from Anson:

> To my friends—The kind offer to raise a large public subscription for me, the first notice of which I received by a chance meeting with Mr. Spalding the afternoon preceding its publication in the daily papers, is an honor and a compliment I duly appreciate. Implying as it does the hearty and close fellowship of the originator of this movement, my lifelong friend and old comrade, A. G. Spalding, causes me to regard it the higher. But there are times when one hesitates to receive favors even from friends. At this hour I deem it both unwise and inexpedient to accept the generosity so considerately offered. Reiterating my thorough appreciation of the proffered kindness, I ask you to believe me, sincerely,
> A. C. ANSON.

The disappointed, and no doubt embarrassed, Spalding told a reporter, "I found myself something in the position of a politician who had announced his candidate, had the wires all set, convention packed, election assured, but my candidate would not run."[5]

Anson expressed his feelings more directly after the meeting. "I refuse to accept anything in the shape of a gift," he said. "The public owes me nothing. I am not old and am no pauper. I can earn my own living. Beside that, I am by no means out of baseball." In his autobiography, Anson explained the matter further. "To me," he said, "it appeared to be something too much in the nature of a charity gift for me to accept, and I felt

I should stultify my manhood by so doing, and that I should sacrifice that feeling of independence that I had always possessed."[6]

The deposed captain may have been correct in his decision to turn down the testimonial. It might have been difficult for Anson to accept a large sum of money from the Chicago club and its supporters and then take a managing job in another city soon afterward. He was only 46 years old, and Anson believed that he had many years of service in the game ahead of him. Besides, he already had a plan to return to baseball. He proposed to buy the Chicago ballclub from Al Spalding and John Walsh.

Somehow, during the first few days after his dismissal, Anson demanded — and received — a 90-day option to buy the ballclub from its main stockholders, Walsh and Spalding. There were 1,000 total shares of stock in the club, 130 of which Anson already owned. These shares had been valued at $100 apiece, but Spalding sent Anson a letter on February 15, 1898, offering 640 shares under his control for the price of $150 apiece. If Anson could buy these 640 shares and add them to his existing 130, he would then own more than three-fourths of the club. He would need to buy the remaining 230 shares as well, since the letter explained that the other stockholders would be allowed to sell to Anson at that same $150 price if they so desired, and the chance to sell out at such an attractive price would have been difficult for the shareholders to ignore. The papers stated that Anson needed to obtain $150,000 to buy the ballclub, but Anson's own holdings in the club totaled $19,500, so he needed to raise $130,500 to buy all 870 outstanding shares. It was a large sum of money, comparable to a few million in today's dollars, and Anson had until April 15 to raise it.

This advertisement for "Captain Anson's Indestructible Score Card" appeared in the back pages of Anson's autobiography, which was published in 1900. Remy A. Fiegal was the captain's brother-in-law. (Author's collection)

Anson scurried about for the next three months, cajoling bankers and friends to join him in what appeared to more levelheaded observers as a fool's errand. Spalding and Walsh never intended to sell their shares, but masterfully turned the offer to their own advantage. They knew that Anson would never be able to raise that much money, and used Anson's interest to establish a share price 50 percent higher than it had previously been. Spalding and Walsh manipulated Anson to increase the value of their franchise, and Anson, once again, proved that he was a novice in the business side of baseball.

Anson's search for funding hit the newspapers, and Spalding unwisely attempted to deny the existence of Anson's option. On April 2 Spalding told the *Chicago Chronicle* that the story of Anson's option "is absurd. In the first place, Anson is not trying to get the franchise. No one has made overtures to me with that end in view. I have set no price on the franchise, because I had not the slightest intention of letting it go."[7] Some papers speculated that no option existed, and that Spalding fixed the $150,000 asking price for the ballclub as a joke that Anson somehow took seriously. The *Cincinnati Enquirer* was probably accurate when it stated, "People who ought to know say that Spalding and Hart would not part with the Chicago Club for $250,000."[8]

Undaunted, Anson continued his quest for investors, but, as he related a few years later, "I was informed by friends that I was simply wasting my time, as the option that I possessed was not worth the paper it was written on, and that there was never any intention on the part of A. G. Spalding and his confreres to let me get possession of the club."[9] In February, international events also conspired against the captain, when the battleship *U. S. S. Maine* exploded in Havana harbor and thrust the nation onto the brink of war against Spain. War news pushed the upcoming baseball campaign off the front pages, and many of Anson's potential partners shied away from investing in baseball with the country poised for battle.

Some investors pledged their support to the former captain, perhaps secure in the knowledge that Anson would ultimately fail and that they would never be required to follow through. Others promised to help but reneged as the deadline approached, and Anson soon suspected that Spalding had passed the word to bankers and sportsmen to back away from his attempt to gain control of the ballclub.

On April 10, five days before the deadline, Anson publicly acknowledged defeat. "Owing to the absorption of public interest in war news," said Anson, "and to the opposition shown by the present managers of the club, it will be impossible to meet the terms of the option."[10] Cap Anson's career in Chicago, as player, manager, and potential club owner, was finally and irreversibly over.

There remained one more unseemly controversy involving Anson and Spalding. In early 1898 Spalding announced a plan to build the nation's first baseball school, to be called the A. C. Anson Base-Ball College, in Calumet, a suburb of Chicago situated on the Illinois-Indiana border. He distributed a prospectus that detailed the proposed workings of the school, promising daily instruction for two dollars per day and requiring that each student "pass an examination made by Captain Anson as to their natural aptitude for being proficient in the game of base-ball." Spalding had not discussed the proposal with Anson, and it appears that Spalding cooked up the scheme as a way to start a real estate boom in Calumet, where he owned land that could be sold at a handsome profit. Anson denounced the project, stating that "it never received any serious consideration at my hands," and that he believed that Spalding was "using me as a catspaw with which to pull the chestnuts out of the fire."[11]

Anson got the last laugh in the battle for control of the Chicago team. In 1900, the ex-captain published his autobiography, which included an image of the letter that Spalding had denied sending. Anson was telling the truth about the offer after all, and the letter caused Spalding no end of embarrassment.

Though Anson retained his 130 shares in the franchise, the papers decided that the name Colts was too closely identified with Cap Anson to be usable now that the captain was gone. The writers began to call the team the Orphans almost immediately after Anson's dismissal, and the nickname stuck for the next several seasons. New manager Tom Burns ran a looser ship than Anson, and the players took advantage almost immediately. Burns appointed Jimmy Ryan as field captain, but the men wanted the more popular Bill Lange to have the post, so they refused to take the field on opening day until Hart gave in and ordered the change. Burns encountered as many discipline problems as had Anson, if not more, but despite the turmoil the Orphans turned in a solid fourth place finish in 1898 for the team's best record since 1891. The club also set a new Chicago attendance record with more than 400,000 paid admissions, and for the first time in seven years the club announced that it turned a profit for the season.

Anson was the most noteworthy unemployed manager in baseball, and his name was mentioned in several cities during the first few months of the 1898 season. The Brooklyn Dodgers fired manager Billy Barnie in May, but the club bypassed Anson and appointed Mike Griffin, the Dodger team captain, to the post. The Phillies struggled under manager George Stallings, and *The Sporting News*, among other papers, reported that Anson was ready to go to Philadelphia, Virginia Anson's hometown, and take over the ballclub. However, the Phillies rejected the idea of replacing one strict disciplinarian in Stallings with another one in Anson, so they hired Bill Shettsline instead. Anson remained in Chicago, watching the standings closely and waiting for the next National League managerial opening.

That next opportunity came in New York, where the widely unpopular Andrew Freedman was still the main owner of the ballclub. Freedman was a powerful figure in politics on the municipal and national levels, and in 1897 became the treasurer of the national Democratic Party. He was the richest owner in baseball, but many of the game's historians call Freedman the worst owner in history. Freedman used his political and financial muscle to gain control of the Giants before the 1895 season began, and quickly alienated the fans with his high-handed and autocratic rule. In his seven years at the helm, Freedman hired and fired 16 managers, barred umpires from the grounds if their rulings displeased him, and carried on feuds with the influential New York sportswriters. Upon his death in 1915, *The Sporting News* said, "He had an arbitrary disposition, a violent temper, and an ungovernable tongue in anger which was easily provoked and he was disposed to be arbitrary to the point of tyranny with subordinates."

Freedman's wrath was not limited to the umpires and press. In 1895 he angered his star pitcher, Amos Rusie, by withholding $200 in fines from his paychecks; Rusie figured, probably correctly, that Freedman used the fines as an excuse to cut his salary without the trouble of negotiations. Rusie sat out the 1896 season in protest and made noises about going to court to test the reserve rule. Freedman would not budge, and the other National League owners paid Rusie his entire 1896 salary to drop the suit and return to the Giants. This was only one of the many controversies caused by Freedman, who almost single-handedly destroyed the popularity of baseball in the nation's largest city.

Anson, almost alone within the baseball world, admired Freedman. Both were stubborn, willful men who demanded much from those around them and paid scant attention to social niceties in doing so. Anson still held a small amount of Giants stock, and was well acquainted with Freedman, team secretary Eddie Talcott, and other club officials. Anson had made many wagers with Freedman and Talcott in the previous few years, most of which the captain lost, but he approved of Freedman's hard-charging style.

Bill Joyce, the first baseman and manager of the Giants, was a favorite of Freedman's, but ran into trouble at the Polo Grounds on June 3. In a hard-fought game against the Cincinnati Reds, Joyce singled and received a forearm to the face from Reds first baseman Jake Beckley as he rounded the bag. The enraged Joyce then grabbed the ball and began beating Beckley on the back of the head with it, touching off an ugly brawl. The fracas grew uglier when umpire Bob Emslie tossed Joyce out of the game and refused to do the same to Beckley, and the game resumed only after Emslie threatened to forfeit the game to the Reds if Joyce did not retire from the field. Beckley was a popular former Giant who was released the year before following a dispute with Freedman, and although the Giants won the game, the New York fans hissed at Joyce for his attack on Beckley.

The fallout was immediate. *The Sporting News* condemned Joyce's assault as "disgraceful" and blamed Freedman, claiming that the Giants owner "affects to despise all baseball authority" and "has encouraged his manager and players to violate the kicking rules under a promise to protect them."[12] Several of the more influential club owners, including Cincinnati's John T. Brush and Boston's Arthur Soden, demanded that Freedman discipline his manager. While the controversy simmered, the Giants lost four in a row at home to the Reds and Orphans as attendance dropped sharply at the Polo Grounds.

Freedman did not particularly wish to punish Joyce, but also did not want the league to step in and take action. He cast about for a way to deflect criticism from his fellow magnates, and soon hit upon a solution. Freedman sent a telegram to Anson, inviting the former Chicago captain to come to New York to discuss the managerial position with the Giants. Freedman promised him full control over the team and its players, and Anson, hungry for a return to baseball, jumped at the opportunity to take over the ballclub. He assumed the post on June 11, 1898, and led the Giants that day to a win over the Brooklyn Dodgers.

Anson told the press that he intended to get into shape and play first base himself, but he quickly discovered the first obstacle to his leadership. Bill Joyce, the former manager, remained on the team as the starting first baseman, and if Anson assumed that Freedman would soon trade the deposed skipper, he soon found out otherwise. Joyce remained on the team and retained his popularity with the other players. This was the first indication that Anson's tenure in New York would not be a long one.

The captain's former Chicago charges expressed satisfaction that their old manager had landed on his feet. Tom Burns, Anson's successor, told the *Chicago Tribune*, "Anson should make a success of the New York team.... If Anson has full command, which he must have been promised, he will win. The team is strong and Anson is popular in New York." Jimmy Ryan sounded a note of caution. "If Anson manages from the bench he will do well," stated Ryan, "but if he goes on first the question of competency will be raised against him as it was in Chicago. He ought to make the team win, and will certainly get the support of the newspapers who are sore on Joyce and Freedman."

One unidentified Colt issued a prophetic warning. "The first time that Anson says 'yes' and Freedman says 'no' there will be a war worth seeing," said the player, "and if Freedman attempts to interfere in the management of the club it will bring about a big clash. Both men have had their way in all things, and it is a question as to who will weaken."[13]

Anson's Giants started off well, with four wins in their first six games, but injuries and player apathy prevented the team from mounting a challenge to the league leaders. New York's main starting pitcher was Amos Rusie, who had set strikeout records in the early 1890s but had suffered from a sore arm for the past two seasons. Rusie defeated Brooklyn with a 1–0 shutout on June 16, but walked six batters and relied more on junk pitches than his legendary fastball. He left his next two starts in the early innings, and his absence left a void in the pitching staff. More importantly, the players retained their allegiance to Joyce, and saw no reason to pay much attention to their new field boss. They knew, even if Anson did not, that Anson was merely a temporary manager.

Anson tried his best to make a success of his new post. Most of the National League's non-playing field leaders managed from the bench in street clothes, but Anson wore a Giants uniform and directed play from the third-base coaching box. He instituted strenuous daily workouts at home and on the road, and the 46-year-old manager took part in every drill. He looked to be in better shape than his much younger players, and the papers said that it was only a matter of time before Anson took the field again. Anson also strictly monitored the nighttime activities of his charges, much to their dismay. He levied fines for breaking curfew, though the players paid scant attention and continued their hard-partying ways.

Freedman, too, ignored Anson whenever possible. He refused to allow Anson to come out of retirement and play first base, which would have made Bill Joyce expendable. The owner also scotched the captain's request to trade away some of the players loyal to Joyce, and refused to collect fines that Anson levied against his rebellious players. When outfielder Tom McCreery dropped a fly ball, costing the Giants a game in early July, Freedman released him that evening without consulting Anson. With no support from the owner and little respect from his players, Anson could only watch helplessly as the Giants drifted in the middle of the National League standings. Freedman had lied when he promised Anson full control of the team, as Anson now realized.

When the Giants traveled to Chicago on June 29 to play Anson's old team, the 9,000 fans in attendance gave their old captain a warm reception, along with a floral horseshoe. Tom Burns and the Orphans then proceeded to trounce the Giants by a 12 to 4 score, leaving the New Yorkers in seventh place, nine and a half games behind league-leading Cincinnati. Another loss to Chicago the next day was the eighth in 11 games for the Giants, but Anson's men rebounded with two wins against the Orphans on July 1 and 2. The Giants then returned to the Polo Grounds for a July 4 doubleheader with Boston, and many observers wondered if Anson could survive another losing streak.

The questions were answered quickly. The apathetic Giants lost both games to the Beaneaters by scores of 6 to 5 and 10 to 3 as the Polo Grounds fans booed loudly. Another loss to Boston the next day left the Giants 13 games out of first place and three games under the .500 mark. Anson looked forward to upcoming home games against tail-enders Brooklyn, St. Louis, and Louisville as a chance to regroup and climb back into contention, but Andrew Freedman would not give him the chance. With the Joyce-Beckley controversy safely buried in the past, Freedman was ready to make his move.

On July 6, Freedman met with Anson to discuss the state of the team. The meeting did not go well, as Anson angrily accused Freedman of undermining his leadership by refusing to trade Joyce and ignoring fines. Freedman was not a man to tolerate criticism, and seized upon this argument as a pretext for his next action. He fired Anson and reinstated Bill Joyce as manager of the Giants.

Joyce was Freedman's man all along, as the Giants owner virtually admitted in a press release. "Anson proved a failure, and no other course but to release him was open to the club," stated Freedman. "I have always had the utmost confidence in Joyce and replaced him by Anson only to save him from the abuse that was heaped upon him by the club's enemies. The men showed that they could not play winning ball under Anson's direction."[14] A group of fans gave Joyce an armful of red roses in his first game back, and the players celebrated Anson's dismissal by winning their next seven games and 10 of their next 11 against the Dodgers, Browns, and Colonels. The Giants appeared to prefer Joyce's loose rein, as opposed to Anson's strictness, and newspaper reports stated that several Giants had deliberately played poorly under Anson in a bid to get him fired.

His one-month term as manager of the Giants represented the second major humiliation inflicted upon Anson in a span of six months, and many onlookers wondered why he would involve himself with such a mercurial character as Andrew Freedman. "Anson, with the prestige of his reputation," suggested Cleveland manager Patsy Tebeau, who began his career with the White Stockings ten years earlier, "should have been able to command an iron-clad contract that would ensure him a salary for at least two years. But he goes blindfolded to New York and is practically turned down by Freedman. I thought the Grand Old Man of the Game, as they call him, wore a larger bump of business in his cranium."[15]

In his autobiography, Anson brushed aside his stay in New York with one paragraph:

> Later I accepted a position as manager of the New York Club, being assured that I should have full control of the team, but at the end of a month finding that there were too many cooks to spoil the broth I resigned, accepting only the amount of salary due me for actual services, though offered a sum considerably in excess of the same. This ended my actual connection with National League base-ball, and its mismanagement.[16]

In late 1898, Anson investigated the possibility of buying the bankrupt St. Louis franchise and installing himself as manager, but Cleveland Spiders owner Frank Robison bought the Browns instead and moved his best players to St. Louis. The captain then discovered that the Western League, which had operated for several years in smaller midwestern cities such as Minneapolis and Grand Rapids, might allow him to buy one of its eight teams and move it to Chicago's South Side. Anson had rejected overtures from the Western League in 1898 because he was convinced that he could purchase the Colts from Spalding, but he was no longer so choosy after a year out of the game. He wanted to get back into baseball, even if it meant assuming the lead of a minor league team. Since the Western League, like the National, operated under the rules of the National Agreement, Anson was required to gain permission from Spalding and Hart before moving a new team into Chicago.

Spalding did not want a rival team in Chicago, not even a minor league outfit, and turned Anson down. "I think a Western League club would have been a success in Chicago," said a hurt Anson to the press, "and so far from injuring the National League team, I think it would have helped it." Spalding's snub of his longtime protégé completed the rupture between the two men and turned Anson into a bitter critic of the National League. "Baseball as at present conducted is a gigantic monopoly," said Anson in 1900, "intolerant of opposition, and run on a grab-all-that-there-is-in-sight basis that is alienating its friends and disgusting the very public that has so long and cheerfully given to it the support that it has withheld from other forms of amusement."[17] He was finished with the National League, and although he lived for another two decades, he would never again hold any official position in organized professional ball.

With no apparent options left open to him in baseball, Cap Anson concentrated on his second favorite sport. He opened a billiard hall on

Michigan Avenue in downtown Chicago, down the street from the A. G. Spalding sporting goods emporium, and hired his nephew, William Anson, as a clerk. William was one of Sturgis Anson's grown sons. Anson also recognized that the sport of tenpins was on an upswing, and installed bowling alleys in his establishment as well. Before long his place was one of the most spacious and best-equipped billiard and bowling establishments in Chicago, if not the Midwest. When a federal census taker entered the names of Adrian Anson and his family onto the rolls in June of 1900, Anson stated his occupation as "billiard hall owner."

The former captain kept busy with family matters. His 20-year-old daughter Grace, who had married a businessman named Walter H. Clough, fell ill with typhoid fever in early 1898, and for a while it was feared that she would not survive. Grace recovered, fortunately, and in May of 1899 she gave Adrian and Virginia their first grandchild, a boy named Anson McNeal Clough. At the same time, Virginia was not finished having her own children. She gave birth to another daughter, Virginia Jeannette, on November 22, 1899.

Anson also took the time to pen his memoirs, with the aid of a ghostwriter. Anson was eager to put his version of events before the public, so he commissioned a Chicago writer named Richard Cary Jr. to interview him at length and put his words in book form. The interviews touched on all areas of Anson's life, from his childhood in Marshalltown to his falling-out with Spalding, Hart, and the Chicago ballclub, and in early 1900 a company called Era Publishing released the book. Titled *A Ball Player's Career: Being the Personal Reminiscences of Adrian C. Anson*, it was the first true baseball autobiography.

The book is an interesting mix of anecdotes from Anson's childhood, his early days in professional ball, and his 22-year career with the Chicago franchise. It is marred by its disproportionate emphasis on the round-the-world tour of 1888-89, which takes up fully half of the book, and by several disparaging and racially insulting references to the former Chicago mascot Clarence Duval. The language that Anson used to express his contempt for Duval was not considered objectionable at the time, but would be condemned as abhorrent in the present day. However, Anson's autobiography illuminated many of the important events of the first two decades of professional baseball, and provides a valuable insight into the sport as it was played more than 100 years ago.

Anson used his book not only to record the events of his long baseball career, but also to burn his remaining bridges with Hart, Spalding, and the National League. His bitterness shone through when he accused some of his Colts of undermining him during his final season in Chicago.

"The team with which I started out in 1897 was certainly good enough to win the pennant with," remarked Anson, but "underhanded work looking toward my downfall was indulged in by some of the players." He named Jimmy Ryan as the "ringleader in this business" and asserted that "the most perfect understanding seemed to exist" between Ryan and club president Hart.[18]

It is not known if the book made money, but the former captain of the Chicagos had made his final break with the ballclub with which he had been associated for 22 years. In December of 1899 he told *The Sporting News*, "My stock in the Chicago ballclub is for sale. With the club properly managed it would pay a handsome dividend, but under present conditions it is of no use to me and I want to clear out ... I will gladly take $100 each for my 130 shares, and this is the first time I have offered to sell under any such terms."[19] No one took him up on his offer, but another proposition was presented to Anson in the final months of 1899. A group of backers enlisted him in an effort to create a new major league.

CHAPTER 22

Baseball, Business, and Politics

> *Anson, I guess, is beginning to realize that those people who told him he was making a mistake in sticking with the magnates at the time of the Brotherhood [in 1890] were right and that he was wrong. He saved the National League then, and now the National League will not even give him a helping hand when it can do so without any sacrifice on its own part.*
>
> —An unidentified friend of Anson's, quoted in the *Chicago Tribune*, 1899[1]

The National League had functioned as a 12-team circuit since the collapse of the American Association in 1891, and by the end of the 1899 campaign the magnates realized that 12 teams were four too many. The league prepared to drop its four least successful teams (Cleveland, Baltimore, Louisville, and Washington) and play in 1900 with eight clubs. This move gave a group of prominent baseball men, which included Francis Richter of *Sporting Life*, former Milwaukee club owner Harry D. Quinn, and *Sporting News* founder A. H. Spink, an idea. They would create eight new ballclubs, some of them in the recently vacated National League cities, and set up a rival to the established league. Cap Anson was immediately interested in the venture, and the backing of the popular former baseball hero gave the proposed circuit a patina of credibility. On September 17, 1899, Anson and representatives of five other cities met in Chicago to announce the formation of a new circuit, the American Association. "Honest competition, no syndicate baseball, no reserve rule, to respect all contracts, and popular prices," were the declared goals of the new league.[2]

The leaders of the American Association offered the presidency of their new circuit to Anson, but the ex-captain turned it down, possibly because his wife Virginia was expecting another child in the next two months. However, Anson and his son-in-law, Walter H. Clough, claimed the Chicago franchise and set to work. Anson expected to fill his roster from the ranks of the four discontinued National League teams, and also with players who were as disaffected with the National League as he was. "We will get [players] from wherever we can," said Anson in October of 1899. "I know positively that two-thirds of the members of the Chicago tem are ready now to join with us, and it will be found that the players of other teams are equally willing to get away from the reserve rule and other laws adopted by the league in which there is no justice."[3]

The new league posed a threat to the established order, mostly because the National League players had never accepted the reserve rule and hated it as much as ever. "By abolishing the reserve rule," stated *The New York Times*, "the new league thinks it will get a hold on the best baseball talent." Many Chicago ballplayers had expressed their dissatisfaction with the management of the local club, and Anson told the papers that Clark Griffith, Bill Lange, Jimmy Callahan and others could be induced to leave the employ of Jim Hart and join the new Association. Lange had announced his retirement in order to marry and enter the business world, but Anson believed that Lange could be enticed to remain in baseball as field captain of the new Chicago ballclub.

The National League magnates realized that an exodus of players to the new circuit would be more disastrous to the sport than the Players League insurrection of 1890, so they quickly mounted an offensive. Jim Hart claimed that the National League owned the name "American Association," having acquired it when it bought out the assets of the failed league eight years before. "The National League," said Hart, "paid something like $15,000 for the second half of its title, and intend to use it. The National League will protect itself."[4] Hart also suggested that the National League might set up its own eight-team circuit and call it the American Association. "We have ballplayers enough ... to have a second league if we want one," said Hart. "...The name is ours. We can put it into active operation if we want to."[5]

At the same time, another potential rival to the National League watched these developments and waited for its opportunity. The Western League, which was founded in 1894 by former Cincinnati sportswriter Byron (Ban) Johnson, had operated successfully with teams in Grand Rapids, St. Paul, and other smaller Midwestern cities. In November of 1899 Johnson changed the circuit's name to the American League and declared his intention of moving into larger population centers, including Chicago and Cleveland. If the American Association proved unable to establish itself as a competitor to the National League, the new American League stood ready to take up the challenge.

Anson secured a lease on the old Players League park at 35th and Wentworth on the South Side, while other would-be magnates searched for financial backing and inspected possible playing fields. One of the most enthusiastic participants in the venture was John McGraw, the 27-year-old third baseman and captain of the Baltimore Orioles. The National League had dropped the Orioles after the 1899 campaign and assigned McGraw's contract to St. Louis, but McGraw owned a bowling alley in Baltimore and did not want to go west. He and his longtime friend and teammate, catcher Wilbert Robinson, gathered a group of investors, obtained an American Association franchise, and spent $3,500 to lease the former Oriole ballpark. With the Baltimore franchise on solid ground, McGraw worked to identify prospective investors in New York and Philadelphia, two important cities in the scheme of things for the new league.

As the months passed, Anson adopted a more conciliatory tone toward the National League. After criticizing the established circuit for months, the ex-captain suddenly revealed that he had held talks with several National League owners. "All of them," stated the captain, "believe just as I do, that friendly competition with a division of schedules and a salary limit is the best advertisement for base ball. Mind you, I did not approach then directly about the question, but the drift of their conversation was along the line I endorse."[6] It was a stunning shift in strategy, but Anson perceived that his fledgling organization could not fight off both the National and American leagues at once. However, the National League showed little interest in Anson's overtures, and the new league resumed its barrage of criticism against the established circuit.

By January, the American Association appeared to possess reasonably viable franchises in six cities, among them Chicago (Anson's club), Baltimore, Milwaukee, Louisville, St. Louis, and Boston. This lineup included four western clubs and only two in the eastern states, and the league found it difficult to find two more eastern clubs to complete the circuit. Two groups of Philadelphia backers had formed and disbanded in quick order, while the creation of a franchise in New York appeared impossible due to the machinations of the politically powerful Giants owner, Andrew Freedman. On the positive side, many established stars of the National League, including Napoleon Lajoie, Ed Delahanty, and several of Anson's old Chicago charges, appeared ready to follow the example of John McGraw and throw in their lot with the new league.

The New American Base Ball Association officially came into being on February 14, 1900. At the Great Northern Hotel in Chicago, the representatives of six prospective clubs (the Boston representative, Tommy McCarthy, was late in arriving) elected Cap Anson as president, named seven of the eight member cities, and declared that the league would begin play on April 16. A Philadelphia group had been assembled after much effort, leaving only one empty slot on the league roster. That space would be filled from a group of cities that included Providence, New Haven, and Washington, and Anson appointed John McGraw and league secretary Philip Peterson to select the location of the eighth franchise from among those three sites.

Adrian Anson had finally become a magnate, but the *Chicago Tribune* was correct when it suggested that "the new enterprise [is] still on the doubtful list in the minds of the public." The league still needed a team in one more eastern city, and Anson doubted that Providence or New Haven were populous enough to support a real major league franchise. Washington was a question mark, since the National League club had failed there, and the new organization was not interested in offers from Worcester, Massachusetts and other smaller venues. A strong New York presence might have increased the Association's chances for survival, but no suitable backing could be found there. A group from Detroit cabled Anson and declared itself ready to join, but Detroit was too far west, and by mid–February it was clear that the new circuit would have to accept Providence as its eighth member in order to get off the ground.

Only two days after Anson assumed the presidency of the new league, the bubble burst. The Philadelphia group was unable to find a suitable ballpark and asked for three more weeks to decide whether or not to sign an agreement to join the league. McGraw then wired Anson that Philadelphia, the linchpin of the eastern half of the new Association, could not be counted upon; McGraw complained to the papers about "the entire lack of business sagacity in the men promoting the deal" in that city[7]. The league was now down to six members, since Providence had offered to join only if Philadelphia did, and the task of finding sufficient backing in two more cities was too great to be accomplished in the short amount of time available. The new league was dead, and Anson regretfully announced its demise on February 16.

"I have suspected something like this for some time," confessed Anson. "I am sorry it has happened. If someone with plenty of time had taken hold of the matter earlier, there is not the slightest doubt that we would have been able to pull it through. As it was we were too hurried and too little time remained to fix our fences. I really did not think there was much hope for the association, but I made up my mind I would not desert the enterprise and was hoping at times that something might turn up that would make it look more favorable.

"I don't know what we will do in the future. One thing is certain: the National League, which has been running base ball into the ground for the last eight years, will have opposition at one time or another and some of us may probably be found in the fray in the sweet some time.

"I have no excuses for the collapse of the enterprise. The cut throat methods of the National League have not been relished for the last few years by the fans and a change is bound to come sooner or later. I have no regrets for myself. I simply wish to emphasize the fact that the American Association on its feet would have been the best thing in the world for the game."[8]

Some of the men involved in the new Association kept fighting to keep it alive, but Anson recognized that the battle was over, with the beginning of the 1900 campaign only two months away. Francis Richter of *Sporting Life*, a key Philadelphia backer, complained that Anson had "made an ass out of himself," while other observers blamed McGraw for pulling the plug on Philadelphia too quickly. However, it appears that the new league simply ran out of time to establish itself firmly enough to take on the National League.

Anson might have retrenched and aimed for a 1901 starting date had not Ban Johnson's American League harbored ambitions of its own. The collapse of Anson's league freed Johnson to shift Charlie Comiskey's St. Paul club to the South Side of Chicago for the 1900 campaign; Jim Hart and the National League gave permission for the move, probably to freeze out Anson and keep a revived Association out of Chicago in the future. Comiskey's team, which he dubbed the White Sox, was an immediate success, winning the first American League pennant in 1900. In 1901, the American League declared itself as major and initiated a war against the National. This conflict ended in 1903 with a peace agreement that led to the creation of the two-league structure under which major league baseball has operated for more than a century.

The backers of the new Association made another attempt to launch it in the fall of 1900, but Cap Anson did not participate in this effort. Instead, Anson devoted much of his time to the sport of bowling, which had fascinated him for several years. Anson, still a fine athlete as he neared his 50th birthday, spent long hours practicing on his alleys until he made himself one of Chicago's leading bowlers. The popularity of the sport grew rapidly, and in January of 1901 the American Bowling Congress, of which Anson was a member, hosted its first national tournament in Chicago. Anson bowled poorly there, but a few weeks later the ex-captain's team set a new national record with a score of 2,974 in a three-game string. In 1904, at the fourth annual ABC tournament in Cleveland, Anson and his team won the five-man national title.

Anson, as the proprietor of one of the largest bowling alleys in the Midwest, became prominent in the affairs of the American Bowling Congress. The sport experienced many of the same growing pains that baseball had faced 25 years earlier, and Anson played a major role in setting the ABC on a steady course. In 1901, when the ABC nearly split in two due to rivalry between its eastern and western factions, Anson helped engineer a compromise in which a man from the neutral city of Indianapolis succeeded to the presidency. Anson served as a vice-president of the ABC for several years, and in 1904 he created a short-lived National Bowling League with franchises in eight cities. Anson enjoyed bowling, partly because it provided an outlet for his competitive passion, and also because it furnished a new opportunity for wagering. The former captain bet on bowling matches as enthusiastically as he had gambled on baseball a few years before.

Anson was too immersed in bowling to pay much attention to the baseball scene, but in late 1901 a battle erupted in the National League which brought Anson to the forefront. Andrew Freedman, owner of the New York Giants, attempted to create a "baseball trust" in which a small group of magnates would own and operate all eight National League teams and distribute players and resources as it saw fit. The Giants, representing the most populous city in the league, would receive 30 percent of the profits from the syndicate, with teams in Cincinnati and Pittsburgh getting less than 10 percent of the pie. Al Spalding publicly opposed the plan, which he claimed would result in the "general demoralization of our national sport in its every interest." With the support of four of the eight National League teams, Spalding mounted a campaign to stop the syndicate plan and drive Freedman out of the league.

Anson professed neutrality in the Spalding–Freedman fight, since both the Chicago and New York ballclubs had treated him shabbily. However, Freedman used the ex-captain's name in his public battle with Spalding, reviving Anson's past claim that the Chicago franchise had not paid the dividends to which Anson was entitled. Spalding replied that Anson had not purchased his 130 shares in the club, but had received them as a gift. "I happen to know as a fact," said Spalding, "for I was president of the club at the time, that every dollar of the stock [Anson] now owns in the Chicago club was presented to him as a gift by the club."[9] This unwise statement brought Anson into the fray, prompting him to write an angry response, which was printed in the *Chicago Tribune* the day after Christmas 1901.

"This statement is not true," stated Anson. "The club was originally organized with a capital of $20,000, of which I owned 10 percent, paid for in cash.... The additional 30 shares were paid for by me out of the amounts earned but not drawn on the club treasury — that is, my compensation was based upon a stipulated salary, and 10 percent of the net earnings of the club, neither of which was connected in any way with the dividends I was entitled to as a stockholder in the Chicago baseball club."[10]

Anson went on to explain that during the presidencies of Hulbert and Spalding, the ballclub paid dividends each year ranging from 20 to 80 percent. Since 1891, when Jim Hart succeeded Spalding, "no dividend whatever has been declared on the stock of the Chicago baseball club." Anson remarked that he still held $5,000 worth of stock in the New York club, which had paid dividends in the previous few seasons despite its troubles on the field and at the gate.

The battle intensified in early January, and Anson decided to cash in the small amount of stock that he held in the New York franchise. Since Spalding was trying to wrest control of the Giants from Freedman, Anson figured that his old mentor might be interested in purchasing his stock in the ballclub. He sent Spalding a telegram that read, "Will sell my New York stock for $4,000. Answer."

Spalding wired back, "All right. Sell it."[11]

The captain soon sold his stock, though he certainly did not come close to recouping his original $5,000 investment. The baseball syndicate plan failed when Cincinnati Reds owner John T. Brush bought the Giants and forced Freedman out of the game, after which Spalding sold his remaining baseball holdings and retired to California. Both Spalding and his former protégé Anson were finished with baseball, and the 130 shares of Chicago stock that Anson still held now represented his only connection to the game.

Political life beckoned Anson in 1902. As a favor to his friend Tom Barrett, an old ballplayer running for sheriff of Cook County, Illinois, Anson gave a few speeches on the candidate's behalf. Anson enjoyed the resulting attention, and reasoned that his name and reputation could translate into success in the political arena. Some Democratic strategists came to that same conclusion, and suggested publicly that Captain Anson could help the party at the polls. Thus began a movement to elect Anson to citywide office. The Chicago city treasurer was scheduled to retire at the end of his term in 1903, and Anson's friends in the party put him forward as a candidate for the position.

The captain was hardly qualified for such an office, as he was an indifferent student in his youth, with no discernable facility for numbers, and 20 years before had been unable to calculate simple interest on an investment for his father. However, the top offices in the city were political jobs first and foremost. If Anson could draw votes with his presence on the citywide Democratic ticket, then his popularity at the polls would serve as the main qualification for the job he sought.

Anson's potential candidacy tempted the party regulars, but the outgoing treasurer demanded the right to name his own successor, and the captain withdrew his name from consideration at the city Democratic convention in March of 1903. The party viewed him as a vote getter, and he campaigned enthusiastically for the ticket. In July of that year, when two-time Presidential nominee William Jennings Bryan came to Chicago and delivered a fiery speech denouncing Wall Street and big business interests, Cap Anson rode at the head of the parade with the other Democratic bigwigs. Anson had opposed Bryan vigorously in the 1896 election, remaining loyal to the conservative Cleveland wing of the Democratic Party, but he was a politician now. If Anson held any reservations about the policies of the populist Bryan, he did not air them in public.

He became more involved in the city political scene, and though some observers suggested that Anson start his career as an alderman and work his way up the political hierarchy, the party brass had higher aspirations for the captain. Democratic incumbent mayor Carter Harrison was set to retire in 1905, and the party bosses wanted to use the ex-ballplayer's popularity to help their next mayoral candidate. In late 1904, the party offered Anson the opportunity to run on the citywide ticket for the office of city clerk.

Anson readily accepted, but only after he made one more attempt to get back into major league baseball. In November of 1904 he learned that the most moribund franchise in the American League, the Washington Senators, was for sale, so Anson asked league president Ban Johnson to set a price for the team. The last-place Senators, with Anson's old catcher Mal Kittridge as manager, had lost 113 of their 151 games in 1904 and finished nearly 60 games behind the pennant-winning Boston club. Fan support was almost non-existent in the nation's capital, but Anson declared that he would buy the club and make it a winner, on the condition that he gain full control.

Johnson told Anson that he could buy the team for $30,000, a much lower price than the $150,000 that Al Spalding had demanded for the Chicago Colts six years before. However, the Washington ballclub had accrued a large amount of debt in its four seasons in the American League, which made the club a less than attractive investment, and Johnson preferred local ownership of the team. Anson dropped out of the bidding after a few weeks, and in early 1905 Johnson arranged the sale to a group headed by a prominent Washingtonian, newspaper editor and Republican Party official Thomas C. Noyes.

With this avenue into baseball closed off, Anson threw himself into Chicago party politics, and on February 25, 1905, he won the nomination for the city clerk's office at the local Democratic convention. Anson was unopposed for the honor, and the local party bosses set him on a tour of the city, giving speeches almost every day in support of the citywide Democratic ticket, headed by mayoral candidate Edward Dunne. Most observers had conceded the clerk's race to the popular ex-ballplayer weeks before the April 5 election, but the party also counted on Anson to draw voters to the other men on the Democratic slate.

Race, an issue that had arisen several times in Cap Anson's public life, became a factor in his political campaign. Many politicians of the era gave speeches warning against the specter of "race suicide," the fear that white couples were producing fewer children than non-whites in America. President Theodore Roosevelt issued stern warnings of the dire consequences of a future non-white majority in the nation, and the national Republican Party tried to make the issue their own in an attempt to appeal to white voters. The Chicago Democrats countered the Republicans with the nominations of Judge Dunne, the father of thirteen children, and Cap Anson, a family man with a long history of animosity toward minorities. As the *Tribune* pointed out, "[Anson's] popularity, personally, was beyond doubt a potent help to the Democrats, who seemed to hugely appreciate his campaign statistics, designed to prove that the Democracy, at least in Chicago, are the original and only genuine opponents of race suicide."[12]

On the evening of the election, Anson and other Democratic candidates gathered in the city council chambers to wait for the returns, but a Democratic sweep materialized early, and at 7:30 P.M. Anson confidently left the assembly to eat dinner. "I guess there's nothing to spoil my appetite," said Anson happily to a reporter, and he was correct. The Democrats won all the major offices in the city, though Republicans retained control of the city council, and Anson won the clerkship by more than 24,000 votes over his Republican challenger. On May 17, 1905, he took the oath of office and began his two-year term.

However, it appears that Anson saw the city clerkship as a mere stepping-stone to higher office. He set his sights on the office of Cook County sheriff, which would come up for election in late 1906, and spent most of his term as city clerk planning his future campaign. Anson seemed to show little interest in the performance of his clerk's duties, and his lax oversight of his department caused political trouble almost from the beginning of his term.

Anson was proud of his election as city clerk, and he was prouder still that his father Henry was alive to see it. Henry Anson was still an active businessman in Marshalltown at the age of 79, managing his brick factory and coal company with the assistance of Adrian's brother Sturgis. The "old gentleman" was revered in Marshalltown, and the federal census of 1900 listed Henry's occupation as "Founder of City." Still, not even Henry Anson was indestructible. In November of 1905, while working at his desk, he was stricken with an attack of fever and chills. He went home to bed, but the fever turned into pneumonia, and on the afternoon of November 28, 1905, Henry Anson died.

Henry's body lay in state in the rotunda of the Marshall County courthouse, and Adrian watched as thousands filed past the casket. The line of people extended out of the building, down West Main Street, and past the site where Henry had built the first log cabin in Marshalltown some 54 years earlier. All businesses in the city closed for the day, and citizens draped the downtown area in black. Henry Anson was the first, and only, person ever honored in this fashion by the city of Marshalltown. His tombstone is, to this day, the biggest and most imposing in Riverside Cemetery.

The old gentleman was not the easiest person to get along with. His second marriage lasted only a few years, and he was a stern taskmaster with high standards. However, Adrian Anson respected and admired Henry above all others, not only as a father but also as a role model. Henry was one of three men who had profoundly influenced Adrian's life, but now William Hulbert was long dead, Al Spalding was no longer his friend, and Henry was gone. Adrian, at the age of 53, had lost his last mentor.

After the funeral, Anson returned to Chicago, where his new career as city clerk was not going well. Less than two months into his tenure, he became embroiled in a controversy over fees. The city paid Anson a salary of $5,000 per year, but the city collector and the city clerk had traditionally shared a 25-cent fee for every bond given by individuals or corporations to the city. The city approved approximately 16,000 bonds per year in the early 1900s, which provided an annual bonus of about $2,000 each for the collector and the clerk. This extra payment made the clerkship a highly coveted position in the city at the time, but political reformers managed to guide a bill through the Republican-dominated council that cut off the fees for the clerk, while retaining the payment for the city collector.

The public no doubt welcomed the measure as a long-needed, if halfhearted, reform of the political process, but Anson complained to the papers. "It isn't fair," lamented Anson. "I ought to be in on any of the fees that are running around loose. I want the ordinance changed back to what it was before, so that I can split up with the city collector. It ought to be share and share alike."[13] The incident made Anson look like one more political hack with his hand out, since voters wondered why a public official should receive extra payment for performing his official duties. A more experienced politician might have found a way to restore the fees without making himself look like the aggrieved party, especially when Chicago voters were in the mood for reform.

Anson found conflict with personnel almost immediately in his new post. He had inherited many men in his department who were Democratic Party workers first and conscientious city employees second. They were accustomed to doing party work on city time, a practice that Anson saw no need to curtail so long as the clerk's office filed its reports and handled its financial matters promptly. Unfortunately, Anson's style of leadership, such as it was, allowed the practice to flourish in a way that drew the attention of the Chicago civil service commission after a citizen filed a complaint against the clerk's office. Anson ignored the situation, but the public was outraged to find that some of his employees barely showed up at their jobs at all. The controversy occupied the front pages of the city's main Republican newspaper, the *Tribune*, in May of 1906.

In response, the city auditor presented Anson with a list of his employees who had missed workdays in the first four months of the calendar year. One man had skipped 50 working days, another 39, and still another 18, while two others had gone out for seven days each. One worker had been docked 10 days of pay for neglect of duty, but the rest had been drawing full pay despite their absences. The civil service commission demanded that Anson file charges against three of the men for shirking their duties, but Anson hesitated, much to the commission's dismay. The commission then summoned the city clerk to a hearing to discuss the matter on May 18, 1906.

The hearing, which lasted only about half an hour, was a disaster for the ex-ballplayer. The *Chicago Tribune* reported that the head of the commission "explained the most elementary principles of government to Anson, who sat coiled at the head of the table, confused, and unable to give any reason why he should continue to refuse to do his duty."[14] Anson appeared to be paralyzed by indecision; he did not want to be seen as incompetent, but he also did not want to bring charges against office holders who were probably not indulging in any practices that were unusual for Chicago city government at the time. Many no-show jobs were dispensed for political patronage reasons, and the ambitious Anson had no desire to anger his party or its bosses.

However, the abuses uncovered in his department were so egregious that the board demanded immediate action from the reluctant city clerk.

22. BASEBALL, BUSINESS, AND POLITICS

"It is wrong," lectured one of the commissioners, "to let the money go to people who did not earn it when you have it in your power to stop such proceedings."

"I think the men could do more to earn their money," replied Anson. "I'll admit that. But how can I remedy it?"

"You can sign these charges against them."

"That's another proposition. I don't want to take the burden of it on my shoulders. I'll take the matter up with the corporation counsel and ask for an opinion."

"We won't wait for it," snapped the commissioner. "We'll take action ourselves."

Anson thought that over. "Won't you let me know in advance what you intend to do?"

An older Cap Anson, sometime in the 1910s. (National Baseball Hall of Fame Library, Cooperstown, New York)

pleaded the former ballplayer. "I would like to be able to get in ahead of any action you may intend to take by taking some other action myself."[15]

The commissioners could not help laughing at this suggestion, and it appeared to all that Anson did not fully appreciate the seriousness of the matter. If he had, he would have sought the advice of counsel prior to his appearance before the board. Instead, he revealed himself as woefully ill prepared for the stormy meeting, and poorly qualified for the position that he held. His evasiveness so angered the members of the civil service commission that they threatened to prosecute the former baseball hero for malfeasance of office if he did not sign the charges.

Two days later, an attorney for the commission laid three sets of charges in front of Anson, who curtly replied, "I'll take a couple of days to think about it." Instead, on the recommendation of counsel, Anson signed and returned the charges in less than an hour.

"I guess the boys have had all the chance they had coming, and maybe a little more," he told the reporters. "I never have excused them. I have been after them ever since I got in office. Every effort was made to bring them to time without causing them to lose their jobs. I talked to them until I was black in the face."[16] This lame explanation was too much for the

Tribune, which editorialized on the matter a few days later. "The democratic voters may raise the question as to whether the ex-baseball captain is, as city clerk, displaying the particular brand of backbone and executive capacity which should characterize a candidate, say, for sheriff," complained the *Tribune*. "When an elective official's eagerness for some other elective office is of the sort which makes him a coward in his present office that cowardice is not a good qualification for another job."[17]

This unpleasant incident gave the voting public an impression of Anson as a political weakling, and effectively destroyed the captain's future in Chicago politics, though Anson was not yet ready to surrender. He campaigned for his party's nomination for the office of Cook County sheriff, but the civil service fiasco derailed his candidacy and spelled the end of his political career. On August 8, 1906, the Cook County Democratic party held its nominating convention, and Anson was included as one of four candidates for the sheriff's position. He finished an embarrassing fourth in the race, receiving only 22 votes from the 1,000 party members, and now even Anson realized that his life in politics was over.

He tried to pass the rest of his term quietly, but another sticky problem emerged mere days before he left office. A Republican named Fred Busse, who won the mayoralty in the election of April 1907, did not want to wait to begin his term. He interpreted the city charter as stating that he would become mayor upon the presentation of his certificate of election to the city clerk, not upon his official inaugural date. Busse appeared before Anson on April 6, nine days before the scheduled inaugural, and demanded that Anson certify his election and swear him into office. Anson, whose political career was over anyway, did not want to become caught in a legal tug-of-war with the victorious Republican mayor-elect, so he took the path of least resistance. He administered the oath of office and posed for newspaper photos with the Republican. This action might have caused innumerable legal headaches, since for nine days the city of Chicago had two mayors, had not the city council convinced Busse not to exercise the powers of his new office until after his inauguration.

Anson paid little attention to the controversy. Instead, he threw out the first ball at the Cubs' opener against the

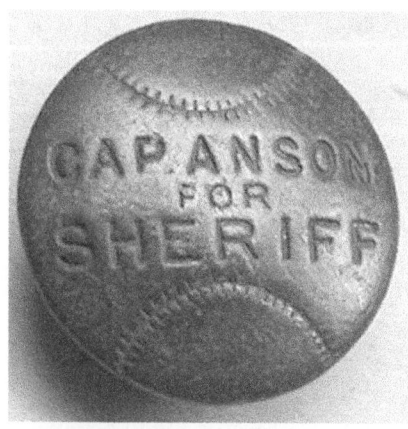

An Anson campaign button from 1906. (Author's collection)

St. Louis Cardinals on April 11, four days before the end of his term, and distributed gifts from the Board of Trade to all the players on both teams. On April 15, Anson left office and returned to his billiards and bowling establishment on Michigan Avenue.

CHAPTER 23

"The Best I Can"

> For every day in the season, for every occasion that might arise, I believe old "Cap" Anson was the best batsman the game ever knew. Just look at that grand record of his through 20-odd years of experience and make up your mind for yourself. He could hit anything. He used an extremely heavy bat, the limit both as to length and as to thickness, and swung easily. It used to do our hearts good to hear the crack when old "Cap" Anson hit the ball squarely.
> — Billy Sunday, 1909[1]

By 1907, Cap Anson had failed at several different careers. He did not receive any offers to manage after his disastrous few weeks with the New York Giants in 1898, and had criticized the National League so harshly ever since that no team owner was inclined to hire him. Anson had tried his hand at stage acting, with spectacularly negative results, and the attempt to create his own baseball league had ended miserably. His once-promising political career lay in ruins, and although he still operated his billiards and bowling place on Michigan Avenue, the business was highly cyclical and unpredictable. The captain had a wife and two children to support (his second daughter, Adele, had been married in 1904), but his financial future was shaky after he lost his $5,000 a year position as Chicago city clerk.

Anson had severed his last link with the Chicago National League team two years before. Though he departed the Chicago ballclub in February of 1898, he had retained his 130 shares of stock in the team. Frank Selee, the former leader of the Boston Beaneaters, became manager in 1902, and brought so many young players to training camp that year that the newspapers began to refer to the team as the Cubs, the name by which it is known to this day. The Cubs steadily climbed in the standings in the following several seasons, but Anson had nothing to do with the team's success, as Jim Hart controlled the other 870 shares of stock. Anson's 13 percent ownership gave him no voice in the club or its operations, and since Hart never distributed dividends, the 130 shares generated no income for Anson and his family.

Al Spalding's treatment of Anson still irritated the former captain, who complained frequently to the papers about his former friend and his business practices. When the widowed Spalding remarried in 1899, he and his new wife became devotees of Theosophistry, a religious movement based in California. When a reporter asked Anson one day about Spalding's newfound interest in religion, the former captain could not contain his bitterness. "Well," said Anson, "I suspected Al was getting 'nutty' in his old age. So he is going to be a Theosophist? I don't know what in thunder a Theosophist is, but if it's something that you can make money out of, you can bet Al Spalding will be one.

"If Spalding has reached that stage of spirituality — is that what you call it? — I think he ought to come back here and pay me my dividends on my Chicago baseball stock which he has held out for fifteen years. Spiritual culture at the expense of the physical, eh? That's a change for your life! He was always developing the physical when I knew him, and he didn't care a tinker's oath for the spiritual."[2]

There may have been another factor involved in the estrangement between Anson and his former mentor. Spalding's second wife was his longtime mistress, who had presented Spalding with a son several years earlier while Spalding's first wife was still living. When Spalding married his second wife, he acknowledged the child as his own and gave him the name Albert Goodwill Spalding Junior.[3] This state of affairs no doubt offended the strictly moralistic Ansons, as Virginia and the first Mrs. Spalding were close friends.

Anson held his Chicago stock for three years after Spalding sold out to Hart. In December of 1905, a former sportswriter and press agent named Charles Murphy bought all 1,000 shares of stock in the team from Hart (who wished to step down due to illness) and Anson. Though Spalding had priced the team at $150 per share seven years earlier, Murphy managed to purchase the club for much less, an indication that Spalding had set the price artificially high when Anson tried to buy the team in 1898.[4] Anson was paid $10,000, or $76.92 per share, for his stake, and the sale ended Anson's 29-year affiliation with the Chicago National League franchise.[5]

However, Anson had a scheme to return to the business he knew best. Chicago had an active semipro baseball scene, and several teams drew sizable crowds in different sections of town. If Anson could not find his way back into the major leagues, at least he could assemble a semipro nine. In the early months of 1907, while waiting for his term as city clerk to end, Anson made plans to obtain and manage his own team. It would be called "Anson's Colts," and Cap Anson would be its sole owner and operator.

Anson's former pitcher-turned-outfielder, Jimmy Callahan, pointed the way for success in the world of semipro ball. Callahan jumped from the National League to the American, joining Charlie Comiskey's Chicago White Sox in 1901. He became manager in 1904, but Comiskey replaced him with Fielder Jones halfway through the 1905 season. Callahan became so disenchanted with major league ball that he quit the White Sox to operate his own semipro team, the Logan Squares, in 1906. Though the majors had blacklisted Callahan for joining what they called an "outlaw" league, he turned a profit with his ballclub, and in October 1906 the Logan Squares defeated both the pennant-winning Cubs and the World Series champion White Sox in exhibition play. Cap Anson apparently thought that if Jimmy Callahan could succeed financially in semipro ball, he could do so as well.

In the same month that Callahan's team made headlines with its wins over the White Sox and Cubs, Anson announced his intention to enter his new team in the Chicago City League for the 1907 season. In typical Anson fashion, the captain did not want to rent a playing field; instead, he proposed to build his own ballpark at 61st and St. Lawrence streets on the South Side. Nearby property owners were less than enthusiastic about the presence of a baseball stadium in their neighborhood, and sued to halt its construction. The suit failed, and work began in the spring of 1907. While construction continued, Anson challenged the White Sox to a match, on the condition that the two club owners, Comiskey and Anson, play first base for their respective teams. Comiskey did not respond, but the gesture garnered Anson some valuable publicity.

Anson intended to manage the Colts, not play for them. By 1907 he was 55 years old and could best be described, in a phrase in popular use at the time, as "aldermanic." He weighed about 270 pounds, some 50 pounds greater than his playing weight some 15 years before. Anson still competed at billiards and bowling, but in 1907 he was content to stay on the sidelines in street clothes and let younger men play baseball under his direction.

The best semipro team in Chicago, next to the Logan Squares, was an all-black ballclub called the Leland Giants. Founded by an entrepreneur named Frank Leland in the early part of the decade, the Leland Giants featured Rube Foster, the greatest African-American pitcher of the era, along with many of the outstanding black ballplayers in the nation. Anson's Colts played the Leland Giants many times during the next few seasons, and if Anson objected to hosting a "colored" nine at his new ballpark, he made no complaints in the newspapers. Perhaps his oft-expressed disdain for minorities had mellowed, but it is more likely that he played against the Leland Giants because he had no choice in the matter. His political career was over and professional baseball had no place for him. If Anson wanted to succeed in the world of semipro ball, he would have to play against all-black nines to do so.

The 1906 season was a banner year for semipro baseball in Chicago, but Anson faced many challenges during the 1907 campaign. Semipro teams relied upon neighborhood support, but the construction of Anson's new ballpark had upset many homeowners in the area, especially since Anson's Colts played many of their games on Sundays. The Logan Squares drew thousands on the north end of town, but Anson's Colts attracted much smaller crowds. In June of 1907, perhaps in an attempt to lure more fans, Anson decided to leave the sidelines and take the field. He had a uniform made to cover his large frame, and began to direct the action from the first-base coaching box.

Anson's Colts won about half of their games in 1907 but lost money for their owner. The 1908 season started poorly for the Colts as well, and in late May Anson informed his team that he could no longer pay their salaries and that they would be paid out of the available gate receipts in the future. Five of his ten players immediately quit, and Anson scrambled to find replacements. The 56-year-old captain then, out of necessity, decided to place himself on the active playing roster, returning to his former position at first base.

Though Anson was 11 years removed from his last major league engagement as a player, he could still hit at least passably well. He retained enough strength to swing his huge bat, and his eyes were still clear, so much so that he was never required to wear glasses at any time in his life. However, the 270-pound Anson could no longer cover any ground near the first base bag, and relied on his pitchers and fellow infielders to assist him. He was never a fast runner, even as a young man, but now was so slow that he was often forced to stop at first on hits to the outfield fence.

Many of the other Chicago semipro ballclubs experienced financial hardship during the 1908 season, but Anson's problems were particularly acute. He carried a hefty mortgage on his ballpark, which he had hoped to pay off by attracting large crowds at a 25-cent admission price. The expected crowds never materialized, and Anson soon fell behind on his payments to the bank. His house on 30th Street was also heavily encumbered, since Anson had taken out a mortgage against it nine years earlier when he furnished his billiards and bowling place. That business also suffered a slump in the summer of 1908, and Anson soon found himself at the end of his financial tether.

The captain's troubles came to a head in early July 1908, when Mrs. Anna Taft, owner of the Michigan Avenue building in which Anson operated his business, filed a suit to recover $6,500 in back rent. Mrs. Taft was the sister-in-law of Republican presidential nominee William Howard Taft, and was not disposed to let the former Democratic city clerk slide on his rent. Within days, several of Anson's other creditors filed legal papers as well, and on July 15, Adrian Anson appeared in court as a defendant before Judge Kenesaw M. Landis.

Judge Landis, the future commissioner of baseball, was an old friend of Anson, but not even he could pull the former captain out of his financial mess. The amount owed by Anson to all his creditors totaled more than $20,000, while the billiards and bowling hall contained only $7,000 to $8,000 worth of recoverable assets. Anson held no other tangible assets besides two pieces of property, one of which included his house, and foreclosure appeared to be the only viable option left to the court.

Anson tried his best to ward off financial disaster. "This is the ninth inning," said an unbowed Anson to the newspapers, "and the score is pretty much against me, according to anybody who has kept tab, but you can't tell anything about the end of the game until it's over. And I don't look as though I were played out yet, do I?"[6] He entertained an offer by Chicago Cubs catcher Johnny Kling to buy his business establishment, but the creditors objected, and Judge Landis appointed a receiver to oversee the business and prevent it from being sold. Kling withdrew his offer, and after the sale of the business and its contents was completed, Anson still owed about $11,000. In September 1908, the court ordered the properties sold, and the Anson family soon lost ownership of the house at 160 30th Street. Though Anson delayed the inevitable as long as possible, the bank took possession of the house in May of 1910.[7] Anson and his family then moved to another place, probably rented, at 320 30th Street.

As if the Ansons did not have enough trouble, their 19-year-old daughter Dorothy chose this moment to elope. In September, at the time of the foreclosure proceedings, Dorothy traveled to New Jersey to visit her sister Grace and brother-in-law Walter Clough. Once there, she left the house and married a bank clerk named Arthur C. Dodge in a ceremony performed by a justice of the peace. No other family members were present, and Dorothy's marriage left only the 9-year-old Virginia Jeannette remaining at home with Adrian and Virginia.

In January 1909, more bad news came Anson's way. Another creditor filed a lien for $111, and Anson found himself in debtor's court once again.

On the witness stand, Anson smiled at the courtroom observers as he discussed his financial woes. "What are you doing at present?" inquired the creditor.

"The best I can," stated Anson.

"I mean," said the creditor, "what occupation are you engaged in?"

"None at present."

"What is the condition of your finances?"

"Busted," replied the former captain.[8]

As Anson's plight elicited sympathy from many of the nation's leading sportswriters, Chicago Cubs team president Charles Murphy asked National League president Harry Pulliam to offer Anson a position as chief of umpires. However, Pulliam was in no mood to accede to the request. In the previous September, Pulliam caused a firestorm of controversy when he supported umpire Henry O'Day in the famous "Merkle Boner" game between the Giants and the Cubs, making it possible for the Cubs to defeat the Giants for the pennant on the last day of the season. The league president did not want to put a Chicago man in charge of the umpires, especially with the New York press still seething over the lost pennant.

Pulliam issued a statement. "There's one thing I want to say," he stated. "I would be glad to give Adrian C. Anson any help he may need, but I can't subscribe to Charley Murphy's proposition to make the old Chicago Captain supervisor of umpires. As President of the National League I am directly responsible for the deportment of the umpires, and I don't intend relinquishing that personal relation. The Chicago club can well afford to make Anson a scout."[9]

Evangelist Billy Sunday, the captain's former baseball protégé, read of Anson's plight in the papers, and wrote a letter to the editor of the *Chicago Tribune* in which he offered to host a public benefit for his old boss. "I regret to hear of anyone's financial troubles, especially Cap Anson's," wrote the former outfielder, "and I am sure that every baseball player and fan in the United States sympathizes with him in his present unfortunate condition. I have a proposition to make ... I will be glad to go to Chicago, bring my entire party, and deliver a lecture free of charge, giving a special musical program preceding the address."

The captain appreciated the gesture, but was no more inclined to accept a public benefit than he had been ten years earlier, when Al Spalding tried to organize a similar affair. "I don't believe I'm ready just yet to admit myself an object of charity," replied Anson. "Not while I have my health, anyway ... I could use the money all right, but I don't want any charity as long as I am able to earn anything. Just thank Mr. Sunday for me."[10]

Cap Anson, despite his personal and financial setbacks, was not a quitter. In the fall of 1908, a semipro football league was formed in Chicago, and Anson assembled a team to play at his park at 61st and St. Lawrence. This unit was also dubbed "Anson's Colts," and after several particularly brutal contests, the Colts won the city championship. Unfortunately, this effort lost more money for the cash-strapped former ballplayer. Still, Anson plowed ahead with ambitious plans for his baseball club. He told reporters that he would rely on his team to support him in 1909, and made arrangements for his Colts to make an exhibition tour of Eastern cities, including Washington and New York, in April. Anson himself would be the star attraction, and the 57-year-old club owner donned a uniform and worked out with his team during the spring months.

The Colts began their eastern swing in Washington on April 5 against a semipro team called the Commissioners. The captain played first base and contributed a single as the Colts won by a score of 11 to 1. After Anson singled, the catcher turned to argue with the umpire, and with the catcher's attention directed elsewhere, Anson set out for second base. He stole the bag cleanly, to the surprise and delight of the crowd.

The Colts found tougher competition when they met some better teams. Anson's club traveled to the Polo Grounds in New York on April 13 for a game against the second stringers of the New York Giants. John McGraw, a longtime admirer of Anson's, arranged the contest as a favor to the man whom McGraw had once labeled "an ornament to the game." Though Anson hoped that his name alone would bring out the fans, only a few hundred people showed up at the park on a rainy, cold afternoon. They saw the Giants, fortified by long-retired former stars Dan Brouthers and Wilbert Robinson, defeat Anson's Colts by a 9–1 count. Anson hit a double in four trips to the plate, but the game provided "much practice and little money," as *The New York Times* put it, for the financially strapped ex-captain. At the end of April, the Colts returned home with a losing record. Anson's trip, like all of his business endeavors since he left the National League, was a monetary failure.

Rube Foster and the Leland Giants won the City League championship in 1909, while Anson's Colts played in front of dwindling crowds even with the novelty of Cap Anson at first base. The Colts managed to stay afloat financially by paying their players from gate receipts, but they played mediocre ball and finished a distant fourth in the six-team league. On October 1, the Chicago Cubs played an exhibition game against Anson's ballclub at West Side Grounds, where the captain had ruled Chicago baseball more than a decade before. Cubs manager Frank Chance used only rookies and second-stringers, but still defeated Anson's men by a score of

9 to 0. The captain appeared as a pinch-hitter in the ninth inning and reached first base when the second baseman fumbled the ball, probably on purpose.

The short-lived boom in Chicago semipro ball died out by the summer of 1909, and the papers claimed that only Jimmy Callahan's Logan Square club made money in the City League that year. At season's end, Anson sold his ballclub to Chicago White Sox pitcher John (Jiggs) Donohue, who chose to leave the major leagues rather than accept a demotion to the minors. Cap Anson's association with baseball was now officially over, and he would never again hold any permanent position in either professional or semipro ball.

He did not stop trying to get back into the game, however. National League president Harry Pulliam committed suicide in July of 1909, and Chicago Cubs owner Charles Murphy surprised many baseball observers when he nominated Anson for the position. "The National League owes something to Captain Anson for his 27 years of continuous service in the game," said Murphy to a group of surprised reporters, "and it would be a fitting tribute to him to be elevated to the presidency of the league." Though Anson had failed miserably in political office and in baseball administration, Murphy convinced the ex-captain that he stood a chance of being elected. Armed with a curiously lukewarm endorsement from Murphy (who said, "I am not prepared to say what the chances of electing [Anson] would be just now"), the hopeful Anson traveled to the league meetings to New York in the fall of 1909 to campaign for the post.[11]

The eight National League magnates were sharply divided on the future of the circuit. League secretary John Heydler had served as acting president following Pulliam's death, but the owners rejected Heydler's candidacy. Four of the owners supported John Ward, the leader of the Brotherhood revolt of 1890, for the presidency, but the other four (representing Cincinnati, St. Louis, Boston, and Pittsburgh) were so bitterly opposed to Ward that they threatened to quit the National League if he gained the office. The opposing faction nominated Robert T. Brown, a little-known sportswriter from Louisville. The magnates found themselves hopelessly deadlocked, while Anson, almost alone among the many baseball figures gathered at the meetings, expected that the owners would turn to him as a compromise selection.

It soon became obvious that neither Brown nor Ward could be elected, and that an alternate candidate needed to be found. However, even Murphy realized that Anson was not the right man for the job. The hard-driving capitalists who owned the eight National League teams would never give power to a man who had experienced nothing but failure since leaving the

Colts 11 years before. Nevertheless, the former Chicago captain was still the "Grand Old Man of the Game," as sympathetic newspaper reports called him. He lobbied hard for the position, though many onlookers regarded his candidacy as nothing more than a sad joke.

Anson was "game to the last," said the *Chicago Tribune*, but the owners selected Thomas Lynch, a former umpire with a reputation for integrity and a long history of run-ins with Anson. The captain, according to the *Tribune*, presented "one of the most pathetic spectacles of all ... [he] did not let a muscle quiver to show his bitter disappointment when told the news of the election of Tom Lynch. Anson immediately sought out President Fogel of the Philadelphia club and made application for the management of the Phillies."[12]

Needless to say, the Phillies did not hire Cap Anson as their manager. By 1910, Anson was a relic of baseball's ever-receding past, and had no realistic chance of being hired for any position in the baseball world. He had once been the most instantly recognizable celebrity in the game, but many team executives at the league meeting in the fall of 1909 had never seen him play ball, and some did not even know who he was. Anson's successes on the diamond were ancient history, while his recent troubles were fresh in everyone's mind.

After this latest disappointment, Anson returned to Chicago to face an uncertain future. The federal census of 1910 found the 58-year-old ex-ballplayer living on the South Side of Chicago with his wife Virginia, daughter Virginia Jeannette, daughter Dorothy, and son-in-law Arthur Dodge, who had found employment as a bookkeeper. The census listed Adrian as head of the household, but it appears that Dodge was now supporting his in-laws, because Adrian gave his occupation as "None."

Adrian Anson's many failures in the business and sporting worlds contrasted with the fortunes of some of his former teammates and rivals. Al Spalding, who like Anson began his baseball career in the green and white uniform of the Rockford

WORLD'S SERIES BASEBALL GAMES

COLISEUM

Every play in Philadelphia Athletics-Boston Braves games duplicated on a real diamond by pick of Chicago's minor leaguers. Direct wires from the East. Games staged by

Capt. Adrian C. Anson

Sox-Cubs Series by Innings   Doors Open 12:30

BEST SEATS 50 CENTS

Another of the captain's financial opportunities. This ad appeared during the 1914 World Series between the Boston Braves and the Philadelphia Athletics. (Author's collection)

Forest Citys, had created the world's most successful sporting goods company and retired to California as a millionaire. Charlie Comiskey's rivalry with Anson began in Dubuque, Iowa in 1879 and continued through the 1885-86 World Series, the Players League rebellion, and Anson's failed attempt to revive the American Association in 1900. While Anson's semipro team floundered, Comiskey owned the Chicago White Sox, the 1906 world champions and one of the most profitable teams in baseball. Comiskey and Anson battled for decades, but it was Comiskey who emerged as the most powerful figure on the Chicago baseball scene.

Cap Anson in a tuxedo, preparing to take the stage. (National Baseball Hall of Fame Library, Cooperstown, New York)

John Ward, whose New York Giants battled the White Stockings for supremacy during the 1880s, built a thriving law practice after his playing career ended, and both of Anson's pitchers from the 1888-89 world tour also attained prominence in other fields. Mark Baldwin became a renowned surgeon at the Mayo Clinic in Minnesota, while John Tener gained election to Congress in 1908 and followed that victory with a campaign for the governorship of Pennsylvania in 1910. Tener won the election in a landslide and served as governor of the nation's second most populous state from 1911 to 1915.

Perhaps the most successful former Chicago White Stocking was Cap Anson's baseball protégé from Marshalltown. Billy Sunday, who gave up the game for religious pursuits, became an evangelist and gained national fame for his fiery, passionate style. He pounded the pulpit with his fists, slid across the stage to illustrate "the Great Umpire in the sky" calling a sinner out at home, and railed against alcohol with the most virulent language ever heard from a minister of the Gospel. Many traditional churchmen criticized Sunday for his antics, but the public adored him, and by 1910 Sunday was America's most popular evangelist and one of the nation's most famous and admired men.

In contrast, Anson found his options severely limited. With no hope of finding a position in baseball, and still steadfastly refusing to accept any form of charity, he turned once again to the stage. He created a monologue of baseball jokes, poems, and reminiscences, and in late 1910 managed to find bookings in small-town vaudeville houses. He cut an impressive figure on stage in top hat and evening clothes, and disarmed the audience with his honesty. "I can't sing, can't dance, can't act," said the captain, "and that leads me to the conclusion that someone must be crazy, myself, the people who hired me, or those who listen to me."[13] He further declared that he was appearing on stage to raise money to buy a baseball club.

In 1911 Anson performed his act in larger midwestern cities such as Milwaukee, St. Paul, and Chicago, and eventually secured a place on the Sullivan-Considine vaudeville circuit. He shared the bill with dog acts, acrobats, and jugglers, but managed to present a friendly, though dignified, demeanor on the stage. His many difficulties had turned the "Grand Old Man of the Game" into a sympathetic figure. The aging ex-captain did not get rich in vaudeville; in fact, it appears that he was barely scraping by, but at least he was able to pay his bills. Besides, he enjoyed the attention, and had stationery printed that bore his picture with the inscription, "A Greater Actor than Any Ballplayer, a Greater Ballplayer than Any Actor."

He also discovered a new hobby. After making his mark in baseball, cricket, billiards, trapshooting, and bowling, Anson turned to golf and soon became obsessed with the game. He played nearly every day, and improved quickly enough to believe that he could compete successfully in tournaments. He applied for membership to the United States Golf Association, but the organization turned him down because, as a former professional athlete, he was no longer an amateur. Anson appealed the decision, and the USGA reversed its stand and admitted Anson to membership.[14]

In 1914, Anson entered a qualifying round for the Western Open, which was (and still is) played in Chicago and was, for many years, one of the most prestigious tournaments in the nation. However, the day was raw and windy, and the 62-year-old Anson found rough going on the wet course. The leaders managed to match par 72, but Anson staggered home with a score of 98, far out of the running. From then on, Cap Anson played golf more for amusement than competition.

His love of the game proved valuable on Christmas Day 1911, when Anson played a round with a doctor friend in unusually mild December weather. The golfers saw two boys fall through the ice on a nearby pond, and Anson waded out and grabbed them as they flailed about in the icy water. The captain was tall enough to walk on the bottom of the pond, enabling him to break a path through the ice and carry the boys to safety.

Anson kept abreast of developments in the baseball world, though, like most old ballplayers, he steadfastly maintained that the men of his era were superior to those of the present day. Connie Mack's Philadelphia Athletics of the American League won three World's Series in four years beginning in 1910, but Anson declared, with his usual certitude, that his White Stockings of the 1880s were the greater team. "The Athletics are a fine playing aggregation," allowed Anson, "but if I had my old Chicago team, with the famous stone-wall infield, I could beat them by a good margin. Could they hit such pitchers as [Chief] Bender and [Eddie] Plank? Sure they could! None of the pitchers of today can equal such men as Clarkson, Goldsmith, Larry Corcoran, and Charlie Ferguson."[15]

The captain was a voracious reader of the sports pages, and in 1918 he noticed an article in *The Sporting News* in which Grantland Rice named his all-time team, weighting it heavily in favor of Ty Cobb and other 20th-century players. This would not do, decided Anson, and he selected his own all-time aggregation and mailed it to the newspaper. He put himself on first base, Fred Pfeffer at second, Ed Williamson at third, and Ross Barnes at shortstop. In the outfield he selected Jimmy Ryan, George Gore, Bill Lange, and Hugh Duffy, and chose John Clarkson, Jim McCormick, and Amos Rusie as his pitchers.[16] King Kelly and Buck Ewing shared the catching duties for Anson's all-star squad. The captain firmly believed that the players of his day were better, as all of his selections except Lange were stars of the 1870s and 1880s, and none played in the major leagues after 1906.

The National League magnates grew disenchanted with Thomas Lynch's leadership, especially after the American League won four World's Series in a row from 1910 to 1913. They dismissed Lynch in 1913, but this time no one championed Cap Anson as a candidate for the post. The owners sought a more prestigious leader, and offered the presidency to one of Anson's former pitchers, Governor John Tener of Pennsylvania. Tener agreed to serve without a salary until his gubernatorial term ended in 1915, which no doubt appealed to the owners. The governor was elected unanimously as league president on December 9, 1913, and the subject of a pension for Cap Anson once again came up for consideration at the league meetings.

The new league president sympathized with his old captain, but knew Anson well enough to realize that he would no doubt refuse any offer of assistance. "Speaking as president of the National League," said Governor Tener, "I will say that I see no reason why a pension should be voted Captain Anson. The captain is strong, physically and mentally, and is appearing weekly on the vaudeville stage. He is entirely satisfied with the renumeration he is receiving for his talent. In common with his many friends I deplore the continued reference to the National League's failure to provide a pension for the captain's support.

A vaudeville advertisement in the *Chicago Tribune*, 1917. (Author's collection)

"Mr. Anson is far from being an object of charity and would refuse any pension that any league would vote him. The National League is not unmindful of its heroes and faithful and if there should come a time when Captain Anson should need the organization's support it will quickly and gladly come to his assistance."[17]

Anson spent the next few years performing his monologue on the vaudeville circuit, a task that became increasingly difficult as his wife's health began to fail. The Ansons had moved from 30th Street to a place on Kenwood Avenue, and it was there, on February 26, 1915, that Virginia Anson died at age 56 after an undisclosed illness. She was buried in the Fiegal family plot in Philadelphia.

In 1917 Cap Anson developed a new vaudeville act with the assistance of sportswriter Ring Lardner of the *Chicago Tribune*. Lardner wrote a sketch, titled "First Aid for Father," in which Anson and his two daughters, 33-year-old Adele Cherry and 28-year-old Dorothy Dodge, sang, danced, recited poetry, and reminisced about the old days of baseball. Armed with a new monologue, "Captain Anson and Daughters" opened at the Majestic Theater in Chicago in late January 1917 to favorable reviews.

Dorothy Dodge recalled the act many years later:

> We had two pretty fair writers—Ring Lardner and George M. Cohan. Cohan wrote a monologue for Papa, Lardner a sketch which included me and my sister Adele, who had a good singing voice.
> Papa wore tails while he delivered his monologue and Adele and I were dressed in fur-trimmed evening gowns for the first part of the act. But the finale was all baseball. We changed to sports clothes and carried a huge bag filled with papier-mâché baseballs made for us by A. G. Spalding....
> As we threw the balls into the audience, we sang:
>> We're going to take you to the game
>> Where dear old Daddy won his fame.

At that point, the 65-year-old captain appeared on stage in his old Chicago uniform, carrying a silver bat that had been presented to him by the alumni of Notre Dame University. Anson took a batting stance and whacked the papier-mâché baseballs tossed his way by the audience.[18]

"The sketch is ideal for the captain's purposes," wrote Percy Hammond in the *Chicago Tribune*, "combining as it does wit, humor, melody, dancing, and a soupcon of the sentiment which is said to cling around the memory of historic personages." The Anson daughters, said Hammond, were "large, blond and affable ladies of the Valkyr type," while the captain displayed "the faculty of assuming a dignified intimacy with his audience." Hammond summed up the effort with the statement, "Vaudeville is full of acts not nearly so good by authors not nearly so mature."[19]

"Cap Anson and Daughters" played the Keith circuit for four years, and while the retired ballplayer could hardly be called a headliner, the act was reasonably well received. Most importantly, it provided Anson with a small income as he approached his 70th year. He had found a way to support himself without accepting charity, and that, to Cap Anson, was a victory as sweet as any earned on the baseball diamond.

CHAPTER 24

Epilogue

> Cap Anson the greatest man that baseball ever knew
> The pitchers feared him and the bleachers cheered him
> And he led the league in 1492.
> — A line from a song in Anson's vaudeville show, 1917[1]

While Cap Anson performed vaudeville, a new baseball scandal threatened the foundation of the national game. Eight members of Charles Comiskey's ballclub, the Chicago White Sox, were accused of accepting money from gamblers to throw the 1919 World Series to the Cincinnati Reds, who won despite entering the fall classic as underdogs. In September of 1920, Chicago pitcher Eddie Cicotte confessed his involvement in the conspiracy and put the long-dormant issue of "hippodroming" on the nation's sports pages. Not since 1877, when the Louisville Grays threw the National League pennant race to the Boston Red Stockings, had major league baseball faced such a monumental threat to its existence.

A three-man National Commission, consisting of both league presidents and a mutually acceptable club owner, had managed the game since 1903, but proved too weak to deal effectively with this latest scandal. Sportswriters and fans demanded that the sport clean up its image, and when Garry Herrmann, owner of the Cincinnati Reds, resigned from his seat on the commission, the magnates decided to identify and select an unimpeachably honest and respected individual to fill the vacancy. The owners considered several candidates, including former President William Howard Taft, war heroes John Pershing and Leonard Wood, and no-nonsense Federal Judge Kenesaw M. Landis of Chicago.

The 68-year-old Cap Anson could not resist. He submitted his own name for nomination to the post.

Most of the press and public ignored the former captain's candidacy, but when the major league owners met in New York on February 11, 1920, outgoing commissioner Herrmann entered Anson's name for consideration. The other candidates included Judge Landis, *Chicago Tribune* sports editor Harvey T. Woodruff, and New York state senator Jimmy Walker. However, Anson "will not enter into the final consideration," wrote Jim Cruisinberry of the *Chicago Tribune*. "Anson said he was a candidate, so the magnates put him on the list just to make him feel good."[2]

The owners eventually disbanded the three-man commission and appointed Landis as the sole Commissioner of Baseball in November of 1920. The new commissioner made headlines when he banned all eight of the accused World Series conspirators for life, following the example of William Hulbert in the Louisville scandal more than 40 years previously. It was a harsh, but necessary, punishment that met with public approval, and within a few years baseball attendance boomed as the game rode a wave of unprecedented popularity.

Cap Anson was an old friend of Landis and paid many visits to the commissioner's Chicago office, but baseball had passed the old captain by. He had outlived most of his contemporaries from the days of underhand pitching and gloveless infielders. All of Anson's teammates on the 1871 Rockford Forest Citys (save for pitcher Cherokee Fisher) were now dead, as were most of the men who played with him on the Philadelphia Athletics. Some of his former Chicago charges, including Fred Pfeffer, Abner Dalrymple, and George Gore, were still living, as was Billy Sunday, who told the newspapers that he would like to "bat Captain Anson into church." However, such players as Mike Kelly, John Clarkson, Ed Williamson, Silver Flint, Tom Burns, and Jim McCormick were gone, as were Al Spalding and Jim Hart.

The widowed Anson, who had moved in with his daughter Dorothy and son-in-law Arthur Dodge on Harper Street in Chicago, retired from the stage in 1921. He had saved no money for his retirement, though he stoutly rejected all offers of charity, pensions, and benefits. John Heydler, who succeeded John Tener as president of the National League in 1918, once interviewed Anson and held out the promise of a yearly pension for the old Chicago captain. Anson replied, "If I need help, I'll let you know," and brusquely terminated the meeting.

The old man was too proud to accept help, despite his gloomy financial picture, but in early 1922 an opportunity presented itself. A new golf club on the South Side, the Dixmoor, was looking for a general manager, and the owners offered Anson the position. The post would allow him to remain in the public eye while pursuing his favorite sport, and Anson, still a golfing fanatic at the age of 69, fairly leaped at the offer. He accepted in April of 1922 and attacked his responsibilities with his usual enthusiasm. "I'm going to have a golf club," boasted the captain to a Chicago reporter, "and it sure is going to be some place. I'm going to manage the new Dixmoor club out on the highway and things are going to hum there once we get started."[3]

This new challenge filled Anson with excitement, but his health failed him at the worst possible moment. In early April, he collapsed with what appeared to be a heart attack while taking his usual Sunday afternoon stroll. He was rushed to St. Luke's Hospital on the South Side, and underwent an operation for "glandular trouble." Though his condition was listed as critical for several days, the old captain seemed to be making a recovery. However, he soon suffered a relapse, and on Friday, April 14, 1922, Adrian Anson died. He was three days short of his 70th birthday.

The baseball world had mostly ignored Cap Anson since his departure from the National League 24 years before, but an impressive array of sporting celebrities attended his funeral three days later. Chicago White Sox owner Charlie Comiskey praised his old rival, while Commissioner Kenesaw M. Landis eulogized Anson, intoning, "We of today should pattern our lives after this man, whose steadiness in crises can be compared only with the pyramids or with Gibraltar." Fred Pfeffer, Deacon White, Abner Dalrymple, and George Gore were but some of the players who returned to say goodbye to their old teammate. Clark Griffith, Anson's long-ago pitcher who by 1922 was the owner of the Washington Senators, sent an impressive floral wreath, as did Anson's onetime protégé Billy Sunday. All the members of the Chicago White Sox and the Detroit Tigers attended the funeral; they were scheduled to play ball that afternoon, but managers Kid Gleason and Ty Cobb agreed to postpone the game until the ceremony was completed.

Cap Anson was buried in Chicago's Oak Woods Cemetery. Shortly after his funeral, the remains of Virginia Anson, who had passed away seven years before, were removed from a temporary resting place in Philadelphia and returned to Chicago to be interred beside her husband. Two months later, in June of 1922, National League president John Heydler sent Dorothy Anson Dodge a check for $750 to cover her father's funeral expenses. Cap Anson, the "Grand Old Man of Baseball," had died penniless.

The National League created a fund to establish a "fitting memorial" for Anson, though many sportswriters wondered in print why the league did not raise money for the captain when he was alive. Francis Richter, editor of *Sporting Life*, offered an explanation in the *1923 Reach Guide*. "It has been meanly stated," wrote Richter, "that this [memorial fund] was a 'belated appreciation of Captain Anson.' In justice to the National League let it be stated that the body for many years stood ready to come to Anson's assistance when necessary. That it was not necessary was due to the fact that the independent old man would not accept a pension, in default of which no position could be created that he could fill satisfactorily owing to his disposition which was self-opinionated and brooked neither advice nor order."[4]

The directors of the memorial fund had originally planned to erect a statue of Anson, but later decided to create a tall marble shaft, decorated with crossed bats and a wreath. In September 1923 Commissioner Landis and members of Anson's family unveiled the marble monument over Anson's grave. The stone read:

CAPT. ADRIAN CONSTANTINE ANSON
BORN AT MARSHALLTOWN, IOWA, APRIL 18, 1852
DIED AT CHICAGO, APRIL 14, 1922

HE PLAYED THE GAME

ERECTED BY THE NATIONAL LEAGUE
OF PROFESSIONAL BASEBALL CLUBS

The National Baseball Hall of Fame opened in Cooperstown, New York, in 1939. The directors of the Hall had sponsored its first elections three years earlier, with pre–1900 and post–1900 players placed in separate categories. The Baseball Writers Association of America voted for both categories in early 1936, and while five men gained election from the post–1900 group, none of the 19th century stars managed to attain the required 75 percent of the votes. There were 78 writers voting for the old-timers, and Cap Anson and Buck Ewing led the balloting with 39.5 votes each. In response, the Hall of Fame created a special commission to recognize older players and executives, and such men as shortstop George Wright and managers Connie Mack and John McGraw were selected for induction in 1937.

Commissioner Landis recognized that some of baseball's foremost pioneers were unrecognized by the Hall committee, so he assembled a panel, consisting of himself and the two league presidents. This group met on May 2, 1939, and selected six 19th-century players and managers for induction. Cap Anson, Landis' old friend, was one of them, as were Anson's former mentor Al Spalding and his longtime rival Charlie Comiskey. Catcher Buck Ewing and pitchers Candy Cummings and Charley Radbourn were the others. All six men were long dead, but it seemed somehow fitting that Cap Anson and Al Spalding would enter the Hall of Fame together.

Cap Anson played his final National League game in a Chicago uniform more than 100 years ago, but is still the team's all-time leader in runs scored, hits, doubles, and runs batted in, and stands second to Ernie Banks in games played and times at bat. When he retired in 1897, he was baseball's career record holder in runs, hits, games played, times at bat, doubles, runs batted in, and wins by a manager. He established the hitting standards that Honus Wagner, Ty Cobb, and others later surpassed, and left managing records for men such as John McGraw and Connie Mack to challenge.

However, Anson's reputation has suffered over the last few decades as his role in the segregation of baseball has come under scrutiny. Few people had heard of Moses Fleetwood Walker until the 1970s, when baseball researchers established the Toledo catcher as the first African-American major leaguer, 63 years before Jackie Robinson took the field. As Walker's name garnered attention from the press and public, so too did Cap Anson's outspoken opposition to the presence of minorities in the national game. Anson became the villain in the story, and though he could not have banned blacks from the game by himself, his actions cast his character in an unflattering light and made the Chicago captain one of the most unpopular men in the Hall of Fame.

Even Anson's membership in the 3,000-hit club has been called into question. For many years, statisticians credited him with over 3,500 base hits during his 27-year career, but in 1969 a special baseball rules committee decreed that the National Association, in which Anson spent his first five seasons, was no longer a major league. This ruling erased more than 400 hits from his total, leaving him with 3,081 in his 22 seasons of National League play. Major league baseball still recognizes that number, but later researchers have found numerous discrepancies in the statistical record of early baseball and have adjusted the figures accordingly. They revised Anson's total to 3,055, and later took away 60 more hits (from Anson's 60 walks in 1887, when walks were counted as hits). *Total Baseball,* by John Thorn and Pete Palmer, credits Anson with 2,995 hits and drops him from the 3,000-hit club; however, *The Baseball Encyclopedia* reports Anson's total as an even 3,000.

Anson was, without a doubt, both the greatest player and the greatest manager of baseball's first three decades. He was a hard hitter, a dedicated athlete, and an innovative and forceful field captain who helped define the role of the baseball manager for all who followed. He was also a highly underrated all-around athlete. Anson was not only an outstanding baseball player, but also competed successfully at the highest level in billiards, trapshooting, cricket, and bowling. On a personal level, Anson was honest to the core, outspoken to the point of rudeness, and so fiercely independent that he refused to accept charity even in his darkest financial hours. He was also a racist, a bully, and a martinet who failed at a myriad of career pursuits after his baseball days were over.

Perhaps historian David Voigt had it right when he described Cap Anson as "a baseball Hercules" who "shared the naïveté and intellectual weakness of that Greek god."[5] The tragedy of Cap Anson lies in the fact that his bluntly aggressive manner, which served him so well on the baseball diamond, prevented him from finding success in any other field of endeavor. He was not the last old ballplayer to suffer financial hardship in his later years; in that, too, he set an unfortunate standard for others to follow.

Appendix A

Cap Anson's First Professional Baseball Contract

Adrian (Cap) Anson's first professional baseball contract, with the 1871 Rockford Forest City team, reads as follows:

Memorandum of Agreement: made and entered into this 31st day of March A.D. 1871, by and between John P. Manny, John C. Barbour, Henry W. Price, Hosmer P. Holland and Jerome C. Roberts of the City of Rockford, Illinois, party of the first part; and Adrian C. Anson of Marshalltown Iowa, party of the second part:

Whereas divers residents of said city of Rockford have associated themselves and contributed a common fund for the organization and maintenance of a first class base ball club, to be known and called "The Forest City Base Ball Club of Rockford Illinois";

And whereas the said party of the second part, being desirous of playing in said club; has represented to the party of the first part that he is a first class base ball player and possessed of the skill, and physically competent, to play said game as a member of a first class club;

Now therefore, this Agreement Witnesseth: That the said party of the second part, in consideration of the premises and of the promises and agreements of the party of the first part, hereinafter expressed, has, and does, covenant and agree, to and with said party of the first part, to play the game of base ball with said Forest City Base Ball Club, and in any position, he may be therein assigned by the Directors of said Club, for and during the season of A.D. 1871, to wit: from April 15th A.D. 1871, to and including October 15th A.D. 1871.

And in further consideration of the premises said party of the second part promises and agrees to keep and observe the following rules of conduct and discipline, viz:

To use his best efforts to advance the interests of said Club, by cheerfull, prompt and respectfull obedience of the Directions and requirements of the Directors thereof, or of any person by said Directors placed in authority over him, as well as the by laws of said Club;

To abstain from the use of Alcoholic Liquors: unless medically prescribed, and to conduct himself, both off and on the Ball Ground, in all things like a gentleman;

To report promptly for duty at the grounds of the Club for all games, and for practice at the hours designated there for by the officers of the Club, and upon the grounds, to abstain from profane language, scuffling and light conduct, and to discourage the same in others.

To practise at least two and a half hours per day. On each and every practice day of the Club, and at all times both in games and at practice, to use his best endeavours to perfect himself in play. Always bearing in mind that the Object in view in every game is to win.

And in further consideration of the premises said party of the second part promises and agrees that he will not make, or procure to be made for him, or in any [way] be concerned or interested in, any bet or wager upon the result of any game, or upon the playing of any member of the club, or upon anything connected with any game, in which said Forest City Club, may engage during the time of his engagement hereunder.

And in consideration of the premises, said party of the first part promise and agree to pay said party of the second part the sum of Sixty six and two third ($66 2/3) Dollars per month for each and every month of the time he may play with said Forest City Club, payable as follows; to wit: Sixty Six and two third ($66 2/3) Dollars on the 1st day of June A.D. 1871, and sixty six and two third ($66 2/3) Dollars on the first day of each and every month thereafter of the term of his employment, as aforesaid, the balance due to be fully paid on the 1st day of November A.D. 1871.

A.C. Anson [signed]

J.C. Barbour [signed]
Hosmer P. Holland [signed]

APPENDIX B

Cap Anson's Statistical Record

Year	Team	League	G	AB	R	H	2B	3B	HR	RBI	Average
1871	Rockford	NA	25	120	29	39	11	3	0	16	.325
1872	Athletics	NA	46	217	60	90	10	7	0	50	.415
1873	Athletics	NA	52	254	53	101	9	2	0	36	.398
1874	Athletics	NA	55	259	51	87	8	3	0	37	.336
1875	Athletics	NA	69	326	84	106	15	3	0	58	.325
1876	Chicago	NL	66	309	63	110	9	7	2	59	.356
1877	Chicago	NL	59	255	52	86	19	1	0	32	.337
1878	Chicago	NL	60	261	55	89	12	2	0	40	.341
1879	Chicago	NL	51	227	40	72	20	1	0	34	.317
1880	Chicago	NL	86	356	54	120	24	1	1	74	.337
1881	Chicago	NL	84	343	67	137	21	7	1	82	.399
1882	Chicago	NL	82	348	69	126	29	8	1	83	.362
1883	Chicago	NL	98	413	70	127	36	5	0	68	.308
1884	Chicago	NL	112	475	108	159	30	3	21	102	.335
1885	Chicago	NL	112	464	100	144	35	7	7	108	.310
1886	Chicago	NL	125	504	117	187	35	11	10	147	.371
1887	Chicago	NL	122	472	107	164	33	13	7	102	.347
1888	Chicago	NL	134	515	101	177	20	12	12	84	.344
1889	Chicago	NL	134	518	100	161	32	7	7	117	.311
1890	Chicago	NL	139	504	95	157	14	5	7	107	.312
1891	Chicago	NL	136	540	81	157	24	8	8	120	.291
1892	Chicago	NL	146	559	62	152	25	9	1	74	.272
1893	Chicago	NL	103	398	70	125	24	2	0	91	.314
1894	Chicago	NL	83	340	82	132	28	4	5	99	.388
1895	Chicago	NL	122	474	87	159	23	6	2	91	.335
1896	Chicago	NL	108	402	72	133	18	2	2	90	.331
1897	Chicago	NL	114	424	67	121	17	3	3	75	.285
NA only, 1871–75			247	1176	277	423	53	18	0	197	.360

Year Team	League	G	AB	R	H	2B	3B	HR	RBI	Average
NL only, 1876–97		2276	9101	1719	2995	528	124	97	1879	.329
Totals		2523	10277	1996	3418	581	142	97	2076	.333

The information used here was obtained free of charge from and is copyrighted by Retrosheet. Interested parties may contact Retrosheet at 20 Sunset Rd., Newark, DE 19711.

APPENDIX C

Cap Anson's Statistical Record (Projected to 162-Game Seasons)

Cap Anson played major league ball for 27 years (including the five he spent in the National Association), but at the end of 2004 season he ranked only 39th on the all-time list of games played. Teams in Anson's day played far fewer games than they do now. In the National League's inaugural campaign of 1876, Anson's Chicago White Stockings played only 66 contests, and the league schedule did not exceed 100 games until 1884, Anson's 14th season of professional ball. Here is Anson's statistical record as presented in Appendix B, projected to 162-game seasons.

Year	Team	League	G	AB	R	H	2B	3B	HR	RBI	Average
1871	Rockford	NA	162	777	187	252	71	19	0	103	.324
1872	Athletics	NA	158	745	206	309	34	24	0	171	.415
1873	Athletics	NA	162	791	165	314	28	6	0	112	.397
1874	Athletics	NA	162	762	150	256	23	8	0	108	.336
1875	Athletics	NA	145	685	176	222	31	6	0	121	.324
1876	Chicago	NL	162	758	154	270	22	17	4	144	.356
1877	Chicago	NL	159	687	140	231	51	2	0	86	.336
1878	Chicago	NL	159	691	145	235	31	5	0	106	.340
1879	Chicago	NL	99	440	77	139	38	1	0	66	.316
1880	Chicago	NL	162	670	101	226	45	1	1	139	.337
1881	Chicago	NL	162	661	129	264	40	13	1	158	.399
1882	Chicago	NL	158	670	132	242	55	15	1	159	.361
1883	Chicago	NL	162	682	115	209	59	8	0	112	.306
1884	Chicago	NL	160	678	154	227	42	4	30	145	.335

Year	Team	League	G	AB	R	H	2B	3B	HR	RBI	Average
1885	Chicago	NL	160	662	142	205	50	10	10	154	.310
1886	Chicago	NL	160	645	149	239	44	14	12	188	.371
1887	Chicago	NL	155	599	135	208	41	16	8	129	.347
1888	Chicago	NL	159	611	119	210	23	14	14	99	.344
1889	Chicago	NL	159	614	118	191	37	8	8	138	.311
1890	Chicago	NL	162	587	110	182	16	5	8	124	.310
1891	Chicago	NL	160	635	95	184	28	9	9	141	.290
1892	Chicago	NL	160	612	67	166	27	9	1	81	.271
1893	Chicago	NL	130	502	88	157	30	2	0	114	.313
1894	Chicago	NL	99	405	97	157	33	4	5	118	.388
1895	Chicago	NL	148	575	105	192	27	7	2	110	.334
1896	Chicago	NL	132	491	88	162	22	2	2	110	.330
1897	Chicago	NL	133	494	78	141	19	3	3	87	.285
NA only, 1871–75			789	3760	884	1353	187	63	0	615	.360
NL only, 1876–97			3300	13369	2538	4437	780	169	119	2708	.332
Total			4089	17129	3422	5790	967	232	119	3323	.338

Chapter Notes

1. Beginnings

1. Adrian C. Anson, *A Ball Player's Career: being the personal reminiscences of Adrian C. Anson* (Chicago: Era Publishing, 1900), pp. 15–16.
2. Some sources, including the 1895 Iowa state census, state that Sturgis was born in Michigan, but the United States Census of 1860, 1870, and 1910 all list Sturgis Anson's state of birth as Ohio. He was named after the southern Michigan towns of Sturgis and Ransome.
3. Paul Dysart, "The Heritage of Henry Anson," *Marshalltimes*, February 1996.
4. *Marshalltown Times-Republican*, December 1, 1905.
5. Ibid.
6. Anson, page 9.
7. Anson, page 10.
8. Anson, page 16.
9. Anson, page 14.
10. Anson, page 13.
11. Anson, page 15.
12. Anson, page 39.
13. *Sporting Life*, November 3, 1886.
14. Anson, page 19.
15. Anson, page 15. Anson's autobiography, which was written by Chicago writer Richard Cary Jr. from a series of interviews with Anson, stated that the future baseball star attended Iowa State College before Notre Dame. However, records from the archives of Notre Dame University and the University of Iowa (the former Iowa State College) show that the Anson brothers attended Notre Dame from 1866 to 1868, and enrolled at the state college in Iowa City in the fall of 1869.

2. From Marshalltown to Rockford

1. Alfred H. Spink, *The National Game* (St. Louis, Missouri: National Game Publishing Company, 1910), page 173.
2. Peter Levine, *A. G. Spalding and the Rise of Baseball: The Promise of American Sport* (New York: Oxford University Press, 1985), pp. 7–8.
3. *Chicago Tribune*, May 3, 1897.
4. Adrian C. Anson, *A Ball Player's Career* (Chicago, Illinois: Era Publishing, 1900), page 45.
5. *Rockford Register*, January 1, 1871, mentioned in Levine, pg. 13.
6. Adrian may have started the 1870 fall term at college in Iowa City. The United States Census of 1870 recorded both Sturgis and "A. C." Anson in Iowa City in August of that year. Adrian also appeared in Marshalltown's census, which was recorded in June.
7. A copy of *The Base-Ball Guide for 1871, Rules and Regulations of the Game of Base-Ball*, adopted at the association's convention in November 1870 and amended in March 1871, can be found at http://www.retrosheet.org/1871Rules.doc.
8. *Rockford Register*, August 16, 1939; AP wire, July 7, 2002.

9. Roger H. Van Bolt, "'Cap' Anson's First Contract," *Annals of Iowa*, April 1953. A copy of the contract can be found in Appendix A.
10. *Chicago Tribune*, July 6, 1871.
11. Anson, page 50.

3. The Philadelphia Athletics

1. Anson, Adrian C. *A Ball Player's Career* (Chicago, Illinois: Era Publishing, 1900). page 62.
2. Anson, page 55.
3. Anson claimed in his autobiography that the ball used in that game was a dead one, but the final score seems to indicate otherwise.
4. *Brooklyn Eagle*, July 1, 1872.
5. *Brooklyn Eagle*, June 26, 1872.
6. *Brooklyn Eagle*, July 16, 1872.
7. *The New York Times*, June 25, 1872.
8. *Brooklyn Eagle*, June 19, 1872.
9. *Brooklyn Eagle*, September 6, 1872.
10. The infield fly rule, which was created to prevent such deception by infielders on easy pop flies with runners on base, did not enter the rulebooks until 1894. It stated that the batsman is out "... if he hits a fly ball that can be handled by an infielder while first base is occupied with only one out." It was revised in 1895 to include runners on other bases with no outs as well.
11. *The New York Times*, May 15, 1873.
12. Anson, page 63.
13. Anson, page 88.

4. Across the Ocean

1. *New York Clipper*, July 25, 1874.
2. Adrian C. Anson, *A Ball Player's Career* (Chicago, Illinois: Era Publishing, 1900), page 57.
3. Anson, page 70.
4. Peter Levine, *A. G. Spalding and the Rise of Baseball: The Promise of American Sport* (New York: Oxford University Press, 1985), page 18.
5. Levine, pp. 18–19.
6. A. G. Spalding, *Base Ball: America's National Game* (New York: American Sports Publishing Company, 1911), page 179.
7. *Sporting and Dramatic News*, undated clipping from A. G. Spalding scrapbook, available on microfilm from the Society for American Baseball Research (SABR) Library.
8. *London Graphic*, undated clipping from Spalding scrapbook.
9. *London Sand and Water*, August 1, 1874; from Spalding scrapbook.
10. Alfred H. Spink, *The National Game* (St. Louis, Missouri: National Game Publishing Company, 1910), page 173.
11. Undated newspaper article from Spalding scrapbook.
12. Spalding, pp. 199–200.
13. Tom Melville, *Early Baseball and the Rise of the National League* (Jefferson, North Carolina: McFarland and Company, 2001), page 78.
14. Anson, page 65.

5. William Hulbert and the White Stockings

1. Robert Smith, *Baseball* (New York: Simon and Schuster, 1947), page 96.
2. *Chicago Tribune*, October 24, 1875.
3. Albert G. Spalding, *Base Ball: America's National Game* (New York: American Sports Publishing Company, 1911), pp. 201–202.
4. Spalding, pp. 200–201.
5. Adrian C. Anson, *A Ball Player's Career* (Chicago, Illinois: Era Publishing, 1900), pp. 92–93.
6. Spalding, page 207.
7. Spalding, page 208.
8. Letter from Spalding to Anson, January 8, 1876, on file at Chicago Historical Society, Chicago Cubs collection; also referenced by Peter Levine in *A. G. Spalding and the Rise of Baseball: The Promise of American Sport* (New York: Oxford University Press, 1985), page 39.
9. *Chicago Tribune*, May 3, 1897.
10. Ibid.
11. Spalding, pp. 520–521.
12. Anson, page 89.
13. *Chicago Tribune*, April 26, 1876.
14. The new rule appeared in the *1877 Spalding Guide*, page 35.
15. *Chicago Tribune*, July 14, 1876.
16. *Chicago Evening Journal*, September 9, 1876.

17. A. C. Bartlett, *Baseball and Mr. Spalding: the history and romance of baseball* (New York: Farrar, Straus, and Young, 1951), page 94.

6. Manager in Training

1. *Washington Post*, September 3, 1878.
2. Tom Melville, *Early Baseball and the Rise of the National League* (Jefferson, North Carolina: McFarland and Company, 2001), page 87.
3. *Chicago Tribune*, July 1, 1877. This may be the first printed description of the hit-and-run play.
4. *Brooklyn Eagle*, September 1, 1877.
5. Adrian C. Anson, *A Ball Player's Career* (Chicago, Illinois: Era Publishing, 1900), page 67.
6. *New York Clipper*, November 17, 1877.
7. *Brooklyn Eagle*, November 12, 1877.
8. Albert G. Spalding, *Base Ball: America's National Game* (New York: American Sports Publishing Company, 1911), page 120.
9. Anson, page 100–101.
10. Bill James, *The Bill James Guide To Baseball Managers From 1870 to Today* (New York: Scribner, 1997), page 22.

7. Captain of the Chicagos

1. *New York Clipper*, April 12, 1879.
2. Dalrymple was named the winner of the batting title in the league's official statistics, but later researchers credit Paul Hines of the Providence Grays as the 1878 batting champ with an average of .358 to .354 for Dalrymple.
3. Robert L. Tiemann and Mark Rucker, editors, *Nineteenth Century Stars* (Kansas City, Missouri: Society for American Baseball Research, 1989), page 35.
4. *1880 Spalding Guide*, page 18.
5. *Brooklyn Eagle*, July 2, 1879.
6. Many modern histories of baseball claim that Spalding was the man who came onto the field and incurred Anson's wrath, but the *Brooklyn Eagle* and the *Chicago Record* both state that it was Hulbert. The account of the game in the *Chicago Tribune* did not mention the argument between the two men.
7. *Brooklyn Eagle*, August 22, 1879.
8. *Chicago Tribune*, August 13, 1879.
9. *Chicago Tribune*, August 24, 1879.
10. *New York Clipper*, August 30, 1879.
11. David Nemec, *The Great Encyclopedia of 19th-Century Major League Baseball* (New York: Donald I. Fine Books, 1997), page 123.
12. From American National Biography Online (www.anb.org).
13. *New York Clipper*, September 13, 1879; referenced also by Tiemann and Rucker in *Nineteenth Century Stars*, page 31.
14. Tiemann and Rucker, page 21.
15. *Brooklyn Eagle*, June 7, 1880.
16. *Brooklyn Eagle*, June 5, 1880.
17. Preston Orem, *Baseball (1845–1881) from the Newspaper Accounts* (Altadena, California: self-published, 1961), page 324.

8. Champions of the National League

1. *Cincinnati Enquirer*, October 7, 1882.
2. Jerome Holtzman and George Vass, *The Chicago Cubs Encyclopedia* (Philadelphia: Temple University Press, 1997), page 7.
3. Preston Orem, *Baseball (1845–1881) from the Newspaper Accounts* (Altadena, California: self-published, 1961), page 351.
4. *Brooklyn Eagle*, September 12, 1888; quoting a report in the *Chicago Sportsman's Referee*. The poem also appears in Howard Rosenberg, *Cap Anson 1: When Captaining a Team Meant Something* (Arlington, Virginia: Tile Books, 2003), page 121.
5. *New York Clipper*, July 30, 1881.
6. John Phillips, *Uncle Nick's Birthday Party* (Cabin John, Maryland: Capital Publishing, 1996), page 71.
7. A case could be made for Lou Boudreau of the Cleveland Indians, who won the Most Valuable Player award in 1948 while managing the Indians to the world championship. However, Ted Williams won his fourth batting title that season and was generally recognized as baseball's best hitter at the time.
8. Holtzman and Vass, page 7.
9. *Chicago Tribune*, September 13, 1882.
10. *Cincinnati Enquirer*, October 9, 1882.
11. David Nemec, *The Beer and Whiskey*

League (New York: Lyons Press, 1994), page 38.

9. Controversy

1. *New York Clipper*, August 27, 1881.
2. Anson, in his autobiography, stated that he became aware of Sunday when he saw the youngster perform in a fireman's baseball tournament during a visit to Marshalltown.
3. Jerome Holtzman and George Vass, *Chicago Cubs Encyclopedia* (Philadelphia: Temple University Press, 1997), page 9.
4. *Toledo Blade*, August 11, 1883.
5. Ibid.
6. Toledo, the home team, batted first. In those days, the two teams tossed a coin to decide which team batted first.
7. *Toledo Blade*, August 11, 1883.
8. Sol White, *History of Colored Base Ball* (Lincoln, Nebraska: University of Nebraska Press, 1995), pp. 76–77.
9. Robert Smith, *Baseball* (New York: Simon and Schuster, 1947), page 96.
10. *Sporting Life*, April 9, 1884.
11. *Sporting Life*, May 28, 1884.
12. *Washington Post*, August 24, 1884.
13. John Phillips, *Uncle Nick's Birthday Party* (Cabin John, Maryland: Capital Publishing, 1996), page 54.
14. *Sporting Life*, July 30, 1884.
15. *The Sporting News*, June 5, 1976.
16. *Washington Post*, September 22, 1907.
17. *Sporting Life*, July 30, 1884.
18. Robert Peterson, *Only the Ball Was White* (Englewood Cliffs, New Jersey: Prentice-Hall, 1970), pp. 43–44.
19. Peter Levine, *A. G. Spalding and the Rise of Baseball: The Promise of American Sport* (New York: Oxford University Press, 1985), page 47.
20. *Sporting Life*, September 21, 1887.

10. Back on Top

1. *Philadelphia Star*, May 15, 1885; also referenced by Howard Rosenberg in *Cap Anson 1: When Captaining a Team Meant Something* (Arlington, Virginia: Tile Books, 2003), page 96.
2. Marty Appel, *Slide Kelly Slide* (Lanham, Maryland: Scarecrow Press, 1996), page 66.
3. Interview with Hardy Richardson in the *Washington Post*, April 10, 1911. Richardson identified Fred Goldsmith as the base runner, but Goldsmith did not appear in the boxscore for that game.
4. Ibid.
5. *Chicago Tribune*, March 27, 1885.
6. *Sporting Life*, April 30, 1884.
7. Mark Rucker and John Freyer, *19th Century Baseball in Chicago* (Charleston, South Carolina: Arcadia Publishing, 2003), page 104.
8. *The Sporting News*, April 6, 1963.
9. Adrian C. Anson, *A Ballplayer's Career* (Chicago, Illinois: Era Publishing, 1900), page 130.
10. *The New York Times*, August 11, 1885.
11. *The New York Times*, October 4, 1885.
12. *Washington Post*, October 7, 1885.
13. Peter Golenbock, *The Spirit of St. Louis* (New York: William Morrow, 2000), pp. 27–28.

11. King of Kickers

1. Albert G. Spalding, *Base Ball: America's National Game* (New York: American Sports Publishing Company, 1911), page 265.
2. *Sporting Life*, May 28, 1884.
3. *The Sporting News*, March 17, 1886.
4. David Nemec, *The Great Encyclopedia of 19th-Century Major League Baseball* (New York: Donald I. Fine Books, 1997), page 290.
5. For a discussion of Anson's 1886 platooning arrangement, see an article by Tom Nawrocki, "Captain Anson's Platoon," in the 1994 SABR publication *The National Pastime*, pp. 34–37.
6. *Washington Post*, September 22, 1907; article reprinted from the *Minneapolis Tribune*.
7. Marty Appel, *Slide, Kelly, Slide* (Lanham, Maryland: Scarecrow Press, 1996), pp. 89–90.
8. Spalding, pp. 523–526.
9. William T. Ellis, *Billy Sunday: The Man and His Message* (Philadelphia: Universal Book and Bible House, 1914), page 41.
10. *Brooklyn Eagle*, June 17, 1888.

11. *The Sporting News*, July 5, 1886.
12. *Chicago Tribune*, July 11, 1886.
13. Nemec, page 291.
14. Adrian C. Anson, *A Ballplayer's Career* (Chicago, Illinois: Era Publishing, 1900), page 137.

12. A New Beginnings

1. Robert Smith, *Baseball* (New York: Simon and Schuster, 1947), pp. 93–94.
2. Jerome Holtzman and George Vass, *The Chicago Cubs Encyclopedia* (Philadelphia: Temple University Press, 1997), page 258.
3. *The New York Times*, January 3, 1887.
4. Holtzman and Vass, page 12.
5. *The New York Times*, February 21, 1887.
6. From American National Biography Online (www.anb.org).
7. *Washington Star*, February 19, 1887.
8. *Brooklyn Eagle*, May 7, 1887.
9. Albert G. Spalding, *Base Ball: America's National Game* (New York: American Sports Publishing Company, 1911), pp. 527–528.
10. *The Sporting News*, January 7, 1888.
11. *The Sporting News*, May 14, 1887.
12. *Brooklyn Eagle*, August 21, 1887.
13. *Sporting Life*, July 27, 1887.
14. *The New York Times*, September 12, 1887.
15. David W. Zang, *Fleet Walker's Divided Heart* (Lincoln, Nebraska: University of Nebraska Press, 1995), page 59.
16. *Sporting Life*, April 11, 1891.
17. Robert Peterson, *Only the Ball Was White* (Englewood Cliffs, New Jersey: Prentice-Hall, 1970), page 30.
18. *Brooklyn Eagle*, August 21, 1887.
19. *Washington Star*, September 5, 1887.
20. *Chicago News*, September 9, 1887.
21. *The Sporting News*, January 1, 1977.
22. *The New York Times*, September 17, 1887.
23. *The New York Times*, October 20, 1887.

13. Second Place

1. Bryan DiSalvatore, *A Clever Base-Ballist: the life and times of John Montgomery Ward* (New York: Pantheon Books, 1999), page 229.
2. *The Sporting News*, September 5, 1887.
3. *The Sporting News*, April 6, 1963.
4. *Washington Post*, November 13, 1887.
5. *The Sporting News*, October 24, 1887.
6. *Sporting Life*, December 14, 1887.
7. Albert G. Spalding, *Base Ball: America's National Game* (New York: American Sports Publishing Company, 1911), page 265.
8. Peter Levine, *A. G. Spalding and the Rise of Baseball: The Promise of American Sport* (New York: Oxford University Press, 1985), page 100.
9. The scene was described in the *Brooklyn Eagle*, April 21, 1888.
10. *Brooklyn Eagle*, March 4, 1898.
11. Adrian C. Anson, *A Ballplayer's Career* (Chicago, Illinois: Era Publishing, 1900), page 148.
12. *Brooklyn Eagle*, June 9, 1888.
13. Anson, page 148.
14. *Washington Post*, June 22, 1897.
15. *The Sporting News*, January 15, 1942.
16. The full title of the piece is "Casey at the Bat: A Ballad of the Republic, Sung in the Year 1888." It appeared in the *San Francisco Examiner* on June 3, 1888.
17. Tim Wiles, "Letters in the Dirt 87" (March 2000) from *The Baseball Archive* Internet site at http://www.baseball1.com/twiles.
18. *1889 Spalding Guide*.

14. Around the World

1. *Chicago Journal*, June 23, 1888.
2. *Washington Post*, October 8, 1888.
3. Albert G. Spalding, *Base Ball: America's National Game* (New York: American Sports Publishing Company, 1911), page 251.
4. Adrian C. Anson, *A Ball Player's Career* (Chicago, Illinois: Era Publishing, 1900), page 150.
5. *San Francisco Daily Examiner*, November 12, 1888; referenced by Bryan DiSalvatore in *A Clever Base-Ballist: The Life and Times of John Montgomery Ward* (New York: Pantheon Books, 1999), page 228.
6. DiSalvatore, page 229.
7. *Melbourne Argus*, December 25, 1888, quoted in the *1889 Spalding Guide*.

8. Anson, page 228.
9. Anson, page 232.
10. Anson, page 256.
11. Anson, pp. 258–259.
12. Joe Clark, "The Spalding Tour: 1888–1889," on http://www.australianbaseballhistory.webcentral.com.au.
13. Spalding, page 263.
14. *Bristol Times and Mirror*, March 16, 1889; referenced by Patrick Carroll in "Baseball in Graceland" on the SABR UK web site at http://www.sabruk.org/examiner.
15. Anson, in his autobiography, stated that the trip "cost me in round figures about $1,500." Anson, page 284.

15. The Brotherhood War

1. *Sporting Life*, January 18, 1888.
2. *Sporting Life*, April 24, 1889.
3. Dean A. Sullivan (editor), *Early innings: a documentary history of baseball, 1825–1908* (Lincoln, Nebraska: University of Nebraska Press, 1995), page 188.
4. *Boston Herald*, March 9, 1894.
5. *The Sporting News*, January 18, 1890; this report made reference to a statement that appeared in the *Chicago Tribune* on January 3, 1890.
6. *New York Star*, April 13, 1889; referenced by Howard Rosenberg in *Cap Anson 1: When Captaining a Team Meant Something* (Arlington, Virginia: Tile Books, 2003), page 187.
7. Adrian C. Anson, *A Ball Player's Career* (Chicago, Illinois: Era Publishing, 1900), page 289.
8. *Washington Post*, August 17, 1890.
9. Unidentified newspaper clipping, dated April 5, 1890, from the Cap Anson file at the National Baseball Library, Cooperstown, New York
10. Bill James, *The Baseball Book 1990* (New York: Villard Books, 1990), page 147.
11. Ibid.
12. Anson, page 293.
13. Peter Levine, *A. G. Spalding and the Rise of Baseball: The Promise of American Sport* (New York: Oxford University Press, 1985), page 61.
14. Albert G. Spalding, *Base Ball: America's National Game* (New York: American Sports Publishing Company, 1911), pp. 287–288.
15. *St. Louis Post-Dispatch*, April 10, 1890; referenced by Rosenberg, page 155.
16. *Sporting Life*, May 10, 1890.
17. *The Sporting News*, July 12, 1890.
18. Reed Browning, *Cy Young: A Baseball Life* (Amherst, Massachusetts: University of Massachusetts Press, 2000), page 12–13.
19. This story was told by Lee Allen in *The Sporting News*, August 24, 1963. Lytle then signed with the Pittsburgh club and played 15 games for them before he drew his release in late August of 1890.
20. *Sporting Life*, October 11, 1890.

16. A Disputed Pennant Race

1. *The Sporting News*, April 23, 1892.
2. *Chicago Tribune*, January 3, 1890.
3. *The Sporting News*, April 4, 1891.
4. Jerome Holtzman and George Vass, *Chicago Cubs Encyclopedia* (Philadelphia: Temple University Press, 1997), page 15.
5. John McGraw, *My Thirty Years in Baseball* (New York: Boni and Liveright, 1923), page 46.
6. Johnny Evers and Hugh Fullerton, *Touching Second* (Chicago: Reilly and Britton, 1910), pp. 81–82.
7. *The Sporting News*, March 1, 1961.
8. *Brooklyn Eagle*, October 1, 1891.
9. *The Sporting News*, October 3, 1891.
10. *Chicago Tribune*, October 2, 1891.
11. *The Sporting News*, October 3, 1891.
12. This scenario seems unlikely, as Kelly played only four games for the Boston Reds before he jumped to the Beaneaters for the remainder of the season. Still, the Boston Association club featured Hugh Duffy, Duke Farrell, and other popular players, and a post-season matchup with the Colts might have drawn well.
13. *The Sporting News*, October 3, 1891.
14. Adrian C. Anson, *A Ball Player's Career* (Chicago: Era Publishing, 1900), page 295.

17. The Grand Old Man

1. John Phillips, *Uncle Nick's Birthday Party* (Cabin John, Maryland: Capital Publishing, 1996).

2. *The Sporting News*, April 16, 1892.
3. *The Sporting News*, March 19, 1892.
4. *The Sporting News*, March 19, 1892.
5. *Brooklyn Eagle*, July 1, 1892.
6. *The New York Times*, September 16, 1892.
7. Howard Rosenberg, *Cap Anson 1: When Captaining a Team Meant Something* (Arlington, Virginia: Tile Books, 2003), page 187.
8. *Brooklyn Eagle*, March 25, 1893.
9. The pitching mound was also introduced in 1893. A team was allowed to place the pitching rubber on an elevated area if it so chose.
10. *Brooklyn Eagle*, October 2, 1887.
11. *Brooklyn Eagle*, September 2, 1892.
12. *Chicago Tribune*, May 18, 1885.
13. *The Sporting News*, September 9, 1893.
14. *The New York Times*, August 24, 1893.

18. Anson and His Colts

1. *The Sporting News*, June 9, 1894.
2. *The New York Times*, February 27, 1894.
3. *The New York Times*, March 1, 1894.
4. *The Sporting News*, March 28, 1951.
5. Fullerton's account of the incident appeared in *The Sporting News*, April 28, 1938, though Fullerton wrongly recalled that it happened on opening day. Other versions of this story have Anson showing the telegram to Hart, only to have the club president inform the mortified captain that the message was a fake.
6. Jerome Holtzman and George Vass, *The Chicago Cubs Encyclopedia* (Philadelphia: Temple University Press, 1997), page 14.
7. *New York Clipper*, January 9, 1892.
8. *The Sporting News*, July 16, 1898.
9. *The Sporting News*, April 23, 1892.
10. *The Sporting News*, January 5, 1895.
11. *The New York Times*, February 16, 1894.
12. Unidentified clipping, dated July 20, 1907, from the Cap Anson file in the National Baseball Library, Cooperstown, New York.
13. Hart explained his side of the story, recounting Anson's indebtedness to the Chicago team, in the *Chicago Tribune*, December 31, 1899.

14. *The Sporting News*, August 24, 1895.
15. *Chicago Tribune*, August 3, 1895.

19. Cap Anson on Broadway

1. *Chicago Tribune*, November 13, 1895.
2. This was not Hoyt's longest title. Two years earlier he wrote a play called "A Milk White Flag: And its Battle-scarred Followers on the Field of Mars and in the Court of Venus. A Tribute to our Citizen Soldiers by one who would gladly join their ranks if he knew how to dance."
3. *New York Daily News*, September 21, 2003.
4. *Brooklyn Eagle*, November 26, 1895.
5. Ibid.
6. *Los Angeles Times*, July 22, 1895.
7. *Washington Post*, November 17, 1895.
8. *Washington Post*, December 29, 1895.
9. *The New York Times*, October 22, 1895.
10. *The New York Times*, November 13, 1895.
11. *Brooklyn Eagle*, November 26, 1895.
12. Ibid.
13. *The New York Times*, December 3, 1895.
14. *New York Daily News*, September 21, 2003.
15. *Chicago Tribune*, December 24, 1895.
16. *Chicago Tribune*, January 5, 1896, in the "Drama and its Devotees" column.
17. *Washington Post*, March 31, 1896.
18. *Washington Post*, February 18, 1896.
19. John Phillips, *Uncle Nick's Birthday Party* (Cabin John, Maryland: Capital Publishing, 1996), page 9.
20. Ibid.
21. Phillips, page 127.
22. Ira L. Smith and H. Allen Smith, *Low and inside: a book of baseball anecdotes, oddities, and curiosities* (Garden City, New York: Doubleday, 1949), pp. 86–87.
23. *Washington Post*, October 18, 1896.
24. Ibid.
25. Phillips, page 126.
26. *The Sporting News*, October 3, 1896.

20. The Final Season

1. Jerome Holtzman and George Vass, *The Chicago Cubs Encyclopedia* (Philadel-

phia: Temple University Press, 1997), page 128.
2. *Brooklyn Eagle*, April 2, 1897.
3. *Chicago Tribune*, May 4, 1897.
4. *Chicago Record*, May 5, 1897.
5. *Chicago Tribune*, May 5, 1897.
6. *Chief Sockalexis and the 1897 Cleveland Indians* (Cabin John, Maryland: Capital Publishing, 1991), May 20 entry.
7. *The Sporting News*, August 7, 1897.
8. Phillips, May 20 entry.
9. Phillips, May 22 entry.
10. *Washington Post*, May 22, 1897.
11. *Washington Post*, March 12, 1897.
12. *Chicago Tribune*, May 27, 1900; also referenced by Howard Rosenberg in *Cap Anson 1: When Captaining a Team Meant Something* (Arlington, Virginia: Tile Books, 2003), page 59.
13. *Washington Post*, May 27, 1897.
14. *Washington Post*, March 4, 1897.
15. *The Sporting News*, December 3, 1942.
16. Ibid.
17. *Chicago Tribune*, October 5, 1897.
18. *Chicago Tribune*, November 10, 1897.
19. *The Sporting News*, November 11, 1898.
20. *Chicago Tribune*, November 12, 1897.
21. *Chicago Tribune*, November 10, 1897. The unidentified speaker was probably either Boston's Frank Selee or Baltimore's Ned Hanlon, who between them won all 10 National League pennants during the 1891–1900 period.
22. *The Sporting News*, December 4, 1897.
23. Adrian C. Anson, *A Ball Player's Career* (Chicago, Illinois: Era Publishing, 1900), page 305.
24. *Los Angeles Times*, January 30, 1898.

21. An Unemployed Manager

1. *Brooklyn Eagle*, April 10, 1898.
2. *Chicago Tribune*, February 2, 1898.
3. Ibid.
4. *Washington Post*, March 4, 1898.
5. *The Sporting News*, February 26, 1898.
6. Adrian C. Anson, *A Ball Player's Career* (Chicago, Illinois: Era Publishing, 1900), pp. 310–311.
7. Anson, appendix, page vi.
8. Ibid.
9. Anson, page 313.
10. *Brooklyn Eagle*, April 14, 1898.
11. Anson, pp. 311–312.
12. *The Sporting News*, June 11, 1898.
13. *Chicago Tribune*, June 13, 1898.
14. *Brooklyn Eagle*, July 8, 1898.
15. John Phillips, *The 1898 Cleveland Spiders* (Cabin John, Maryland: Capital Publishing, 1997), page 67.
16. Anson, page 313.
17. Daniel Okrent and Harris Lewine, editors, *The Ultimate Baseball Book* (Boston: Houghton Mifflin Company, 1981), page 28.
18. Anson, page 302.
19. *The Sporting News*, December 16, 1899.

22. Baseball, Business, and Politics

1. *Chicago Tribune*, January 19, 1899.
2. *Brooklyn Eagle*, September 18, 1899.
3. *Chicago Tribune*, October 6, 1899.
4. David Pietruzsa, *Major Leagues: the formation, sometimes absorption, and mostly inevitable demise of 18 professional baseball organizations, 1871 to present* (Jefferson, North Carolina: McFarland and Company, 1991), page 137.
5. Ibid.
6. *Brooklyn Eagle*, January 6, 1900.
7. Charles Alexander, *John McGraw* (New York: Viking Penguin, 1988), page 69.
8. *Brooklyn Eagle*, February 16, 1900.
9. *Brooklyn Eagle*, December 16, 1901.
10. *Chicago Tribune*, December 26, 1901.
11. *Chicago Tribune*, January 12, 1902.
12. *Chicago Tribune*, April 5, 1905.
13. *Chicago Tribune*, June 3, 1905.
14. *Chicago Tribune*, May 19, 1906.
15. Ibid.
16. *Chicago Tribune*, May 22, 1906.
17. *Chicago Tribune*, May 21, 1906.

23. "The Best I Can"

1. *Washington Post*, January 10, 1909.
2. *Los Angeles Times*, March 31, 1903.
3. Albert Goodwill Spalding Junior had the same name as J. Walter Spalding's son (and Al's nephew), who was born in 1888 and became a famous concert violinist.
4. Reports stated that Murphy paid

$105,000 for the team. If that sum was paid for Hart's 870 shares only, Murphy bought the stock for about $120 per share, but if the $105,000 was paid for all 1,000 shares, then he paid $105 per share.

5. The *Washington Post* of December 11, 1905, gave the price received by Anson as $10,000, while the *Chicago Tribune* of December 11, 1905 stated that Murphy paid $13,000 to Anson. Perhaps Anson received a lesser sum due to the loans that the ex-captain had carried against the stock for several years.

6. *Los Angeles Times*, September 17, 1908.

7. *Chicago Tribune*, real estate transfers listing, May 29, 1910. Both of Anson's properties were listed as reverting to the Hibernian Bank of Chicago.

8. *Washington Post*, January 17, 1909.

9. *The New York Times*, January 21, 1909. Oddly enough, Charles Murphy's business partner and co-owner of the Cubs was Charles Phelps Taft, the husband of Anna Taft, who had set the foreclosure proceedings of Anson's business into motion the previous summer.

10. *Chicago Tribune*, January 27, 1909.

11. *Washington Post*, November 17, 1909.

12. *Chicago Tribune*, December 19, 1909.

13. *Chicago Tribune*, February 7, 1911.

14. *Christian Science Monitor*, March 6, 1914. The USGA had reinstated another prominent ex-ballplayer and golfing enthusiast, John Ward, as an amateur several years before.

15. *The New York Times*, October 13, 1913. Charlie Ferguson was a pitcher for the Phillies who appeared to be on his way to a stellar career when he died of typhoid at the age of 25 shortly before the beginning of the 1888 season.

16. *The Sporting News*, January 17, 1918.

17. *Chicago Tribune*, December 20, 1913.

18. Interview with Dorothy Anson Dodge in the *Chicago Tribune*, April 17, 1968.

19. *Chicago Tribune*, February 4, 1917.

24. Epilogue

1. *Chicago Tribune*, April 17, 1968.
2. *Chicago Tribune*, February 12, 1920.
3. *Chicago Tribune*, April 15, 1922.
4. Bill James, *The Baseball Book 1990* (New York: Villard Books, 1990), page 256.
5. David Q. Voigt, *American Baseball, Volume 1* (University Park, Pennsylvania: Pennsylvania State University Press, 1983), page 101.

Bibliography

Books

Alexander, Charles. *John McGraw* (New York: Viking Penguin, 1988).
Allen, Lee. *The National League Story* (New York: Hill & Wang, 1961).
Anson, Adrian C. *A Ball Player's Career* (Chicago: Era Publishing, 1900).
Appel, Marty. *Slide, Kelly, Slide: The Wild Life and Times of Mike "King" Kelly, Baseball's First Superstar* (Lanham, Md.: Scarecrow Press, 1996).
Bartlett, A. C. *Baseball and Mr. Spalding: The History and Romance of Baseball* (New York: Farrar, Straus, and Young, 1951).
Baseball as America: Seeing Ourselves Through Our National Game (Washington, D.C.: National Geographic Society, 2002).
Brown, Warren. *The Chicago Cubs* (New York: G. P. Putnam's Sons, 1946).
Danzig, Allison, and Joe Reichler. *The History of Baseball* (Englewood Cliffs, N.J.: Prentice-Hall, 1959).
DiSalvatore, Bryan. *A Clever Base-Ballist: The Life and Times of John Montgomery Ward* (New York: Pantheon, 1999).
Ellis, William T. *Billy Sunday: The Man and His Message* (Philadelphia: Universal Book and Bible House, 1914).
Evers, Johnny, and Hugh Fullerton. *Touching Second* (Chicago: Reilly and Britton, 1910).
Golenbock, Peter. *The Spirit of St. Louis: A History of the St. Louis Cardinals and Browns* (New York: William Morrow, 2000).
Holtzman, Jerome, and George Vass. *The Chicago Cubs Encyclopedia* (Philadelphia: Temple University Press, 1997).
Ivor-Campbell, Frederick, and Robert L. Tiemann, editors. *Baseball's First Stars* (Cleveland: Society for American Baseball Research, 1996).
James, Bill. *The Bill James Guide to Baseball Managers from 1870 to Today* (New York: Scribner, 1997).
_____. *The Bill James Historical Baseball Abstract* (New York: Villard Books, 1986).
_____. *The New Bill James Historical Baseball Abstract* (New York: Free Press, 2001).
_____. *The Politics of Glory: How Baseball's Hall of Fame Really Works* (New York: Macmillan, 1994).

Levine, Peter. *A. G. Spalding and the Rise of Baseball: The Promise of American Sport* (New York: Oxford University Press, 1985).
Light, Jonathan Taylor. *The Cultural Encyclopedia of Baseball* (Jefferson, N.C.: McFarland, 1997).
McGraw, John. *My Thirty Years in Baseball* (New York: Boni and Liveright, 1923).
Melville, Tom. *Early Baseball and the Rise of the National League* (Jefferson, N.C.: McFarland, 2001).
Myers, Doug. *Essential Cubs: Chicago Cubs Facts, Feats, and Firsts* (New York: McGraw-Hill/Contemporary Books, 1999).
Nemec, David. *The Beer and Whisky League* (New York: Lyons Press, 1994).
_____. *The Great Encyclopedia of 19th-Century Major League Baseball* (New York: Donald I. Fine Books, 1997).
Okrent, Daniel, and Harris Lewine, editors. *The Ultimate Baseball Book* (Boston: Houghton Mifflin, 1981).
Orem, Preston. *Baseball (1845–1881) from the Newspaper Accounts* (Altadena, Calif.: self-published, 1961).
Peterson, Robert. *Only the Ball Was White* (Englewood Cliffs, N.J.: Prentice-Hall, 1970).
Phillips, John. *Chief Sockalexis and the 1897 Cleveland Indians* (Cabin John, Md.: Capital Publishing, 1991).
_____. *The 1898 Cleveland Spiders* (Cabin John, Md.: Capital Publishing, 1997).
_____. *The '99 Spiders* (Cabin John, Md.: Capital Publishing, 1988).
_____. *Uncle Nick's Birthday Party* (Cabin John, Md.: Capital Publishing, 1996).
Pietrusza, David. *Major Leagues: The Formation, Sometimes Absorption, and Mostly Inevitable Demise of 18 Professional Baseball Organizations, 1871 to Present* (Jefferson, N.C.: McFarland, 1991).
Rosenberg, Howard. *Cap Anson 1: When Captaining a Team Meant Something* (Arlington, Va.: Tile Books, 2003).
Rucker, Mark, and John Freyer. *19th Century Baseball in Chicago* (Charleston, S.C.: Arcadia, 2003), page 104.
Seymour, Harold. *Baseball: The Golden Age* (New York: Oxford University Press, 1971).
Smith, Ira L., and H. Allen Smith. *Low and Inside: A Book of Baseball Anecdotes, Oddities, and Curiosities* (Garden City, N.Y.: Doubleday, 1949).
Smith, Robert. *Baseball* (New York: Simon and Schuster, 1947).
Spalding, Albert G. *Base Ball: America's National Game* (New York: American Sports Publishing Co., 1911).
Spink, Alfred H. *The National Game* (St. Louis: National Game Publishing Co., 1910).
Sullivan, Dean A., editor. *Extra Innings: A Documentary History of Baseball, 1825–1908* (Lincoln: University of Nebraska Press, 1995).
Tiemann, Robert L., and Mark Rucker, editors. *Nineteenth Century Stars* (Kansas City, Mo.: Society for American Baseball Research, 1989).
Voigt, David Q. *American Baseball, Volume 1* (University Park: Pennsylvania State University Press, 1983).
Ward, Geoffrey C., and Ken Burns. *Baseball: An Illustrated History* (New York: Knopf, 1994).
White, Sol. *The History of Colored Base Ball* (Lincoln: University of Nebraska Press, 1995). Originally published in 1907.

Zang, David W. *Fleet Walker's Divided Heart* (Lincoln: University of Nebraska Press, 1995).

Newspapers

Boston Herald
Brooklyn Eagle
Chicago Evening Journal
Chicago Herald
Chicago Inter-Ocean
Chicago News
Chicago Record
Chicago Tribune
Christian Science Monitor
Cincinnati Enquirer

Los Angeles Times
Marshalltown Times-Republican
New York Clipper
New York Star
The New York Times
Rockford Register
Toledo Blade
Washington Post
Washington Star

Magazines

Baseball Digest
Baseball Magazine
Baseball Research Journal
Literary Digest
The National Pastime

Sport
Sporting Life
The Sporting News
Sports Illustrated

Internet sites

American National Biography Online (*http://www.anb.com*)
Australian Baseball History (http://www.australianbaseballhistory.webcentral.com.au)
The Baseball Archive (http://www.baseball1.com)
Baseball Reference (*http://www.baseball-reference.com*)
National Baseball Hall of Fame and Museum (*http://www.baseballhalloffame.org*)
Project Retrosheet (http://www.retrosheet.org)
Society for American Baseball Research (SABR) (*http://www.sabr.org*)
The Sporting News (*http://tsn.sportingnews.com*)

Index

Addy, Bob 26, 60, 70, 73
American Bowling Congress (ABC) 282–283
Anson, Adrian Constantine (Cap): aggressive play 73; autobiography 270, 275–277; bankruptcy 296–297; batting style 12, 20; betting activities 78–79, 120–121, 162–163, 192, 233–235, 283; and billiards 124, 234, 275–276, 292, 295–296; birth 6; and bowling 282–283; and boxing 51–52; Broadway career 239–246; business affairs 158–159, 275–276; and cricket 44–46, 179–180; death 308; discipline as manager 91–92, 114, 117–118, 123, 136–139, 150–151, 155, 193, 219–220, 232, 249–251, 257–258; drinking 39–40, 51–52, 232; and football 298; and golf 302, 307–308; hit-and-run play 71 72; and the Irish 192–193; kicking and bullying 12, 30, 66, 90–91, 97–98, 126–127, 140–141, 177–178, 260; leadership style 82–83; manager of Philadelphia 58; marriage 69; newspaper criticism 149–150; nicknames 24; as pitcher 110–111, 116; political career 284–291; racial attitudes 111–114, 118–119, 152–153, 176, 186, 276, 286, 310; and segregation 111–114, 118–119, 152–153; semipro ball 293–299; strategy 91, 135, 152; superstitions 164–166; and the theater 167–168, 239–246; tour of England (1874) 43–48; town baseball 11–15; vaudeville career 302, 304–305; world tour (1888–89) 172–187; youth 8–9

Anson, Adrian Constantine, Jr. (son) 159
Anson, Adrian Hulbert (son) 101
Anson, Henry (father) 4–14, 17–19, 48, 56–57, 123–124, 175, 216, 226, 231, 266, 287
Anson, Jeannette Rice (mother) 5–6, 8
Anson, John Henry (son) 216
Anson, Melville (brother) 8
Anson, Sturgis Ransome (brother) 5, 8, 11, 13–14, 17–19, 266, 287
Anson, Virginia Fiegal (wife) 40, 52, 59–60, 62, 69 70, 78, 101, 104, 159, 163, 174, 176–177, 216, 242, 270, 276, 279, 293, 296, 300, 304, 308
Anson, Virginia Jeanette (daughter) 276, 296, 300
Anson, Warren (grandfather) 4
Anson, William (nephew) 276
Austin, John 4
Austin, Silas Jr. 4

Baldwin, Charles (Lady) 136
Baldwin, Mark 147–148, 150–151, 162, 166–167, 170, 172, 175, 181, 184, 189, 191–192, 196, 220, 301
Banks, Ernie 310
Barnes, Ross 19, 38, 56, 62–64, 71–72, 75–77
Barnie, Billy 228, 270
Barrymore, Ethel 254
Barrymore, Maurice 254
Bartholemew, Professor 174, 179–180
Bastian, Charlie 191–192
Beckley, Jake 271–272
Bell, Digby 167, 174

333

Bender, Charles (Chief) 303
Bennett, Eddie 165
Bennett, Frank 230
Bond, Tommy 49, 74
Borden, Joe 49
Bradley, George 63, 70, 72–73, 76
Briggs, Herbert (Buttons) 256
Brotherhood of Professional Base Ball Players 190, 192, 194–195, 199, 201–202, 211
Brouthers, Dan 136, 156, 170, 298
Brown, Joe 121
Brown, Jonathan 85, 118, 198
Brown, Robert T. 299
Brown, Tom 173, 255
Brush, John T. 233, 272, 284
Bryan, William J. 234, 285
Buffinton, Charlie 116
Bulkeley, Morgan G. 59
Burney, H. P. 229–230
Burns, Tom 88–89, 91, 96, 100–101, 105, 109–110, 126, 138, 145, 166, 172, 191, 195–196, 204, 208, 215, 262–263, 270, 272–273, 307
Bushong, Doc 143
Busse, Fred 290

Callahan, Jimmy 253–254, 257, 259, 261, 279, 294, 299
Canavan, Jimmy 215–218
Carroll, Cliff 196, 208–209
Carroll, Fred 173
Caruthers, Bob 142
Casey at the Bat 168
Chadwick, Henry 33, 41, 76, 171
Chance, Frank 298
Cherry, Adele Anson (daughter) 174, 292, 304–305
Cicotte, Eddie 306
Clapp, John 37, 58
Clarke, Fred 227
Clarke, William (Dad) 236
Clarkson, John 121–123, 125–130, 132, 134, 136, 140–144, 147–148, 151, 159–161, 164, 170, 190, 193–194, 196, 208, 210, 217, 227, 303, 307
Cleveland, Grover 137–138, 173–174, 188
Clifford, John 23
Clough, Anson M. (grandson) 276
Clough, Grace Anson (daughter) 78, 174, 276, 296
Clough, Walter H. 276, 279, 296
Cobb, Ty 220, 303, 308, 310
Comiskey, Charles 130, 132, 142, 148, 153, 164, 194–199, 201, 203, 282, 294, 301, 308–309
Cone, Fred 19
Connor, Jim 257, 259
Connor, Roger 194, 210, 256
Cooney, Jimmy 196, 208, 215, 218
Corcoran, Larry 88–92, 94, 98–101, 103–105, 109–110, 112, 114–116, 121, 123, 125–126, 150, 193, 231–232, 303
Corcoran, Mike 116
Crane, Ed 172, 176, 185
Crosby, George 114
Crusinberry, Jim 307
Cummings, W. A. (Candy) 33, 35, 49, 60, 64, 70, 88, 309
Cuthbert, Ned 35, 36, 41

Dahlen, Bill 204–205, 207–208, 217–218, 222–223, 226–227, 235, 237, 240, 246, 250–251, 256–258
Dalrymple, Abner 81, 87, 91–93, 105, 110, 135, 137–138, 143, 145, 149, 307–308
Daly, Tom 148, 150, 153, 172, 185–186, 191
Darling, Dell 148, 164, 191
Day, John B. 125, 194, 198, 266
Deauvray, Helen 241
Decker, George 220, 223, 229–230, 235, 246–247, 255, 257, 260–261
Delahanty, Ed 248, 280
DeMontreville, Gene 255
Devlin, Jim 62, 75, 120
Dickinson, Lew 96
Dodge, Arthur 296, 300, 307
Dodge, Dorothy Anson (daughter) 159, 296, 300, 304–305, 307–308
Donohue, John (Jiggs) 299
Donohue, Tim 235, 237, 256
Doscher, John 96
Dowd, Tommy 254
Doyle, Jack 229, 261
Duffy, Hugh 166–167, 191–193, 195–196, 203, 208, 215, 231
Dungan, Sam 215
Dunlap, Fred 92, 100, 115
Dunne, Edward 286
Duval, Clarence 165–166, 175–176, 179, 181, 186–187, 197, 266, 276
Dwyer, Frank 191, 193, 196

Earle, Billy 176, 180
Emslie, Bob 260, 272
Esper, Duke 254
Esterbrook, Dude 164
Everitt, Bill 235, 261

Ewing, John 210
Ewing, William (Buck) 163, 168–170, 201, 309

Farrell, Charles (Duke) 162, 167, 191, 204, 208, 215
Ferguson, Bob 64, 76–77, 79
Ferguson, Charlie 303
Ferguson, James 44
Fiegal, John (father-in-law) 40, 62, 216, 236
Fiegal, Remy 124
Fisher, William (Cherokee) 23, 26–27, 37, 307
Fisler, West 30, 36, 38
Flick, Elmer 257
Flint, Frank (Silver) 82–85, 87–88, 90–91, 98, 110, 117, 133, 135, 145–146, 148, 152, 175, 190–191, 219, 232, 307
Flynn, John (Jocko) 135–136, 141–142, 147
Fogerty, Jim 173, 181
Force, Davy 50, 59, 69, 122
Foster, Andrew (Rube) 294, 298
Foster, Elmer 206–207
Foutz, Dave 142, 227
Fowler, Bud 154
Foy, Eddie 254
Freedman, Andrew 233, 271–275, 280, 283–284
Friend, Danny 260
Fullerton, Hugh 206, 228, 248, 258–259

Gaffney, John 140–141
Galvin, Jim (Pud) 102, 150
Gambling in baseball 33–34, 54–55, 120–121
Gastright, Charlie 227
Glasscock, Jack 194
Gleason, William (Kid) 308
Glenalvin, Bob 200–201
Glenn, John 74
Goldsmith, Fred 88–90, 92, 98, 100–101, 104–105, 110, 112, 114–115, 117–118, 120, 123, 303
Gore, George 82, 87, 89, 91–94, 97–98, 122, 127, 130, 132–133, 136, 138, 145–146, 149–150, 307–308
Grace, W. G. 267
Grant, Frank 152
Green, Chief Johnny 6, 9
Griffin, Mike 270
Griffith, Clark 222, 226, 230, 233–235, 237, 246, 248–249, 252–253, 261, 279, 308

Gumbert, Ad 169–170, 191–193, 196, 204, 207, 211, 216, 218, 220, 222
Guth, Charlie 92

Hackett, Charlie 116, 152
Hahn, Willie 165
Hallinan, Jimmy 74
Hamilton, Billy 248
Hammond, Percy 305
Hankinson, Frank 77, 82
Hanlon, Ned 173, 177
Hardie, Lew 135
Harrison, Benjamin 173, 188–189
Harrison, Carter 285
Hart, Jim 178, 192–193, 207–208, 215, 218–219, 221, 224, 228, 232, 235–236, 248–249, 251, 253, 256–257, 259, 261–265, 275–277, 279, 282, 284, 293
Hastings, Winfield S. (Scott) 24–26, 49
Hatfield, John 36
Hawley, Emerson (Pink) 255
Healy, John 172, 241
Herrmann, Garry 306–307
Hersh, George 234
Heydler, John 299, 307–308
Hicks, Nat 77
Hines, Paul 63, 73, 86, 164, 229
Hippodroming 50, 75, 120–121, 142–143, 306
Hopper, DeWolf 167–168, 174, 186
Hoskins, Pete 19
Hoyt, Charles 239–245
Hudson, Nat 143
Hulbert, William 42–43, 49–51, 55–62, 69, 71, 73–80, 84, 90, 92, 94–96, 98–99, 102, 108, 114, 120, 137, 148, 207, 221, 236, 287, 307
Hutchison, Bill 169–170, 175–176, 190–193, 195–196, 200–201, 204–205, 208, 216, 218, 221–223, 226, 230–231, 235, 254

Iowa State College 14
Irwin, Charlie 226, 235

James, Bill 20, 80
Jennings, Hugh 258
Johnson, Byron B. (Ban) 279, 282, 285–286
Jones, Charley 74
Joyce, Bill 241, 245, 271–274

Kalakaua, King of Hawaii 179
Keefe, Tim 125, 128, 168, 170, 246

Kelly, John 131
Kelly, Mike (King) 87–88, 90, 92, 94, 96–98, 100–101, 104, 110–111, 120–123, 127, 130, 135–137, 139, 142–147, 149–150, 160–161, 173, 175–176, 190, 193–194, 196, 201, 204, 212, 216, 219, 223, 232, 241, 246, 307
Kelly, Ray 165
Kennedy, Ted 126
Kittridge, Malachi (Mal) 196, 208, 219, 226, 237, 248, 256, 285
Kling, Johnny 296
Knight, Lon 57, 68
Krock, Gus 161–162, 170, 191–192

Lajoie, Nap 280
Landis, Kenesaw M. 296, 306–309
Lange, Bill 220, 222–223, 226, 229, 248, 258–259, 261, 270, 279
Lantz, James 40
Lardner, Ring 304
Larkin, Terry 77, 82, 88
Latham, Arlie 133–134, 196
Lawler, Frank 173
Leland, Frank 294
Leo XIII, Pope 182
Leonard, Andrew 46
Luby, Pat 196, 200, 204, 206, 208–209, 218, 220
Lynch, Leigh 178, 181
Lynch, Thomas (pitcher) 116
Lynch, Thomas (umpire) 209, 228, 300, 303
Lytle, Ed 200–201

Mack, Connie 152, 303, 309–310
Mack, Denny 32, 36–37
Macullar, Jimmy 105
Malone, Fergy 35, 36
Manning, Jack 57, 116
Manning, Jimmy 173, 180
Marshalltown, Iowa 3, 6–14, 16–17, 67
Marylebone Cricket Club 42, 45–46
Mathews, Bobby 32, 49
Mauck, Hal 220, 223
McBride, James Dickson (Dick) 30, 32, 35, 37, 38, 44, 46, 54–55, 57–58, 68
McCarthy, Tommy 281
McCormick, Barry 259
McCormick, Jim 100, 126, 128–130, 134, 138, 140–142, 144, 146–147, 149, 190, 193, 307
McCreery, Tom 273
McGeary, Mike 32

McGill, Willie 220, 223, 226, 235
McGinley, Tim 64
McGraw, John 204–205, 258, 280–282, 298
McKee, Frank 244–245
McKinley, William 234
McLean, Billy 51
McMullen, John 36
McPhee, John (Bid) 105
McVey, Cal 38, 46, 56, 62, 70, 72–73, 75–77, 84–85, 87
Meyerle, Levi 30, 34, 36
Mills, A. G. 158
Mills, Everett 38
Moolic, George 135, 148
Morton, Charles 112, 118
Mullane, Tony 216
Murnane, Tim 33, 37, 47, 166
Murphy, Charles 293, 297, 299
Mutrie, Jim 125, 162–163, 192

Nash, Billy 246
National Association of Professional Base Ball Players (NA) 21, 41, 50–51, 53, 55–56, 58–59
National Baseball Hall of Fame 3, 309
Nichols, Charles (Kid) 209–210, 216, 222
Nicol, Hugh 94, 100–101, 105, 109
Nimick, W. W. 162
Notre Dame, University of 10–11, 14
Noyes, Thomas C. 286

O'Day, Hank 297
O'Neill, Tip 196
O'Rourke, Jim 64, 89, 214, 223

Palmer, Pete 310
Parker, Frank 124
Parrott, Walter (Jiggs) 217, 235
Pearce, Dickey 143
Pershing, John J. 306
Peters, Johnny 63, 76, 82, 89
Peterson, Philip 281
Peterson, Robert 154
Pettit, Bob 162, 167, 172, 191
Pfeffer, Fred 105, 109, 113, 137, 142, 148, 152, 155, 159–161, 166, 172, 180–181, 190–191, 193, 195, 199, 204, 207, 211, 214–216, 247, 249, 256–257, 307–308
Phillips, Bill 84
Pike, Lipman (Lip) 32
Plank, Eddie 303
Players League 190, 194–203
Pottawattamie Indians 6, 9

Powell, Jack 259–260
Pulliam, Harry 297, 299

Quest, Joe 82, 88, 98, 100–101, 108
Quinn, Harry D. 278

Radbourn, Charley 115, 123, 309
Radcliffe, John 38, 50
Reach, Al 30, 35, 55, 161
Reserve clause 86–87, 89, 94, 279
Rice, Wells 5–6
Richardson, Hardie 122, 136
Richmond, Lee 91
Richter, Francis 278, 282, 308–309
Robinson, Jackie 119, 310
Robinson, Wilbert 280, 298
Robison, Frank 259, 275
Roe, Elwin (Preacher) 93
Rogers, John 262
Roosevelt, Theodore 286
Rose, Pete 233
Rowe, Dave 101
Rowe, Jack 98, 136
Rusie, Amos 210, 223, 230, 271, 273
Ruth, George (Babe) 117, 165
Ryan, Jimmy 135, 143, 148, 150–151, 162, 166–167, 172, 184, 191–193, 195–196, 204, 206–207, 210, 216, 219, 222, 226, 228, 235, 248, 255–256, 270, 272, 277

Sager, Sam (Pony) 19
Schriver, William (Pop) 219, 226, 230, 235
Scott, Milt 102–103
Selee, Frank 233, 292
Sensenderfer, John 30
Shaffer, George (Orator) 82–84, 90
Shettsline, Bill 271
Smith, Robert 114, 142
Snyder, Charlie (Pop) 40, 104
Soden, Arthur 102, 272
Spalding, Albert Goodwill 16–19, 21, 23, 35, 42, 44–51, 55–64, 66–67, 69–80, 83, 85–86, 88, 90, 92–94, 99, 102–104, 107–108, 110–111, 113–114, 118, 120, 123, 125–126, 130–132, 134, 136–139, 144–151, 155–163, 167, 169, 172–175, 177–183, 185–186, 188–191, 194, 197–202, 204, 207–208, 212, 218–219, 221, 252, 263–264, 266–270, 275–276, 283–285, 287, 293, 300, 305, 307, 309
Spalding, Albert Goodwill, Jr. 293
Spalding, J. Walter 70, 218
Spalding and Brothers 70–71, 76

Sperling, C. H. 50
Spink, A. H. 220, 278
Stallings, George 261, 270–271
Start, Joe 77
Stearnes, Frederick 156
Stein, Ed 226
Stenzel, Jake 261
Stewart, Ace 235, 237
Stovey, George 152–153
Sullivan, Dave 130
Sullivan, Marty 148, 150, 162, 164, 166–167, 172, 191
Sunday, Billy 109, 111, 122, 130, 133–134, 137–140, 148, 151, 162, 173, 297, 301, 307–308
Sunday ball 235–236
Sutton, Ezra 37, 38, 56–58, 60–61, 74, 81
Sweeney, Charlie 115

Taft, Anna 296
Taft, William Howard 296, 306
Talcott, Eddie 225, 271
Tebeau, Oliver (Patsy) 211, 217, 274
Tener, John 169–170, 172, 181–182, 191–193, 196, 301, 303
Terry, Bill (Adonis) 226, 235, 248
Thayer, Ernest L. 168
Thorn, John 310
Thornton, Walter 237, 257
Treacy, Fred 50
Truby, Jack 237, 247
Twain, Mark 186

Umberto, King of Italy 183

Van Haltren, George 147, 150–151, 162, 170, 176, 191, 193, 203, 208, 215, 247
Veeck, William 165
Vickery, Tom 210
Voigt, David 311
von der Ahe, Chris 153

Wagner, Honus 310
Waite, Charles 70
Waldo, Hiram 23–24, 27, 175
Wales, Prince of 185
Walker, Jimmy 307
Walker, Moses F. 111–113, 119, 152–154, 309
Walker, Welday 119
Walsh, John 218, 259, 263, 268–269
Ward, John M. 90–91, 128–129, 168, 172, 175–178, 182, 185–186, 189–190, 193–195, 211, 241, 299, 301
Watkins, Bill 156

Welch, Curt 143, 153
Welch, Mickey 127
White, Harmony 149
White, James (Deacon) 56, 62, 70, 74, 136, 214, 308
White, Sol 113, 154
White, Will 104
Williams, Wash 126
Williamson, Ed 73, 82, 84, 87, 89–90, 92, 94, 103, 105, 109–111, 114, 117, 136, 142–143, 145, 148, 151–152, 159–161, 166, 169, 172, 174, 184, 190–193, 195–196, 199, 203, 208, 219, 232, 307
Wilmot, Walt 196, 208, 222–223, 226, 228, 233, 236

Wood, Jimmy 19
Wood, Leonard 306
Woodruff, Harvey T. 307
Wright, George 35, 46, 89–90, 101, 174, 180, 182
Wright, Harry 19, 21, 39, 42, 44–48, 54, 66, 71, 74, 90, 93, 97, 111, 134, 155, 170, 199, 266
Wrigley, Phil 165

Young, Denton (Cy) 200, 221–222, 247
Young, Nicholas 59, 141, 246

Zettelein, George 50, 68

www.ingramcontent.com/pod-product-compliance
Ingram Content Group UK Ltd.
Pitfield, Milton Keynes, MK11 3LW, UK
UKHW041922140426
5217IPUK00014B/277